WHAT IS TRUTH?

This book studies the nature, growth and prospects of Roman Catholic culture, viewed as capable of appropriating all that is noble both from internal and external sources. John Rist tests his argument via a number of avenues: man's creation in the image of God and historical difficulties about incorporating women into that vision; the relationship between God's mercy and justice; the possibility of Christian aesthetics; the early development of the see of Rome as the source of an indispensable doctrinal unity for Christian culture; the search for the proper role of the Church in politics.

He also argues that such an understanding of Catholic culture is necessary if contemporary assumptions about inalienable rights and the value of the human person are to be defended. The alternatives are a value-free, individualist universe on the one hand, and a fundamentalist denial of human nature and of history on the other.

JOHN M. RIST is Emeritus Professor of Classics and Philosophy at the University of Toronto, where he taught from 1959 to 1980 and again, following three years as Regius Professor of Classics at the University of Aberdeen, from 1983 to 1996. Since 1998 he has been part-time Visiting Professor at the Institutum Patristicum Augustinianum in Rome. In 1976 he was elected a Fellow of the Royal Society of Canada, and in 1991 he was elected a life member of Clare Hall, Cambridge. In 1995 he was the Lady Davis Visiting Professor in Philosophy at the Hebrew University in Jerusalem. He is the author of over one hundred scholarly articles and numerous books including *Augustine: Ancient Thought Baptized* (1994) and *Real Ethics* (2002).

WHAT IS TRUTH?

From the Academy to the Vatican

JOHN M. RIST

CAMBRIDGE
UNIVERSITY PRESS

CAMBRIDGE UNIVERSITY PRESS
Cambridge, New York, Melbourne, Madrid, Cape Town, Singapore, São Paulo, Delhi

Cambridge University Press
The Edinburgh Building, Cambridge CB2 8RU, UK

Published in the United States of America by Cambridge University Press, New York

www.cambridge.org
Information on this title: www.cambridge.org/9780521717755

First published 2008

Printed in the United Kingdom at the University Press, Cambridge

A catalogue record for this publication is available from the British Library

ISBN 978-0-521-88901-8 hardback
ISBN 978-0-521-71775-5 paperback

To the memory of Eric Osborn

"What is Truth?", said jesting Pilate, and did not wait for an Answer.
Francis Bacon

Contents

Acknowledgments

Over a number of years many individuals and institutions have helped me construct this book, parts or themes of which have been discussed at Cambridge and Oxford Universities, at the Catholic University of America in Washington D.C., at Leuven and in Rome. Among individuals I must particularly acknowledge constructive comments (oral or in writing) on earlier versions of parts of my text by Allen Brent, Robert Dodaro, Douglas Hedley, the late Eric Osborn, Emile Perreau Saussine, Kurt Pritzl, Robert Sokolowski and Benedetta Selene Zorzi. But as usual the main supporter both of myself as author and of the text as finally generated was Anna Rist who read the entire manuscript in great detail twice and corrected hundreds of misdescriptions of fact or sloppinesses of argument and style. It could not have been completed at all adequately without her kind, loving and severe help.

As usual, the staff of the Cambridge University Press, especially Kate Brett and my copy-editor Joanne Hill, have been patient and constructive with a manuscript of indeterminate academic nature which, as I am inclined to boast, has something to annoy everyone – thereby, one can only hope, provoking further debate.

John Rist
Rome

Abbreviations of Journals and Series

AJP	*American Journal of Philology*
ANRW	*Aufstieg und Niedergang der römischen Welt*
AS	*Augustinian Studies*
BA	*Bibliothèque Augustinienne*
BR	*Bible Review*
CIA	*Congresso Internazionale su s. Agostino 1987*
CP	*Classical Philology*
CQ	*Classical Quarterly*
CSEL	*Corpus Scriptorum Ecclesiasticorum Latinorum*
DS	*Encheiridion Symbolorum*, ed. Denzinger and Schönmetzer
GCS	*Die griechischen christlichen Schriftsteller der ersten drei Jahrhunderte*
HTR	*Harvard Theological Review*
JBL	*Journal of Biblical Literature*
JECS	*Journal of Early Christian Studies*
JHBiol	*Journal of the History of Biology*
JHS	*Journal of Hellenic Studies*
JTS	*Journal of Theological Studies*
JWCI	*Journal of the Warburg and Courtauld Institutes*
LTP	*Laval Philosophique et Théologique*
MusHelv	*Museum Helveticum*
NT	*Novum Testamentum*
NTS	*New Testament Studies*
PAS	*Proceedings of the Aristotelian Society*
PCPS	*Proceedings of the Cambridge Philological Society*
PG	*Patrologia Graeca*
POC	*Proche-Orient Chrétien*
REA	*Revue des Etudes Augustiniennes*
RM	*Review of Metaphysics*

RSPT	*Recherches de Sciences Philosophiques et Théologiques*
RSR	*Recherches de Science Religieuse*
SC	*Sources Chrétiennes*
SJT	*Scottish Journal of Theology*
SVF	*Stoicorum Veterum Fragmenta* (ed. H. von Arnim)
TLS	*Times Literary Supplement*
TS	*Theological Studies*
TU	*Texte und Untersuchungen der Geschichte der altchristlichen Literatur*
VC	*Vigiliae Christianae*
ZKG	*Zeitschrift für Kirchengeschichte*
ZKTh	*Zeitschrift für Katholische Theologie*

Introduction: Partial and universal truth

Jesus and Paul did not belong to the Church of England.
K. Hopkins, *A World Full of Gods* (London 1999) 81

TRUTH, SCRIPTURE AND CHRISTIAN CULTURE

"It is no less sure that both patristic and medieval theology recognized that the whole of saving truth is to be found in the Bible and that the Church is bound to its rule."[1] The words of a modern scholar echo those of Gregory of Nyssa in the fourth century: "We make the Scriptures the rule and the measure of every teaching."[2] Such comment may look obvious and self-explanatory, but it is not: neither as the complete expression of a theological principle since it leaves unanswered questions of interpretation – as, how literally is Scripture to be read?; nor in its implications, since "saving truth" needs to be identified and distinguished from other forms of truth; nor even as a fact about the history of the Church, for it leaves us uncertain about Christianity before the "Bible" – or more specifically the canon of the New Testament – was established, let alone what Christians were thinking and doing before the composition of the earliest New Testament texts (let us say before 55 AD, or some ten years later for the appearance of the earliest canonical Gospels[3]). Some of the apostles, in the early days the ultimate court of appeal,[4] were long-lived. By 120 they were all dead and the four-Gospel canon had not yet been established.[5]

---

[1] J. H. Walgrave, *Theological Resources: Unfolding Revelation* (London 1972) 188–189.

[2] *De an. et res.*, PG 46. 49C, 52C.

[3] Although this is occasionally challenged (e.g., by P. Rolland, *L'origine et la date des évangiles* (Paris 1994) who wants to date a hypothetical text of Aramaic Matthew to before 40), the earliest plausible date for Matthew and Mark would seem to be in the sixties.

[4] For Papias' "sources" of Christian knowledge see especially E. Norelli, *Esposizione degli oracoli del Signore* (Milan 2005).

[5] For the absence of written sources of Christianity in Clement of Rome and Ignatius of Antioch (late first and early second century) see Y.-M. Blanchard, *Aux sources du canon: Le témoignage d'Irenée* (Paris 1993) 21–43.

At some point in the middle of the second century, however, the Christian Churches determined it – which means that, though in later patristic times the manner of that determination had been long forgotten, we know that there was a Christian age when "the whole of saving truth" was *not* decided by reference to the Scriptures, and when the acceptability of the candidate Scriptures would depend on their compatibility with privileged teachings derived orally from the apostles and other early witnesses to the life of Jesus, or from writings now lost.

The historical facts of the relation of primitive Church tradition to Scripture were no clearer to the Catholic Fathers of the Council of Trent than to their Protestant rivals, but, whatever their reasoning, they were right to treat of Tradition as a source of Christian truth. Therefore, if we consider the development of "Christian doctrine" – let alone of "Christian culture" – since it is not the case that saving truth has always been determined by simple transparent reference to the Scriptures, it must be correct in principle that much more general metaphysical, religious and social truth need not – indeed cannot – be so immediately determined. Tradition will always need to be invoked. The question is: how is it to be approached?

Clearly the Church has recognized that the Scriptures (viewed as a living organism) have now become the touchstone for acceptable doctrinal development, but Christian history has shown that the formulation of even saving truth need not, perhaps cannot, be precisely determined by what is self-evidently clear to the casual reader, and that there are elements of enriching theological and philosophical truth (though perhaps not of essentially saving truth, however determined) to be revealed elsewhere. Yet to be recognizably Christian such elements must be *compatible* with the Scriptures, however interpreted. Anything incompatible is beyond the pale, but the most stringent argument would be required to dismiss anything compatible as non-Christian, let alone anti-Christian.

And what Scripture teaches is not always easy to determine. We have to interpret, and interpretation has proved, and still proves, exceptionally tricky. But we must already retrace our steps amid so many uncertainties. We need to clarify the relationship between "saving truth" and "truth", and between both these truths and the connected but not identical themes of "Christian doctrine" and "Christian thought". And then there is "Christian culture": in some sense a wider term, though without Christian doctrine and Christian thought there is no Christian (or not even post-Christian) culture.

If there is a distinction between "truth" and "saving truth", then "truth" in all its forms must be compatible with "saving truth". Augustine – a pivotal figure in the present essay – offers an interesting example pointing to the required distinction. All his life he was puzzled about the "origin" of the soul, but frequently, when frustrated at his failure to resolve the matter, he observes that to know the origin of the soul is not necessary for salvation. Which does not prevent him from continuing his search, nor probably from recognizing that, if he could find the answer, it would illumine "saving truth" and make that easier to accept. We can therefore agree that "truth" is wider than "saving truth", that the truth about God is wider than saving truth, and that those who possess and hand on saving truth may not know as many truths about God as later generations. Yet the wider knowledge of these later generations may be ill assimilated with saving truth itself.

Thus "saving truth" may be comparatively narrow and – controversially – impede the acceptance of wider truths. It is possible to be so concerned with the most important theological truths as to blind oneself to truths arising from unexpected sources. In reviewing some of the history of the expansion of "Christian truth" and of the knowledge of "truth" more generally by Christians, we frequently find situations where Christian possession (though not necessarily comprehension) of saving truth has rendered its possessors incapable of recognizing other truths compatible with saving truth and possibly illuminating it.

Some further distinctions should be made between "Christian doctrine", "Christian dogma" and "Christian thought". Stipulative definitions will serve our turn, provided we are consistent and our stipulations more or less follow current practice. "Thought" (including "belief") is clearly the widest term, and it will refer to all ideas that have a certain consistent circulation within a Christian culture. A Christian "belief", such as in limbo, may have little or no official status; it is simply an idea held by a number of Christians *qua* Christians. "Dogmas" and "doctrines" have a more official ring, and in current usage signify ideas derived directly from Scripture or expounded by official or semi-official Christian bodies such as Church councils, popes or synods. The great majority of such ideas – especially about the person of Christ and the Trinity – are of considerable antiquity, often deriving from the first five or six centuries of Christianity, though if we admit "doctrinal development" as a legitimate principle we must assume that this may continue into the future.

Perhaps we can get away without a distinction between "doctrine" and "dogma", but both of these must be distinguished from longstanding Christian beliefs seeming to underlie them, of which some may predate any tightened propositional formulation. Indeed, such propositions, especially if clearly formulated, will normally involve later expansions (or contractions), since it seems that Christians (as other groups) have been happy to deploy ideas only broadly understood, provided they can be explained historically or seem to be useful: perhaps in liturgical or other worshipful practices.

Good examples of such general notions are the concepts of omnipotence and creation. Descriptions of God as "omnipotent" go back well into Old Testament times,[6] but generations of Christians used the term before much thought was given to its precise connotation, or to what it might or might not imply about what a tolerably intelligible God could or could not do. At an early stage of its use "omnipotent" probably meant something like "indescribably more physically powerful than anything else". Similarly, God seems to have been described as "maker of heaven and earth" long before Christians began to ask whether he made heaven and earth out of nothing or whether he perhaps brought order out of some kind of formless chaos.[7]

When modern writers treat of the development of Christianity, they normally follow Newman in treating of the development of doctrine, that is, of those propositional utterances, however determined, which are supposed to sum up the essentials of Christian belief, thus formalizing saving truth. And the development of such "doctrines" depends on the development of Christian thought in the broader sense, so that the development of Christian doctrine will go hand in hand with the development of Christian culture.

Which brings us to the fundamental difficulty, that primitive Christianity was not in the most obvious sense a set of doctrines at all; it might be better described as a set of Jewish attitudes, or as the relationship of a group of Jews to Jesus of Nazareth. Whatever these Jews and their successors knew of Christianity in a more "doctrinal" sense – namely of the nature of Christ and the God of Christ, "God the Father" – they acquired through this personal relationship and by unavoidable reflection on its significance in their immediate place and time. So that, from being the story of the words and deeds of Jesus, Christianity came to be seen as the interpretation of those words and deeds. Thus, on the one hand there is no need to suppose that the disciples ever considered the best (even if inadequate) way to describe Jesus "propositionally" which the Church later claimed to identify; yet any such developing descriptive propositions would – if adequate – have to demonstrate a fidelity to the tradition about what Jesus had meant and what he had revealed to the original group.

[6] See N. J. Torchia, *Creatio ex Nihilo and the Theology of St. Augustine* (New York 1999) 1–4.
[7] See generally G. May, *Creatio ex Nihilo* (Eng. trans. A. S. Worrall, Edinburgh 1994).

Hence not only will "Christian" doctrinal understanding (or misunderstanding) develop from the time of the original apostles, but also there must have been a set of foundational beliefs which the original apostles held, and which, in a later phrase, we can refer to as the original rule of faith (*regula fidei*). The existence of such a rule, even though implicit, provides the test of whether or not ideas coming originally from outside the minimum of Christianity "necessary for salvation" can be accepted as Christian truth in some wider sense. Since Jesus is said to have told his disciples that they will be led by the Spirit into all truth (John 16:13), there is no *a priori* reason why a process of expansion should not last as long as humanity itself.

In any full-scale consideration of Christian thought, it will be necessary to identify, as far as possible, the foundational elements of the Christianity of the earliest days of the movement: that is, the Christianity identifiable from New Testament texts and other early writings. Naturally the present investigation – concerned not with Christian origins but with the growth of a wider Christian "culture" – is being carried forward from a Christian perspective: that is, I am hypothesizing that Christianity is in some sense "true" and asking what historical facts can show us about the nature of that truth as it worked itself out as a culture. If the development of Christian culture, considered historically, were to show itself to be utterly random, with no clear line of intelligible progression, that would be a strong argument that my hypothesis about the "truth" of Christianity was unfounded. Pilate would have the last laugh.

CHRISTIAN TRADITION

In *Dominus Iesus* (AD 2000), that briefly notorious Declaration of the Roman Catholic Church's Congregation for the Doctrine of the Faith, we find a claim about the nature of various Christian Churches and their relationship to the Church of Rome, and by implication about the development of Christian doctrine. "The ecclesial communities which have not preserved the valid Episcopate and the genuine and integral substance of the Eucharistic mystery are not Churches in the proper sense." Here we have not only what amounts to an Aristotelian definition of "Church" as a centre of "focal meaning", whereby other Churches are understood to be such in varying degrees and with reference to a Church of Christ founded on the rock of Peter and his successors, but an implied thesis that proper development will always involve addition to (or exposition of), and never subtraction from, a fundamental deposit.

In *Dominus Iesus* Cardinal Ratzinger (as he then was) and his colleagues discussed doctrine in the strictest sense: creeds, the documents of councils and of the magisterium. In these cases, they argued, exposition of Christian truth is constructed on an original deposit taught by Jesus to the apostles and through them to the developing Church. As Newman was well aware, that leaves the problem of how to determine proper from improper development, but Newman's solution – which is roughly to identify the teaching of the fourth and fifth centuries and imply that such beliefs were in the mind of the Church (rather than in the mind of Jesus) from the beginning – takes us on to dangerous ground inasmuch as it would infer historical facts and more or less conscious beliefs on the basis of the evidence of later epochs. Indeed, in tempting us to misread earlier intentions in the light of later ones, it subverts the principle of doctrinal development itself.

Dominus Iesus itself comes close to offending in this regard by availing itself of a common habit of re-using ancient formulae while endowing them with meanings unlikely to coincide with the intentions of the original authors. After citations of the Fourth Lateran Council, Vatican II and a letter of the Holy Office to the archbishop of Boston, we read that Cyprian's formula "there is no salvation outside the Church" (*extra ecclesiam nulla salus*, *Letter* 73.21, etc.) is to be interpreted as allowing for the salvation of non-members of the Church "by virtue of a grace which, having a mysterious relationship to the Church, does not make them formally part of the Church" (pp. 31–2 and note 82).

Modern scholars have pointed out that Cyprian (and Origen in similar contexts) was speculating on the fate of those who leave the Church for conventicles, and not on the possible salvation of pagans.[8] That is not to imply that he would have been any more "generous" (to use our jargon) to them; his insistence on the necessity of baptism suggests that had he been asked the wider question his answer would have been equally "ungenerous". And among later Fathers of the ancient Church, especially after Augustine (whose views will be discussed in chapter 2), as well as among their medieval successors, the "ungenerous" attitude prevailed.

An earlier view, strikingly adduced in the bold claim of Justin Martyr (*First Apology* 46.1–4), that Socrates and Heraclitus are to be numbered among those "Christians" who recognized something of the Logos without

---

[8] For a recent history of the question see B. Sesboué, *Hors de l'église pas de salut: Histoire d'une formule et problèmes d'interprétation* (Paris 2004). Sesboué's account of Cyprian, as I argue, is tendentious, but he comments helpfully on the effect on the debate of the discovery of millions of non-evangelized Indians in America, as well as on the background to the formulations of Vatican II.

benefit of any institutional sacrament (and that they have contemporary parallels), was not followed up until much later. There may be something similar in Clement of Alexandria (*Miscellanies* 6.6.45.6), but Augustine – more characteristic of the ancient Church *when it began to consider* the possible salvation of pagans – is inclined to think that even the salvation of the Penitent Thief on the cross is only intelligible if he had already been baptized.[9]

On this point the attitude of *Dominus Iesus* is rather similar to Newman's: what is later explicit (in this case some sort of baptism of desire) is not merely compatible with the earlier "essentials" of the faith but would have been readily accepted (if presented to them) by all earlier "orthodox" thinkers. That seems to confuse the mind of the Church with the mind of God, nullifying Jesus' words that the Holy Spirit will lead us into all truth. We do not need to be led where we have already arrived, and to argue that even Cyprian (let alone Augustine) understood "outside the Church" (*extra ecclesiam*) as we understand it is to play down the importance of the challenges the Church faced at particular periods of its history and to imply that by easy deduction an ancient Christian could have teased out later doctrinal assumptions.

Attitudes of this sort, though consistent and multivarious, are dangerous, causing scandal in the strict theological sense and laying Christians open to the contempt of historically literate unbelievers and those who listen to them.[10] In this book I shall try to maintain the distinction between theology and the history of theology, recognizing that without that distinction history has to be falsified in the interests of what can be called a fundamentalism of tradition which confuses and perverts the uninformed as much as a crude biblicism. In making the distinction, I am immeasurably assisted by the fact that the modern scholar has better tools and opportunities to get history "right" than any of his predecessors – though we have only approximated to that position since the beginning of the nineteenth century.

If problems about theology and its history arise with matters of faith, how much more do they arise in matters of morals where it is impossible to deny that the Church has radically modified its earlier condemnations, as

---

[9] See below p. 120.
[10] A second variety of "scandalous" material – less about the beliefs of historical figures than their mentality, yet similarly liable to provoke scepticism – can occasionally be found, for example, in A. Scola's generally illuminating *The Nuptial Mystery* (1998; Eng. trans. M. K. Borras, Grand Rapids/Cambridge 2005). Thus Scola rather implausibly insists (p. 48) that "Their [the Cappadocians', especially Gregory of Nyssa's] position [on double creation], however – we repeat – cannot be confused with a fear of sex." That is unnecessarily to provoke in the less pietistic the reaction "Oh yeah?"

notoriously of usury and of religious freedom as well as its toleration of slavery, torture and capital punishment. Development, whether strictly doctrinal or more broadly of Catholic culture, occurs when particular challenges from the outside world – from Gnosticism to modern feminism – have to be met. Which means that if we could identify with sufficient accuracy the challenges the Church will face, we should be able to predict some of the developments of Catholic culture in coming years, decades and centuries.

For development of doctrine, as of Catholic culture and society, is substantially a matter of what is compatible with what has gone before, not simply of what can be deduced from it – or so it is my present aim to propose. If, for example, we look at the history of the Pauline doctrine that in Christ there is neither male nor female, slave nor free, we can see how modern interpretations of the text are possible and legitimate extensions of the primal deposit brought to the surface by external events, and not such deductions from it as could easily have been made in earlier ages. Or rather, they might have been and occasionally were made, but were as readily forgotten because the spirit of the age found it easy to ignore, pervert or deny them.

Given enough time, I could draw examples from virtually any period of Church history. Given the shortness of human life and the tiredness of age, I shall focus primarily (as did Newman) on the early centuries, when patterns and principles of constructive development were firmly fixed, where problems demanding solution can easily be identified, and hence where present and future advances may the more readily be foretold, and where the basic Christological and Trinitarian dogmas of Catholic Christianity – on which I have little to add to the current consensus – were broadly established. But the period embracing the Renaissance, the Reformation and the Enlightenment will demand more attention than the more "homogeneous" medieval West. In those dramatic times unexpected challenges arose, and in coping with them the Church not infrequently found itself, and still finds itself, falling back on varieties of historical fundamentalism, as in the misrepresentation of Cyprian's famous text, or alternatively bending over backwards – a posture at least as common among clergy and ex-clergy as among the laity – to adopt the premises of their opponents. In purporting to expand what they believe to be their own civilization, they manage to recycle many of the cultural errors of their opponents along with their metaphysical incoherences.

Cultural investigations cannot be limited to the credal or narrowly doctrinal. Christianity is a historical religion or of no more than scholarly interest, and the development of historical institutions such as the Roman see are as much a part of our story as is the complex relationship between Christian thinkers and Platonists over the nature and significance of Beauty, the human body and of art, or the still far from completed Christian analysis of sexual differentiation, or the indispensability of divine grace if salvation is to be found. Hence I shall suggest that lines and laws of development can be identified in the growth of Christian institutions similar to those in the development of Christian thought and doctrine. And all along Newman's question will keep returning: what is proper, what improper development? For only if similar lines of growth and development can be discerned in a wide range of Christian "activities" can we be sure that unfolding Catholic Christianity is ever more coherent and therefore ever more a candidate for truth.

Protestantism will turn out to be both a hero and a villain in the play: villainous in that it has tended to run down Christ to the preached and printed word, and thus too often to an emotionless and philistine rationalism against which modern generations are in revolt – and usually thinking they are rejecting Christianity as a whole. (Which is neither to say that Protestants are all emotionless philistines nor that historically speaking many such have not had even excessive influence in the Catholic Church.) Villainous in another way too, in that, by encouraging biblical literalism, the Protestants have laid Christianity as a whole open to attack on strictly historical grounds.[11]

But Protestantism has also been heroic (in an almost Wagnerian sense) in that it has raised intriguing possibilities of moral, spiritual, scientific and philosophical advance, many of which have turned out to be blind alleys; yet without our finding (even hitting) the end of the cul-de-sac, proper development both doctrinal and cultural would have been much the slower. Yet where Protestant culture in its originally religious and later secularized forms has been the most successful, that is, in its promoting of scientific and technological progress, it is now increasingly having to recognize that science without ethics – as also art, as we shall see – is haunted by two vices: first by what used to be called *curiositas*: that is, misplaced curiosity (who, apart from those wishing to help the victims, should want to know the psychological and physiological effects of electric shocks on the human genitals?); second, by an irresponsibility fuelled by fear, arrogance or just love of power: as Tom Lehrer expressed it: "'If the rockets go up, who cares

---

[11] For a test case against any strictly literalist inerrancy in the New Testament see J. M. Rist, "Luke 2:2: Making Sense of the Date of Jesus' Birth", *JTS* 56 (2005) 489–491.

where they come down?/ That's not my department,' said Werner von Braun."

The Protestant thesis of "Scripture alone" seemed the more plausible and seductive when the historical genesis of the New Testament could hardly be known; indeed, as I have implied, the decline of "mainline" Protestantism as an intellectual form of Christianity – and its consequent collapse either into liberal (i.e., more or less non-Christian) theism and even atheism, or into a narrow biblicism – is in part the direct result of failure to withstand the assaults of a modern historical criticism itself in origin the product of a Protestant "scientific" culture. And biblical fundamentalism can only flourish not only by denial of the development of doctrine but by a wholesale rejection of historical enquiry and a consequent willingness to accept logical absurdities.

"Developmental" enquiry, as I have observed, has been suspect not only among Protestant fundamentalists and fideists but among their Catholic counterparts; it is so still and not least among the more fervid. There are two major reasons for this, one understandable, the other wholly misguided. The first is the undoubtedly ultra-sceptical, if not frequently perverse notion of historical enquiry which has prevailed among New Testament scholars, some of them purporting to discern truth by "democratic" voting-procedures among members of their special guild. At its worst such "historical" enquiry operates on principles unrecognizable by other historians, and such activity has rightly brought the subject into contempt in the secular world as well as among more rational (and usually more devout) Christians.

But to identify abuses is not enough; historical enquiry is not to be dismissed on account of the inadequacy of some of its practitioners. Nor is it appropriate to look solely for "spiritual" guidance to resolve historical problems such as the *development* of the Roman see, of the concept of omnipotence or of the theology of baptism. Such appeal to "spiritual" guidance – in effect constituting a denial of secondary causation – not only negates any meaningfully human account of doctrinal development, but constitutes an alternative form of fundamentalism: not biblicist but "traditionist", and in irrational opposition to serious historical enquiry, the results of which, its adherents fear, will undermine the faith. That is paradoxical indeed in the mouths of those who claim allegiance to a "historical" religion which can no more be reduced to an emotional acceptance of authority than to a variety of metaphysics (as with the deists); but which, on the other hand, cannot be justified intellectually without metaphysics – as was supposed by many of the first Protestants in their distorting of the Bible into a replacement for not historical but philosophical enquiry.

THE NATURE OF THE PRESENT STUDY

The present book aims to address primarily two classes of readers: those Christians who wish to make a considered attempt to deploy the richness of their tradition in serious debate with the "secular and godless" world, and those members of that world who, as honest seekers after truth, are willing to consider the radical alternative to the prevalent mode of viewing the nature and prospects of man. Although it contains historical, philosophical and theological material, some of it detailed though by no means inaccessible, it is a work of neither history nor philosophy nor theology. Necessarily offering little more than a sampling of its potential subject-matter, it remains an investigation of certain historical, philosophical and theological phenomena and an attempt to project the findings of that investigation – proposed as a thesis – in their implications for the future development of an institution.

That institution is the Roman Catholic Church, and the thesis is that, in confronting and surmounting its present challenges (Western secularization, intolerant Islam, its own transformation into a world religion no longer overwhelmingly Western), it must become either more catholic in the broad sense or forfeit its original and developing identity, in succumbing to the age-long temptation to become lazy, ignorant, outdated and spiritually emasculated: that is, to become sectarian. Hence it must nourish the long-recognized power within itself to expand beliefs and doctrines into a cultural structure capable of assimilating all that is good, true and necessary from outside its formal limits. In all this it must retain "organic" unity with the divine seed from which it has grown and from which springs its zeal to show itself the uninhibited lover and promoter of all that is good and the only defensible conduit for any human "salvation". As Paul taught, such "saving truth" is encapsulated in its belief in the historical, bodily Resurrection of Christ.

Augustine observes in *On Christian Teaching* (2.18.28) that the good Christian should recognize truth wherever he finds it. Part of the concern of this study will be with the "internal" development of Christian ideas and doctrines, or rather with the development of the understanding of such doctrines. But as integral to that "internal" examination, as urged by Augustine, I shall discuss the appearance or reappearance, from outside the Church's visible boundaries from one age to the next, of ideas sometimes surprisingly compatible with its "deposit", and thus able to enrich and render it more comprehensive, and hence more comprehensible and persuasive to those willing and able to think.

To complete such an assignment, the strictest concern for historical accuracy is required. One cannot make a case for the development of the understanding of doctrine unless one is prepared to admit that doctrine was not fully understood – even if correctly formulated and "lived" – in preceding ages; and I cannot make a case for an extended cultural horizon for Catholicism if I do not admit that in earlier times Catholicism's horizons were seriously restricted. Nor can I make a case for the necessity of an ongoing reinterpretation of the socio-political contents of a Catholic culture unless I recognize the inadequate (though often inevitable) socio-political structures within which the Church has allowed itself to operate, even prided itself on operating.

I have chosen six themes through which to indicate my view of the expanding horizon of Catholic culture. As I have indicated, much of my discussion will centre on the first five centuries of the Church's history, since in those five centuries a large measure of dogma, belief and practice was established in councils and without them. Clearly, if significant expansion of mental horizons can be shown in this early period, a pattern has been set which we should expect to be repeated in later centuries. That is, not only will a given core of belief and precept become more or less fixed, but the possibility of incompletenesses in understanding will emerge. And such incompletenesses may involve matters of importance, as in our understanding of human nature and human society as well as of the nature of God. I shall take as axiomatic that in any religion (or at any stage of religious development) a believer's understanding of the nature of God will be intimately reflected in his account of human nature, human obligation and human good.

As I have already noted, a major tactic of the present study will be to show that in patristic times there is a partial assimilation of "outside" material to the Christian core, hence that this early period provides a model both for what happened in later centuries and for what could and should continue to happen. The "Christian core" is identified by writers as early as Irenaeus and Tertullian at the end of the second century as the "rule of faith" or "rule of truth". Further growth must therefore be either a logical expansion of that rule of faith or the accumulation of new ideas not incompatible with it – by which further understanding of the "rule" itself may be achieved. My thrust, therefore, is that there have occurred, should occur and will occur additions to "Catholic" culture – that is to a Catholic mentality – that have themselves to be re-informed by their meeting with Catholic dogma, theology, and a wider but compatible "thought" and "culture", before in their own turn informing further aspects of Catholic life.

A serious obstacle to which I have already alluded needs further preliminary comment. There has existed – and in many quarters still exists, despite massive evidence in favour of a more nuanced presentation – a belief that the great intellectual and ecclesiastical structures in Catholicism have, if authentic, always been visibly identical with those of the past; thus, for example, that contemporary moral teaching is in practically every area virtually identical with what has always been taught. And in many respects that is true. The Ten Commandments and the Beatitudes are still with us, teaching on abortion has remained constant, and we still subscribe to the Apostolic Succession; yet – to mention two of the questions I shall discuss in this book – we do not now preach the same view of human nature (especially in relation to autonomy and sexuality) as we did in the past; but a different "anthropology" has led to a rather different attitude to the various parts of morality. Nor do we view the authority of the bishop of Rome in the same way as, for example, did Cyprian, author, as already noticed, of the famous "Outside the Church there is no salvation".

Hence I shall make it a matter of principle to keep theology distinct from the history of theology, and insist that the truth of contemporary theological and moral claims provides no justification for historical misreadings of past beliefs. The history of theology, let alone of Christian thought and culture, cannot be written *a priori* on the basis of the contemporary state of our understanding. On the contrary, if understanding has developed, it was underdeveloped in the past (though it is also importantly true that, under local pressures, we are always prone to forget what we once knew); and the effects of such underdevelopment (as, for example, in the case of religious persecution) may make for unwelcome "memories" in the present. "Unwelcome" does not entail "untrue", and true but unwelcome propositions about the past in no way invalidate more refined claims made in the present or future. Here we have a serious problem, but refusal to recognize the difference between theological and historical truth will not only lead to what I have dubbed fundamentalist "traditionism" – a mentality that has as one of its essential components the fostering of wilful ignorance when "ignorance" is judged more "spiritually" acceptable – but will attract condemnation under a famous Augustinian principle: that the worst kind of untruthfulness is lying in matters of religion.

A ROMAN ROAD-MAP

The topics to be discussed in this book may look disparate. I begin with a Christian theme fundamental in any exposition of Christian "anthropology",

Christian ethics, indeed any seriously Christian account of God, and which will set the tone for my study: namely that *Homo* – humanity – has been created in the image and likeness of God. The immediate aim of my first chapter will be to provide a philosophical, theological and historical discussion of how our understanding of a key aspect of this theme – the created godlikeness of women – has been a very slow process, and is still incomplete. That is, I shall try to explain how the Church came first to recognize (rather than understand) that women, as well as men, are created in the image of God, and how such recognition was both forwarded and inhibited by originally extra-Christian philosophical and theological ideas about what it is to be specifically human, and in what way what is specifically human could intelligibly be said to have been created in the image and likeness of God.

In chapter 2 I turn to more unfinished business, about man and about God. Traditionally, Christian accounts of human free will are associated with the doctrine of original sin, namely that after the Fall we are not particularly "free", but need to be freed by God's grace; at best we are incapable of the regular choice of the good. In the past these assumptions have encouraged the coercion of unbelievers and heretics (not to speak of artists) to enter or re-enter the fold. Enforced "choice", however, came to clash with ideas about autonomy, often now accepted blindly and in unassimilated form by the Church – this and related matters will be discussed in chapter 6. That a "human" act is not human merely in virtue of being performed, but in virtue of being performed in accordance with the reflections and dictates of a formed conscience, the Church has gradually come to recognize, and so to repudiate the error of the enforcing of orthodoxy in defiance of a "right to religious freedom" – while maintaining its scepticism on the possibility of an autonomous and well-formed conscience without grace in our "fallen" condition.

If an autonomous conscience is now so important, indeed central, in Christianity, how should it be understood in relation to theories of fallen man's sin and God's justice? Those earlier theories – as expounded – tended to make God's justice unintelligible, implying that man, in a world in which he is created in God's image, is yet helplessly dependent on God's arbitrary power. But an arbitrary God – as distinct from an ultimately unknowable God – leaves man little more than a puppet. As already implied, in pursuing the present and future of this dilemma I shall treat it as axiomatic that, however we understand God, we shall understand the worth of man in a God-reflected light: an axiom which can be seen working itself out at least in all monotheistic religions.

My third chapter also is both philosophical and theological. It is concerned with how theories of beauty, largely of Platonic origin and especially of the beauty of Christ, influenced a developing Christianity in the third and especially the fourth century, enabling it eventually to offer a Christian account of beauty and hence of artistic creativity. Such development has allowed Christianity to free itself from the narrowness of a puritanical, or even "philistine", account of art and the artist, and at the same time to resist a view of aesthetics as a quasi-religion of "art for art's sake", or the corresponding cult of the creative artist or writer – in more secular theology of the pop-star, well-endowed starlet or soccer-player – as the self-inspired prophet of moral and anthropological truths. For as to the latter, a modern Wordsworth might declare, "Juvenal, thou shouldst be living at this hour, England hath need of thee"!

Chapter 4 is more strictly historical, aiming to point to a certain parallel development of Catholic institutions and thought, as well as offering further reflection on the necessity of the papacy for the future development of a specifically Catholic culture. It attempts to outline the gradual recognition by the pre-Constantinian Roman Church of something of its later theological and historical role – although the "political", social and even theological nature of that role was to become clearer only many centuries and many temporary way-stations into the future. Thus the historical (and related doctrinal) enquiry of chapter 4 reflects on the temptation to a theocratic (and necessarily anti-intellectual and anti-cultural) "Catholic" state, and to questions of the proper relationship between the Church and civil society. These are more specifically the subject of chapter 5, where I also consider the more "secular" medieval (and even post-medieval) alternative of Caesaropapism.

Within Christianity theocratic claims are now a thing of the past and, in order to investigate the possibility of an honest relationship between the Church and civil – and not only Christian – society, I turn finally to the wider principles of modern and post-modern culture, and to consider how the development of the post-Christian West reveals a certain failure of the Church to come to grips with many of man's broader aspirations, as well as with what can be learned from recent secular thinking and what should be unambiguously rejected. In this chapter the doctrine of man's creation in the image of God returns to centre stage as a rediscovered resource through which substantive foundations, rather than mere wishful thinking, can be developed to justify a "moral" concept of man and hence human rights.

In our age, and the more readily because of the power of the mass-media, Catholics are known to call a mere accommodation to contemporary fashion, driven by a fear of being caught naked opposing it – "The important thing is not to be out of communion with the *New York Times*" – a "development" or even an *aggiornamento*.[12] Chapters 4, 5 and 6 infer connections between the historical development of the central Catholic institution of the papacy and the possibilities for the ongoing expansion of a recognizably Catholic culture.

Some readers may be surprised that I shall say rather little about Orthodoxy, the "other lung of the Church". My reasons will become clearer as I proceed, but I should briefly notice two fundamental (and perhaps sadly – and dangerously – irreformable) weaknesses of the Orthodox world: its originally Byzantine Caesaropapism (transformed later into fragmented national and nationalist Churches), and its tendency to interpret tradition as the idolization of an undevelopable past. This can be seen strikingly in its refusal of the *filioque* clause added by Westerners to the Nicene Creed and in its claims to find full-blown versions of the late Byzantine theology of Gregory Palamas in texts composed centuries earlier. I shall notice tendencies to the latter sleight-of-hand within the fold of Catholic Christianity too – as evidenced in my comments on the relationship between theology and the history of theology.

Some readers may be surprised at how much space in a book about Catholic Christianity is given over to non-Christian thinkers, especially to Plato, Aristotle and Plotinus; and may mutter about hobby-horses. But if they continue to mutter when they have reached the end of the book, they will either have wholly failed to understand it or will logically have rejected it lock-stock-and-barrel. The role of Plato, Aristotle and Plotinus in the present study is to illuminate in the most concrete fashion how, from its earliest times until now, the "saving truth" of Christianity has been rendered to us in an enriched and – to be frank – surely more divine form than would appear to have been possible without their divine inspiration. Greek philosophers have not only enriched Christian culture; they have shown how that culture can be enhanced by all that is good in the apparently non-Christian world.

Throughout this book I argue that there is a continuous development of "Catholic" thought from the time of Jesus himself. Surprisingly, perhaps, I shall also show that in most cases this development has been achieved outside of Rome: an early example is the growth of understanding of man's creation in the image of God. Only in very recent times has development seemed frequently to derive immediately from the Roman see, and that model may also be a delusion. For although in recent times popes have been seen (not least by themselves) as expressing expansions of Christian ideas,

---

[12] See the comments of Jonathan Robinson on Charles Taylor in *The Mass and Modernity* (San Francisco 2005) 226–227.

there has been no substantial change in the way these ideas have originated. The function of the Roman bishop, *qua* Roman bishop, has always been not that of innovator but of confirmer of what has been established within Christian society as a whole. His apparent contemporary role as instigator is a function less of a new role within the Church than of his being the easy focus of media attention. His real role has throughout history been to confirm and to restrain.

Two final and more personal words should be added by way of introduction. The author of this book has had no formal training in anything except a broadly understood classical philology – and hence in the contemporary world would never have secured an academic post – yet from that discipline, among other goods, has acquired a lifelong admiration for Plato: not least for his ability to mingle the entertaining and the disrespectful with the important – in fact to write in the character of the *spoudaiogeloios*, the mixer of the serious and the comic. It is a great gift, found also in Shakespeare. I can admire but not lay claim to it. If at times I attempt to imitate, it is in tribute to my Master, whom I hope also to have imitated in his love of Truth: and to have made the important distinction between the properly serious (*spoudaion*) and the merely earnest.

Second, in 1993 I rashly accepted to submit an essay (I entitled it "Where Else?") for a volume to be edited by Kelly J. Clark and called *Philosophers who Believe*. The present book may be seen as a vastly enlarged and better documented exploration of the summarized thinking behind and beyond that autobiographical snapshot, the inadequacies of which I well realize. Nevertheless, it can only sketch an approach to many of the topics it treats; and necessarily much secondary literature has been left unexamined. But though my material is diffuse and in parts cannot but remain difficult, I have tried to ensure that this book can be read without reference to footnotes. These, plus the bibliography, are designed for those who wish to pursue purely technical as well as more peripheral questions further than my available space and present aims permit.

CHAPTER I

The human race, or how could women be created in the image and likeness of God?

Mulier non Codex

Trimalchio in Petronius' *Satyricon*

1.1 THE IMPORTANCE OF THE PROBLEM

Despite its gamut of heroines, the unreconstructed Old Testament preaches an essentially male religion. That is true even more of the Qu'ran, where women may be accorded a certain respect in their place, but where in subsequent law (and common practice) they are exactly half as valuable as men; as is notorious, a man may have up to four wives at a time (Mohammed himself was eventually conceded an indefinite number, plus concubines), while no woman can have more than one man at a time, who may be shared, without risking death as an adulteress. Despite the plain and remarkable attitudes of its founder, Christianity too could (humanly speaking) have become an essentially male religion, and in periods when the Old Testament (plus a few ambiguous passages of Paul) were given special weight, both in Catholicism and Protestantism – not to speak of Orthodoxy – it tended to revert to earlier Near Eastern attitudes to the relationship between man, woman and God.

In important respects such attitudes were confirmed by certain features of the Greek philosophy (not to speak of the Greco-Roman culture) that lent Christianity so much help in the formulation and development of its dogmas. So that it is of particular interest for any study of the development of Catholic culture that Catholic Christianity has eventually *not* become a "male" religion. In search of some part of the explanation of that historically surprising fact I shall review the long struggle in early and later Christianity – a struggle still incomplete – to understand how, why and in what sense the axiom that man has been created in the image and likeness of God implies that women have been equally so created.

A historical and theological enquiry into woman's creation in God's image can do more than shed timeless light on human nature and human

18

sexual differentiation in a Christian context: the primary and explicit aim of the present chapter. It will also introduce ramifications of the doctrine of the creation of all human beings (of man as *Homo*) in the image of God. These will be considered further in chapter 6, where, discussing intellectual challenges and temptations for the Church in modern and post-modern society, I shall argue that the doctrine is beginning to prove of capital importance in responding to some fundamental questions of contemporary ethical and political theory. In particular, it is becoming clearer that it provides us with the rational foundation for human rights and the equal dignity of men and women which the secular post-Christian world sadly – and (especially for women) dangerously – lacks.

According to Genesis, "man" is created in the image and likeness of God. At least two major problems arise in every Christian interpretation of those words: "What is the sense of 'man'?" and, "What is the sense of 'image'?" I want to consider some of the answers to these questions, especially the first, offered during the patristic period and beyond, as well as the enduring confusions which the ancient answers leave us to clear up and the intellectually undistinguished solutions which in recent times we have too often been offered. I have also a subsidiary purpose: to investigate, in this specific instance, the relationship between ideas deriving from the Bible and those also influenced by Greek philosophy, in particular from the Platonic tradition, but also from Stoicism.

In considering the philosophical question "What is a man?", Western thought in general has offered two kinds of answers. The first may be called a moral explanation; that is, it identifies a man with his moral personality, with his ability to make moral decisions, or more widely with his existence in "moral space". Broadly speaking, that approach is represented in early Christian times by a philosophical tradition which takes its origins from Socrates and Plato and which tends to identify a human being with his soul or self. A second tradition, complementary to the first, is also well represented in antiquity, in particular by Aristotle; it offers what may be called an ontological account of man: that is, an account of what metaphysically makes a man a *man*, and not, say, just a soul, or a mind, or a body.

Despite a continuing strand in Christian teaching (deriving from the Old Testament and importantly reinforced by Paul) that humans should be viewed "holistically", that is, without an ontological body–soul dualism, this second tradition had a rather limited impact on Christianity in antiquity; and that despite a strong, albeit early, Christian interest in Stoic vitalism. Aristotelianism, however, came into its own in the Christian Middle Ages, and I shall argue that within the "platonizing" traditions of late antiquity, and particularly in Augustine, tensions developed which might – indeed should – have pushed ancient Christians to extend their platonizing accounts of man in a more broadly Aristotelian direction.

Thus, while considering the image and likeness of God in patristic times, and in particular the interpretation of that tradition through "moral" terms largely derived from Platonism – man, that is, is, like God, some sort of moral agent (free, authoritative, etc.) – I also look at the very incomplete attempts of ancient Christians to think not merely biblically but also philosophically in a more ontological and holistic tradition. I then progress to a specific application of the re-emergence of that tradition in its Thomistic version, arguing that although at first sight it might seem that the "platonizing" approach adopted increasingly from the time of Clement of Alexandria (*c.* 200) had obvious weaknesses in its tendency to "depersonalize" humanity seen as God's image, it was also, in its patristic manifestations, more sensitive than its more "biblical" rival to a number of philosophical distinctions that need to be observed in any satisfactory account of human nature.

So that, as developed in ancient times at least, both the more "platonizing" and the more "holistic" traditions had their own inadequacies, some of which we still need to overcome. Two-substance theories, which use soul and body language, may seem to account better than their ontologically superior rival for some important phenomena (not least the godlike phenomena) of human nature. Which does not entail that they are not ultimately misleading or inadequate or that they may not cause much damage in passing, whether theoretical or social.

Frequently, not least in Augustine but also generally in antiquity, Christianity defined itself over against its real or perceived enemies. Such enemies, at the outset, were represented either by "semi-friends" such as Jews and "heretics" or by pagans in the particular context of the hostile if seemingly eternal Roman Empire. That Empire was still dominated by the pagan gods – or demons as the Christians regarded them.[1] Roughly speaking these "gods" encouraged two false loves: idolatry of sex (or "Venus") and of power (or "Jupiter"), both of which purported to give the highest satisfactions, and the latter of which might contribute substantially to facilitating the former. On the sexual side, one of the more extreme Christian positions was unashamedly propounded by Ambrose: "How can sensuality recall us to Paradise, when it alone robbed us of its delights?" (*Letter* 63.11–14). In an ideal

---

[1] For an early identification of gods and demons (by Tatian) see K. Gaça, *The Making of Fornication* (Berkeley/Los Angeles/London 2003) 221–246. Augustine's *City of God* is the classic treatment.

society, as many Christians dreamed, perhaps both loves – of power as of sexual activity – might be eliminated.

But if idolatry of sex can or should be erased, what becomes of the divinely made distinction between men and women? Why did God create sexual difference at all? And how ultimate is that difference in the entire human? Is not sexual difference – or at least sexuality, as even now (for example) von Balthasar often seems to believe – not part of the original image of God in man?[2] Much of the present chapter will reflect Christian interpretation of or reaction to the apparently "dangerous" and subversive power of human sexuality, more particularly in females. In later chapters I shall treat of the other false god, the god of power: in Augustine's phrase the "love of domination". Roughly speaking, as we shall see, love of sex for its own sake is seen by the *bien-pensants* of Christian antiquity as a "feminizing" vice even among heterosexual males;[3] love of power, even of omnipotence, as so obviously masculine as to stand as a challenge to the supreme patriarch, God himself. To decide whether such categorizations are well taken and what stage they represent in the development of Christian culture will be among the goals of the present enquiry.

In Christian antiquity as it developed, one of the broadest questions of all – still unresolved after the Emperors Constantine and Justinian had long left the stage – was whether "secular" societies, dominated by the love and worship of sex and power, should be replaced by some form of theocracy or "divine right" kingdom. And if not that, then what? And if that, how should relations between the sexes be managed within the desired régime? Clearly that would depend on the answer to a prior question about who is the "man" who is intended to be (in) the image of God and when "he" is so intended. Problems about the status of women in relation to God cannot be separated either theoretically or historically from problems about the social status of women, whether in a theocracy or in alternative and more appealing Christian forms of society.

According to the Synoptic Gospels (Mark 12:25; Matthew 22:30; Luke 20:36), in replying to the Sadducees' questioning of resurrection, Jesus observed that in heaven there will be no marrying and giving in marriage (and specifically that a much-married woman will then be no-one's "woman") since we shall then be like the angels. Although these texts do

---

[2] H. U. von Balthasar, *The Glory of the Lord* VI (Edinburgh 1991) 99, note 22: "Sexuality cannot be derived from man's original state as image of God." For further comment on Balthasar's views see notes 27, 115, 196 and 197 below.

[3] For some basic data, pagan as well as Christian, see J. W. Knust, *Abandoned to Lust* (New York 2006).

not say that women will not be women, and although they were frequently misunderstood, they form part of the background – and in the fourth-century notion of living the "angelic life" part of the foreground – of Christian debate about the best human condition, not least because angels (though seeming formally male) have no sexual nature, organs or activity. For in an angelic life sexuality – at least if read merely genitally – will become unnecessary for those who will in any case survive death and need no earthly progeny to give them "immortality". But equally important may be the wider assumption that "neutral" sexual beings can be thought of as male, since "sexuality" is only activated by the introduction of a second, specifically female, type of human being.[4] As "male/neutral" angels are perfect of their kind, so are male/neutral human beings, as created (or recreated) in the image of God.

1.2 FROM MYTHOLOGY TO PHILOSOPHY

Students of Greek mythology know that apparently all the women seduced or raped by Zeus become pregnant,[5] and that with a single exception the child born is male. The exception is Zeus' daughter Helen: not male, merely the most beautiful woman in the world.[6] The explanation of such myths lies in the widely current Greek assumption from earliest times – strikingly set out in the *Eumenides* of Aeschylus (552ff.) – that conception is to be explained on the analogy of sowing a field. Both human and divine seed will grow into a human being (or demi-god), provided only that it is embedded in nourishing soil. Thus the female (as the word *thēlus* may indicate) is nurse both before and after birth.

Yet even before the discovery of the ovaries by Herophilus in third-century BC Alexandria, during a brief period when dissection of cadavers was

---

[4] See K. E. Børresen (ed.), *Image of God and Gender Models* (Oslo 1991).
[5] The Homeric Poseidon observes that the embraces of the gods are always fruitful (*Od.* 11.249–250).
[6] The effects of Zeus' amours with goddesses are more varied, as is appropriate to the rank of the divine partner: thus Artemis as well as Apollo is generated. At least some goddesses, such as Hera, can produce both male and female offspring parthenogenically. As for Helen herself, her mother Leda bore seven sons and just the one daughter. And we should also note other versions of the Helen story (for example, in Apollodorus): in one case the real mother of Helen is Nemesis, a more-than-mortal. She it was who laid the egg (after being raped by an apparent gander) which eventually fell into the hands of Leda and was hatched into Helen. In a second version it was Leda herself who had intercourse with Zeus, but also on the same night with her husband Tyndareus. Some of her brood were thus by Zeus, others, it was said, by Tyndareus – though the mythographers regularly claim that it was Zeus, not Tyndareus, who was the father of Helen. (Note, however, the widespread belief in antiquity that intercourse after conception is liable to cause defects (including being female); cf. Aristotle, *GA* 2.748A; *HA* 6.577AB, 584B–585B.)

permitted, such a view of conception was not universally held by doctors and philosophers. Empedocles, Democritus, the author of the apparently pseudo-Aristotelian *History of Animals* book 10, and later Epicurus, as well as a minority among the Hippocratic writers who discuss gynaecology, argued that both male and female parents contribute "seeds" – sometimes adding the refinement that both contribute both male and female seeds – and that the sex of the newborn child is determined by whichever seed in each particular combination proves to be the stronger. A similar theory was later adopted by Galen and was very important in Christian times. But "two-seed" theories do not imply that the "seeds" are different in kind, as would be implied by modern theories of conception. The seed is the same, even if it comes from both the male and the female partners, and the female version is still inferior to that derived from the "canonical" male body.[7] As for Aristotle, his "mature" view, which I take to be a sophisticated and metaphysically motivated development of popular (and, as we shall see, Platonic) belief about the dominant role of the male, is that the male seed provides the form of the foetus while menstrual discharge contributes the matter. Form, of course, is dominant over matter.[8]

We turn from the amours of Zeus to Hesiod's accounts of Pandora. The standard Greek assumption was that *males* (at least "real men" as distinct from natural slaves or passive adult homosexuals) are fully human beings: that is, that they are unambiguous members of a recognizable class in the world. In early Greek societies, both in myth and in philosophy, the idea circulated that women might be very different: not merely defective males but something yet more "other". So to consider Pandora. Two versions of her story are told by the eighth-century BC poet Hesiod (*Works and Days* 57–105; *Theogony* 512–589), though her name does not appear in his *Theogony*.

After the gods have constructed males, Zeus, in anger at Prometheus and with the co-operation of Athene, Aphrodite and Hermes, forms Pandora, the first woman. Like the men, she is made of clay and given life, but she is significantly different from the males, not least in that Hermes has endowed her with "impudence" and trickery – and she opens up a jar filled by the gods with evils and diseases. Presumably (though there are sceptics) the jar

---

[7] This has been well described as constituting a one-sex model for all bodies by T. Laqueur, *Making Sex: Body and Gender from the Greeks to Freud* (Cambridge, Mass. 1990).

[8] For some of those who held versions of the two-seed theory, see D. M. Halperin, "Why is Diotima a Woman? Platonic Eros and the Figuration of Gender", in D. M. Halperin, J. Winkler and F. I. Zeitlin (eds.), *Before Sexuality* (Princeton 1990) 278; also M. Boylan, "The Galenic and Hippocratic Challenges to Aristotle's Conception Theory, *JHBiol* 17 (1984) 83–112. The fullest account of Aristotelian and pre-Aristotelian gynaecology is probably L. Dean-Jones, *Women's Bodies in Classical Greek Science* (Oxford 1994).

symbolizes her femaleness, standing for the vagina and uterus.[9] When men "know" her (or her female descendants), they know what is other than and inferior to themselves, so releasing and bringing on themselves the evils and diseases in the jar.[10] Pandora's femaleness thus introduces, both for women and for males, the problems of active sexuality. In the myth there is no "problem" with male sexuality as such – it is a neutral part of being a human – but only with its activation by the new female. As we shall see, here is a foreshadowing of much ancient theory: female sexuality is intended for use, liable to be non-sacred or idolatrous, and prone to engender "soft" and "womanish" characteristics in males; whereas male sexuality is of itself properly asexual (if and when inactive) and potentially sacred.

Leaving the Dog-Days of Hesiod's Boeotia and returning to Aristotle, we find the "problem" of Pandora in metaphysical guise. As often in ethics and psychology, Aristotle is ready with a rational version of widely held beliefs. In the *Metaphysics* (1058A29ff.)[11] and the *Generation of Animals* (1.730B35) he alludes to the popular notion, also current among a number of philosophers,[12] that men and women do not belong to the same species. An ancestor of that view is what we have found in Hesiod's account of Pandora – as well as in what the same poet says elsewhere about the "race" of women (*Theogony* 591).

Although Aristotle dismisses the "two-race" theory more or less out of hand, he takes the alternative that men and women are radically different *sorts* of human being more seriously. Indeed, whereas we might expect him to say that he distinguishes men and women only in terms of their significantly different reproductive functions, he infers a more radical variation. Since there are two types of human being, he assumes, they cannot be "equally" human beings; for that would imply that there are two *perfect* human beings, or perfect sorts of human beings: perfect male and perfect female. But for Aristotle, following his own cultural tradition and that of many others, there can be only one perfect type of human being: the perfect male, as the mythographers had normally assumed. And to the mythographical accounts Aristotle can add some science: women's *pneuma* (a quasi-hormonal substance

[9] So F. I. Zeitlin, "The Economics of Hesiod's Pandora", in E. Reeder (ed.), *Pandora* (Baltimore 1995) 49–56.
[10] For further comment see (e.g.) N. Loraux, "La race des femmes et quelques unes de ses tribus", *Arethusa* 11 (1978) 43–89; J. Rudhart, "Pandora: Hésiode et les femmes", *MusHelv* 43 (1986) 231–246; J. N. Bremmer, "Pandora or the Creation of a Greek Eve", in G. P. Luttikhuizen (ed.), *The Creation of Man and Woman* (Leiden 2000) 19–33.
[11] Cf. 1044A34–35; 1071A13–17; 1071B14–31.
[12] Perhaps alluded to in the *Timaeus* (42B, 90E). Cf. G. Sissa, "The Sexual Philosophies of Plato and Aristotle", in P. S. Pantel (ed.), *A History of Women* I (Cambridge, Mass. 1992) 60–61.

which somehow relates form and matter almost as a fifth element) is cooler than required for a male.

In what sense does Aristotle, following popular traditions, believe that such "science" is borne out by empirically observed facts? First of all, as I observed in the case of Zeus – the perfect example – males alone can produce seeds which, given more or less appropriate assistance in women, will grow into newborn members of the human race, possessed of our characteristic humanity. For Aristotle this male physiological superiority is to be explained in terms of the *pneuma*. Pneumatized or boiled blood is the refined product of human processes of nutrition, and males, being hotter than females, pneumatize their blood to a higher degree of perfection; hence in this very specific sense women are inferior and incomplete males (*Generation of Animals* 737A28). Even more particularly, one of the most advanced of the "pneumatized" products is male semen; lesser products, less well cooked in women, are menstrual discharge and milk. At conception, the semen, which consists of *pneuma* plus water, sets or concocts the menstrual blood, rather as rennet or fig-juice sets milk. It is active on female passivity: a thesis which will be extended well beyond the biological and reproductive spheres.

What then about the mental, moral or spiritual superiority of the male? Is it to be connected with his physiological superiority? Aristotle does not want to claim – in this rejecting at least part of the traditional wisdom – that women have no intellect (*nous*), that highest quality of human beings. If they were defective in that, they would strictly not be human beings at all, or at best only natural slaves.[13] But he argues in the *Politics* that, though women possess a certain intellectual capacity, their bodily weakness makes it appropriate for this capacity to be exercised in the home. More interesting, however, is the further claim that in respect to their specifically deliberative powers women are generally *akuroi* (1.1260A13): not, that is, that they are less intelligent but that their deliberations tend to be ineffectual. They are less able to enforce what they know to be right over their emotions; they are less "controlled", hence more suitable for the home than for the assembly, more fit to be ruled than to rule (1254B). That is not to say that they are *acratic* in the technical sense Aristotle developed in his *Ethics*. The *acratic* is a sinner in that he knows the better and does the worse; he could, in some sense, do better and hence is blameworthy. Women are just congenitally weak, hence not to be blamed but guided and strengthened.

---

[13] For an argument that Aristotle's account of the natural slave is widely misread, see J. M. Rist, *The Mind of Aristotle* (Toronto 1989) 249–252; for women see 246–249.

It has been widely recognized that the two practical female deficiencies, in generative power and in weakness of the mind in moving from deliberation to effective action, have a common "metaphysical" aspect. Certainly they are both connected by Aristotle with the indefiniteness, the unformed and hence imperfect and incomplete nature of females at the physical level, but for him material differences must reflect differences of form or soul. And indefiniteness is also an indicator of passivity – "natural" in females who are passive *qua* females (*Generation of Animals* 729A28[14]), but "womanish", and hence to be despised, in passive homosexuals who play an "inferior" role without the justification of being female.[15] Among the Greeks it was normally held to be a mark of subordination merely to *experience* something at the hands of another, even in the case of receiving presents or acts of kindness.

In reflecting on the "degradation" of "suffering" or "experiencing" and on the Greek notion of the superiority of acting and therefore also even of inflicting, we should recognize that Socrates' contention in the *Gorgias* that it is better to suffer injustice than to do it is particularly remarkable. No matter what Socrates said he was prepared to suffer, no-one in antiquity ever called him womanish – as they might Alcibiades, who, juxtaposed with Socrates in Plato's *Symposium*, sometimes appears in medieval chronicles as a *mulier pulchra*; Socrates, despite his "passivity", as a real man.

To conclude this preliminary survey of the Greeks, and noting that the social implications of two-seed theories, in Galen's influential version,[16] could be very similar to those of Aristotle, I will glance at two further apparently unrelated cultural phenomena: the world of "high" art and the numerological speculations of various generations of Pythagoreans. Both offer support for the view that human (and therefore divine) perfection is originally "male", though gradually and hesitatingly alternative possibilities were opened up.

If we look at the history of Greek sculpture in the fifth and fourth centuries BC, we discover an expansion of idealized (and therefore godlike) subject-matter from the nude male to the nude female to the nude hermaphrodite. In less than high art – as in vase painting – naked women, representing common eroticism or simply as fertility symbols, can be found in the sixth and fifth centuries, but in sculpture of the same period nude figures are almost exclusively male.[17] The same situation obtains in painting: Zeuxis' nude

---

[14] Cf 728A18 on impotence.

[15] For comment see Maud W. Gleason, "The Semiotics of Gender", in Halperin, Winkler and Zeitlin, *Before Sexuality*, esp. 396–399.

[16] For details see especially O. Temkin, *Galenism: Rise and Decline of a Medical Philosophy* (Ithaca, N.Y. 1973).

[17] See M. Robertson, *A History of Greek Art* (Cambridge 1975) 390–395.

Helen was a novelty, and in any case, as we have seen, Helen is special. At this period of Greece respectable women, and especially goddesses, are draped; in the Ludovisi throne (*c.* 400) – I take it to be genuine – though one of the supporting figures is nude, the central goddess is still covered – though only transparently above the navel.

No doubt there were many reasons for such conventions, but two at least may be mentioned. First, and most important in our present enquiry, is that the male anatomy is the perfect human version, and thus the more suitable for idealization. Second, apart from the down-to-earth world of popular eroticism and famous mythological scenes represented on vase paintings (such as the rape of Cassandra), naked females – as Hesiod's depiction of Pandora would imply – are dangerous socially and religiously. When Praxiteles (in the fourth century) sculpted his Aphrodite – the first major nude statue of a goddess, presented as an ideal type – it was rejected as *too* dangerous by the people of Cos and taken in by the Cnidians. His mistress and model Phryne – the incarnation of female perfection – was held to be a representative of the goddess in her own lifetime: her gilt and (probably) nude form stood in bronze at Delphi between representations of a Spartan and a Macedonian king.[18] But Phryne was an opportunity lost: despite her unchallenged beauty, she made little dent in the belief that, somehow, the male form is superior. That was not the effect of an argument – for the argument was not yet made – but of an assumption. Presumably it would be somehow "agreed" that the beauty of Aphrodite could not match the beauty of Zeus. We shall return, if not to Phryne, at least to her descendants.

To say that masculinity is not the only form of human perfection is not necessarily to conclude that there are only two perfect forms, the male and the female. Perfection need have no sex at all – an option only theoretically open to the Greek sculptor – or it might be bisexual.[19] Hence the rapid development of the bisexual ideal in the Hellenistic age. There is no need to reject *in toto* the older "puritanical" view that the hermaphrodite in art represents a corrupt taste; sometimes it doubtless did. But more theoretical considerations

---

[18] Phryne's appearance half-naked in an Athenian courtroom was enough to secure her acquittal (as a fitting servant of Aphrodite) when the pleas of the distinguished orator Hypereides were likely to fail. It seems, however, that, even if naked, her bronze statue would have lacked vulva or pubic hair: the latter at least would have lowered the tone to popular eroticism. See J. Kilmer, "Genital Phobia and Depilation", *JHS* 102 (1982) 104–112.

[19] See R. Mortley, *Womanhood: The Feminine in Ancient Hellenism, Gnosticism, Christianity and Islam* (Sydney 1981); L. Brisson, "Bisexualité et médiation en Grèce ancienne", *Nouvelle Revue de Psychanalyse* 7 (1973) 27–48. For comment on the first created humans being hermaphrodite in Jewish *haggada* (and in Gnosticism) see M. C. Horowitz, "The Image of God in Man – Is Woman Included?", *HTR* 72 (1979) 184–186.

can be adduced to explain this limited phenomenon and are probably at least
as important as any pruriently sensationalist motive.

Even here, however, the old priorities had not entirely changed.
Hermaphroditus himself is originally male: the *son* of Hermes and
Aphrodite. His bisexuality is biassed towards the (effeminate) male: he is
a womanly male rather than a masculine female. The penis, symbol of
a complete humanity with its actively procreative ability and associated
ideas of dominance and deliberative superiority, is retained.

Asexuality or bisexuality: the choice, oddly enough, also presented itself
to the Pythagoreans. The earliest evidence, especially that of Aristotle
(*Metaphysics* 1.985B22ff.), suggests that Pythagoreanism was originally a
dualism with its famous column of opposites, of goods and bads. Unity,
limit and maleness are among the goods, multiplicity, indeterminacy and
femaleness among the bads. The male is thus superior to the female – for
reasons that should now be apparent. Male unity and determinacy are
imposed on female plurality and indeterminacy.

In such matters, as elsewhere, Plato was influenced by Pythagoreanism,
but the influence also ran the other way. In Plato's late metaphysics the One
and the Dyad are both first principles, but the One is superior, and by the
first century BC "Neopythagoreans" such as the Alexandrian Eudorus,[20]
developing this superiority, hold that the Dyad itself is derived from the
One, thus converting the dualism into a monism. What does this do to the
principles of male and female? To answer that we need to look at the history
of the number one. Originally it was just a number; it would be the first odd
number, and hence viewed as male, while the first even number, two, would
be female. Two would be "derivative" of one, but both would be classed as
numbers. But then, for Pythagoreans, one becomes not just a number but
the source of number: of odd and even. If it is the source of odd and even, it
might seem to be neither male nor female, but that was not the conclusion
drawn, or at least not immediately. Instead, it came to be spoken of as
bisexual, as male-female, *arsenothēlus*, like Hermaphroditus or a bearded
Aphrodite or the male-and-female Zeus, also – as we should expect – not
unknown in later antiquity. The option of non-sexuality is seen as difficult
for the numerologist, not merely for the sculptor, and with male–female
units, as with hermaphrodites, male predominance is retained.

Returning from such wider cultural considerations to more narrowly
philosophical material, we bear in mind that in Greco-Roman culture there

---

[20] For more on Eudorus, see especially J. M. Dillon, *The Middle Platonists* (London/Ithaca, N.Y. 1977)
115–135.

are all sorts of semi-mythological ways in which, even when the male–female dichotomy appears about to be transcended, male dominance – and correspondingly female subsidiarity – persists.

1.3 PLATO AND THE PERFECT (MALE) SOUL

Plato observes four times that the goal of human life is to obtain likeness to God,[21] but the *Theaetetus* (176AB) is the dialogue most frequently cited in this connection by Christian (as by pagan) authors: not least, perhaps, because there Plato not only urges us to seek likeness to God as far as we may, but speaks of a "flight" from this world to the world of the gods, that is, to the immaterial (and non-bodily) world of Forms. We may assume that such flight will not only involve a degree of asceticism in matters of food, drink and sex, and this especially if eating, drinking and sex involve a pursuit of pleasure for its own sake, rather than cheerful acceptance of pleasure as a by-product: thus we may enjoy moderate drinking but not drink because we like drinking. It will also involve withdrawal from the more corrupting aspects of public life, at least where public life is recognizable as a mere power struggle.

Beyond such transient activity we are to find truth and moral strength in a world of Forms recognized by a mind informed by *eros*, the philosophical love of wisdom. In such a "flight" our desire and our love will be directed in the first instance to the search for and contemplation of those moral and spiritual realities in virtue of which, according to the *Phaedrus* (249C5–6), the gods are divine. In recognizing these, we too shall become godlike, indeed divine, and if we return to our more normal setting we shall act in godlike ways and as sharers in the providential activities of the gods themselves. By knowing the good, we shall be obligated (and want) to do good.[22]

In this Platonic vision we recognize an underlying metaphysical claim about what Plato calls the "soul", namely that this is an eternal being or immaterial substance condemned to its present existence in a body. (Plato is never clear about the reason for this, or perhaps is not particularly willing to speculate.) Metaphysically, we are immortal souls temporarily existing

---

[21] *Rep.* 10.613B; *Theaet.* 176AB; *Tim.* 90Aff.; *Laws* 716B. A recent discussion is that of D. Sedley, "The Ideal of Godlikeness", in G. Fine (ed.), *Plato 2: Ethics, Politics, Religion and the Soul* (Oxford 1999) 309–328 (though Sedley's remark about the paucity of "studies which take it seriously" is open to question; some of the older treatments are mentioned in J. M. Rist, *Eros and Psyche* (Toronto 1964) 15–19, etc.).

[22] For a more extended treatment see J. M. Rist, "Desiderio e azione", in L. Alici (ed.), *Azione e persona: Le radici della prassi* (Milan 2002) 29–44.

"within" a material frame, and in this like the ship in the bottle. Morally, however, the ship-and-bottle language is inadequate because the ship turns out to be in charge of the bottle, able to make the bottle do what it wants if it tries hard enough. Socrates, described in the *Phaedo* as deciding not to run away to Thebes when the Laws tell him to stay in prison in Athens, acts less like a ship in a bottle than an embattled soul, like that captain of a threatened ship with whom the ideal philosopher is compared in the *Republic* (6.488AB). Thus in our present state, when we are urged to seek likeness to God, we are challenged to live as far as possible the life we hope eventually to enjoy as disembodied souls – provided we do not abandon moral responsibility to the society in which we live for as long as we are "with and in the body".

With all this in mind there remain a number of questions to be tackled before we leave Plato and turn to his direct or indirect Christian heirs. The first is whether all human beings are capable of obtaining likeness to God, and to which god? Surely for a male not to a goddess! The second is the role of pleasure in that "happy" state to which we are naturally – and erotically – drawn. In other words what is the relationship, for Plato, between the love of beauty and the love of the pleasure that beauty gives us?

To that too the answer is clear: it is beauty, not pleasure, that inspires us; pleasure in beauty is a side-effect to be enjoyed (it forms part of our erotic motivation), but it should not be pursued for its own sake. On the other hand, to seek beauty while rejecting pleasure, as some of Plato's would-be heirs seem to have intended, would be like looking for a square circle.

It would appear, especially in the *Phaedrus*, that Plato believed that *all* men are capable of a certain likeness to God, but not to the same degree. In his mythological language, some are capable of "joining the choir" of Zeus, while others will attain only a lower divine level. But among the lesser divinities there appear to be differences of quality and of moral standing. He who is capable of attaining likeness to Ares would surely be of lesser stature than he who is capable of attaining likeness to Apollo. And what about likeness to a goddess?

In the *Phaedrus*, reflection on such themes revolves around the ultimate fates and possibilities of males, since the context of the debate is the success or failure of male lovers, in joint pursuit of truth and beauty. Then what does Plato think about the ultimate prospects of the other half of the human race? An indication of his position in the same dialogue is that he speaks tradition-ally of male ejaculation as "sowing children" (251A1): further evidence of the dominant view that the female is a nurse before and after birth. And there are texts in the *Timaeus* in which, whether speaking the language of the

Pythagoreans or also that of the streets of Athens, he tells us that after the creation of males, those who lived badly were reincarnated as women (*Timaeus* 90E, cf. 42AB and *Politicus* 271–274): an indication that women are again inferior males, or conversely that males are a superior (and thus more idealizable) version of humanity.

In Plato, as in all classical literature, there is, as we have seen, a pervasive use of "male" to mean more virtuous and "female" to mean intellectually or morally inadequate. Masculinity is superior to femininity, and the *Politicus* passage (271–274) states specifically that females were brought into existence for the sake of reproduction; males would apparently be of more spiritual and/or intellectual use – a point about to be reiterated in various forms in many Christian texts.

But this cannot be the whole Platonic story. In the *Republic* there are female guardians, and although Plato seems to suppose that their highest attainments will be lower than those of the best men, there is no doubt as to their capacity both to philosophize and to rule. Such ideas, common to many within the Socratic circle[23] (fascinated as it apparently was by the example of the political skills of Aspasia, the Milesian mistress of Pericles and principal speaker in Plato's own dialogue *Menexenus*), were translated into historical reality in the Academy, of which there were at least two female members during Plato's lifetime. Their names (Axiotheia (= Diotima) and Lastheneia of Mantinea, DL 3,46; 4.2) may be combined into the figure of Diotima of Mantinea, Plato's fictitious character and principal spokesperson on philosophical *eros* in the *Symposium*. For Diotima – whether or not she is Socrates in drag[24]– is the exponent not only of the mysteries of the erotic ascent to the world of Forms, but of the first detailed introduction to that world, or at least to its perhaps first-recognized member: that inspirational Form of Beauty which to be inspirational must itself be perfectly beautiful.

A key to such apparent contradictions in Plato's account of female potentialities vis-à-vis those of males can be found if we hypothesize that, while he held the traditional view that the male is the perfect human type, he also supposed that, if females are able to bracket out the weaknesses and indeterminacies somehow inherent in their receptive (and/or submissive) role in procreation, they can function mentally and volitionally as males. Thus Plato would hold that sexual difference is a purely bodily aspect of the

[23] Cf. the comments of C. H. Kahn, *Plato and the Socratic Dialogue* (Cambridge 1996) 23–29 and in P. A. Vander Waerdt (ed.), *The Socratic Movement* (Ithaca, N.Y./London 1994) 87–106. For further comment on Plato's school, Diotima, etc., see Rist, *The Mind of Aristotle* 192, 311–312.

[24] See Halperin, "Why is Diotima a Woman?"

human condition and that the immortal soul of itself – and of both bodily males and females – is male, or at least not female. That would explain in part why in the *Meno* Socrates argues, against the unthinking traditionalist after whom the dialogue is named, that virtue (like the soul itself) is the same for males and females. Aristotle, as we have seen, was a neo-traditionalist when he holds that radical bodily differences must be paralleled by differences in the soul and therefore in the virtues.

Plato's position apparently entails that morally and spiritually femaleness is something to outgrow: a claim represented mythologically by the passage of the *Timaeus* to which I alluded where inferior men are said to have been reincarnated as women; while presumably superior women will be reincarnated as men. Again, mistaken theories about conception could have contributed to such a thesis: Plato – as we saw in his describing ejaculation as "sowing children" (*Phaedrus* 251A1) – seems to have subscribed to the view that in the process of conception the woman provides the fertile field – the appropriate space (*chōra*) – in which the seed, a sort of homunculus, can be sown and grow up. Similarly, according to the cosmic biology of the *Timaeus*, the Demiurge introduces the images of the Forms into a cosmic womb or matrix (*ekmageion*): the male principle thus actively inseminates the female field,[25] and constructs the universe – *with* time, as Aristotle properly recognized – in a mode which in Christian centuries came to be known as creation *de deo*; that is, purely from God's own substance operating in something like a cosmic void.

How then are we to interpret Plato's thesis that it is our aim to seek likeness to God as far as possible? What shall we be like in that perfect state? Certainly we shall have no bodies; we shall be simply souls, or rather minds, and as minds we shall all be male, like the universe-generating Demiurge. Femaleness is a bodily phenomenon necessary for the production of children (and thus for a surrogate immortality), but of no relevance to an eternal existence. That view would help explain why homosexualists in Platonic dialogues, like Pausanias in the *Symposium*, despise lovers of women as satisfied to live at an ultimately subhuman, and so part-female, level. And it would clarify an apparent anomaly in the speech of Phaedrus in the same dialogue when he declares the female Alcestis to be a hero, though less than Achilles (179B). Like a Platonic guardian, and inspired by her love of a male, she is already in this life able to act as a male. As a soul, she is able to live according to her proper masculinity and as captain of her ship. Indeed it is

---

[25] For Plato's cosmic biology, see Rist, *The Mind of Aristotle* 191–205. Note the language of *Laws* 8.838ff., cited with typical approval by Clement of Alexandria (*Paed.* 2.10.91–92).

Diotima (who also adverts to Alcestis) who indicates that mere procreation is a rather low-level way to secure the good of immortality (*Symposium* 208E).

In light of all this we can recognize a general and not merely a cultural reason why Plato's *Symposium* and *Phaedrus* demand a homosexual setting. The soul is male, and the male body, at least in traditional circles, is regarded as more beautiful than the female. Hence a "higher" love, directed at the good as beautiful, will be directed in the first instance by males towards male bodies. Thus what appear to be self-serving, even cynical, apologies for pederasty on the part of the earlier speakers in the *Symposium* should be viewed in a more nuanced way. Phaedrus, the first speaker, talks the ordinary language of the lover of (male) beauty, though he pleads that such love is beneficial to both parties, but Pausanias, who succeeds him, introduces the crucial distinction between "vulgar" and "heavenly" Aphrodite. Vulgar Aphrodite (with vulgar Eros) is concerned exclusively with the body, but celestial Aphrodite (which in Pausanias' view exists only among males (181CD)) is above all concerned with the well-being of the soul and with virtue.

Once the distinction between soul and body has been introduced, Plato can develop its implications further, until eventually, in the speech of Diotima, he can say that the lover who genuinely recognizes the beauty of the soul will neglect bodily beauty altogether. But if that is the case, and if it is the soul (male in women as well as in men) which is the more beautiful, we can see why eventually (in the *Phaedrus* and more fully in the *Laws*) Plato draws the conclusion that homosexual acts are no proper culmination of an erotic desire for the beautiful but a mere distraction for the erotic philosopher – and that having no other social utility they are to be forbidden.[26] Between love for the Good itself and love of a mere physical body comes love of the properly male soul present in men and women alike.

Plato's theory of the nature of men and women depends on his account – rejected by Aristotle – of the relationship between the soul and the body. In recognizing that, we can see why, as a necessary corollary to that rejection, Aristotle must reject the associated Platonic claim that the virtue of women is identical with that of men. Yet Aristotle's variously improved account of the metaphysical union of soul and body in both males and females led him to propose a much greater inferiority of females than Plato believed warranted by the evidence: for Aristotle women are simply defective males: defective as such and not merely as possessing weaker and inferior human bodies.

---

[26] For detailed analysis of the texts see J. M. Rist, "Plato and Professor Nussbaum on Acts 'Contrary to Nature'", in M. Joyal (ed.), *Studies in Plato and the Platonic Tradition: Essays presented to John Whittaker* (Aldershot 1997) 65–79.

I.4 INTERPRETING GENESIS

It is time to move from Athens to Jerusalem. Though this is no place to speculate in detail on the intentions of the two "writers" of the Old Testament accounts of the creation of mankind, the following comments are intended to set the scene for the interpretations put upon those two accounts by Christian authors. Suffice it therefore to say that in the later account in Genesis Chapter 1 – the so-called Priestly version – the writer first describes "man" being created in God's image (which may refer to his being a shadow of God's material greatness) and likeness (perhaps in certain character-traits, or as a representative of divine authority) and then continues with the explanatory line, "Male and female he created them."

The author's intent is hard to discern.[27] He could simply be stating as a fact that human beings, male and female, were simultaneously all created – even equally created – in the image of God; that interpretation would be supported by Genesis 5:1–2 where *adam* ("mankind") is clearly identified as plural. Or he could be suggesting that maleness together with femaleness affords a better composite picture of God's nature and power. Or could there perhaps be an echo of a more ancient and long-discarded belief in a bisexual divinity ("Let *us* make man in our image and likeness"; a number of rabbis supposed that the original "man" was androgynous[28])? Or is the male–female distinction

---

[27] K. Barth (*Church Dogmatics* 3.2 (Eng. trans. Edinburgh 1961) 285–324) argued that the relationship between man and woman was intended to indicate the Trinitarian relationship within God. For appropriately critical comment (with further references) see H. U. von Balthasar, *Theo-Drama* II (Eng. trans. Graham Harrison, San Francisco 1990) 318, 321. But Balthasar (cf. notes 2, 115, 196, 197), in accepting G. von Rad's exegesis (*Genesis* (London 1972) 60) as theologically correct, holds that man's procreative capacity, though blessed, "is removed from God's image" (see note 2 above).

Interpreting the text of Genesis itself is the more difficult in that the emphases in the Septuagint version of creation-stories are at times different from those of the Hebrew Bible. Both versions influenced early Christians, incompatible though they may be in their details. For an introduction to the problems see W. Loader, *The Septuagint, Sexuality and the New Testament* (Grand Rapids/Cambridge 2004).

[28] The idea of a bisexual divinity seems to have been revived in later Judaism, perhaps in parallel to later Greek ideas about the hermaphrodite; see *The Treasure* 2,13 and the comments of J. Jervell, *Imago Dei* (Göttingen 1960) 96–106; also, with strong rabbinic evidence, G. M. G. Teugel, "The Creation of the Human in Rabbinic Interpretation", in Luttikhuizen, *Creation* 107–127. See also – on the original meaning of the Genesis text – J. C. de Moor, "The Duality in God and Man: Genesis 1: 26–27", in J. C. de Moor (ed.), *Intertextuality in Ugarit and Israel* (London 1998) 112–125. But the "us" in "Let us make . . . " may refer to God as the Elohim (with whatever implications for plurality in the Hebrew concept of divinity). And against De Moor's view that Genesis itself advocates an androgynous divinity see E. Noort, "The Creation of Man and Woman in Biblical and Ancient Near Eastern Traditions", in Luttikhuizen, *Creation* 1–18. Noort, however, does not discuss Genesis 5.2: a text which at least encouraged some of the rabbis to think of God himself (and his image) as androgynous.

irrelevant to the matter of imaging God and was Adam – as "man" (with all its ambiguity) – the perfect and original image?

The latter reading opens the text to the almost inevitable misinterpretation that God created in two temporal, or at least two metaphysical, stages: first "humanity", then individuals of two sexes, a male and a female. In that case we cannot avoid wondering what "humanity" means: one solution would be that it refers to a sexually inactive though not necessarily sexless condition (i.e., as male), another would invoke a Form of Man. The idea that "humanity" is originally male, made in the image of a "male" God, is a rather Greek-sounding, though also strictly Semitic, option. The Septuagint version of Genesis, however, renders "humanity" as *anthrōpos*, though even that is not definitive evidence that femaleness is supposed to be included, as the author of Genesis 5:1–2 seems to have thought.

The second but older account in Genesis chapter two, the so-called Yahwist version, describes the creation first of a man, then of the woman Eve from the man. There is no mention of God's image; the man seems to be historically prior and the woman is made from him. This text may – perhaps unintentionally – suggest an original, prelapsarian subordination of the woman to the man, as it did to a number of Christian exegetes – and if blended with the Priestly version is easily read as confirming that only the male (or at least non-female) Adam is in God's image. Certainly for the original Yahwist author woman is subordinate on earth after the Fall, a view congenial to the author of 1 Timothy 2:13–15; she is more like Adam's servant – not least in that she is at his mercy sexually and thus liable to endless pregnancies – than his companion.

1.5 PHILO JUDAEUS AND PAUL OF TARSUS

Christianity was born in a Jewish environment, but that environment was ringed and permeated by Greek ideas. Many of these ideas had become part of the common intellectual air of the Greco-Roman world, including the world of the Septuagint translators, so that when they appear in a Christian text it is not easy to propose a specifically non-Christian source. They may be cited by Christians with little or no notion of their ultimate origin. What makes the problem worse is that the vast majority of Hellenistic philosophical and historical texts are lost or survive only in fragments, sometimes, for all we know, misquoted or quoted out of context to such a degree as to be wholly unreliable evidence for the intentions and language of their original authors. Nevertheless, we do well to consider the writings of Philo Judaeus of Alexandria, both because they survive in bulk and because we can be

certain that, though little noticed by later Jews, they were widely read by
Christian authors, especially those like Origen who wished to comment on
the Old Testament.[29] But in examining Philo we must remember that
"Philonic" ideas may indicate either familiarity with Philo's own text or a
more general familiarity with the form of Hellenistic Judaism which Philo
represented but which was largely eclipsed – though perhaps less so in
Philo's native Alexandria – after the sack of Jerusalem in AD 70.

Philo was much influenced both by the Stoics and by Plato, especially by
Plato's *Timaeus*. His sources for both Platonism and Stoicism are indirect as
well as direct; the middle-men include Antiochus of Ascalon and especially
his fellow-Alexandrian Eudorus. He believed that the soul is buried in the
body as in a tomb, and probably cited Plato's *Gorgias* (*sōma-sēma* 493A),[30] as
evidence for a claim that the goal of the philosophical life is the suppression
of the passions (*apatheia*),[31] and that there are two types of human soul, of
which the superior, and that which survives death, is rational and "male".[32]
For Philo femaleness denotes the world of the senses, maleness the world of
the intellect and hence of God,[33] though there are traces of the notion,
developed later by Origen, that in relation to God the souls of the devout are
analogous to the best kind of female, that is to a virgin.[34] However, it is the
intellect which is made in the image of God. In our present individual life
the intellectual male soul needs the female sensible soul if it is to function in
its bodily context, just as Adam needed Eve as a field for procreation: a view
with obvious analogies to that of Pausanias in Plato's *Symposium*.

Philo proposed a platonizing account of the Genesis story of the creation
of the universe whereby God (apparently asexual, but to whom maleness is
more germane than femaleness) first constructed the Forms (*On Creation*
16), including a Form of Man (probably also asexual) in his own image and
likeness, and then the male and female individuals Adam and Eve as two
different sorts within the genus man (*anthrōpos, On Creation* 76).[35] Of these
only Adam – or rather the soul of Adam (and hence the souls of his male

---

[29] For Christian knowledge of Philo see D. T. Runia, *Philo in Early Christian Literature* (Assen/Minneapolis 1993).
[30] See conveniently Dillon, *The Middle Platonists* 149, citing *Leg. Alleg.* 1.108.
[31] Cf. *Leg. Alleg.* 2.100–102.
[32] I shall return to the question of how it may be better to think of "non-female" rather than "male".
[33] See especially R. A. Baer, *Philo's Use of the Categories Male and Female* (Leiden 1970) 14–44.
[34] So *De Cher.* 49. Beyond Philo there seems also to have been rabbinic talk of the rabbi as a "wife of God": see H. Eilberg-Schwartz, *God's Phallus* (Boston, Mass. 1994) 163–194.
[35] Philo probably follows Plato (*Pol.* 263A). Note that Philo's God *constructs* the Form of Man: an un-Platonic position (despite *Republic* 10) which could bring him into metaphysical difficulties (though certain Christians like Gregory of Nyssa still are willing to follow him). For Philo the Forms – apparently even moral Forms like Justice – are not divine attributes.

descendants) – approximates *in se* to the image of God. Before the coming of woman, who (like Pandora) loosed carnal desires, he was sinless (*On Creation* 58, 151).[36]

As I have suggested, the final compilers of Genesis may have believed that the male Adam *in toto* was created in the image of God inasmuch as God himself is envisaged as male and material.[37] Philo proposes a very different explanation, dependent on a platonizing account of man as composed of two separate substances: soul and body.[38] The real "man" is the male soul. As for women, they will normally – and unplatonically – be condemned to remain female. And also unlike Plato, Philo explains why females must be inferior to males: femaleness, being strictly sensual, is distinct from the immaterial nature of God and unfitted to reason effectively or to hold authority.

While admitting the existence of female *souls* – perhaps in an echo of Aristotelianism or Stoicism – Philo ties the female version more radically to the body. He is, however, prepared to admit, and in this he is a precursor of much pre-monastic and "monastic" Christian thinking, that if a female abandons sexual activity altogether – a novel and unplatonic course – she can become some sort of male.[39] "Progress is indeed nothing other than the giving up of the female gender by changing into the male, since the female gender is material, passive, corporeal and sense-perceptible, while the male is active, rational, incorporeal and more akin to mind and thought" (*Questions on Exodus* 1.8). Indeed, in more clearly Aristotelian mode Philo concludes that the female is simply an imperfect male (1.7).

For "male", however, one may apparently substitute "virgin": that is, sexually inactive. "When souls put on God, from being women they become virgins, throwing off the female corruptions of the senses and the passions . . ." (*Questions on Exodus* 2.3). And again: "When God begins to consort with the soul, He makes what before was a woman into a virgin again, for he

---

[36] In *The Male Woman: A Feminine Ideal of the Early Church* (Uppsala 1990) 86, K. Aspegren rightly observes that although Philo alludes to Plato's *Symposium* (189C–193D), his reading is very different: in Plato the division into needy males and females is a consequence of human sin; in Philo the existence of woman is the cause of sin.

[37] See also P. A. Bird, "Sexual Differentiation and Divine Image in the Genesis Creation Texts", in Børresen, *Image of God and Gender Models* 11–34.

[38] For recent comment see A. van den Hoek, "Endowed with Reason or Glued to the Senses: Philo's Thoughts on Adam and Eve", in Luttikhuizen, *Creation* 63–75.

[39] Philo uses the notions of "becoming male", "becoming a virgin" and "becoming one" in ascetic contexts for both men and women. For the female Therapeutae as examples see Baer, *Philo's Use of the Categories* 98–101.

K. Vogt has no discussion of Philo, but cites Baer: see "'Becoming Male': A Gnostic and early Christian Metaphor", in Børresen, *Image of God and Gender Models* 172–187; "'Becoming Male': A Gnostic, Early Christian and Islamic Metaphor", in K. E. Børresen and K. Vogt (eds.), *Women's Studies of the Christian and Islamic Traditions* (Dordrecht/Boston, Mass./London 1993) 217–224.

takes away the ignoble and emasculate passions which made it womanish
(*ethēluneto*) . . . (*Cherubim* 50).[40] Note again the difference from the Plato
of the *Republic* where neither male nor female guardians are to renounce
sexual activity, only to order it. Heterosexual activity has no necessary
connection with their success or otherwise in becoming "like God".[41]

If we look at certain apparent similarities between Philo and his contemporary Paul of Tarsus, we realize that Philo's solution to the "woman-
problem" – two types of souls in their male and female bodies – is not
available to those who reject the metaphysical claim that there is difference of
substance between soul and body. In making this split Philo prefers the
Platonic tradition not only to that of most of his own less hellenized
Jewish contemporaries (who may be more in the spirit of the original authors
of Genesis) but also (if less radically) to the materialist (or, better, vitalist)
account of the relationship between soul and body which he would have
found among the Stoics. For although the Stoics were "Hellenic" enough to
make a distinction (albeit material) between soul and body – and in this
"materialism" were followed by Tertullian and other Christians who hoped
thereby to promote the intelligibility of bodily resurrection – the option of a
substantially separate and distinct non-sexual (or more male) soul for women
was not philosophically available to them.

That Philo is both Jew and hellenizer becomes clearer if we compare him
with the Paul of 1 Corinthians 11:7. Paul's discussions of the image of God are
often connected with the idea that Christ (as second Adam) is the perfect
image (2 Corinthians 3:18–4:6; Colossians 1:15: "image of the invisible God").
In 1 Corinthians 11:7, however, a passage construed – perhaps rightly – by
most patristic authors (except the later Augustine) as implying or asserting
that males but not females are formed in the image of God,[42] he (hebraically)

---

[40] D. Gourevitch (*Le mal d'être femme: La femme et la médecine dans la Rome antique* (Paris 1984) 96)
comments that for many ancient doctors a non-menstruating female is not really a woman (but
perhaps something better).

[41] In Plato, as we have seen, homosexual intercourse (as well as recourse to prostitutes) is eventually
ruled out. Seed (pre-embryonic humanity) should not be deliberately sown where pregnancy is
impossible or unwanted.

[42] A. G. Hamman (*L'homme, image de Dieu* (Paris 1987) 29) asserts without comment that 1 Cor. 11:7
"selon une interprétation rabbinique" concerns itself with men and not women, merely observing
that this "contrasts" with Col. 3:11 and Gal. 3:28.
        For preliminary discussions of patristic views see Børresen, *Image of God* and F. G. McLeod, *The
Image of God in the Antiochean Tradition* (Washington 1999). Hamman (following Jervell, *Imago Dei*
108) notes that the rabbinic tradition (known to Paul) was divided on whether women are created in
God's image, even if such imaging is denied to Eve herself. The view of Paul, however, is not quite as
clearly a *denial* that women are created in God's image as Børresen maintains. In 1 Cor. 11:7 he says
that man should not cover his head, since he is the image and glory of God, but woman is the glory of
man. His thinking, of course, is governed by Gen. 1:26–27a and Gen. 2:7, but he blends them in a

declines to avail himself of the Greek distinction between soul and body – a distinction indeed generally alien to his thought, centred as it is on the resurrection of the whole bodily individual. Hence he expresses our moral ambiguity not in terms of the soul–body distinction but in the – probably conventional[43] – language of "flesh" and "spirit", or of the inner and outer man.[44] Earlier language of that latter sort has come down to us only in Plato's *Republic*.[45] That may be an accident of transmission and there is no need to suppose that Paul read the *Republic*, or that his view of the "inner man" was identical to Plato's, let alone to Plato's interpreters.[46]

As has been widely observed, once a flesh–spirit dichotomy was current in Christian circles, it was tempting – and not always resisted – to interpret "flesh" with reference, at least primarily, to sexuality, and "spirit" to a flight from the sexual and thus feminized universe into the world of a non-female God. In sum, Paul's probably "hebraic" view that women are not (at least directly) created in God's image – even if eschatologically there is no male and female in Christ – has similarities with the position of Philo. Yet as a non-hellenizer Paul has no inclination to use any radical ontological distinction between the immaterial substance of the soul and the material

strange way, saying not that *anthrōpos* but that *anēr* (the male) in created in the image of God. (See the discussion in L. J. Lietaert Peerbolte, "Man, Woman and the Angels in 1 Cor. 11:12–16", in Luttikhuizen (ed.), *Creation* 76–92.)

Paul's words could be interpreted as implying *either* straightforwardly that woman is not created in the image of God (the normal later view of the "Antiochene" school), *or* – in the light of Ephesians 4:13 (assuming that Ephesians was written by Paul himself or at least that it is "Pauline") – that since our aim, whether as men or women, is to "arrive at full knowledge of the Son of God, *unto a perfect male*", that women can attain to a *more* perfect likeness by "becoming male" or "becoming virgins". That possibility could entail that they have received a certain "creational" image-like nature inasmuch as they "descend" from the image Adam. Their relationship to the image would be indirect, chiefly defective only insofar as they are female in *body*. That would be closer to Augustine's understanding of the matter, as we shall see.

In favour of Børresen's reading, however – and prescinding from the question of which rabbinic interpretation of Genesis Paul favoured or followed – is the fact that he considers human beings to be a single substance. He cannot, like Augustine and other platonizers, think of females as male (or asexual) souls in a female body, so he is apparently committed to the view that those female in body (and *therefore* female as such) must "become male", somehow, as Ephesians 4:13 seems to suggest. Thus they would not be created in the image of God, though they would possess the capacity to acquire an image-like nature (as Ambrosiaster and others later believed). Perhaps Paul has not thought the problem through; he certainly could not have foreseen the effect of his ambiguities. I shall return to the problem at the end of the present chapter.

[43] Outside, that is, platonizing circles – and in the light of the facts that "flesh" seems to find a related philosophical sense among the un-Pauline Epicureans, and (again) that most Hellenistic prose literature is lost!

[44] *esō anthrōpos*: cf. Rom. 7:22; II Cor. 4:16; Eph. 3:16. [45] *Rep.* 9.589A6, *ho entos anthrōpos*.

[46] For the clash of motifs and the tendency of a version of the Platonic motif to dominate in Christian circles, see C. Markschies, "Die platonische Metapher von 'innerem Menschen': Eine Brücke zwischen antiker Philosophie und altchristlicher Theologie", *ZKG* 105 (1994) 1–17.

substance of the body to buttress a position that nothing female could be created in God's image. *If he had made use of such a distinction*, however, he would have been driven *either* to advocate the Platonic (and later largely Augustinian) view that it is only in bodily terms that females are radically inferior, *or* – maintaining the claim of created female inferiority – to advocate something like the inferior Philonic female soul inhabiting the inferior female body. If, that is, he had been driven to defend himself "philosophically". Among later Christians, once the soul–body dichotomy – understood more or less platonically – had been introduced, both strategies found their advocates.

1.6 CARNAL AND SPIRITUAL, CORPOREAL AND NON-CORPOREAL

As Origen first pointed out in the third century AD,[47] the word "incorporeal" (*asōmatos*) does not appear in the New Testament, though before Origen's time it had been widely adopted into Christianity as a result of the influence of Greek thought. In the New Testament God is recognized as "spirit", and he is to be worshipped "in spirit and in truth". Frequently in a human being "spirit" is contrasted with "flesh"; the contrast is between a willingness to act according to the divine spirit within, which is the mark of the Pauline "inner man", and a desire, in our actual and fallen condition, to act contrary to God's will, that is "carnally", or "after the flesh" (*sarx*): hence "the spirit is willing but the flesh is weak". A correct understanding of "flesh", however, is made more complex since the term is sometimes used simply to refer to the human created condition as distinct from God, as "the Word became flesh": that is, became man. In what follows I shall ignore this second and wider understanding of "flesh" and concentrate on "flesh" as contrasted with spirit in the more restricted moral or spiritual, non-ontological, sense.

The "moral" antithesis "spirit–flesh" leaves unclear whether the "spirit" is material or immaterial, corporeal or incorporeal. Indeed, one might suppose that when the categories "corporeal" and "incorporeal" were introduced into Christianity (largely as a result of the influence of Platonism from the time of Justin in the second century), it would have been wise to argue either that the "spirit" which is God is transcendent over the corporeal–incorporeal distinction or that such a distinction is unrelated to the nature of God as spirit. That, however, did not happen; hence when Christians turned to the platonizing dichotomy (corporeal–incorporeal) to prevent God's being construed as

---

[47] *De Princ.*, proem. 8–9, with the note of Crouzel-Simonetti in *SC* 253, *ad loc.*

a pantheist Stoic "spirit", they began to assimilate the notion that the spirit is "invisible" (as the New Testament had it) to the idea that it is incorporeal and immaterial. They came to suppose – though Tertullian bucked the trend – that to speak of God's immateriality and incorporeality was the best way of protecting his transcendence. But if the spirit is incorporeal, it is easy to change the meaning of "flesh" as well; now "flesh" tends to become identified with the corporeal, that is, for us, the body – with disastrous results for an ascetic tradition and a radical misconstruction of the Pauline usage of "flesh" to indicate not the body so much as the fallen inner man: the self that struggles against God and the good.

Thus for good or ill, the New Testament distinction between our spiritual and our fallen selves tended to resolve itself into a distinction between a soul capable of living in an immaterial world and a body that lives in a world of sense-objects. It is not difficult to recognize the likely effect of this on an account of the difference between males and females for those who believe – and those who do not – that strictly speaking the soul is the real self. I have roughly distinguished the two groups as hellenizing (or platonizing) and hebraizing. Obviously both tendencies will talk about human beings as some sort of complex of soul and body, but the first group will hold that all of us are (and have always been) really male souls destined to live in an immaterial world, while the second group will tend to suppose (as did many second-century Christians) that, since our souls as well as our bodies are material (though the "matter" in question is of a superior and more luminous, "spiritual" kind), sexual differences, being certainly corporeal, are more plausibly characteristic of the whole person, the corporeal soul–body complex. Hence if femaleness is inferior, then the whole female person is inferior.

As a further effect of the shift from spirit–flesh (as originally understood) to soul–body, a third, perhaps superior, possibility will tend to disappear altogether: namely that we all have a "spiritual" component which has nothing to do with the sexual differences of our bodies or the arguably sexual differences of our souls, but which should permeate both body and soul: that is, the whole human agent, male or female. In any case all these varying possibilities are reflected in ancient accounts of who is created in the image of God as well as in later attempts to improve on them.

1.7 BECOMING MALE: PLATONIZING AND NON-PLATONIZING VERSIONS

In the wake of Ephesians 4:13 Christian texts, both orthodox and those which would be judged to be "heretical", were quick to develop the notion that to become perfect is to become a "male" (*andra*)[48]. Since to become perfect is to acquire likeness to God, in Christian terms by imitation of Christ, becoming male comes (somehow) to be seen as part of the journey towards likeness to God. My immediate concern is how such ideas about attaining likeness to God affected early Christian answers to the question of whether, or in what way, women were seen as created in God's image. The answer to such questions varied with the different theories about the nature of females. If they are born capable of being *mentally* males in female bodies – the Platonic position – that generated an answer unavailable to those who avoided the soul–body split, arguing that in their totality women – at least as created – are wholly female. In the latter case perhaps only males are created in the image of God, while it may (or may not) be open to women to become male "as a whole" as a result of their choice of life. In Christian terms that could mean that they must live in such a way that their *resurrected body* (and not merely and platonically their soul) will be male. However viewed, many ancient theories diverged from the theological view that both males and females are equally created in God's image.[49] Given the modern consensus, however, our concern must be to recognize the *development* – whether or not legitimately achieved – of a Christian (but arguably non-Pauline) understanding of the creation stories of Genesis.

"In Christ there is no more male and female"(*arsen kai thēlu*) (an echo of Genesis in Galatians 3:28): the natural interpretation (that in Christ it will not matter whether we are male or female because the physical union of bodies in marriage will no longer occur) may look simplistic. There are other logical possibilities: for example, that of future hermaphrodites[50] – a revival of a Hellenistic motif – or that there will no longer be males and females because we shall all be males (that is, asexual), in imitation of the maleness of Jesus. As already implied, there could be platonizing or non-platonizing – we might say "holistic" – explanations of this latter possibility.

---

[48] See (e.g.) Vogt, "'Becoming Male': A Gnostic and Early Christian Metaphor", and "'Becoming Male': a Gnostic, Early Christian and Islamic Metaphor"; G. Sfameni Gasparro, "Image of God and Sexual Differentiation in the Tradition of Enkrateia", in Børresen (ed.), *Image of God* 138–171. There is a "carnal" parallel in lesbian relationships; for the superiority (and dominance) of the "male" partner see Knust, *Abandoned* 30–31.

[49] Every discussion of woman in the image of God should recognize the work of K. E. Børresen, especially (ed.) *Image of God* and "In Defence of Augustine: how femina is homo?", in B. Bruning, M. Lamberigts and J. van Houten (eds.), *Collectanea Augustiniana: Mélanges T. J. van Bavel* (Louvain 1990) 263–280.

[50] See Vogt, "'Becoming Male': A Gnostic, Early Christian and Islamic Metaphor" 223; W. Meeks, "The Image of the Androgyne: Some Uses of a Symbol in Earliest Christianity", *History of Religions* 13 (1974) 165–208.

The thesis that only in his soul is man created in God's image was attractive not least because, if God is immaterial, his image might seem better understood as immaterial. But such arguments could be dangerous; they might suggest not the new Christian doctrine of the resurrection of the body, understood as the holistic person, but the old pagan notion of the natural immortality of the soul: a thesis anathematized in the late second century both by the "orthodox" Justin (*Dialogus* 6) and the "heretical" Tatian (*Address to the Greeks* 13.1). Hence we can identify a divergence between those who look to a more materialistic account of God – thus tending to favour the notion that woman could not be created in his image – and the more spiritualizing "Alexandrians", like Clement and Origen, who use Genesis 1.27b to emphasize woman's creation in the image of a spiritual God, at least in her masculine soul.

Presumably the holistic (often materialistic) version appeared first – that is, before the appearance of an "Alexandrian", platonized Christianity. Perhaps the best example is the notorious *logion* 114 of the *Gospel of Thomas*: "Simon Peter said to them, 'Let Mary [Magdalene] leave us, for women are not worthy of life.' Jesus said, 'I myself shall lead her in order to make her male, so that she too may become a living spirit resembling you males. For every woman who makes herself male will enter the Kingdom of Heaven.'" There is little doubt that such "becoming male" entailed giving up or losing the possibility of sexual activity, that is, retaining one's virginity or living in celibate widowhood. Virgins, in this tradition, are (happily) not yet women while consecrated virgins have accepted a call not to become women and celibate widows have finished with being women.[51] In such ultra-ascetic or "encratite" texts all trace of a desirable female self is abandoned; unless they activate their possibility of "becoming male", women cannot be the image of God.

Yet Justin, perhaps close in date to the *Gospel of Thomas*, seems to follow a more "platonizing" line, arguing in the spirit of the *Meno* that circumcision is far from indicating a superior virtue in males. On the contrary, God created females equally able to live a just and virtuous life. Unfortunately he does not connect this claim with any specific commentary on creation in God's image (*Dialogus* 23.5).

---

[51] See P. Brown, *The Body and Society* (New York 1988) 113–115 and especially M. W. Meyer, "Making Mary Male: The Categories 'Male' and 'Female' in the Gospel of Thomas", *NTS* 31 (1985) 554–570. Similar ideas of destroying "the works of the female" are to be found in the *Gospel of the Egyptians* (cited by Clement in *Strom.* 3.9.63.1).

1.8 CLEMENT OF ALEXANDRIA AND THE FEMALE: PLATONIC EROS AND STOIC APATHEIA

It has often been observed that Clement of Alexandria, platonically influenced and well read in Philo, is the first "orthodox" Christian to cite Ephesians 4:13 ("until we all reach the oneness of faith . . . the perfect man . . ."; *Miscellanies* 6.14.114.4). Hence it is unsurprising to find him distinguishing between being female in body and having a male – or perhaps a neutral, certainly non-female – soul (*Miscellanies* 6.12.100.3): "Souls by themselves are equally souls, neither male nor female (*oute arrenes oute thēleiai*), when they neither marry nor are given in marriage. And is not woman (*gunē*) changed into man (*andra*), the woman who has become equally unfemale and perfect and manly (*andrikēn*)?"[52] Elsewhere in the *Miscellanies* (4.21.132.1) we all are apparently urged to become perfect men (*andra*). Such ideas of change are to be viewed symbolically rather than physiologically, at least for platonizers who view only the soul as properly male; but their cultural impact may be recognized if we look at the more physiological dream of Perpetua, about to face the beasts in the amphitheatre at Carthage: "I was stripped naked and became a male (*masculus*)" (*Passion* 10.7).[53]

Clement avoids discussing the image of God in the language of 1 Corinthians 11:7,[54] preferring to follow Galatians 3:28 that there is no male or female in Christ – and hence at creation – so that "platonically" woman (*qua* soul) was created in God's image. This again implies that femaleness is a bodily phenomenon created solely for purposes of reproduction, and that since Eve derives from Adam she is subordinate to him in the earthly order. Hence, although Clement defends marriage against the "encratites", he follows Philo and the Stoic Musonius Rufus in maintaining that sexual activity should occur only for purposes of procreation.[55] Any wider use would feminize the *soul* not only of the women, to whom such femininity is the more natural, but of the men who consort with them. As with Philo, so with Clement, femaleness symbolizes sensuality and its desires.[56]

---

[52] Cf. *Paed.* 3.19.1–2 (activity is male, passivity is female), *Strom.* 4.8.59.4–5. See Aspegren, *The Male Woman*.

[53] Cf. the legends of Thecla, with the comments of Meeks, "Image" 196.

[54] Cf. Børresen, "God's Image, Man's Image? Patristic Interpretations of Gen. 1,27 and 1 Cor. 11,7", in *Image of God* 194–196.

[55] Cf. *Strom.* 2.23.141.1; 3.6.52.1; 3.6.58.2; 3.11.71.4; 3.12.79.3; 3.12.81.4; *Paed.* 2.10.83.1; 2.10.90.3; 2.10.98.2, etc.

[56] For Clement's ambiguous view of women in society, see D. Kinder, "Clement of Alexandria: Conflicting Views on Women", *Second Century* 7 (1990) 213–220.

Ephesians enabled Clement to develop what was perhaps latent in Philo. Although in Christ we are to be neither male nor female, we are then assimilated to the *perfect* or "real" kind of man. In other words, whereas being labelled "male" "carnally" would indicate an active sexual life (where in a sense males are corrupted by females), when males escape from sexual activity they become "real men" (like Jesus). Women too, in abandoning the female, become not ordinary (sexually active) males, but "real men". Thus in *Miscellanies* 6.12.100.3, as we have seen, when a woman becomes "unfemale" she becomes not "male" (which would designate active male sexuality) but manly (*andrikē*) and perfect.

For the platonizing Clement the real "woman" is her soul; hence the effect of ceasing to be sexually active is to allow this "manly" soul to be rid of its femaleness (as the male its mere maleness) and become like Jesus. Strictly speaking it is the Logos-Christ that is the image of God. As Clement says, "The image of God is the divine and royal Logos, a passionless human... the image of Christ is the human mind" (*Miscellanies* 5.14.94.5). As in Philo, it is the (manly) soul, not the body, that is created in God's image; human sexuality, being bodily, is no feature of what was so created.[57]

Yet Clement has varied Philo's position. If the male is to rid himself of his active sexual "maleness" in becoming a "real man", it seems that, though femaleness is an obvious weakness, there is something wrong (though less wrong) with maleness too. Clement invokes the language of Plato's theory of the tripartite soul to explain the problem: the female represents desire (symbolized by the black horse of the *Phaedrus*), while the male drive (*arrena hormēn*) is energy (*thumos*) (*Miscellanies* 3.13.93.1).[58] Beyond these analogues of male and female, however, is the charioteer of the *Phaedrus*, the reasoning part (*logistikon*) of the *Republic*.[59] As Clement explains elsewhere (*Miscellanies* 4.23.151.1), God (the goal of our imitative life) is *apathēs*, without (male, white-horse) *thumos* and (female, black-horse) desire.

In brief, Clement thinks (platonically) that all souls are by nature manly – hence created in the image of God and thus capable of virtue (*Miscellanies*

---

[57] H. von Balthasar wants to deny this, claiming that Clement "elsewhere does regard the body as part of the 'image'" (*Theo-Drama* II. 322, note 24 (citing *Paid.* 3.11.64.3 and 3.11.66.2). But for denials of image-quality to the body see *Prot.* 10.98.4; *Strom.* 2.19.102.6; 6.14.114.4; 6.16.136.3 (the latter, along with 2.19.102.6, cited by Balthasar).

[58] See T. H. C. van Eijk, "Marriage and Virginity, Death and Immortality", in J. Fontaine and C. Kannengiesser (eds.), *Epektasis: Mélanges patristiques offerts au Cardinal Jean Daniélou* (Paris 1972) 220 and D. G. Hunter, "The Language of Desire: Clement of Alexandria's Transformation of Ascetic Discourse", *Semeia* 57 (1992) 95–111, esp. 101; cf. S. R. C. Lilla, *Clement of Alexandria* (Oxford 1971) 81–83; W. Völker, *Der wahre Gnostiker nach Clemens Alexandrinus* (Berlin 1952) 130–132.

[59] For more on Clement's appropriation of Plato's charioteer see Lilla, *Clement of Alexandria* 97.

4.8.59–60; 6.12.96.3) – but that among the sexually active we have to
recognize a bodily distinction between males and females which can affect
the souls of both, and this effect (unsurprisingly) may be called "feminizing". Clement, however, has another, potentially conflicting, concern: he
wants to uphold the goods of marriage and procreation against the "encratites".[60] How then does he square this with the view that real men (even if
physiologically they are female) are not sexually active? The answer is to be
found in a distinction, also already in Philo, between moderation of the
passions (*metriopatheia*) and *apatheia* (which I shall for the moment leave
untranslated). The perfect man, rid of femaleness, and also of maleness, is to
be *apathēs*[61] (as, somehow, God is *apathēs*).

As has been widely recognized, Clement's extensive use of the concept of
apatheia is both novel among Christians and of immense significance for later
Christianity, and here again Philo is his predecessor.[62] Clement declines to
follow his "Middle Platonist" contemporaries who normally hold *metriopatheia* to be the highest state of virtue, preferring a more Stoicizing ideal
of man as of God.[63] For Clement *metriopatheia* is a way-station, either a
merely "ordinary" morality (leading to an ordinary salvation) or a means of
advancing further. He fails to recognize, however, that he will find it difficult
to combine a platonizing metaphysics with a strongly Stoicized ethics: something Christians had to learn as their culture developed. The process took a
long time, indeed is still incomplete.

The sense of *metriopatheia* is clear enough, indicating a disposition whereby
the virtuous man controls the non-rational parts of his soul to prevent them
from overwhelming the dictates of reason. Such a project, obviously, is
acceptable only to those who hold that there *is* a non-rational *part* (or parts)
of the soul; it is accordingly anathema to orthodox Stoics.

For the metriopathist a *pathos* is an impulse which is to be kept in check;
the good man will experience *pathē*. But for the Stoics every *pathos* is
irrational; according to their standard definition a *pathos* is an impulse

---

[60] For discussion of some of the philosophical background see Hunter, "The Language of Desire".
Hunter omits to explain that Clement's praise of marriage should be set against the background of his
views on the superior status of *apatheia*.

[61] *Strom.* 7.2.10.1; 7.14.84.2; *Paed.* 3.6.35.2, etc. For a survey of Christian *apatheia* see M. Spanneut,
"L'apatheia chrétienne aux quatres premiers siècles", *POC* 52 (2002) 165–302; for Clement
pp. 197–202, 247–259.

[62] *Apatheia* is not unknown in Christian writings before Clement, but it is marginal. For Justin, see
1 Apol. 10.2; 57.2, etc.; for comment see M. Spanneut, *Le stoicisme des Pères de l'église* (Paris 1957) 246
and "L'apatheia chrétienne" 173–174.

[63] The situation may be rather different for the Neoplatonists, as Lilla claims, but Clement predates
Neoplatonism. Lilla is mistaken in suggesting *Platonist* influence on Clement's account of *apatheia*.

which is out of control (DL 7.110; Clement, *Miscellanies* 2.13.59.6). Hence the wise man has no *pathē*, only the proper emotional feelings or sentiments (*eupatheiai*) which are the accompaniments and satisfactions of rational behaviour.[64] If we were to ask Clement (and also Philo), "What kind of *pathos* are you alluding to in your discussions of *apatheia* and *metriopatheia*?", perhaps all they need reply is that there is nothing irrational about the emotional condition of the good man, that he is never led astray by his emotions. If the good man is "*apathēs*", this means he is free of those *pathē* deemed sinful because excessive; his remaining *pathē* are not irrational and are always controlled. But in effect what Philo and Clement say, stoically, is that the good man has no *pathē* at all (adding that the *pathē* of the metriopathist are merely contained). That leaves the good man with only an emotional "colouring" of rational acts, with a *eupatheia*; something like a "feel-good" but non-motivating experience.[65] Yet Clement allows that the good man not only has a proper fear of God (*Paedagogus* 1.9.87) without ceasing to be *apathēs*, but is capable of feeling pity and repentance.

According to the Stoics an important feature of *apatheia* is invulnerability; the sage is not touched, let alone swayed, by emotional appeals or by grief at the suffering of others. This is the heartless side of a Stoic ethic – as well as the claim that whatever emotional colouring there may be to the wise man's actions and beliefs, these are all driven by impersonal rationality. But whatever may be acceptable for Philo, such ideas pose problems for the Christian Clement, and we recognize them in his account of the goal of the good life, namely obtaining likeness to God. In considering that likeness, we also recognize that whether women can be said to be in God's image, or rather in what sense they can be said to be in his image, will depend on our view of the nature of God.

Clement certainly associates *apatheia* with the search for likeness to God.[66] He connects it not only with Genesis but with the Platonic likeness-to-God as the goal of human aspirations. For Clement man is created in God's image and attains his likeness, platonically, by his mode of living,

---

[64] For recent comment see R. Sorabji, *Emotion and Peace of Mind* (Oxford 2000) 47–51; M. Nussbaum, *The Therapy of Desire: Theory and Practice in Hellenistic Ethics* (Princeton 1994) 398–401. According to Spanneut ("L'apatheia chrétienne", 199, note 99), Clement uses *eupatheia* once of Christ. Spanneut also notes that in his enthusiasm to attribute *apatheia* to Christ Clement tends to diminish his full humanity (200).

[65] Spanneut holds that Clement's *apatheia* is not "essentially insensibility". I argue that the problem is that Clement is confused. He sometimes makes things more difficult for himself by denying even the Stoic rational condition of "joy" (*chara*): as in *Strom.* 6.9.71.3.

[66] See already H. Merki, ὉΜΟΙΩΣΙΣ ΘΕΩΙ: *Von der platonischen Angleichung an Gott zur Gottähnlichkeit bei Gregor von Nyssa* (Freiburg in der Schweiz 1952) 48–52; A. Mayer, *Das Gottesbild im Menschen nach Clemens von Alexandrien* (Rome 1942).

though in specifically Christian wise by following and imitating Christ (*Protrepticus* 8.3). But to become like God one has to know God's nature, and for Clement, following Philo, God is *apathēs* in the Stoic sense: he is pure rationality, possessed of no non-rational features. Yet the Stoic God is *apathēs* not only as purely rational, but also as invulnerable, being ultimately unconcerned with human happiness or unhappiness, even though also in effect providential. Such unconcern is impossible for Clement, though he not only agrees with Philo that God is *apathēs*, but adds that Christ is *apathēs*, and that it is by attaining likeness to Christ that we attain likeness to God.[67]

Since normally for Clement we seek to attain likeness to the Father, we might suppose that we should become like him in our manly soul. But Clement offers a certain modification of this, and thus a further apparent modification of the Stoic version of *apatheia*. In *Which Rich Man is to be Saved* (37.2), we read as follows:[68] "In his ineffability he is father; in his 'sympathy' to us he became mother. The Father by loving (*agapēsas*) became female, and a great sign of this is he whom the Father begat from himself. And the fruit begotten of love is love." God the Father, says Clement, became mother to the Son, and hence our mother. That indicates not only God's loving care – far removed from the indifferent providence of the Stoics – but characterizes that care as explicitly both "female" and divine. God the creator is characterized as father, while God the loving and incarnate saviour is characterized as mother. That in its turn might suggest the "divinity" (and imaged divinity) of female characteristics as such; yet Clement, typical of his age, makes little further use of this idea.

Sympathy of this sort (very different from the Stoic "sympathy" of the parts of the universe) indicates a further breach in God's character as *apathēs*. Not only is it no product of a non-rational part of the divine being, but it has no connection with matter, since for Clement God is wholly immaterial. Nor does it appear the mere colouring of the sentiments which we have recognized as *eupatheia* in Stoic texts. It is much more full-blooded, indicating that we too, if we are to be like God, must exhibit similar "female" characteristics.

"Sympathy" is related to love, specifically to *agape*. We ask therefore what kind of love Clement has in mind.[69] The problem, at least, is clear: since

---

[67] See Lilla, *Clement of Alexandria* III.

[68] Part of the text is quoted by J. Behr, *Asceticism and Anthropology in Irenaeus and Clement* (Oxford 2000) 161, note 144.

[69] Clement is influenced by the specifically Stoic determination of *eros*. The wise man, for the Stoics, will welcome *eros* but not in any way as "madness", let alone as compromising his *apatheia* and self-sufficiency. For Clement, I shall argue, *agape* seems to be passionless *eros* (cf. Spanneut, "L'apatheia chrétienne" 257). Platonists like Plutarch denied that such a state is properly designated *eros* at all; for a good discussion (without reference to Clement) see M. Nussbaum, "Eros and the Wise" in J. Sihvola and T. Engberg-Pedersen (eds.), *The Emotions in Hellenistic Philosophy* (Dordrecht 1998) 271–304, esp. 289–298.

God is love, we too must become love; hence we are concerned not only with God's love for us but with our love for God. According to a tradition of interpretation best represented by the Swedish theologian Anders Nygren, "Clement uses the New Testament term Agape, but the reality he intends to convey corresponds most closely to what Plato calls 'the heavenly Eros'".[70] Nygren is right to recognize the influence of the Platonic tradition on Clement's analysis of love (though his radical distinction between Agape and Eros is historically, philosophically, theologically and psychologically untenable[71]). Clement certainly believes that in our likeness to God we are somehow divinized (*Miscellanies* 4.23.148.8; 7.10.56.6, etc.) – a view he shares with his near-contemporary Irenaeus (*Against Heresies* 4.33.4) – and that love (normally called *agape*) is the means by which we thus become "gods":[72] a state seen primarily as immortality, and to which we advance not by nature but by God's grace.

On at least one occasion (*Protrepticus* 11.117.2) Clement speaks of a heavenly and divine *eros* (using apparently Platonic terminology): "The heavenly and really divine *eros* is present to mankind whenever in the soul itself the really beautiful is able to shine out re-kindled by the divine Word." Nygren is right, however, to observe that he normally avoids the word *eros*, though he misunderstands the reasoning behind this. That becomes clear in passages like *Miscellanies* 6.9.73.3. Defending *apatheia* against its critics, Clement tries to purge the perfect love (this time *agape*) of the "gnostic" (i.e., perfect) Christian of any element of "desire". *Agape* is beginning to look like a Stoicized, colourless and impassive *eros*.

Clement's opponents ask, "How can the man who desires fine things (*tōn kalōn*) remain *apathēs*, if all familiarity (*oikeiōsis*) with fine things arises with desire?" To which Clement replies that "these people" do not understand the divine nature of *agape*:

Love is no longer the desire (*orexis*) of the lover, but a respectful familiarity which has restored the "gnostic" to the unity of the faith ... He will not strive to become like beautiful things since he possesses beauty through *agape*. What need has he of energy and desire [the two Platonic horses again], since he has obtained familiarity from love with the God who is *apathēs*?

[70] A. Nygren, *Agape and Eros* (trans. P. S. Watson, Philadelphia 1953) 364.
[71] Cf. Rist, *Eros and Psyche*. For detailed rebuttals of Nygren see especially M. C. D'Arcy, *The Mind and Heart of Love* (London 1962), J. Burnaby, *Amor Dei* (London 1938) and several of the essays in C. W. Kegley (ed.), *The Philosophy and Theology of Anders Nygren* (Carbondale, Ill. 1970).
[72] See generally *Quis dives*, 7.3; *Strom.* 2.19.97.2; 5.3.19.4; 7.2.13.1–3.

Desire is at best a mark of the incomplete Christian, not of the perfect "gnostic" or of God himself. True *agape*, generating godlike behaviour, does so without any desire. Like fellow-feeling, it is an expression – perhaps one might say the exterior face – of goodness and beauty.

Clement's position is anomalous. He seems to start with the basic Stoic notion of *apatheia* or *eupatheia*, of which *agapēsis* – as a sort of wish (*boulēsis*) or kindly rational affect – is a regular Stoic species.[73] He then modifies his Stoicism with the help of a more Platonic notion of love of beauty, while trying to avoid any suggestion of erotic desire in a final heavenly condition with desire eradicated into *apatheia* (*Miscellanies* 6.9.74.1). As we saw earlier, treating specifically of divine *eros*, he says it shines out in the presence of beauty and is the face of goodness. But *eros*, in effect, is emasculated, to look like a Stoic colouring of the virtues, and enable Clement to maintain rational imperturbability; this seems the right phrase for his *apatheia* – *pace* the rational fear of the Lord – as the mark both of God and of the perfect, "gnostic", Christian. There is certainly a vestige of Platonism about Clement's position, in that when a genuine Platonic *eros* "begets and gives birth in the beautiful", it is productive rather than merely desirous. But Clement's version is bloodless and it is easy to see why in his stoicizing account of goodness he normally steers clear of the word *eros*, with its associations with Platonic "madness".

Clement's position is expressed most clearly when he states that when the "gnostic" sees a beautiful body, his "holy *agape*" leads him to *think* of the beautiful soul: just as when he is amazed at a fine statue he *thinks* of the artist and of what is really beautiful (*Miscellanies* 4.18.116.2). It looks like the Stoicized, impersonal and ultimately unintelligible Platonism – thought without desire – by which, as Spanneut observed,[74] compassion is reduced to beneficence.

The lengths to which Clement – as I noted a defender of marriage against the "encratites" – will go in such matters becomes clear when he observes that even love-making between married couples, undertaken solely for procreation, is performed not with desire (*epithumia*) but with a "rational impulse" and a "strict and chaste intention" (*Paedagogus* 3.6.58.2), bringing with it no dreaded pleasure but a "controlled satisfaction" (*engkratēs apolausis*) – presumably at a duty well performed.[75]

---

[73] Cf. Ps.-Andronicus, *On Emotions* 6 (= *SVF* 3.432).   [74] Spanneut, *Le stoicisme* 249.

[75] For more detailed analysis of Clement's fateful views (and their roots), see Gaça, *The Making of Fornication*, esp. 262–266.

Yet, as we have seen, there remain chinks in Clement's armour, visible if we revert to his view that it is only the manly soul that is created in the image of God. Since *eros*, even its heavenly version, cannot avoid some kind of sexual connotations, if sexuality is only a matter of the body, not of the holistic human being whether male or female, it seems better to disconnect it altogether from true manliness. In this, however, Clement does not succeed, since he cannot entirely free his *agape*, his "gnostic" love, from the sense of beauty – and beauty, in a Greek context, always has open or sublimated erotic connotations.

Was there implicit here the threat that if *eros* or love by any other name could be entirely separated from beauty, then beauty would disappear from the perfect Christian life and from descriptions of God? The question reveals a more basic historical problem: beauty in Clement's time rarely is an attribute of the Christian God,[76] and Clement himself, though influenced by Platonic Ideas both of intelligible beauty and of the distinction between visible and invisible beauty (as in *Paidagogus* 3.1.3,3), seems hesitant about introducing it – albeit he was encouraged in that direction by reflection on Christ's Transfiguration. Yet introduce it he does; even the suspect word *kallos* is applied to the beauty of the soul. *Agape* is true beauty; the Saviour is beautiful, the sole object of love in our yearning for true beauty (*Miscellanies* 2.5.21.1) – yearning which we presumably lose when we are perfected.

In ancient times the Platonists regularly thought of Christians as enemies of the Good and the Beautiful, and although modern historians of early Christian attitudes to art (and hence to beautiful representations of human and divine figures) have rejected the older view that the earliest Christians were proto-iconoclasts,[77] and have even challenged the weaker claim that a

[76] A more detailed treatment of beauty must be reserved for chapter 3.
[77] In the Iconoclast controversy itself both sides claimed that their opponents were "Hellenists", the Iconoclasts rejecting all icons as "Greek", that is, pagan and diabolically inspired, their opponents attempting to distinguish between a Christian and a "Hellenic" use of images; see A. Giakalis, *Images of the Divine: The Theology of Icons at the Seventh Ecumenical Council* (revised edition, Leiden 2005), esp. 32; for evidence Mansi 13, 276B, 293B, 296C–E. It is interesting to note that neither side was able to cite much pre-fourth-century support, and that the Iconoclasts had to drag in as early evidence a letter of Eusebius to Constantine's sister (*PG* 20, 1545–1549) – unsuccessfully because theologically dodgy and written by an officially dodgy (that is "Arian") theologian – together with a piece falsely attributed to Epiphanius of Salamis.
   For the early period see M. C. Murray, "Art and the Early Church", *JTS* 28 (1977) 303–345. The merit of this detailed paper is to show that the once widely held idea that Iconoclasm grew from early Christian beliefs is historically false; the Iconoclasts' view of earlier times was often self-serving. But Murray offers little positive evidence for the idea that before the fourth century there was much Christian enthusiasm for aesthetic *beauty* (rather than for mere representation of biblical scenes and symbols), and pagan Platonists maintained that such enthusiasm was grimly absent. The theological and sociological problem of iconoclasm – not only in its Byzantine variety – therefore remains: does "real" Christianity regularly and properly throw up an ambivalence, if not a hostility, towards artistic representations of men and of God, and does it also engender a specific hostility to physical beauty, especially to the beauty of the

love of art was initially suspect to the Christian leadership, there is no doubt that, either under the influence of traditional Jewish fears of idolatry – particularly in the case of portraits – or concerned about Greco-Roman worship (implicit or actual) of physical (sexual) beauty,[78] most Christians before the fourth century set little store by art, still less felt impelled by revelation to think of beauty as a divine attribute. (I shall argue in chapter 3 that it is mistaken to suppose that Irenaeus' account of the glory of God marks a significant change in this regard.) But if beauty is substantially discounted, then creativity – not least sexual creativity – becomes a matter not of desire but of a noble will to a rational duty, as we have seen: in marriage the duty of procreation.[79]

In a remarkable understatement Eric Osborn observes that "Clement never quite reconciles his belief in marriage as the gift of a good creator with his conviction that sexual intercourse is a sign of imperfection."[80] Perhaps in his fear of physical beauty, and his un-Platonic but deeply Stoic determination to reduce proper emotion to the mere colouring or expression of virtue, we can begin to see why. In Clement there is virtually no sense of the *inspiration* of beauty: certainly not of sexual beauty. And the fruit of *agape* is "lordly beneficence" (*Miscellanies* 4.6.28.2).

Clement dubs the supreme example of God's beneficence *philanthrōpia*,[81] a word widely used to describe the providential actions of Hellenistic kings

human body, as distinct from natural beauty which can be sanitized more easily as revealing God's powerful splendour? For discussion of early Christian avoidance of portraits and preference for New Testament narratives see also R. M. Jensen, *Face to Face* (Minneapolis 2005) 23.

Relevant to the early debate was the interpretation of Isa. 53:2–3 – as also, but in different prospective, Ps. 45 – which before Clement was regularly taken to refer to Jesus (before the Resurrection) as lacking *eidos*, *doxa* and *timē* (being thus neither handsome nor glorious): so Justin, *Dial.* 36.6; 49.2; 85.1 (*aeidēs*); Tertullian, *De carne Christi* 15.5; *Adv. Iud.* 14.1–3 (no *species* or *decus*). And note Clement's contrast between admirers of (physical) *kallos* and contemplators of the intelligible world (*Strom.* 6.17.151.3). Later, of course, Christ will return in glory (cf. *Dan.* 7): so Justin, *Dial.* 49.2; 110.2 etc. For helpful comment see J. Taubes, "La giustificazione del brutto nella tradizione cristiana delle origini", in *Messianismo e cultura: Saggi di politica, teologia e storia* (Cernusco 2001) 255–281.

[78] The importance of the fear of "idols" (often depicted in heroic or erotic nudity, thus uniting the two causes of suspicion) is not to be underestimated, and might have led to a formal distinction between idolatrous and non-idolatrous art, though, and despite later hesitant moves in this direction by "iconophiles", it failed to do so. Any such distinction would at least initially be necessarily indeterminate: we might expect quasi-religious portrayals of "secular" subjects and, more frequently, "secularized" portrayals of religious themes. Interestingly, when the old gods were dead, a new iconoclast arose, and Luther, now apparently fearing neo-paganism, held that "idolatrous" Christian images should be replaced by speech, that is by preaching of the "word"of God.

[79] Cf. *Strom.* 2.20.118ff., 3.7.58ff. for loving a wife without "desiring" her. Behr (*Asceticism and Anthropology* 175) rightly observes that there is more concern for mutual love and devotion in Musonius than in Clement.

[80] E. Osborn, *Ethical Patterns in Early Christian Thought* (Cambridge 1976) 74.

[81] For interesting comment see C. Osborne, *Eros Unveiled: Plato and the God of Love* (Oxford 1994) 164–184.

and of the God of Stoicism and Middle Platonism. In Theophilus, a second-century bishop of Antioch, it indicates God's beneficent reaction to man's disobedience (*To Autolycus* 2.27). In Clement it is used in a special way: the extreme example of God's *philanthrōpia* is his becoming man (*anthrōpos*) for us (*Paidagogus* 1.8.62.1–2).

For Clement *philanthrōpia* is an expression of God's *agape*, and, so far from being incompatible with God's *apatheia*, is an indication of it. Yet it would seem to detract from God's *apatheia*, and provide another instance of Clement's confusion. We have seen Clement tell us that, in his love and compassion for us, God became our mother. His incarnationalism might have induced him to abandon his insistence on the ideal of divine and human *apatheia*, but it scarcely does so. Perhaps from fear of the sexual associations and implications of love and compassion – even in the more "acceptable" form of the femininity of a motherly love – Clement prefers to stay with the imperturbable Father God and the duty-driven "gnostic" Christian. Perhaps his ambivalence (at best) about beauty (despite a certain platonizing in his account of love and his recognition of the "female" aspect of the Incarnation) prevented him from offending the puritanism and at least potential icon-oclasm characteristic of many of his "orthodox"[82] – not to say "encratite" – contemporaries. In the end his account of the Incarnation adds little to his picture of the godlike character of the original female who just might have been created in the image of God not merely in her (stoically) impersonal rationality but in her love and compassion. Or even in her beauty?

1.9 "PLATONIZING" AFTER CLEMENT

By the time of Origen the main approaches to man's creation in the image of God had been established. Exegesis depended on several factors, the most important being the degree to which the individual writer accepted a two-substance theory of man, namely that we consist of an ontological (rather than merely moral) "mixture", combination or association of soul and body. Those, like Clement, who suppose us to be a compound of material and immaterial substances normally believe that it is the immaterial soul of each human being

---

[82] Christians naturally inherited a concern about images of God from the Jews – and something of the Jewish aversion to "Hellenic" beauty. But synagogue art at this period (as at Beth Alpha in Galilee) was apparently less strict about images than it later became, and Christians fairly quickly began to paint (as in the Roman catacombs) images of Christ as (for example) the Good Shepherd. Yet there apparently remained a certain fear of representing Christ as suffering: until the fifth century, for example, we have no representations of the crucifixion. People who had seen crucifixions may have been concerned about indicating the degradation of the penalty rather than simply the pain – as Plato had declined in the *Phaedo* to represent the physical details of hemlock-poisoning.

that is created in God's image; hence that that soul is somehow pre-sexual, and thus likely to be thought of as male, not least because the male Jesus was held to be the "perfect man" for likeness to whom we should strive – a likeness normally seen as to a God who is unchanging, whose "emotions" are best viewed as colourless and dispassionate, who is *apathēs*. Thinkers in this camp are inclined to see sexuality – especially in its female form – as not properly human but added as a temporary bodily property for reproductive purposes, and to be left behind in heaven. In broad terms I have identified this as a platonizing interpretation both ontologically and with reference to sexuality, though it is primarily mediated through Philo's influential Jewish version.

The second type of exegesis is rather traditionally Jewish and Pauline, deriving from the idea of a single-structured human being, often represented rather materialistically. According to this view the whole person perishes with the death of the body; an extreme version can be recognized in the doctrine of the Sadducees that there is no resurrection. In Christianity, on the contrary, it is represented by an insistence on the resurrection of the body and/or the flesh: that is, of the whole person. It may or may not be accompanied by the corollary of the immortality of the soul.

Neither of these positions will always appear in an unambiguously complete form; I use them rather as benchmarks. But every variation will depend on one of the two ontological theses I have identified: that is, either on a "Platonic" or on a "Pauline" (or "holistic") account of human nature. As scriptural exegesis develops, however, strains on the two-substance theory of man become greater, especially in Augustine. Before leaving the ancient world, therefore, I want to look briefly at those strains – and their relation to the question of who is created in the image of God – as they approach the situation of their ontological first principles becoming unsustainable. I shall consider them under a number of heads: *apatheia*; the origins of sexuality in the platonizing traditions; the continuation of the Pauline tradition in what may be broadly, if slightly inaccurately, called the Antiochene version; the interpretation of 1 Corinthians 11:7. Finally I shall look at aspects of Augustine's theory of the human person. That will bring my rather disparate problems into focus, thereby setting the stage for further developments.

1.9.1 Origen: Apatheia and Eros

It might seem that theories of *apatheia* have only marginal relevance to the question of who is created and how in the image of God, but that is not the case. We saw in Clement an attempt to impose a supposedly Platonic account of the "passions" – broadly thought of as acts of the two lower and irrational parts of a "tripartite" soul – on to a Stoic base. Thus the achievement of *apatheia*, with its eradication of the irrational parts of the soul, would indicate not only a purification of the person and the elimination of a pathology, as in a properly Stoic schema, but a removal of unnecessary (or no longer necessary) features of the empirical self. Were that claim to be true, it would imply that only the "mind" (however understood, and Clement's account of it is in many ways more Stoic than Platonic) is really "us"; neither the body nor the "lower" affective parts of the soul are ultimately necessary. If we add that to the idea that only the "masculine" mind is the image of God (the platonizing version of my broader theme), the possibility that women are created in God's image remains, for souls are asexual, understood as masculine. The price paid, however, is the removal both of our affections and of our bodies from our real selves. Women's creational equality is thus preserved at the price of an inadequate account of human nature as a whole. A corollary of that is that it becomes increasingly difficult – a difficulty already visible in Clement – to offer more than a bloodless, Stoicizing account of Christian love either for God or for one's neighbour. Christ becomes reduced to the Stoic or Kantian sage.

Here we need a brief outline of some of the fruits of this "platonizing" attempt to blend *apatheia* with the Christian life – and the obvious start is with Origen, who was in some sort successor to Clement in his teaching role in Alexandria. But complications arise immediately, the first of which makes Origen's position on sexuality significantly more rigid than that of Clement and bequeaths a tradition of extremism to his successors, especially the Cappadocians. Origen believed that the original asexual soul of Adam *fell* into a body, and that somehow "in his loins" or "in some other ineffable manner" was the entire human race.[83] Adam's original *body* was etherial but already sexually differentiated. Eve was physically different from Adam in the Garden (*Commentary on Matthew* 14.16), though physical intercourse was as yet unnecessary – but in the act of disobedience to God the original couple became "corporeal" or "animal".[84] The "use" of sexuality began after

---

[83] *Comm. in Rom.* 5.2 (*PG* 14, 1029D).

[84] Any account of Adam's original condition and its relationship to the general fall of rational creatures into bodies (according to Origen) must remain speculative. It is not clear how many "falls" Origen proposed; indeed it is not even clear that he held a single consistent position throughout his life. I am especially indebted to the discussion of C. Bammel, "Adam in Origen", in R. Williams (ed.), *The Making of Orthodoxy: Essays in Honour of Henry Chadwick* (Oxford 1989) 62–93, esp. 68–69. The most interesting alternative is that proposed by G. Bürke, "Die Origenes Lehre vom Urstand des Menschen", *ZKTh* 72 (1950) 1–39. More recent comment (with some treatment of eschatology) is to be found in E. Prinzivalli, "L'uomo e il suo destino nel Commento a Giovanni", in E. Prinzivalli (ed.), *Il Commento a Giovanni di Origene: Il testo e i suoi contesti* (Villa Verruchio, RN 2005) 361–379, esp. 373–374.

the Expulsion, and hence is not merely an unfortunate necessity but a phenomenon of sin which must be transcended if our original paradisal state is to be restored. In "fallen" marriage, every sexual act involves pollution and impurity from which baptism absolves us.[85]

Origen, to put it bluntly, is a revisionist encratite.[86] He does not hold (with many of the encratites) that the original sin was sexual, or with Clement that it was an "anticipation" of marriage by Adam and Eve.[87] He does believe, however, that without sin – a movement of self-satisfaction or boredom with the contemplation of God[88] – the actualization of sexuality and indeed the very phenomenon of the female would not have occurred, and that sexual differentiation will disappear in the angelic body we shall acquire in heaven. By then the physical, fleshly body, a necessary site for the progress of the soul, will have outgrown its usefulness.

In the late fourth century Rufinus seems to have attempted to pin a radical version of such ideas on Jerome, in a tendentious attempt to portray him as the most extreme variety of Origenist:

May we husbands cherish our wives as our souls cherish their bodies, so that the wives may change into males and the bodies into souls, and there may be no difference of sex; but just as among the angels there is neither man nor woman so we – who will be like the angels – may even now begin to be what has been promised us in heaven.[89]

Perhaps it is a distortion of Origen's position that the body will be changed *back* into a pure soul; for Origen even the angels have spiritual and etherial *bodies*. He does seem to have thought, however, that the fleshly body will again become etherial; it will be "bodiless" (*asōmatos*), but in the sense of without *fleshly*, corporeal or animal characteristics – and without the organs of sexual differentiation.[90] At times, however, he seems to have hesitated

---

[85] *Comm. in Matth.* 17.35. Cf. P. Pisi, "Peccato di Adamo e caduta dei NOES nell'esegesi origeniana", in L. Lies (ed.), *Origeniana Quarta* (Innsbruck 1987) 322–335.

[86] For details a convenient summary is that of Sfameni Gasparro, "Image of God", esp. 146–150.

[87] See recently Behr, *Asceticism and Anthropology* 143–144.

[88] Cf. M. Harl, "Recherches sur l'origénisme d'Origène: La satiété (kóros) de la contemplation comme motif de la chute des âmes", *Studia Patristica* 8, TU 92 (Berlin 1966) 373–405.

[89] Rufinus, *Apologia* 1.24.

[90] For this and similar matters see H. Crouzel, "La doctrine origénienne des corps ressuscités", *Bulletin de littérature ecclésiastique* 81 (1980) 175–200, 241–266, esp. 188–197. It would be interesting – and tend to confirm the story of Origen's self-castration – if he thought (as Basil of Ancyra later denied) that by castration one ceases to be a male in this present life. Thus the casting off of bodily sexuality would be the first stage in the shedding of the *animal* body in general – though for Origen such an "desexualized" body must somehow continue to provide a "context" for the purification of the soul until that purification is complete (see again Brown, *Body and Society* 165).

about making the risen "body" wholly immaterial and wholly incorporeal; that may characterize God alone.[91]

Following in the footsteps of Philo, Origen proposes a two-stage creation: first the soul, or rather the mind (*nous*) – the Pauline "inner man",[92] according to the image of God[93] – then the differentiated body. In paradise, Adam had a spiritual body and was in some sense male, but he had no intercourse with Eve. He remained, and should have remained, spiritually and physically virgin.[94] Hence it is the goal of human life, in the first instance, to recover that virginal condition, and thus approximate to the asexual soul of the original Adam.[95]

Although Origen follows Clement in making *metriopatheia* a stage in the journey to *apatheia*, he makes substantially less use of *apatheia* than did his predecessor,[96] and he significantly modifies its sense. For Origen a *pathos* is an experience of the non-rational parts of the soul understood platonically rather than stoically; he teaches not a complete suppression of the emotions, but the elimination of those that are sinful. Furthermore, in contrast to Clement, he adopts a Christianized version of Platonic *eros*, holding love to be superior to *apatheia*. Even God the Father is not unambiguously *apathēs*,[97] for Origen resists the view that *agape* is *eros* without passion.

In order to grasp the importance of this, we must digress briefly to the earlier Christian history of *eros*. Before Origen – as we have noticed with Clement – the word is usually avoided by Christians, chiefly no doubt because

---

[91] See Prinzivalli, "L'uomo e il suo destino" 374–379.

[92] *Entr. Her.* 12; cf. *in Joh.* 20.22.183 (*GCS* 4.2, p. 355, 11ff.).

[93] H. Crouzel, *Théologie de l'image de Dieu chez Origène* (Paris 1956) 145, 148.

[94] Cf. C. Jenkins (ed.) "Origen on I Corinthians II", 29, *JTS* 9 (1908) 370. The matter is complicated by Origen's (Philonic) use of the distinction within each human being between a male *spiritus* and a female (more sensual) *anima*: cf. *Homily on Genesis* 1.13.15. Thus the Fall might be symbolized as a complaisance of the *spiritus* in the adultery of the *anima* with the flesh (and Redemption as its recovery of an original union with the spirit).

[95] For Origen's attenuated view of the resurrection see Crouzel, "La doctrine origènienne".

[96] So Crouzel, *Théologie de l'image* 244; W. Völker, *Das Vollkommenheitsideal des Origenes* (Tübingen 1931) 153–156. Origen's latter-day disciple Evagrius restored *apatheia* to a central position in his account of ascesis, but that takes us too far from creation and will not be discussed here.

[97] For Origen and the Cappadocians on *apatheia* see also the summary of A. and C. Guillaumont, *Evagre le Pontique: Traité pratique*, SC 170 (Paris 1971) 100–108. For a denial of *apatheia* to the Father (where no allegorical interpretation is suggested) see *Hom. in Ezech.* 6.6; for further discussion, L. Perrone, "La passione della carità: Il mistero della misericordia divina secondo Origene", *Parola, Spirito e Vita* 29 (1994) 223–235; T. Kobusch, "Kann Gott leiden? Zu den philosophischen Grundlagen der Lehre von der Passibilität Gottes bei Origenes", *VC* 46 (1992) 328–333; Spanneut, "L'apatheia chrétienne" 204.

Origen certainly allegorizes references (for example) to God's anger in the OT, and normally thinks of the Father as *apathēs* insofar as he is unchangeable, sinless, etc., but he makes use of the Stoic concept of preliminaries to passion to explain the "anger" of Jesus in the Temple (see Spanneut, "L'apatheia chrétienne", 205–207).

of its normal reference to sexual desire. With philosophers in the Platonic tradition, however, such desire had been set in a profound metaphysical and psychological context. Following the *Symposium* and *Phaedrus*, the Platonists especially identified *eros* (as Longus puts it in the preface to his novel *Daphnis and Chloe*) not simply as desire – whether for sex or for anything else – but specifically as the inspirational love and desire for beauty: "For without a doubt no-one has succeeded in escaping *eros* nor will anyone in the future, so long as beauty (*kallos*) exists and there are eyes to see."

In this tradition, "real" beauty, the beauty that abides unchanged, is to be found only among the Forms. Yet although in comparison with Beauty itself earthly beauty is trivial, the Platonists never developed that anxiety about the images of beauty, not least of the beauty of the human body, widely found in early Christianity. Although like Philo the earliest Christians were happy to echo the Old Testament and reflect on the glory of God in the beauty of his created world, *eros*, concerning itself in the first instance with the beauty of the human body, was generally feared by them.[98]

Philo's language should be carefully noted: he is sufficiently Platonist to think of man's striving for God as *eros*, but he often tries to separate *eros* from beauty – not least because of its possible connections with pederasty.[99] He prefers to think of *eros* as a yearning for wisdom (*On Creation* 1.5; 1.70), and dismisses its more vulgar varieties as directed not so much towards beauty as simply towards "pleasure", thus distorting the connection between *eros*, beauty and pleasure that Plato had carefully established.[100] In the footsteps of Philo (as well as of the Stoics, for whom both Platonic and popular *eros* are viciously excessive), we have found Clement making use of the *concept* of *eros* while normally avoiding the *word* itself, though occasionally connecting a "heavenly and divine" *eros* – in the Platonic manner (*Protrepticus* 11.39ff.) – with what is "really beautiful".

In light of this background it is significant that Origen not only begins to reformulate Clement's account of *apatheia* but, especially in his *Commentary on the Song of Songs*, presents God as *eros* and Christ as a lover of beauty: "I do not think that one could be blamed if one were to call God Eros" (*On the Song*, prologue 71). The soul, he tells us in his *Homilies* on the same text, must become "beautiful" (*Homily* 1.3, cf. 2.4). And although he holds that "carnal love" comes from Satan (*Homily* 1.2), Origen retains the sensual aspect of *eros*, even (or perhaps especially) though the soul is originally male (but sexually

---

[98] For the development of Christian ideas of "erotic" beauty see chapter 3.
[99] On which see *De Vita Contemplativa* 7.57.   [100] So *Leg. Alleg.* 3.113.

inert), through a novel thesis of the "spiritual senses", by which, analogously to our use of the physical senses, we can see, taste and touch the beauty of immaterial reality.[101] Such experiences, caused by the "darts" of love,[102] are the sensual joys of the intelligible world, to be experienced by the naked spirit (*Homily* 2.8). They make the joys of physically sexual "knowledge" a mere distraction in comparison (*On John* 19.4.20).[103]

As we have seen, in the Platonic tradition to which Origen is indebted, erotic desire is a predominantly male characteristic, but Origen associates its sensual features with the perfected soul, which, though *qua* soul it is "terrestrially" non-female in both men and women, becomes female in relation to God.[104] Femaleness – in a strictly human context a debased version of maleness – becomes at the higher level (by reason of its sensual analogue) a mode of our humility and dependency in relation to the Creator. Whereas in human procreation (according to Origen) the male is the active partner, at the spiritual level it is the soul (of both men and women) on whom the "male" God – both beautiful and a lover of beauty – acts. Origen no doubt failed to recognize all the implications of this "re-sexualization" of the soul.

According to Origen, physical sexual difference is to be outgrown as the soul passes through the ages. True love of beauty and true reproductive desire are erotically directed elsewhere. All of which enables him not only to stand with Clement and Philo in supposing that women – insofar as they have a manly soul – are created in the image of God, but also to reconstruct a Philonic idea that insofar as the soul is in love with God it becomes female to Christ: thus suggesting, at least, that while only the originally manly soul is in God's image, the manly soul reconstructed as female attains to greater "likeness".[105] A version of this last idea could also be a plausible, indeed

---

[101] Cf. K. Rahner, "Le début d'une doctrine des cinq sens spirituels chez Origène", *Revue d'Ascétique et de Mystique* 12 (1932) 113–145; J. M. Dillon, "Aisthêsis Noêtê: A Doctrine of Spiritual Senses in Origen and in Plotinus", in *The Golden Chain* (Aldershot 1990) essay XIX. The thesis has ramifications for the later disputed issue of the nature of God's knowledge of particulars. For developments in Gregory of Nyssa and possible connections with *apatheia* see J. Daniélou, *Platonisme et théologie mystique* (Paris 1944) 100.

[102] For darts see Osborne, *Eros Unveiled* 72–74.   [103] *SC* 290, pp. 22–25.

[104] Importantly in Origen's account of the Bride in the Song of Songs both the Church and the individual soul (though as yet no special emphasis on the virgin female) are in a sense the new Eve – previously identified only with the Church (cf. Tert., *De Anima* 43.10). I have commented on a tendency to view the soul as female in relation to God in both Philo and the rabbis.

[105] In the fourth century we often find a combination of ideas: the male soul is to be female to God but "manly" in ordinary life, while the female soul is to be made manly (or angelic) by the suppression of its female body, for example by fasting which can suppress a woman's periods, dry up her breasts, etc. For detailed discussion see T. M. Shaw, *The Burden of the Flesh: Fasting and Sexuality in early Christianity* (Minneapolis 1998).

more than plausible, feature of theories about who is created in God's image and likeness in the eyes of those who – resisting the "platonizing" notion that every soul is always essentially "asexual", "male", or at least "unfemale" – hold that "terrestrially" male souls go with male bodies and female souls with female bodies.

1.9.2 Didymus, Basil and Gregory of Nyssa

The influence of Origen's revised encratism, coupled with his platonizing account of sexual differentiation as existing only at the bodily level – while "female" sexual characteristics come into their own in the relationships of all human beings, "male" and "female", to the divine – is strong both among his immediate successors such as Didymus the Blind in Alexandria and among the so-called Cappadocians. I therefore allude briefly to Basil – as well as Didymus – before looking in rather more detail at Gregory of Nyssa, who in many ways may be considered the culmination of the variety of platonizing Christianity that ultimately draws its inspiration from Philo – though, as we shall see, Gregory's account of psychosexual unity differs considerably from Philo's.

Didymus follows Origen in holding that only the inner man, the *nous*, is created in God's image, but he thought (as later did most of the Antiochenes) of the image primarily in terms of the exercise of legitimate authority. Agreeing too with the tradition whereby male and female indicate active intelligence and passive soul, Didymus follows the Origen of the *Commentary on the Song of Songs* in applying the same principle to the relationship of humankind to God; the human soul is female in relation to her divine master.[106]

As for Basil of Caesarea, he too accepts that in her masculine soul woman is created in the image of God: but he uses the somewhat ambiguous phrase (which will also occur among the Antiochenes and where its true implications are the more visible) that the two sexes are "equal in honour".[107] That might allow the possibility that they are both created in the image of God, being thus far "equal in honour", but that one is more in the image than the other. But for the extreme version of the "platonizing" – rather, the hyper-platonizing – version of our story we must look to Basil's brother, Gregory. Unlike Basil, Gregory follows the neo-encratite position of Origen

[106] For comment see K. Børresen, "God's Image, Man's Image? Patristic Interpretations of Gen. 1,27 and 1 Cor. 11,7", in *Image of God* 196–197.
[107] *Sermo de creatione hominis* 1.18 = *Hom.* 10 (SC 160, 212–216).

in proposing a "two-stage" creation:[108] insofar as man is created in the image of God he is created sexless, but, foreseeing man's sin and consequent mortality, God added the sexual distinction. Indeed, misreading Galatians 3.28, Gregory goes so far as to claim that Christ himself (as the perfect Image) is sexless.

Gregory thinks of human beings in their fallen state as prisoners on the inexorable march towards death. We can only ward off death's effects by an endless sequence of marriages and the generation of children[109] – apart from the hope that we may foreshadow the restoration of our unfallen condition through the practice of virginity.

At the ontological level, this view seems to put an end to the ambiguity between a male and an asexual Adam that characterized much of the previous debate; reverting to something more like the position of Clement, Gregory holds that even masculinity is not good enough for an image of God, and he is unambiguous:

The creation of our nature is in a sense twofold: one made like God, one divided according to the sexes: for something like this the passage obscurely conveys by its arrangement where it first says, "God created the human being in the image of God" and then, adding to what has been said, "male and female God created them" – a thing which is alien from our conception of God.[110]

Gregory's argument is clear: God is spirit, spirit is asexual, therefore the image of God is asexual. That entails that to attain likeness to God we must become as asexual as possible, at best by pursuing virginity. We are in effect double beings, an angel–beast combination, and sexuality is a mark of the bestial: useful to fill up the required number of humanity,[111] but with no characteristics imaging the divine. At the resurrection, which is "nothing more" than a restoration of Adam's intended condition before the Fall, we shall return to the state of spiritual (fleshless) asexual angels (*Creation of Man* 17; *Soul and Resurrection* (*PG* 46, 148A)).

For Gregory the two chief effects of human sinfulness, arising from our fall into time, are death and sexuality: perhaps viewed as the extremes of the old enemies of Greek wisdom, pain and pleasure. But after the upheaval

---

[108] The early *De Virginitate* gives no indication of double creation. For a recent discussion of how to interpret double creation (is there an historical or a logical sequence?) see S. Taranto, "Esiste una 'doppia creazione' dalle origini in Gregorio Nisseno?", *Adamantius* 8 (2002) 33–56.

[109] See especially J. Daniélou, *L'être et le temps chez Grégoire de Nysse* (Leiden 1970). For an imaginative reconstruction of Gregory's state of mind see Brown, *Body and Society* 293–299.

[110] *De hom. op.* 16 (*PG* 44, 181B). God made "man" in his image and likeness, then added the sexual distinctions (*phuseōs idiōmata*, 181D).

[111] *De hom. op.* 16.

over the Origenist concept of resurrection and its rebuttal by Methodius
and others,[112] Gregory has no wish to diminish, let alone to deny or even
seem to deny, the resurrection in some sort of the body. Indeed he defends it
vigorously, apparently holding that the unity of the human person demands
it: the incorruptibility of the resurrected body, he thinks, is a mark of its
divine nature;[113] hence it seems that were it not for his hostility to sexual
difference Gregory would have been close to arguing for a more radically
metaphysical unity of bodies and souls, including sexed bodies if not sexed
souls. But Gregory's resurrected body (as his immortal soul) is precisely
divine in that it is devoid of sexuality as of associated corruptibility. It is a
non-fleshly, asexual and etherial body – which ought to have looked too
Origenist for "orthodox" taste. According to Gregory, I conclude, men and
women are created in the image of God, and – in Basilian language – are
"equal in honour" (*Soul and Resurrection* 157AB; Basil, *On the Creation of
Man* 1.18), but that is because they are not properly men and women at all,
but fallen angels. The platonizing version of the thesis that "woman" was
created equally in God's image is retained, but at an even more excessive
price than that paid by Origen.[114]

The heart of Gregory's position, the thesis that sexual activity was only
planned by God as a remedy for the Fall, was repeated by Maximus Confessor
(who specifically names Gregory in *Questions to Thalassius* 1), by John
Damascene (*On the Orthodox Faith* 4.24) and by Scotus Eriugena (*Division
of Nature* 2.534A, 539D11–13; 5.893D). Eriugena indeed secures this ultra-
Alexandrian result by an "end-run" round Augustine.[115] Interestingly, another

---

[112] See E. Prinzivalli, *Magister Ecclesiae: Il dibattito su Origene fra III e IV secolo* (Rome 2002) 24, 87–89.

[113] *De an. et res.* 157AB, though pace Hamman (*L'homme, image de Dieu* 219) he does not say that the
whole man is "in the image of God", as Hamman himself seems to recognize later (p. 236).

[114] For further comment on Gregory's continuing use of the Origenist notion of all souls as female in
relation to God, and on the standard description of heroic sanctity by women as "manly", see
Børresen, "God's Image", 198.

[115] See E. Jeauneau, "La division des sexes chez Grégoire de Nysse et chez Jean Scot Erigène", *Eriugena,
Studien zu seinen Quellen* (Heidelberg 1980) 33–54. All these texts are discussed by Balthasar (*Theo-
Drama* II, 379–382, and see note 2 above) who, while apparently finding the Gregorian position more
satisfying than other alternatives, concludes that "we must leave the question open". In favour of the
Gregorians, he thinks, is that they recognize that the sexual is "only a secondary 'echo' of total
humanity", by which he refers to the Church's teaching that in heaven there will be no sexual acts.
That does nothing to illuminate the fact that sexuality was created by God for human life on earth
and is more than merely genital; indeed it appears to accept the Gregorian and pre-Gregorian line
that sexuality is limited to genital acts of the body.
  Gregory's thesis depends on the view that heaven is the restoration of an unfallen Adamic state,
which must "therefore" have been non-sexual. Since Balthasar appears to reject that part of the
Gregorian account, one wonders why (against the mature Augustine) he is concerned to deny a
genuine original sexuality in favour of an apparently "decorative" account of the originality of the
physical differences between Adam and Eve: a problem which does not arise if we accept the

fourth-century Cappadocian, Basil of Ancyra, claims that Mary is a "statue" (*agalma*) of God "in her soul and in her body".[116] He makes no metaphysical comment on this, however, and draws no conclusions about the creation of women in general, perhaps thinking that Mary's (male and passionless) virginity outweighs the creative femininity of her motherhood.

1.10 THE NON-PLATONIZING TRADITION: IRENAEUS AND TERTULLIAN

So much for versions of the platonizing solution to the question of whether women are created in God's image. In that tradition women are so created because the soul, both of men and of women, is in its essence either male or asexual, and the body (in some sense not really us, as the "Platonic" *Alcibiades* would have it) is certainly not created in the image of God. As I have noted, this tradition has difficulties with the idea of resurrection, which it tends either to deny or to attenuate. Before considering its deeper and more challenging development in Augustine, I turn to the more "Pauline" or "Hebrew" alternative whereby we make less resort to the soul–body distinction but ask directly whether the whole human being, male or female, is created in God's image. In turning to this alternative tradition, however, I first recall my working premiss that in Western thought as a whole accounts of "man" are usually of two types: the first of which (broadly Platonic and so among those we are considering here) emphasizing man as a moral agent, the other more concerned with the metaphysical problem of the unity of the human being's "body" (often material) and "soul" (often immaterial).

Whereas the "platonizing" tradition is liable to consider us, from the moral point of view, as more or less spiritual beings, the metaphysical-unity route (whether philosophical or more commonsensical) will imply a greater importance for the sexed body. In other words and in the context of our

---

consequences of rejecting all "platonizing" (or "angelizing") solutions to the problem of sexual difference.

Balthasar appears to confuse the issue further at *Theo-Drama* 6, 100, where in discussing Genesis he concludes (validly against Barth) that "marriage ... is not an image of God in the protological sense ... marriage [in the New Testament] transcends itself to become the virginal and eucharistic reciprocity between Christ as the Man and the Church as the Woman" – thus sidestepping the question of whether and in what sense *sexuality* is part of the divine image, and tending to identify "sexual" with "carnal" in the patristic mode, as something to be "transcended".

[116] As noted by Hamman, *L'Homme, image de Dieu* 236. For Basil of Ancyra see *De Virginitate* (*PG* 30, 785C). As noted earlier, Basil interestingly suggests, but does not develop, the idea that castration leaves a man still sexually (*kata phusin*, 787CD) a male. This is probably an attempt to disassociate himself from "Origenist" extremism – or does *phusis* merely refer to the penis? For an interesting discussion of Basil as a spokesman for the "homoiousian" version of ascetic progress see S. Elm, *'Virgins of God': The Making of Asceticism in Late Antiquity* (Oxford 1994).

present debate, if we "platonize", we tend to deny the importance of the body and explain away bodily resurrection; if we are more "Pauline" (working with a less radical distinction between spirit and flesh), we are liable to dissolve the ontological "soul–body" problem – that is, the problem that greatly worried ancient Platonists like Plotinus as to how a material body could be mixed or united with an immaterial soul – by some sort of materialist or vitalist account of the soul itself: by tending, that is, to make the soul and body similar physical substances. The up-front Stoic materialism (or, better, vitalism) of Tertullian and the *de facto* materialism of many early Christians before and even after Clement are logical results of this process.

Let us first consider Irenaeus, bishop of Lyon. Unlike Philo and many of the "platonizers", he proposes no two-stage creation.[117] Nor does he offer any direct help with the question of whether woman is created in the image of God, though he maintains that it is the soul–body compound that is in that image: "The perfect man is the mixing and union of soul and flesh" (*Against Heresies* 5.6.1). "It is man, and not a part of man, who is made according to the likeness of God."[118] If that is the case, however, there could be a corollary about the original nature of women, but Irenaeus does not mention it.

A very similar pattern can be found in Tertullian, not least in his *On the Resurrection of the Dead*: "Everything is planned for man and given not to the soul alone but also to the flesh" (34.1–2). It is man in the flesh for whom Christ died (cf. *On the Flesh of Christ* 4.3–4). It is into human flesh that Christ was incarnated. Both Incarnation and resurrection demand that the flesh be treated as essentially and desirably human, no "afterthought" in creation, no necessary occasion of sin or mere adjunct of our fallen nature. As I have observed, it is not least the closeness of soul and body that encourages Tertullian to explain their union in the Stoic language of the materiality of the soul. Yet so far from such ideas encouraging him to think that the differences between male and female bodies are irreducible and must indicate that both are created in the image of God, the contrary is the

---

[117] Cf. recently Behr, *Asceticism and Anthropology* 87. Somewhat like Clement (and many other earlier Christian writers), Irenaeus regards Adam and Eve as childlike, and so not yet mature enough in paradise for procreation, but unlike Clement he does not associate the first sin with an anticipation of marriage. The original sin is caused by their immaturity; they were easily tempted into self-indulgent pride (*Dem.* 15). Their childlike (or for them is it childish?) innocence, in which they were naked and not ashamed, was thus lost. There seems a certain confusion (common in patristic times and beyond) of childlikeness with childish immaturity.

[118] Cf. Hamman, *L'homme, image de Dieu.* Cf later the anti-Origenist Ps.Athenagoras, *De Resurrectione* 15, though the text avoids direct reference to the relation of the image to the body: "Man, who consists of both soul and body, must survive for ever; but he cannot survive unless he is raised." For fuller discussion see G. Stroumsa, "Caro salutis cardo: Shaping the Person in Early Christian Thought", *History of Religions* 30 (1990) 25–50, esp. 42–43.

case; it seems the old notion of a single perfect form of mankind reasserts itself, reinforced by the doctrine that the male Christ is the perfect man. In any case, as Børresen put it, Tertullian's attitude to the female is not "innocent": Eve is the gateway to the devil who has destroyed the image of God that is man (*On Women's Dress* 1.1.2). Women will be resurrected as sexually male (though in a "spiritual" form of matter (1.2.5)).

If Tertullian's view of the material unity of soul and body may be seen as a "philosophical" rendering of Paul's account of the human person as a unitary substance, on the more specific question of women in God's image, I have noted that there is no reason to deny that in Paul himself, even if women are not so created, they can attain to a state of perfect manliness by Christian virtue and God's grace. A variation on that was offered in late fourth-century Rome by "Ambrosiaster", an unidentifiable commentator on Paul whose work attained later importance by being falsely attributed to Ambrose or Augustine and according to whom women are not created in God's image. For Ambrosiaster female deficiency arises not because God transmitted "dominion" over the animals only to Adam (as some of the Antiochenes were later to suggest) – Eve at least shares in that dominion – but because "authority" has been transmitted from one God to one man/male, to whom Eve is subordinate. And as God the Father begot the Son, who is of the same substance as himself, so Adam is the origin of Eve.[119]

1.11 THE ANTIOCHENE TRADITION

One of the few exceptions to the rule that patristic writers ignored Aristotelianism is provided by the philosophically erudite Nemesius, a fourth-century bishop of Emesa. In discussing the difficulties of the two-substance theory of human nature, Nemesius seems to have tried to reformulate the Aristotelian theory of the soul as the form of the body, but eventually settled for the notion that there is an "unconfused unity"

---

[119] Cf K. Børresen, "Imago Dei, privilège masculin? Interpretation augustinienne et pseudo-augustinienne de Gen. 1,27 et 1 Cor. 11,7", *Augustinianum* 25 (1985) 213–234; D. G. Hunter, "The Paradise of Patriarchy: Ambrosiaster on Woman as (not) God's Image", *JTS* 43 (1992) 447–469. Cf. Ambrosiaster, *Liber quaestionum veteris et novi testamenti* 21, 24, 45, 2–3 (*CSEL* 50, 47–48 and 82–83), 106; *Ad Corinthos prima* 11, 7–10 and 14, 34 (*CSEL* 81/2, 121–123, 163), etc.

Hunter thinks (p. 457) that Tertullian may have influenced Ambrosiaster's admittedly different account of woman's created inferiority, though *De cultu fem.* 1.1, with its reference to "*hominem Adam*", is not by itself compelling evidence that Tertullian supposed the image of God to be only male.

between the two: a thesis deriving from a certain Ammonius which seems to do little more than redescribe the original problem.[120]

Nemesius was marginally influential on Christianity in the later Antiochene tradition, but that tradition, largely busying itself with the literal exegesis of Scripture, remained illiterate philosophically, if not downright hostile to philosophy. Of the Antiochean "school" I limit myself to Diodore of Tarsus, John Chrysostom,[121] Theodore of Mopsuestia and Theodoret of Cyrrhus. The views of this group about the possible creation of woman in the image of God have recently received detailed attention,[122] and it is clear that, although Theodoret offers a richer picture of godlike human nature whereby God's image is indicated by our unique ability to make a free choice of the good life, the majority of the group accepts that it is the authority vested in males which indicates that only they have been created directly in God's image. Even Theodoret accepts the conclusion that woman is something like an image of an image (*PG* 82.312C). For Chrysostom, woman is subordinate to man, as Eve to Adam, and therefore she cannot have been created for a position of authority such as to be a divine image.[123] She is subordinate because no family (or other social unit[124]) can have two heads; in such a situation strife would be unavoidable,[125] and in any case (in accordance with

---

[120] On Ammonius see J. M. Rist, "Pseudo-Ammonius and the Soul–Body Problem in Late Antiquity", *AJP* 109 (1988) 402–415. For a recently renewed interest in the Aristotelianism of Nemesius see B. Motta, *La mediazione estrema: L'antropologia di Nemesio di Emesa fra Platonismo e Aristotelismo* (Padua 2004), esp. 157–185; P. F. Beatrice, "L'union de l'Ame et le Corps: Némésius d'Emèse, lecteur de Porphyre", in V. Boudon-Millot and B. Pouderon (eds.), *Les Pères de l'église face à la science médicale de leur temps* (Paris 2005) 253–285, esp. 261–263; M.-O. Boulnois, "L'union de l'Ame et du Corps come modèle christologique de Némésius d'Emèse à la controverse nestorienne", ibid. 451–475, esp. 454–459.

[121] Chrysostom cites Plato frequently (see P. R. Coleman-Norton. "St. Chrysostom and Greek Philosophy", *CP* 25 (1930) 305–317), but despises philosophers and identifies "true philosophy" (as a way of life) with monasticism and virginity, leaving little room for intellectual activity. The Cynic diatribe forms part of the background to Chrysostom's writings; cf. A. Uleyn, "La doctrine morale de saint Jean Chrysostome dans le 'Commentaire sur saint Matthieu' et ses affinités avec la diatribe", *Revue de l'Université d'Ottawa* 27 (1957) 5*–25*, 99*–140*. For Chrysostom's attitude to philosophy see chapter 5 below.

[122] See especially McLeod, *The Image of God*; N. V. Harrison, "Women, Human Identity and the Image of God", *JECS* 9 (2001) 205–249 and "Woman and the Image of God according to St. John Chrysostom", in P. Blowers et al. (eds.), *In Domenico Eloquio: In Lordly Eloquence: Essays in Patristic Exegesis in Honor of Robert Louis Wilken* (Grand Rapids 2002) 259–279.

[123] For male superiority by nature see *Hom.* 26 on 1 Cor. 4 (*PG* 61, 218); cf. *Hom.* 2 on Gen. 2 (*PG* 54, 589). E. A. Clark (with others) claims that Chrysostom is ambivalent on whether Eve's subordination is due to the Fall, but concludes that the controlling position in his thought is that the pre-eminence of the male pertained already in unfallen nature (*Jerome, Chrysostom and Friends* (New York/Toronto 1979) 2–5). Probably before the Fall Eve was only equal in honour (on which more below) and her sin only serves to justify her originally inferior position. We have already met the ambiguous and long-enduring phrase "equal in honour" in Basil.

[124] Cf. *Hom.* 23 on Rom. 1 (*PG* 60, 615).   [125] *Hom.* 26 on 1 Cor. 2 (*PG* 61, 216; *PG* 62, 141ff.).

"holistic" theory) women are inferior to men in their more "childish" mind as well as in body (*PG* 62.148).

It is implausible that the more "Pauline" Antiochenes, for whom 1 Corinthians 11.7 ("woman is the glory of man") is a favourite text, would not have supposed that only the male or asexual soul is created in God's image – still less that women could have been created with male and godlike souls. The female body (designed to defeat death by childbearing) indicates a non-imagelike character in the whole woman. Admittedly as human beings men and women have the same nature (*phusis*) and are equal in honour[126] – the ambiguous phrase again – but women possess this nature in a weaker version (if the body is weaker, the mind is weaker) and thus, as Chrysostom says, they are not created in the image of God (*PG* 54.589).[127] The same apparently necessary conclusion was drawn by Diodore and Theodoret, though perhaps Theodore at times and also Nestorius dissented.[128] The dominant view was taken to be that of "the blessed Paul",[129] though there is no specific indication of the use of Ephesians 4:13 to claim that we should strive to be like Christ the perfect male.

Perhaps we can recover an underlying axiom: what is not assumed is not saved. Hence if the male body has been assumed by Christ and if females are also saved, then to assume a male body entails assuming a female body. Hence, unless to assume a female body entails assuming a male body – which is presumed impossible – then the female body, and hence the female as a whole, is less godlike (that is, at creation, for the Antiochenes, not in the image of God) than the male. But although not created in the image of God, women can acquire that imaging by living well: that is, again, by successful approximation to the male, by having a "manly" spirit.[130] Theodoret even holds with Gregory of Nyssa that at the resurrection there will be no sexual distinction, that is, we shall be like angels. How he could justify such

---

[126] So Chrysostom, *Hom.* 4 on Gen. 1 (*PG* 54, 594), also *Hom.* 26 on 1 Cor. 2 (*PG* 61, 214–215).

[127] So rightly McLeod, *The Image of God*. V. Karras, "Male Domination of Women in the Writings of John Chrysostom", *Greek Orthodox Theological Review* 36 (1991) 131–139 and D. C. Ford, *Women and Marriage in the Early Church: The Full View of John Chrysostom* (South Canaan 1996) suppose that because of Chrysostom's view of equal honour he must have argued that woman was created in God's image. This is rightly rejected by Harrison in "Women, Human Identity and the Image of God" and "Woman and the Image of God according to St. John Chrysostom".

[128] For more recent comment on Theodore see F. G. McLeod, *The Role of Christ's Humanity in Salvation: Insights from Theodore of Mopsuestia* (Washington 2005) 138–142.

[129] *PG* 80, 107–110. So also Diodore at *PG* 33, 1564–5, where the view that the image is to be identified with the soul alone is rejected. According to Diodore's holistic view both soul and body are male or female.

[130] The martyrs above all live "male" lives; so Pelagia who threw herself off a roof to avoid being raped is "female in sex, male in spirit" (*De S. Pel.* 2 (*PG* 50, 585)); for further examples see Clark, *Jerome, Chrysostom and Friends* 15 and note 102.

a position without also holding with Gregory the more platonizing view that the original image is both non-corporeal and asexual – that is *de facto* male (though sexually inactive) – is difficult to determine, as is his concept of the non-corporeal and non-sexed *resurrected* body in general. But, as I have noted, the Antiochenes were rather against philosophy.

If we accept the essential correctness of the Pauline view that the whole person, not just the male or asexual soul, would have to be created in the image of God, then anyone who wishes to claim that women are so created – as modern theology does – must confront the Pauline texts that apparently deny this possibility, offering women only an eschatological image. This necessary confrontation has not yet been completed, whether because it has proved too difficult to determine when Pauline texts need not be taken *au pied de la lettre*, or because of the inveterate insistence on confounding theology with the history of theology. Before turning to that, however, we must consider whether the more platonizing version of woman's creation in God's image finds a more satisfactory defence in Augustine – and in would-be correctors of Augustine.

1.12 AUGUSTINE'S DILEMMA

Augustine, following the platonizing tradition, holds that woman is created in the image of God in her rational soul; that she is not so created in her female *body* is symbolized by her wearing of the veil.[131] But Augustine is the first Church Father eventually to argue that not only Genesis, but also Paul in 1 Corinthians 11:7, teaches that woman too is (to some degree) created in the image of God (*Literal Commentary* 3.22). To understand the significance of that claim against the wider background of his maturing beliefs on creation in God's image we must review the relevant texts in chronological order.[132] In so doing, we shall in effect recapitulate much of the development, both spiritual and ontological, of our theme throughout the patristic period, noticing its strengths and also, especially at the ontological level, its weaknesses.

As ever with Augustine, we must begin with biography. When Augustine first reached Milan, he was worried by Manichaean charges that, if man is material and created in God's image, then God too must be material (*Confessions* 6.3.4): an opinion widespread both in the Christian West – including Africa where we have found a version of it defended by Tertullian

---

[131] *De Op. Mon.* 32.40; *GenLitt.* 3.22.
[132] See generally K. Børresen, "In Defence of Augustine" and "Patristic Feminism: The Case of Augustine", *AS* 25 (1994) 139–152.

(*Against Praxeas* 7) – and elsewhere, and from which he was liberated by Ambrose who in the wake of Origen (perhaps mediated in part by Basil and Gregory of Nyssa) taught that God must be immaterial.[133] Ambrose's preaching, probably on Genesis,[134] soon coagulated in Augustine's mind with the famous "books of the Platonists". For the bishop of Milan had been encouraged by his advanced theological sources to believe not only that it is the mind which is created (for both men and women) in the image of God, but that (as Philo held) the "male" mind must remain in charge of the "female" bodily senses.[135]

A few years after these dramatic events in Milan, Augustine's ongoing treatment of our theme is first found in his *Commentary on Genesis against the Manichaeans* (388/9) – a text grounded on the platonizing belief that sexuality is a strictly bodily phenomenon.[136] Following in the mediating steps of Origen and Gregory of Nyssa, he claims that before the Fall Adam and Eve had spiritual bodies (2.7.9) and that "reproduction" was not sexual.[137] The "Be fruitful and multiply" of Genesis refers to the multiplication of "good works of divine praise" or the "spiritual offspring of eternal joys" (1.19.30). But already in this commentary Augustine modifies Ambrose ("Some who before us were distinguished defenders of the Catholic faith" had associated Eve with the *bodily* senses[138]) and ultimately Philo, though he still holds that in the story of Adam and Eve the male signifies the intellect and the female the animal part or appetite of the soul (2.14.20–21): the male intellect, left to itself, would have resisted temptation.

In line with such interpretation, it is the *souls* of Adam and Eve that Augustine holds to be created in the divine image. But what did that entail?

---

[133] Cf F. Masai, "Les conversions de s. Augustin et les débuts du spiritualisme en Occident", *Le Moyen Age* 67 (1961) 1–40; R. Teske, "Vocans Temporales, Faciens Aeternos: St. Augustine on Liberation from Time", *Traditio* 41 (1985) 24–47.

[134] See G. A. McCool, "The Ambrosian Origin of St Augustine's Theology of the Image of God in Man", *TS* 20 (1959) 62–79.

[135] In one passage of the *83 Quaest.* (51.2) Augustine is still prepared to propose that in some diminished sense the body too could be in God's image.

[136] "*Sexus in carne est*", *CD* 14.22; cf. *CFaust.* 24.2.2; *DeAgChr.* 11.12; *De Trin.* 12.7.10; *GenLitt.* 3.22.34; 6.7.12. According to *Serm.* 280.1 the "inner man" of the Carthaginian martyrs Perpetua and Felicity was neither male nor female – which shows Augustine groping for the more biblical notion that the inner man is not simply the (male) mind, in which he thinks women are inferior, but something wider, more "pneumatic" and more transcendent over sexual differences however explained. Augustine is not the only patristic writer whom the exemplary behaviour of female martyrs (often admitted to be superior to that of males) challenged to second thoughts about female mentality. Unfortunately they stopped short of more basic reflection on the nature of sexual difference. Mary Magdalene too invited such speculation, but here again, as we shall see, Augustine leaves it tantalizingly undeveloped.

[137] Cf. Solignac in *BA* 49, 519.   [138] *GenMan.* 2.14.20–21; cf. Ambrose, *De Paradiso* 2.11–3.12.

Certainly immortality and sinlessness, for as late as the *Literal Commentary* (6.27.38) Augustine rashly remarks that with sin the image is lost: a phrase he censures as excessive in his *Reconsiderations* (2.24.2).[139]

Similar views about the absence of sexuality in the Garden seem to have lingered in Augustine's mind at least until the time of the *Confessions* (cf.*Catechizing the Simple* 18.29 and *Confessions* 13.24.26). Even later, in *The Good of Marriage* (2.2), he hesitates over sexual acts before the Fall, presumably because the bodies of Adam and Eve are still "spiritual". However, whereas at the beginning of the *Literal Commentary* (soon after 405) he ponders whether *caritas* alone might have sufficed for reproduction in paradise, by the time he reaches book 6 he is sure that sexual activity would have been necessary.

Already in 412, in a letter to Marcellinus (143, 6), and with reference to 1 Corinthians 15:42ff., Augustine had alluded to the possibility that in paradise Adam had an "animal" body, and in the sixth book of the *Literal Commentary* (6.19.30ff.) that possibility has become a certainty. In book 9 Eve is said to have been created for ("animal") procreation (9.5.9), while in the *City of God* (13.19–23) there is a long argument against "spiritual" bodies. Thus some time after 412 Augustine's final position – Adam in paradise before the Fall had an animal body intended for procreation – is laid out in full. Which might well raise the question of the relationship of that animal body to the soul, hence, by implication, of the nature of the image of God and the implications for its presence in Eve as well as in Adam.

Already in book 3 of the *Literal Commentary* (3.22.34) Augustine is not only sure that in her soul Eve is created in the image of God, but he is prepared in unprecedented fashion to explain the Paul of 1 Corinthians 11:7 as teaching that *qua* her rational soul Eve too is godlike, even though apparently less so.[140] Her inferiority remains, however, in that she symbolizes not the *bodily* emotions as against reason – the view of Ambrose and the earlier tradition which Augustine had already rejected in 389 – but active reason in contrast to the higher reason of contemplation: a claim repeated in *On The Trinity* (12.3.3). In the latter much controverted passage it is clear that *qua* helpmate to Adam (and therefore in her procreative function) Eve is not in the image of God, but her soul is, as such, so created (even if to an

---

[139] For similar excessive language elsewhere see J. M. Rist, *Augustine: Ancient Thought Baptized* (Cambridge 1994) 272, note 43.

[140] For Augustine's earlier insistence that the soul of Eve is rational see *Conf.* 13.32.47. The importance and originality of Augustine's "neutralizing" of 1 Cor. 11:7 is well brought out by Børresen, "God's Image, Man's Image?" 199–200.

inferior degree).[141] She is inferior *qua* childbearer to man in the "world",[142] but not *qua some* sort of image of God. She is created so that procreation can take place; otherwise a superior, male mind would have been "better" (*Literal Commentary* 9.5.9) – and her reproductive features have nothing to do with her imaging God; yet insofar as she is human, her soul, like that of Adam, is an image of the Trinity.[143]

That *could* mean that in every non-bodily respect Eve is exactly like Adam – but this cannot be the case since her mind is held to be "inferior". Yet there may be the germ of the idea that she has psychological strengths complementary to Adam's. Perhaps that is in Augustine's mind when he observes that Mary Magdalene was honoured as the first to see Jesus after the Resurrection because of her womanly emotional strength, her love (*affectus*).[144]

So we now find Augustine in the familiar position of holding that the souls of Adam and Eve (despite Paul) are created (if unequally) in the image of God, but that their animal bodies, even if eventually to be recreated in glory, are not. It has been widely recognized that the developments in Augustine's account of the human body and its relationship to the soul are related – at least after the arrival in Carthage in 411 of Caelestius, the lieutenant of Pelagius – to his growing concern about the transmission of that original sin which seems to require the baptism of infants. In looking, however briefly, at that debate – I shall return to it in the next chapter – I shall argue that some of its problems involve not only the relationship between human souls and human bodies,

---

[141] Cf T. J. van Bavel, "Woman in the Image of God in St Augustine's 'De Trinitate XII'", *Signum Pietatis* (Würzburg 1989) 267–288, esp. 269ff.; R. J. McGowan, "Augustine's Spiritual Equality: The Allegory of Man and Woman with Regard to *Imago Dei*", *REA* 33 (1987) 255–264; D. G. Hunter, "Augustinian Pessimism? A New Look at Augustine's Teaching on Sex, Marriage and Celibacy", *AS* 25 (1994) 153–177; Børresen, "Patristic Feminism".

[142] Augustine's reasons for this seem to vary, apart from the need to explain Genesis and Paul. They arise either from female physiological "submission" in intercourse (*Conf.* 13.32.47) – for which see also below, pp. 98–99 – or because the weaker mind should be subservient to the stronger (*QHept.* 1.153), or more generally because the male sex is more honourable: Jesus was male "since it was fitting that he should take the human nature of man, the more honourable of the two sexes" (*Quaest.* 83.11). Why more honourable? Perhaps because less "passionate" and not primarily ordered for reproductive acts; or more basically because – as I have noted – although woman's soul is in the image of God, it is less so insofar as it is "active" rather than "contemplative". Cf. also *GenMan.* 2.13.18; *De Mor. Eccl. Cat.* 1.30.63.

[143] Cf. *CD* 12.24. For the development of Augustine's account of the image see R. A. Markus, "'Imago' and 'Similitudo' in Augustine", *REA* 10 (1964) 125–143. Augustine's mature view, that Adam and Eve's creation in the image of God refers not merely to God the Divine Image, that is, to Christ, but to the whole Trinity, afforded scope for seeing other aspects of the soul than "mind" (such as the power to love) as significant evidence of imaging (see especially the *De Trinitate*). For a comparison of Augustine and Marius Victorinus (who thought that only the Father is imaged), see P. Hadot, "L'image de la Trinité dans l'âme chez Victorinus et chez s. Augustin", *Studia Patristica*, TU 81 (Berlin 1962) 409–442.

[144] *Sermo Guelf.* 14.1 = 229L.1; *IoEv.* 121.1 (*fortior affectu*), etc.

but more specifically the relationship between a woman's soul and her body's sexuality.

I have examined elsewhere Augustine's unwearying attempts to determine the origin of the human soul, and his inability or unwillingness to propose an unambiguous resolution in favour either of standard traducianism – the thesis that the soul is handed down from one's parents in the processes of reproduction – or the "creationist" alternative that each individual soul is created by God for its appropriate body. I argued that Augustine's apparent indecisiveness is related to his inability to explain the nature, in our fallen state, of our soul–body complex and its imperfect phenomenological unity.[145] I might have added that difficulties arise in the case not only of our present state but of what would have been our nature had we not "fallen". Let us then return to these wider issues, to see what Augustine resolved, and what he might have resolved, about the nature of the divine image in woman as well as in man. For although he made progress in his understanding of the ontological structure of the human being – that is, of the intelligible relationship between the soul and the body – his eventual failure in that regard made his solution of the "traducianist" problem much more problematic and a solution of the "woman-problem" impossible.

In his early years as a Christian Augustine's even exaggeratedly platonizing account of man as primarily a moral agent is clear. We are our souls; "Our bodies are not what we are" – or perhaps not strictly what we are (*On True Religion* 46.89). It is our souls that recognize an immaterial God and his attributes, and it is our souls that sin (as in *On Order* 2.11.34). That is why, in the *Soliloquies* and elsewhere, Augustine wants to understand only God and the soul: that is, ourselves and our Maker, the image and that which is imaged. But since we are our souls, perhaps Porphyry was right in urging that "all body must be escaped": a text plainly echoed in the *Soliloquies* (1.14.24): "Flee sensible things completely" – but specifically recanted in the *Reconsiderations* (1.4.3).

"What do we consist of?" asks Augustine in an early letter: "Body and soul" (3.4).[146] Soul and body are two separate substances, and their "mixture" or "blend" is us.[147] The language of blending is probably Stoic, derived from Varro, but in 411, in a letter to Volusianus, a pagan aristocrat, Augustine (following Tertullian) introduced a new, and less Stoicizing terminology: the blend is a *persona*. The arrival of this new terminology roughly corresponds in

---

[145] Rist, *Augustine* 320.
[146] Cf. *De Mor. Eccl. Cath.* 1.4.6; *GenMan.* 2.7.9; *QuAn.* 1.1; *Sermo* 128.7.9.
[147] For further comment see Rist, *Augustine* 99–100.

time to that of Augustine's replacement of Adam's spiritual body in Eden by a
body of flesh: a claim first mooted in the following year in letter 143 to
Marcellinus. And if Adam's *persona* was originally a blend of a *fleshly* body
with a *spiritual* (and immaterial) soul, we can see both that the fleshly body
(marked by the organs of an active but as yet docile sexuality) would have
more value – and that Augustine would have to face in a sharper form the old
dilemma facing the Neoplatonists, of the relation between a material and a
non-material substance. That problem in its turn would – or should – lead to
the question of whether a two-substance theory of man is ontologically viable
or whether the "holism" of the Pauline tradition (as well as of Tertullian
and the Antiochenes) had in some respects – though certainly not in all – the
makings of a better solution. If Augustine could not resolve those problems
adequately, what new data or theory might have enabled him to do so?

It might seem as though *persona*-language (as with the somewhat analogous thesis we noticed in Nemesius) does little but reformulate the problem:
the "mix" of soul and body is now a *persona* – which, however, should at least
make clear that it is not an "accidental" union.[148] Perhaps the immediate
advantages of that are largely negative: it should be more difficult simply to
identify the self with the soul. But examine more closely the language of
mixture. So long as we are supposed, in a Stoicizing manner, to be a mix
of two more or less material elements, the language seems not inappropriate,
but what kind of a *mix* could be possible between the material and non-
material? We can recognize the temptation to continue with materialist
language after straight materialism has been abandoned, but in the revised
theory what could it mean to speak of a mix of soul and body – and what did
Augustine think that it meant?

The ancients were often willing to talk about something being a mixture
of being and non-being, to indicate that the object in question is capable of
passing away. Thus we are a mix of being and non-being; God is not. In
modern terminology, we might say that if we use the language of mixing
in such a case, "being" and "non-being" are formal concepts, not ontological
realities: there is no such "thing" as non-being. If a somewhat similar approach
is applied to the mix of spiritual and material "elements" in us, an author
using such language would seem to be saying that we have "immaterial" and
"material" characteristics. In linguistic terms, two kinds of predicates can
be applied to us. One is applied to us as bodily (thus we are tall, fat, round-
shouldered, etc.), the other indicates whether we are people of such a moral

---

[148] Cf. *De Mor. Eccl. Cath.* 1.27.52.

sort (just, unjust, good, bad, devious, etc.). Thus we are a mix of material and immaterial characteristics and the word "I" stands for a being who can display these two different kinds of non-assimilable properties "mixed" together.

If Augustine's word *persona* were intended (*inter alia*) to indicate a being capable of possessing a "mixture" of such different properties, it would indeed have a philosophical use. It would not solve the problem of the ontological relation of soul and body, but it might at least suggest that we are not two substances but one substance identifiable in terms of two different sets of properties. And without necessarily attributing all this to Augustine, we may recall that it is at least true that even though he regularly claims that we are a mixture of soul and body he only rarely describes the body as a "substance".[149] What he may be trying to say is that it is the nature of our "soul" which primarily (i.e. spiritually) makes us what we are, and that in that sense the soul can be properly described as an image of God. In all this we can view Augustine as apparently on the edge of abandoning the two-substance theory, but never quite managing to do so.[150]

There may also be a theological explanation. It is well known that *persona*-language is used of another kind of "mixture", that of the divine and the human in the Incarnation. It is probable that Augustine is invoking what seems a theological given to solve human nature. The notion that Christ is one person with two natures looks analogous to what we have been saying about the human "person" consisting in soul and body. Just as Christ's human and corporeal nature (and accompanying properties) are not identical with his divine nature, indeed are "unconfused" with it, so in the mixture of soul and body the incorporeal is inmixed with the corporeal without confusion.[151] The analogy is far from exact, since in orthodox Christology Christ's human nature is both body and soul, but at least would seem to offer a parallel for the blending of a wholly incorporeal and immaterial substance with an enmattered being, i.e., a living physical body. The use of the word *persona* may indicate Augustine's willingness to see the soul–body "mixture" as somehow

[149] See L. Hölscher, *The Reality of the Mind: Augustine's Philosophical Arguments for the Human Soul as a Spiritual Substance* (London/NewYork 1986) 304, note 8: cf. *ImmAn.* 2.2; *DeTrin.* 1.10.20.
[150] If such were Augustine's underlying ideas, perhaps he was influenced by the Plotinian concept of the empirical "I" (*to hēmeis*) so prominent in *Ennead* 1.1. Plotinus too knew that the Stoic challenge of how we can be a compound of the material and the immaterial had to be answered, though his answer is certainly more etherializing than should have suited Augustine.
[151] For parallel ideas in Tertullian see E. Osborn, *Tertullian: First Theologian of the West* (Cambridge 1997) 130–142.

"imaging" the divine Incarnation. Such language is paralleled in Eastern Christian writers like Nemesius and Theodore of Mopsuestia.[152]

Or perhaps Augustine more consciously considered that what matters is not the ontology but the genealogy of the *persona*. That could have been an effect of his arguments with the Pelagians and indeed of his concern about the origin of the soul itself. Augustine's objection to (ordinary) "creationism" was precisely that, if each soul is newly created by God at conception, then original sin – somehow derived from Adam – is impossible, since it is the soul that sins. Somehow the soul *must* be handed down; and what is handed down cannot be newly made but must be already present in the male seed which, according to Augustine's old conception theory, is nurtured and brought to birthable condition in the womb. Hence the "homunculus", growing from the male seed – which is "seminal reason" plus matter (*City of God* 14.17, *On the Good of Marriage* 20.23) – must already have some kind of soul: that soul which, in Augustine's language, is the bond of our "common life" in Adam.[153] As for Eve, she too is derived from Adam and originally inherits the potential weakness of his character though not yet his coming sin – which in fact she anticipated.[154]

Thus from conception the human being is a mix of soul and body and at least something of soul is inherited as part of our common humanity. Were there no soul in the "homunculus" it would not be alive, so that in a sense Augustine views the soul simply as the body's life – while the body might be the way in which that life is best physically expressed, as well as the only way in which the *soul* (as image of God) *could* be expressed. Perhaps that is what Augustine could have said, but did not say. Had he done so, he could hardly have avoided asking whether female souls (created in the image of God) must necessarily reveal themselves as equally well-expressed female bodies.

That Augustine needed to address this is confirmed by his insistence at the end of the *City of God* that female bodies are restored in enhanced physical beauty as female at the resurrection (*City of God* 22.17–18). In making that claim we find him well aware that he is contradicting a tradition:

---

[152] But it may be easier for Nemesius, for whom man is patristically unusual in having specifically Aristotelian features (see Motta, *La mediazione estrema*). For further comment see Rist, *Augustine* 100, and note 31, and especially H. Drobner, *Person-Exegese und Christologie bei Augustinus* (Leiden 1986), esp. 221–232.

[153] For further discussion see Rist, *Augustine* 121–129, 317–320.

[154] Note that in holding that Adam (and Eve) were created not as children (morally or physically), as many of his predecessors had supposed, but in the full vigour of life (*GenLitt* 6.15.26), Augustine rules out any possibility that their sin was ultimately a sin of immaturity (as in Irenaeus and Clement): hence less culpable.

Because of these sayings, "Until we reach the perfection of manhood, the stature of the full maturity of Christ" (Ephesians 4:13), and "Being shaped in the likeness of God's Son" (Romans 8:29), some people suppose that women will not keep their sex at the Resurrection; but, they say, they will all rise again as men, since God made man out of clay and woman out of man. For my part I feel that theirs is the more sensible opinion who have no doubt that there will be both sexes at the Resurrection ... for a woman's sex is not a defect; it is natural ...

Bodily sex, that is, but what about a possible psychological concomitant?

Further Augustinian development is hindered by deep-seated traditional language – reflecting cultural patterns among both Christian and pagan: thus brave women are seen as behaving like men, in a virile manner. To see how he works this out, I return to Perpetua's dream. Thinking of her coming ordeal in the amphitheatre, and dreaming of it as single combat, she says, "I was stripped naked and became male." Augustine, preaching at her memorial and elsewhere, observes that she did not actually change physiologically – indeed speaking of her dream Perpetua herself says *she* became male ("*facta*" is feminine) and her trainer continues to refer to her as female. According to Augustine (*Sermon* 280.1) she was male in her "inner human" (*interiorem hominem*). Filled with Christ (*Sermon* 281.2) she was neither male nor female (as in Galatians 3.28), but "in that contest she was running towards the perfected male" (*in virum perfectum*, Ephesians 4.13). In interpreting Perpetua's dream Augustine is thus able to rely on the idea that if a woman is courageous she behaves like a male; indeed, with Ephesians, like the perfect male with whom she is united.[155]

In *On the Usefulness of Fasting* (4.5) Augustine says that each person's flesh is dear (and therefore appropriate) to him; that there is "a kind of conjugal union of flesh and spirit"; and at *City of God* 13.6 that at death the soul is torn unnaturally from its embrace with the flesh.[156] What he never explains is why a female body would be appropriate to some "male" souls

---

[155] My reading of Augustine's account of Perpetua's dream is indebted to the perceptive commentary of G. Gillette, "Augustine and the Significance of Perpetua's Words: And I was a man", *AS* 32 (2001) 115–125. Whatever residual doubts may remain about her comment "although the 'vir' [of Ephesians] is meant to include both man and woman", Gillette is right to continue that "it retains its masculine character from its Head who is Christ" (p. 123) – insofar as Augustine means to interpret Perpetua as identifying with Christ as the strong (but also on the cross humbly weak) male. However, the basic question – for further comment see below – is why in Ephesians Paul wrote the Greek equivalent of *vir* when, had he wished to emphasize man and woman inclusively, he could have written the equivalent of *homo*. Augustine writes as though Perpetua knew that she was physiologically still female but that her humanity, her soul, was masculine. For further Augustinian comment see *AnOr*. 4.18.26, where an argument is developed against Vincentius Victor's notion that in creating the human soul an immaterial God "blows" out a materializing substance; also *CD* 22.18; *Sermo* 64A3.

[156] For further discussion see Rist, *Augustine* III.

while a male body is appropriate to others: that the image is in the soul and (at least) cannot be feminine (despite the superior love of Mary Magdalene) stands in his way. So the ontological problem involves not only the nature of a *persona* – that special mix of soul and body in which the soul so loves its particular body – but more ultimately the relationship in certain *personae* between a male soul and a female body.

As with Origen and others, so in Augustine, the notion of the femaleness of the soul in relation to God is not invoked to overcome the deep-seated conviction of the "inferiority" of what is specifically female in women: not only in regard to women's bodies which are, by definition, "different" from the original human version and therefore inferior to those of men,[157] but also to their souls in which the active rather than the superior contemplative element is dominant.[158] Of course that very claim, misguided or not, would suggest that the differences between men and women are more than merely "bodily" (as Augustine would understand "sexual"), but, as we have seen, Augustine does not take the opportunity further to develop the metaphysical (rather than the anthropological and moral) possibilities of a "sexed" account of the soul. And we are left with the further oddity that, though at creation woman's imaging of God is inferior to that of man, in the end such differences apparently make no difference. Differences of heavenly beatitude have nothing to do with sexual differences, whether bodily or of the soul. Thus much confusion still remains.

Augustine's movement in the direction of an abandonment of the two-substance theory finds a parallel in a perhaps unlikely contemporary. Jerome, whose relations with the younger Augustine had been stormy, stood with him wholeheartedly against the Pelagians. More immediately to the point is his volte-face over Origen and the Origenist account of the transcendence of sexuality. In his younger days Jerome, like Ambrose, had worked hard to spread the spiritualizing reading of divine as of human nature in the West. He had dedicated his translation of Origen's *Homilies on the Song of Songs* to Pope Damasus, and in his *Commentary on Ephesians* (*c.* 388) he had offered an etherialized account of perfection, but although his high estimate of Origen's scholarship remained till the end, he came to object violently to his view of human nature, to the doctrine of *apatheia* taught by his follower Evagrius, and in particular to the claim that human nature once was and should be again non-sexual. For Jerome the aim is not to become angelic but to imitate Christ and Mary (*Ep.* 22.18).

---

[157] So K. E. Børresen, *Subordination and Equivalence: The Nature and Role of Women in Augustine and Thomas Aquinas* (Washington 1981) 30.
[158] See above on *QHept.* 1.153, etc.

Jerome came to see sexuality [159] as so dangerous precisely because it ever is a part of human nature – and here we see him moving in something of the same direction, if for very different and far less sophisticated reasons, as Augustine. For as Augustine moved away from the Origenism and near-angelism of Ambrose,[160] so Jerome moved away from the Origenism of his one-time friend Rufinus and his own earlier self.[161] Whatever their differences, Augustine and Jerome had this important theological belief in common: a growing insistence on the importance of bodily resurrection in some "ordinary" sense of bodily:[162] resurrection, that is, as personal and individual human beings with sexual characteristics (though without desire for sexual union). For Jerome as for Augustine, the option was becoming available of combining a belief that the "whole woman" is created (however inadequately) in God's image with a more philosophically satisfactory version of the soul–body relationship than "mix" language could provide – but the philosophical will to explain the phenomena was lacking.[163] Better, apparently, sexual characteristics without sexuality!

1.13 CAN ARISTOTELIANISM HELP? THE CASE OF THOMAS AQUINAS

As we have seen, a remarkable phenomenon of most patristic thought is the limited use of Aristotle. In his investigation of philosophical schools, Justin lost interest in the Peripatetics because (unsocratically) they demanded payment. In Origen's vast array of ancient philosophical learning, Aristotelianism is little represented. When Tertullian wants a holistic model for the human agent he looks to the Stoics rather than to Aristotle. In the fourth century there is a certain polemical mention of Aristotle, as the man who denied the

---

[159] So, rightly, Shaw, *Burden of the Flesh* 212.

[160] Ambrose was prepared to offer a less than angelic account of the good life for much of humanity, but his aspirations for the best of us remained angelic. See M. Colish, *Ambrose's Patriarchs: An Ethics for the Common Man* (Notre Dame 2005).

[161] Lack of appreciation of Jerome's change of heart about the overcoming of sexuality vitiates Clark's treatment in *Jerome, Chrysostom and Friends* 55–56.

[162] See Brown, *Body and Society* 384, on Jerome's *Ep.* 75 to Theodora.

[163] At *De Trinitate* 12.7.10 we can still hear the tones of the pre-Christian, even pre-Platonic, version of male perfection, though in a new and attenuated version: "The wife with her husband is the image of God, so that the totality of this human substance forms a single image; but when woman is considered as man's helpmate, a state which belongs to her alone, she is not the image of God. *By contrast, man is the image of God by being solely what he is, an image so perfect, so whole, that when woman is joined with him it makes only one image.*" That is, *qua* image man is the perfect image, so that *qua* image woman adds nothing, but the converse would not be the case. It must be admitted, however, that Augustine's language is almost casually unclear in its exact implications: a mark of lack of concern with underlying issues.

operations of providence below the level of the moon and can thus be denounced as an atheist. But Nemesius excepted, it is largely in the context of claims and counter-claims of logic-chopping among Arians and anti-Arians or pro-Nicenes: the study of Aristotle, it is then suggested, leads to the intrusion of inappropriate logical minutiae into theology. Yet the continuing neglect of Aristotle is the more remarkable in that after Plotinus Porphyry finally resolved the problem of the admission of Aristotelian writings into the predominantly Platonic culture of later philosophical paganism: Aristotle could be used as a preliminary to Platonic studies; his work "read" in a Platonic spirit. Hence, apart from Themistius, most of the "Aristotelian" commentators after Alexander of Aphrodisias were Neoplatonists.[164]

Perhaps more than anyone else Plotinus was responsible for the continuing virtual exclusion of Aristotle from late patristic thought in the areas with which I am immediately concerned. Plotinus considered it a major part of his own philosophical enterprise to update the work of Plato and to reply to Plato's critics, not least the Aristotelians and Aristotle himself. Part of this project involved extended discussion of Aristotle's theory of the relationship between the soul and the body. For Plotinus was well aware, not least from the anxieties of his own supporters such as Porphyry, that in this area unreconstructed Platonism is vulnerable. In Plotinus' view, however, Aristotle's theory that the soul is the substantial form of the body is little more than a slightly revised version of the notion – rebutted both by Plato and by Aristotle himself – that the soul is a "harmony" of the body or bodily parts.[165]

Augustine seems to have been convinced that Plotinus was right about this, and presumably similar conclusions were reached by most of those (few) Christian thinkers who took Aristotelian criticism of Platonism seriously. In any case, although, as we have seen, Augustine (like Nemesius, though less specifically) sometimes develops a "hypostatic" union of soul and body in ways that might point towards a more genuinely Aristotelian explanation than the version of Aristotelianism dismissed by Plotinus – and although it would have been very helpful in many ways if he and others had taken Aristotelian hylomorphism more seriously – they did not do so.

The adoption of Aristotle by his Neoplatonic commentators in late antiquity meant much more than the use of his writings as a source for the logical defence of platonizing positions. As is now becoming ever clearer, it meant the transmutation of Aristotle into a philosopher much more acceptable to a theistic world, whether Christian, Jewish or Muslim – not least after

---

[164] For a wide-ranging introduction to the topic see R. Sorabji (ed.), *Aristotle Transformed* (Ithaca 1990).
[165] *Enn.* 4.7.8[5]; cf. the cursory remarks of Augustine at *ImmAn.* 10.17.

some of his more unwelcome doctrines (shared by the Neoplatonists) such as the eternity of the world had been challenged by Christians like the sixth-century Philoponus. The "need" for a Christian Aristotle was recognized in the sixth century by Boethius, though his project to translate Aristotle's writings into Latin, thus making them available to the more-or-less mono-lingual Western world, was fated to remain substantially incomplete.

For all the labour of Boethius and the commentators, in the matter of the soul–body relationship substantial philosophical difficulties remained – some of them involving uncertainties in the thought of the historical Aristotle – if a Christian acceptance of Aristotle was to be achieved. For although Aristotle was sure that the soul is the form of the body, in his notorious fifth chapter of *On the Soul*, as in the *Generation of Animals*, he left at best unclear the relationship between the soul as form and the "intellect from outside" or "active intellect". Such unclarity generated longstanding medieval debates which are not our present concern, but one of their effects was to enable Thomas Aquinas to maintain both that the human soul is the substantial form of the body and that it can exist separately. It is not difficult to recognize that this could muddy the effects of hylomorphism in general and the case of the female soul in particular – if, that is, there are female souls; yet in other respects Thomas' Aristotelianism enables him to develop the holistic aspects of the "Pauline" or "Hebraic" tradition about human nature and avoid many of the difficulties inherent in the alternative "two-substance" theory of the person which – whether he realized it or not – had been handed down to him in the dominant platonizing tradition of his patristic predecessors.

As we saw earlier, Aristotle holds that the virtue of men and women is in some respects distinct, and specifically that women lack the deliberative persistence of men, so that their ability to act effectively in public life is correspondingly weaker. This psychological weakness – which is not a matter of intelligence, since women are, as far as one can see, as intelligent as men – is the mental counterpart of the inferiority of the female body. Since in physiological terms a woman is a defective male, that defect must have some kind of psychological analogue. Female deficiency, of course, is not, in Aristotle's view, caused by upbringing or social factors; it is "natural" or, as we would say, genetic.

As I have observed, many of these ideas – however philosophically con-sistent – derive from what would now be considered bad science: an inad-equate account of conception and embriology, the one-seed theory, the view of female *pneuma* as insufficiently heated compared with that of males.[166] For

---

[166] For further comment see above and Rist, *The Mind of Aristotle* 152–153, 246–249.

Plato, sexual difference is a purely bodily phenomenon; it need not affect the psyche of a philosopher-queen. For Aristotle such a one-sided account of human nature is necessarily inadequate: there must always be psychological counterparts to basic bodily data.

Thomas Aquinas took over Aristotelian biology, including the theory that there is a sense in which females are physiologically defective males,[167] and together with that biology developed a predictably clearer account of female *psychological* inferiority, problematic though that might have been for aspects of the Augustinian version of woman's creation in God's image. Yet although Augustine insisted that women are created in God's image, and attempted to interpret Paul in that sense, he also gave certain indications of what might look like a more Aristotelian view: that psychologically too – and therefore with repercussions for the quality of the image of God creationally present in women – women are inferior. The male sex, as he sometimes put it, is superior in rank not least because it is more rational, or because its rationality is more typically the higher rationality of contemplation as against the lower, more "active" and bodily female version.

Like Augustine, and largely following him – not least in holding that man is an image of the whole Trinity (e.g., at *ST* Ia.93; 75.2.6) and that that image is to be recognized "principally" in the mind[168] – Aquinas believes that woman is created in the image of God, but also that sexuality, again as purely bodily and more or less identifiable with strictly genital and reproductive activity, is not part of that image. Had he pursued a less conventional and more coherent version of "Aristotelian" hylomorphism, he would not have been entitled to such a view; presumably the religious and social pressures he faced made it impossible for him to recognize its difficulties. Above all he had to retain the "platonizing" notion that the soul can exist apart from the body before the general resurrection.

Aquinas also seems at times to follow Aristotle in arguing that the inferiority of women is not simply bodily but is also apparent in the mind.[169] Woman is by nature subordinate to man "because among human beings the power of rational discernment varies considerably" (*ST* Ia.92.1 *responsio 2*

---

[167] Cf *ST* Ia.92.1, ad 1.; *CGent.* III.94, etc. Cf. A. Mitterer, "Mann und Weib nach dem biologischen Weltbild des hl. Thomas und dem der Gegenwart", *ZKTh* 57 (1933) 491–556. For a more recent, well-documented, but eventually disappointing account of Aquinas' situation see C. J. Pinto de Oliveira, "Homme et femme dans l'anthropologie de Thomas d'Aquin", in P. Bühler (ed.), *Humain à l'image de Dieu* (Geneva 1989) 165–190.

[168] "*Principaliter*", though for Aquinas a *repraesentatio* of the image also exists in the human body (*in corpore hominis* – therefore presumably both male and female); cf. *4 Sent.* d.49, q.4, a.5b.

[169] Cf. *Scripta super Libros Sententiarum* 2 d. 16,1,3, *contra*, sol.; *ST* Ia.93.4.1 *responsio*. As in Paul, man alone is the glory of God.

and 3);[170] and again: "Woman is subject to man because of the weakness of her nature, of both the spirit and the body" (*Supplement* 81.3, ad 2).[171] What is lacking here, however, is a discussion of whether female mental weakness might be derived from the *sexuality* of the female soul: for all his Aristotelianism Aquinas cannot propose that possibility, assuming as he does that the soul is not sexed, or at least not female – though he may have thought that the female soul's inferiority is connected with its necessary association with the female body.

For Aquinas women's inadequacy as incomplete males does not imply that they are defective in *their own* nature (*ST* 1a.92.1 *responsio*): nature as a whole needs a woman as such, for the purpose of women is to assist in procreation, broadly understood as including domestic life (*ST* 1a.92.2 *contra*, following Aristotle, *Nicomachean Ethics* 1182A19) – and nothing could do that job better.[172] The incompleteness of women only comes out when they are compared with men, as the process of conception itself indicates, for "the active power in the seed of the male tends to produce something like itself, perfect in masculinity" – and Aquinas offers various Aristotelian explanations as to why at times the active power fails and a female is generated. In brief, for Aquinas woman is created in God's image, but not to the same degree as man.

There is clear incoherence here, and its primary cause is Aquinas' insistence on the old "platonizing" view that sexuality is purely a bodily function, combined with an unspecified belief that to be female is less "rational" than to be male – and that despite the tradition from Philo and Origen (to which I shall return) that all properly religious souls are as if female in relation to God. As we shall see, in his view of what it is to be female Aquinas ignores the implications of "symbolical" and "theological" femaleness in relation to God the Creator for a proper evaluation of female human beings. His view of the latter, deriving largely from inadequate biology and the effects of social conventions, mistakenly identifies apparent female incapacities with the notion of femininity itself, though without proper consideration of the

---

[170] Cf. on 1 Cor. *lectio* 2 (*vir specialius dicitur imago Dei secundum mentem*). *ST* 1a.92.1 *responsio* 2 is often misconstrued as simply saying that in males (wrong for *in homine*) the power of reason is greater. But the sense is not changed by correcting the translation: the fact that among human beings some are more "reasonable" than others is offered as an explanation of male psychological superiority.

[171] Cf. IIaIIae 149.4 (she is more prone to concupiscence); *SCG* III.122.

[172] Cf. *In Sent.* 4.44.1.3. The significance of the contrast between *natura particularis* and *natura universalis*, insofar as it affects Aquinas' conclusions about the "chance" incompleteness of each individual woman when viewed in an Aristotelian context, is exaggerated by M. Nolan, "The Defective Male: What Aquinas Really Said", *New Blackfriars* 75 (1994) 156–166. Nolan is followed uncritically by P. F. De Solenni, *A Hermeneutic of Aquinas's Mens Through a Sexually Differentiated Epistemology: Towards an Understanding of Woman as Imago Dei* (Rome 2003) 101–103.

relationship between femininity as such and female genital and reproductive activity.

It seems that a non-platonizing thesis that women are created *equally* in God's image can only be consistently maintained – and not necessarily even then – if a more full-blooded version of the Aristotelian account of the body–soul relationship is accepted. That version might have to include claims both that genital and reproductive differences between males and females entail parallel differences in the soul and that those psychological differences (which would need to be spelled out) do not imply deficiency in either case. Certainly the old and pre-Christian notion that there is a single type of perfectible human being would have to be abandoned, and with it the "Christian" defence that since Christ is male the perfect human is also (somehow) male. Also to be abandoned would be the notion that a virgin is asexual, rather than merely genitally inoperative.

Although Aquinas is in no doubt that woman is created in the image of God, he is in immediate difficulties over the equality of her creational image – for several reasons:[173]

1   Because he seems to combine a belief in the male as the superior type – for there must be a superior type – with an adherence to Aristotle's principle that bodily differences reflect psychological differences and that bodily weakness must reflect psychological weakness: in modern language that hormonal differences, physical though they are, indicate unequally valuable psychological differences between males and females and therefore a necessary and essential difference in the quality of the original divine image between the sexes.

2   Because although he adhered to the wider version of the traditional account of God's purpose in the creation of woman – she is designed not merely for reproduction but for other aspects of domestic life[174] – he retains the older view that in the secular world women are *exclusively* intended for the private and family sphere, having a weaker capacity for the public domain.

---

[173] J. M. Finnis (*Aquinas: Moral, Political and Legal Theory* (Oxford 1998) 172) "translates" *tam mulier quam vir est ad imaginem dei* in Aquinas *ST* 1 q.93a.4 ad 1 (cf. *In 1 Cor.* 11.3 ad v.10) as "as much in man as in woman" rather than "both in man and in woman". From this and other passages he offers to infer that Aquinas accords them equal rights (in some sense of "equal"). For according to Finnis Aquinas "clearly has the concept" of rights (136). That is *inter alia* because he is occasionally able to speak of *iura* (rights) as the plural of *ius* (right). But the sheer paucity of such passages indicates how unimportant an emphasis on rights must be for Aquinas. What matters is the justice or injustice of the moral agent; much less of a moral "player" are the "rights" of the victim. They are rather the domain in which justice should be exercised. A doctrine of rights could be *developed* from Aquinas – which is not to say that he had thought of developing it. The question will be discussed further in chapter 5.

[174] *ST* 1.92.2c; cf. 93.4 ad 1.

3 Because of scriptural texts saying that women should not exercise authority
over men (e.g., 1 Timothy 2:12, 1 Corinthians 7; cf. *ST* 1a.92.1, ad 2) – as
well as the inherited tradition, apparently supported by Scripture, whereby
maleness as such is a superior form of humanity. From patristic times
authority is traditionally one of the more plausible criteria for the (male)
imaging of God.

A rejection of what appears to be Aquinas' view demands a revised view of
women scientifically and socially, but also – of fundamental importance for
Christians – scripturally. Here, however, the difficulty is far from limited to a
mere correction of Aquinas; it would involve the elaboration of a defensible
account of how one can – in good faith[175] – diverge from what has often seemed
the immediate sense of Scripture and much tradition on woman as image of
God. As I noted when discussing the Antiochenes, this challenge has so far been
imperfectly met by theologians and exegetes, and hence by the "magisterium",
though theologians and magisterium imply the possibility of success whenever
they assert woman's equality in regard to her creational image.

When the challenge is met successfully, however, it seems to be realized
that sexual differences are of the whole person – *that is* of both soul and
body – and that therefore they are included in our essential nature as images
of God. Just as consecrated virginity is not a sexless state but a state in which
the genital expression of sexuality is renounced, so that sexualized state which
we cannot renounce can only be a permanent part of human nature as an
image of the divine. In such an account of human nature, of course, there is
no need to treat "male" and "female" as absolute and distinct categories – not
least because we are all to be "female" in our relationship to God.

Thus there is a larger question on the horizon: if the creational equality
of woman as image of God is possible within the confines of Catholic
Christianity – as is now widely, indeed officially, believed – what does this
tell us about the present philosophical state of Christian "anthropology" and
the present stage of the development of our understanding of Christian
doctrine in general?

I have not yet, however, done with Aquinas. Whatever the truth about the
inequality of image, a number of recent writers have pointed to other texts
in his writings which they believe make him look more "modern" and in
line with current Catholic thinking. Some claim that Aquinas himself would
introduce these texts to correct the account of his thought that I have

---

[175] By "in good faith" I mean without falsifying the history of theology and thus wishfully misdescribing
inadequate or incomplete theologies of the past.

offered.[176] I doubt the historical plausibility of that claim, which seems to depend on extensions and clarifications proposed especially by Karol Wojtyła, before and after he became Pope – and which are therefore of interest less to the expounder of Aquinas than to the historian of the development of doctrine. For there are parts of Aquinas' thought about women and God's image, some of them inherited from his patristic past – indeed from Augustine in particular – which are in effect rejected, and which, when studied, show that his position needs to be reworked.

Recent interpretation of Aquinas has sought to find texts on which a Thomistic theory of the complementarity of men and women could be built, but if such a theory is to satisfy claims about equal human imaging of God, it must show not only that woman is complementary to man (and vice versa), but that in that complementary relationship neither party is inferior to the other even if both are necessary. For the moment, therefore, I leave aside contemporary developments and treat only the themes in Aquinas that might contribute to such developments and show that, however incomplete, they are an improvement on what Aquinas himself puts forward in his more immediate treatment of the topic.

It should be obvious that a more thorough-going Aristotelian account of the soul–body relationship will be a prerequisite for a revised Thomistic theory; that is, an Aristotelianism that disallows the underpinning of metaphysics by an inadequate biology. Such a correction would certainly have to include an abandonment of the notion that sexuality can be limited to the body, and that therefore the image of God should be limited to the soul. Aquinas himself has hesitatingly pointed in this direction in observing that it is "chiefly" in the soul that the image is to be found, and in his suggestion that a *praefiguratio* of that image can be recognized in the body of human beings in general, both male and female.

There are other Thomistic themes which, though hardly connected with Aquinas' account of the image, could be useful in a contemporary reconstruction – indeed have been so used: his account of Eve as a "helpmate" to Adam, his account of the role of receptivity (not mere passivity) in the process of thinking; and the related theme of receptive love (instantiated concretely in Mary Magdalene as well as more generally in the traditional femininity of the human soul in relation to God: a tradition which, as we have seen, dates back at least to Origen's understanding of the necessary femininity of every human soul). When these themes – plus others of more contemporary provenance – are developed, it is possible to construct an account of the complementarity of

---

[176] Most extensively perhaps De Solenni, *Towards an Understanding*.

the sexes that does not imply that one is superior to the other as such; though in relation to our condition as images of God, it may suggest a certain superiority of the female, at least in our fallen state.

According to Aquinas the marriage of Adam and Eve, and thus every marriage, was intended to be a *socialis coniunctio* (*ST* 1a.93.3 *responsio*): a condition where the woman has no authority over the man, but at the same time is no slave. This Aristotelian reading is further developed in the *Summa Contra Gentiles* (3.124–125) where, in rejecting marriage between those closely related, Aquinas argues that if, for example, a parent were to marry his child, the natural subordination of one party to the other built into the earlier relationship would interfere with the "social bond" of marriage. It does not follow from either of these passages that the spouses are simply "equal".[177]

The passage from the *Summa Contra Gentiles* explains more exactly – again with apparent reference to Aristotle – how *socialis consortio* is to be understood: marriage is a form of friendship between free persons. It is not a servile condition but a kind of equality (*amicitia in quadam aequalitate . . . consistit*) which would be destroyed by polygamy. The Aristotelianism on which Aquinas relies, however, signifies that marriage is a kind of friendship not between equals. According to Aristotle the friendship between husband and wife, which he sometimes calls "political" and elsewhere "aristocratic", is between mutual beneficiaries; hence it is a friendship of utility.[178] But if one were to ask Aquinas why such friendship cannot be between equals, we might find him giving a merely culturally conditioned reply – leaving the path open for improvement.

Aquinas emphasizes that in the process of thinking the mind's receptivity is not a mere passivity but an openness to truth. One has to want to receive; that is well illustrated by Mary's *fiat* and "keeping all these things in her heart".[179] In this respect thinking is analogous to the receptivity to God required of the Christian, a receptivity also represented scripturally, as Aquinas recognized, in the account of Mary Magdalene as the first witness to the Resurrection of Christ. Augustine, we observed, made a similar point, claiming that Mary Magdalene was thus selected because her love was stronger (*maior affectu*).[180]

---

[177] The text is grossly over-interpreted by De Solenni (ibid. 121–122) when she writes that the spouses should be "innately equal", thus concluding (misleadingly) that Aquinas "recognized the mystery of the complementarity between man and woman". Yes, but viewed as an unequal complementarity.

[178] Aristotle, *E. E.* 7.1238B; 1242A (where the word "partnership" (*koinōnia*) is used for such friendships of utility); *Pol.* 1.1256a ff.; cf. Rist, *The Mind of Aristotle* 150–154.

[179] Cf. De Solenni, *Towards an Understanding* 116–117.   [180] Cf. Rist, *Augustine* 119.

Aquinas cites Augustine, asserting that it was because of Mary Magdalene's love that Christ appeared to her.[181]

1.14 THE WAY AHEAD

1.14.1 The present situation

A revised Aristotelian ontology (rather than some variety of the patristic two-substance theory, devised as it originally was not for an ontological but for a moral/spiritual account of man) is needed to account for core difference in the soul–body complex between men and women – though this will always vary somewhat in individual cases. But being a descriptive ontology – and one trusts at last freed from the assumption that one sex must be intrinsically superior, rather than a complementary variety of human being – it could have nothing to say on the disputed question of which sex, if either, is closer to the image of God. Changes in social structures have thrown up evidence that many women are capable of functioning effectively in the public domain, though such observations, being empirical, reveal nothing as to any individual or average abilities so to function.

That means that so far as our biological and sociological knowledge is concerned, nothing supports the view that women are not created to an equal degree in the image of God. Faulty biological and sociological assumptions cannot be used, as in the past, to demonstrate that women are inferior human beings and hence, necessarily, either in no way, or in a lesser way, created in God's image.

In the past, however, such assumptions have been regularly used to back up apparently clear interpretations of a number of scriptural texts seeming to point to original female inferiority. Had such a thesis been unambiguously denied in Scripture, it would have been much harder to rely on faulty assumptions to promote it; however divinely inspired the Scriptures, they are mediated by the hand of fallen man-males, in fact themselves conditioned by the societies of their day. Nevertheless, even if key texts have been misleadingly written or tendentiously misread under the influence of bias deriving from social and biological beliefs, the unmasking of those beliefs must be free of that alternative subjectivism which negates biblical teachings in favour of the causes espoused by the exegete – as is currently attempted by defenders of homosexual acts.

---

[181] *S. Evan. S.Io. Lectura* 20.1, cited (with other texts) by De Solenni (*Towards an Understanding* 110–111).

In the present case the Catholic Church in its official documents now proclaims the equality of the sexes as equally created in the image of God, leaving the exegete free of the charge of subjectivity: his revised exposition (and therefore its underlying principles) is not his own reading but that of the Church which, as its Founder promised, would be led into all truth. What *is* demanded is that his explication of his exegetical principles be coherent and consistent. If this approach be taken as implying that the Church knows the right answer without knowing (or knowing fully) why that answer is right, it can be replied that this has happened before over both major and minor teachings.[182]

1.14.2 Some underdetermined "Pauline" texts and explanations

In reviewing patristic traditions I noted that, apart from Genesis, a group of "Pauline" texts has dominated the debate over whether woman is created in the image of God. These are:

1 1 Corinthians 11:7: Man is the image and glory of God and woman is the glory of man;
2 2 Corinthians 3:18–4:6 (and Colossians 1:15) which explain that Christ is the perfect image (the question of the import of his maleness is left unresolved);
3 Ephesians 4:13: We should arrive at the unity of faith and of knowledge of God, "unto" (with reference to?) a perfect male (*andra*), to the fullness of Christ;[183]
4 Galatians 3:28: In Christ there is neither male nor female.

To these I add another, whose "after-life" I have not discussed, namely Ephesians 5:12: the relationship between man and wife is like that between Christ and the Church. That enables exegetes to compare males (as Christ and the new Adam) with females (as the Church or as Mary the new Eve).

---

[182] *Humanae Vitae* is an interesting example from recent times. When it was written, the arguments set out for its conclusions seemed at best incomplete, while claims about the risks of a "contraceptive mentality" looked far-fetched. The present demographic disaster now confronting Western Europe (substantially generated by the separation of sexual acts from procreation) indicates that such risks were far from exaggerated and that even on consequentialist grounds we were on a slippery slope. If we turn from moral to "dogmatic" teaching, it is hard to deny that, as subsequent history showed, many, even most, of the bishops who voted for the basic doctrines of the Council of Nicaea had only a limited understanding of the "right" ("orthodox") position on the divinity of Christ, let alone of the arguments for it.

[183] A glance at the translations and glosses on *andra* shows the fudging by the interpreters of this extraordinarily obscure passage. The fourth-century rhetor Marius Victorinus provides an example (not discussed above) of the sort of extreme conclusion to which the text can lead. In his *Commentary on Galatians* 4.4 (*CSEL* 83/2, 140) Victorinus asserts that in our present fallen state we live like (imperfect) women, but that when we are united with the male Jesus we shall be perfected.

I will consider the last passage first. The problem in the comparison, if pressed, is that Christ as head of the Church (as his body) is superior to the Church (or to Mary). This is taken as confirming – at an ontological, not merely a "fallen" social level – the traditional assumption of the superiority of Adam to Eve. But whatever Paul's conscious intent, there is no need to read the text thus timelessly. It was easy and natural for Paul to use the marriage-relationship as understood in his day as an analogue of the Christ–Church relationship. That presents no problems, which only arise when the analogy is read backwards and given universal application: when it is argued, that is, that the hierarchical relationship between Christ and the Church – indicating the superiority of God, the model, to man, the image – symbolizes an ontological truth about the superiority, not least in respect to being originally and directly in the image of God, of males over females.

There is no need so to construe Paul's deeper meaning; indeed such construal was rejected in John Paul II's 1989 encyclical *Mulieris Dignitatem*, where the Pope, in addition to pointing out that the Church – in effect the (Origenist) woman of God – is made up of both males and females, by implication denies that Paul understands females to be created unequally in God's image – though his discussion ignores some of the scriptural texts adduced in patristic times to contrary effect – and claims that Ephesians insists not only on the "submission" of the Church, that is, of all human beings, to Christ, but on the *mutual* and *reciprocal* submission of man and wife in marriage (24): a bold elaboration of the text to which – and to the apparently necessary underpinnings of which – I shall return.

Which brings us to Galatians 3:28, which, though probably teaching simply that Christ makes no distinctions and that slaves and free, men and women, Jews and Gentiles are all equally valued and loved, is often taken in a narrow eschatological sense as teaching that at the resurrection there will be no more sexual activity; or more widely, as in various patristic authorities, that in some "spiritual" sense we shall all be males, even if physiologically women will still look like women; or again – with more dubious social application – that although in this "present age" men and women fill different social roles demanded by an original female inferiority, in the world to come such social and institutional distinctions will cease to exist – just as the teaching that there will be no slaves in heaven may be understood to suggest that *then* but not now we shall all be masters. Finally, as we have seen, Galatians 3:28 has encouraged the view that if women become "unfemale" (which they can do merely by renouncing sexual activity or not undertaking it at all, that is by becoming "manly"), they can anticipate the state of paradise.

Quite apart from the inadequacies of such an account of sexuality – identified simply in terms of genital acts – the text demands no such exotic interpretation. It might teach that just as in the beginning all are in Christ, so that state is restored at the end: human nature as such, whether male or female, was created (as some interpretations of the Genesis texts demand) as a strictly equal image of God.

Such preliminary ground being cleared, I turn to the two texts that most immediately influenced the patristic debate – or confirmed patristic prejudices. I Corinthians 11:7, as we have seen, was confronted by Augustine who, driven by the need to reconcile Paul with a plausible interpretation of at least parts of Genesis, defended a less plausible reading of the explicit sense of the text, producing a reading nearer to our own contemporary teaching. But Augustine, as we saw, had the advantage of a flawed ontological description of the soul–body relationship whereby he could separate sexuality from the soul and defend the creational equality of males and females by reference to the platonizing notion that we are all "really" our male (understood as asexual) souls.

In any case, although Augustine tried to argue that women (as "really" males with female bodies added for primarily reproductive purposes) were created in the image of God, he seems to allow them only an inferior version of the image – since they are inferior *qua* bodily structures which do after all affect the "mind" – and to leave underdeveloped his own view that females *qua* female display a number of qualities superior to those regarded as typically male: Mary Magdalene's superior capacity to love enabled her to be the first witness of the Resurrection – and Augustine even declines the move of suggesting that in this she is behaving in "manly" fashion. But even here Augustine is too much prisoner of his age to follow up his fruitful idea; just as Clement had failed to make significant use of his claim that in the Incarnation – in God's "saving" rather than "creational" mode – he became "female": a "mother".[184]

Which brings us to perhaps the most problematic text of all. Ephesians 4:13 was frequently held to teach that we should strive to be like Christ not as a perfect human being but as a perfect male. There are a number of possible approaches to this. Perhaps Paul unhappily was careless; he meant perfect human being with no specific reference to being male and was misinterpreted by those with social reasons to do so: a number of modern translations seem to imply this weak solution. Or perhaps by referring to a perfect male he

---

[184] Note that John Paul II drew attention to OT descriptions of God as "female", though without citing patristic comment (*Mulieris Dignitatem* 8).

assumed that perfection of the virtues is ultimately a male phenomenon and that he wanted women to reach a state of "manliness" which their original female anatomy (and hence psychological state) makes more difficult. In favour of that view would be the passage from 1 Corinthians where he seems to deny women a direct imaging of God.

Some might try to save the situation by denying at least the direct Pauline authorship of Ephesians, but that route is fraught with uncertainties. In any case the Church has always insisted that whether strictly Pauline or not Ephesians is canonical. A third possible reading is that in Ephesians Paul is only or primarily speaking to males (perhaps as heads of families) and perhaps even to the eligibility of males for certain tasks in the Church. That could be dismissed as too forced and self-serving even if males are addressed in the first instance. Yet Paul's use of "man" (*andra*) in 1 Corinthians 11:2–16 may reflect a tradition that, like *anthrōpos*, it could refer to all human beings, while also implying that "men" (even in the image of God) could – to some extent – include "women", though "women" would not include "men".

I conclude provisionally, therefore, that either Paul was somewhat careless and has therefore been misinterpreted, or, as most patristic writers believed, but which the Church now reinterprets, that he did teach that females must somehow become sexually – or rather asexually – "manly". Of these two possibilities the second is by far the more likely, but even if it is correct, it is much less significant than has often been supposed. For though the perfect man was indeed a physiological male, that is, Christ, it does not follow – as was widely held – that Paul's culturally driven interpretation of this has to be accepted as a doctrine that "asexual" maleness is a *sine qua non* of all human perfection. Indeed, it could be argued from the history of Christian spirituality that in important respects the reverse is the case.

It may have been symbolically better that God become incarnate as a male; I shall return to that possibility. Yet if God for his own good reasons willed to be incarnate in first-century Palestine, and within the Jewish society of first-century Palestine, it is inconceivable that he could have been incarnate as a *female* teacher. And because Paul lived in a society in which virtues were habitually thought of as ideally "male" (as characteristics of an apparently male God) while "female" nature (as we see in Philo) was typically held to be "sensual", it is inconceivable that he would not follow the convention of supposing and calling the virtues "manly", despite the corollary – obvious to us – that females would be considered inferior or that possible female virtues would be neglected or downplayed.

There is no point in speculating further about Paul's intentions. It suffices to show that his words can be construed at least as ambiguous as

to whether directly or indirectly woman was created in the image of God
and whether Christ's maleness has any necessary connection with the facts
about that image for the rest of us. It is more profitable to think immediately
in terms of hints in Augustine and in Clement of Alexandria – not to speak
of the tradition deriving from Origen that in relation to God all souls are
female. Indeed, it is best to start not with Paul, let alone with interpretations
of Paul, but with the recorded words and actions of Jesus: perhaps best
of all with his conversation with the Samaritan woman at the well (John
4:24).[185]

The subject of that conversation was how (and where) God is properly
worshipped; Jesus tells the woman that God is spirit and that those who
worship him worship him in spirit and truth. The disciples, according to
John, were astonished at Jesus' talking to the woman in the first place – which
confirms our estimate of the conventional role of women in contemporary
Palestine. That he tells her that God is "spirit" may seem less surprising, until
we attempt to see what Christians have taken this to mean.

If "spirit" is simply to be understood in contrast to "flesh", that would have
caused little difficulty, but it is clearly much more than that. Before very long,
as we have seen, "spirit" began to be rendered as some sort of "non-material"
substance (where the New Testament limits itself to "invisible" substance).
And before much longer the whole thesis of a contrast between the immaterial and intelligible world, the world of God, and the physical world of the
senses, had arrived in Christianity, and inevitably, not least because of the
opposition of spirit to "flesh" (with the easy inference that sexual activity
is peculiarly tainted), arose the interpretation that, because in the next world
(seen as "immaterial") there is no marrying and giving in marriage and that
sexual distinctions indicate no "genital" value there, sexuality itself is either
purely bodily or ultimately (at least in females) the mark of a second-class
humanity.

That is why a better version of Aristotelian "anthropology" is required,
whereby sexuality, if bodily, is also psychological, and if properly male, then
also properly female, with no suggestion that either male or female is more
fundamental or more earthy. If Augustine (in the *City of God*) was right to
suppose that females would be resurrected with female bodies, then they must
also be resurrected with female souls; in brief, being male or female has
of itself nothing to do with whether one is (created) in the image of God.
Aquinas, despite his ontologically flawed account of female nature, defined

the image of God in terms of a natural capacity to know and love God (*ST* 1a.93.4 *responsio*). And God, as the Samaritan woman is told, is "spirit" – which is to be interpreted neither in contrast to what is (pejoratively) "flesh" nor as simply an ontologically intelligible substance. Inasmuch, then, as we all possess a capacity to know and love this spirit, and thus to become like him, it is inconceivable that women – unless we are to regress to the old pagan position that they are not strictly human at all – are not equally created in his image.

Which is not to say that women are "ideally" identical with men; simply – as is now taught – that they share equally with men in the fact and dignity of being in God's image. Clement's suggestion that in the creation God is like a father (despite its partially unscientific biological assumptions), while in the Redemption he is "femaled" like a mother, may be helpful here, as may Augustine's insights (accepted by Aquinas) into the superior love of Mary Magdalene: not to speak of the common view among the Fathers that the female martyrs – not all of whom were virgins or widows – often outshone their male counterparts in their devotion to God.

Such considerations should have been more influential in explaining (rather than merely asserting) that woman is created in the image of God than forced extensions of the marital and social situations of husbands and wives in the first century AD, where – for extraneous reasons – the male is compared to Christ, the female to the Church. In relation to the image of God, Peter vis-à-vis Mary Magdalene would be a helpful parallel: Peter because we are dealing with fallen human images, and similarly Mary Magdalene because – whether or not she is the sinner of all the Gospel-writers who anointed Jesus with costly ointment and wiped his feet with her hair – she also had need of repentance. But then Mary the mother of Jesus is also an obviously vital symbol, for as uncorrupted humanity – and at the same time a genuine female and not an angel – she can hardly be denied the title of created image of God, and type of that femaleness of the soul in relation to God which Origen and subsequent tradition held to be the properly receptive disposition of humanity as a whole.

Deriving as it did from the religion of ancient Israel – not to speak of the extremely masculine version of that religion proposed by Philo and encouraged by various purely Hellenic traditions of thought – Christianity inherited (or acquired) many features of patriarchal religion. Yet it bore within itself – not least in its account of the image of God – the means both to accept the insights of patriarchalism and to transcend them. I conclude with recent attempts to advance further along this path, and with their continuing limitations.

1.14.3 Some proposals of Karol Wojtyła and others[186]

Karol Wojtyła, both before and after becoming Pope John Paul II, argued that males and females are complementary, suggesting that sexual difference pertains not only to the physiological but also the psychological structure of men and women:[187] "Man is a person, man and woman equally so, since both were created in the image and likeness of the personal God" (*Mulieris Dignitatem* 6). The context of this passage shows that the ambiguity surrounding certain forms of "equality" in earlier texts has been eliminated. Later in the same document, speaking of marriage, he claims a mutual subjugation of the partners, despite 1 Timothy 2:11–15.

In treating the complementarity of the sexes, Wojtyła emphasized the necessary receptivity of all human beings – as modelled by the Canaanite woman and Mary Magdalene – insofar as they aspire to be Brides of Christ.[188] And he insisted that the "one flesh" of marriage indicates God's desire for a unity at all levels of personal identity, with no superior and inferior party, no domination and submission. Yet in *Mulieris Dignitatem* there is still a marked unwillingness to speak of a female soul; the Pope preferred to speak of female persons or a female personality. A cynic might suppose that this enabled him to avoid formally rejecting (or explicitly re-writing) the defectively Aristotelian view of Aquinas and much Catholic tradition that female physiology indicated an inferior soul, and therefore an inferior version of God's image.

Wojtyła clearly did not believe that women's souls are inferior, nor that women are unequally created in God's image, so he presumably had good reasons (perhaps as well as bad) for preferring to speak not of a female soul but of a female person. A bad reason could indeed have been that, in keeping with the recurrent tendency within Catholicism to confuse theology with the

---

[186] The "others" are obviously important and demand detailed treatment in a study specifically devoted to the theme of modern "nuptial" theology, but in view of my broader aims in the present book I limit myself largely to "official" pronouncements. It should be noted, however, as it is by Scola (*Nuptial Mystery* 48–49), that both Barth and Brunner, in different ways, thought that the reciprocity of sexual difference indicates that sexuality is an essential part of our imaging of God. But reciprocity as such, without some kind of "spousal" theology, does not entail the need for specifically physical and *sexual* difference. Indeed the idea, once held and then rejected by Augustine, that before the Fall reproduction would not have involved physical sexual acts (even though Adam and Eve were still somehow "sexually" differentiated) would, if mere reciprocity were the criterion, satisfy Barth's thesis.

[187] K. Wojtyła, *Love and Responsibility* (New York 1981) 48; also *Mulieris Dignitatem* and elsewhere.

[188] *Mulieris Dignitatem* 25.

history of theology, and implicit truths of the "deposit of faith" with their explicit formulation, he believed – which if so would have been an error – that he shared the view of Aquinas, and indeed of a large part of Catholic tradition.

But Wojtyła may have had better reasons – connected with a revised and developed concept of the human "person" and of its relationship with the divine Persons of the Trinity – for talking cautiously about female persons rather than female souls. I shall consider recent developments of the Christian concept of "person" more generally in a later chapter, particularly in the context of current discussions of human rights.[189] For the present, however, it is sufficient to add two points to my earlier discussion: first that the philosophical and theological "school" to which Wojtyła belonged argued that it is an essential part of our proper humanity to be in a relationship with another person or persons, and that at their best (particularly in the marriage of a man and a woman) such relationships image the interpersonal relationships of the Trinity, the triune God. But the Persons of God are equal; hence the human persons – males and females, adults and children – whose relations reflect them must be of similarly equal dignity.

The second point, however, is philosophically more fundamental, concerning the relationship between souls and persons, and the fact that relationships imply an underlying substance. To be a person one must have a soul, and possession of that soul marks one as a human animal. To be human is more basic than to be male or female, though all humans are male or female. To make the soul – as distinct from the human "person" – male or female might suggest a revised version of the primitive view that men and women are of different species: an intolerable position. So perhaps one must conclude – against a large part of the tradition – that if the soul cannot be female it cannot be male either: "asexual" in no sense entails "male". But, as we shall see, there is more to be said.

In line with Wojtyła's approach to relationships, two sections of the *Catechism of the Catholic Church*, themselves dependent on Vatican II's *Gaudium et Spes*, are significant: the first maintains that it is because each individual human being is created in the image of God that he or she may be described as a "person" (357); the second that man and woman have the same dignity and are of equal value, not only because they are each, in their differences (bodily and psychological), created in the image of God, but

---

[189] See chapter 5 below.

more profoundly because the dynamic of reciprocity that gives life to the
"we" in the human couple is an image of God (369–371).[190]

Such "official" moves are a characteristically modern development, reflecting in theology something of new and serious concerns current in secular
philosophy. Since the seventeenth century, in debates – originally largely
among Christians – about the self and personal identity, three phenomena
have been constantly evoked, and the absence of any one of them has usually
been castigated as a weakness of the theory in question: the "possession" of a
body, the capacity to reflect, and the ability to enter into human relationships.[191] The latter question has involved more than a re-run of Aristotle's
view that we are social and political animals, or of Boethius' formal "definition" of the "person" as an individual substance of a rational nature, though
those views are still rightly on the philosophical table. To them has been
added in more recent times a greater emphasis on the individual, with a
developed individual character and personality. It is that aspect of contemporary thought that the Catholic concept of an individual human person,
male or female, equipped with powers of reason, free will and autonomy,
because formed in the image and likeness of the Trinity, attempts to justify.

Augustine, as we have seen, concluded that "I am not my soul". Aquinas
agreed: the soul is not the whole human being (*Super 1 Cor. 15.1, 11*). Yet
traditionally it is the soul that (at least chiefly) is said to be formed in
the image of God. Recent arguments – influenced by Jung – about receptivity, relations between persons and that all souls must be Brides of Christ,
re-emphasizing as they do a "feminine" aspect to the well-ordered male
personality (and implying a masculine aspect to the best female parallel),
point to the conclusion that that tradition now needs to be revised. We have
to admit that the soul – though certainly *qua* soul neither male nor female –
in each particular case, like the body, is sexed; and that the body, like the
soul, in a material way expresses the image of God which is the whole
person. Soul and body have complementary characteristics, reflecting in
complementary fashion the divine original. It is in fact misleading – and has
long misled – to view *either* soul or body as in the image of God; a properly
"Aristotelian" view would apply that description in the first instance to the
whole person. Sexuality itself – which is not merely bodily or genital – is an

---

[190] For the role of *Gaudium et Spes* in basing Catholic meta-ethics and hence morality squarely on the
imago Dei theme (and the influence at the council in this regard of Congar and (the patrologist)
Daniélou), see the comments of C. J. Pinto de Oliveira, "Image de Dieu et dignité humaine",
Freiburger Zeitschrift für Philosophie und Theologie 27 (1980) 425. See further chapter 5 below.

[191] For a synoptic account see J. Siegel, *The Idea of the Self: Thought and Experience in Western Europe
since the Seventeenth Century* (Cambridge 2005).

essential part of the human being as image of God. That seems to have been the view – also doubtless "sensed" though not expressed in earlier times – of Edith Stein;[192] it is also, despite a certain nervousness, the considered view of Scola who (in traditional manner) perhaps rather over-interprets *Mulieris Dignitatem*.[193] It has had precursors, but in its fullness is new in Catholic understanding: something for which Western secular as well as more narrowly "Christian" thought had prepared the way.

1.14.4 Why does it matter now?

This chapter began with a discussion of the influence of theories and of real and supposed facts about sexual intercourse and conception on ideas of the "male" and "female" in Jewish and Christian thought, as well as in Greco-Roman antiquity. It also alluded to significant pagan tendencies – visible also in many forms of neo-paganism (as well as in other forms of religion) – to the worship of sex (Venus) and power (Jupiter or the emperor). I conclude by returning to these themes.

In the description in Genesis of the effects of the Fall, the author tells Eve of God's "prophecy" that the man will dominate the woman (3:16). Historically, that domination has taken the form of the use of physical violence not only by husbands against wives, but by rapists against women whether on dark streets or military campaigns. It has also appeared in the claim that women are to be treated as inferiors because (physically and mentally) they *are* inferiors. The language of sexual acts, both in antiquity and more recently, both literal and metaphorical ("He was really fucked up", and further abusive and contemptuous usage of this "four-letter" English word), has emphasized this: a woman is conquered, possessed: that is, fucked; she is often made to accept sexually what she does not

---

[192] See *Self-Portrait in Letters (1916–1942)* (trans. J. Koeppel, Washington 1993), letter 100, with the comments of S. Borden, *Stein* (London/New York 2003) 76.

[193] Cf. Scola, *Nuptial Mystery* 5, 9–10, 32–52: "We must affirm the fully human, that is, personal, character of sexuality. In this sense the body expresses the person, and expresses it even [*sic*] in its being masculine and feminine." With an ambiguity characteristic of the "tradition" Scola (5) speaks of this as "in continuity with the Church's perennial teaching", but as expanding this "teaching in an original way". Yet, in accordance with that ambiguity, he still hesitates at times: "The question of whether or not human sexuality participates in the *imago Dei* is, on many counts, still open" (32). And the "continuity" to which Scola alludes should, as often, be read as a continuity of logical development, not of personal awareness. See also A. Scola, "L'*imago Dei* e la sessualità umana", *Anthropotes* 1 (1992) 61–73. Scola's work is of particular interest in that he is aware of the need to align Catholic positions with aspects of social orthodoxy in the contemporary world, thus challenging that orthodoxy, as when he notes (23): "In a world which seeks to eliminate God, it becomes impossible to consider sexual difference." See chapter 6 below and more generally J. M. Rist, *On Inoculating Moral Philosophy Against God* (Marquette 2000).

want.[194] (Which does not mean that she does not manipulate her man or men.)

In antiquity, from Genesis to Paul and later, sexual acts were regularly treated as (ideally) the exercise of male mastery: in ancient Greece and Rome if a householder apprehended a burglar, he might hand him over to his slaves to be raped – to show sexually who has the power, who is humiliated. In the Old Testament prophecy of Ezechiel (16:37–38) there is sexual humiliation for the deviant woman who, "suffering the punishment for unfaithful women" is to be stripped and her genitals exposed to her assembled "lovers"; or for the unfaithful wife of Hosea (2:3) who might have expected to be stripped and left in the desert to die of thirst.[195] All this is not to be dismissed as simply figurative; it represents treating guilty female sexuality with brutality and contempt. The mentality – not least the religious mentality – of a culture is signified by its symbols. Marriage, as then understood, was important and highly esteemed in the Old Testament as symbolizing the Covenant. The punishment of female sinners ("whores") is also revealing of the accepted social norms. If *we* no longer understand that, Osama bin Laden and his ilk certainly do.

From the Christian point of view, all this is excess, or should be: Christ took a different view of the guilt of a woman "taken in adultery" – and that, it seems, even before she repented.[196] Yet to be an excess is to be an excess of

---

[194] For a helpful discussion of Augustine's (and Andrea Dworkin's) view of this kind of fucking – the issue is whether intercourse is possible without domination; Dworkin, speaking rather like a Stoic who thinks all sins are equal, assimilates it to rape – see J. C. Cavadini, "Feeling Right: Augustine on the Passions and Sexual Desire", *AS* 36 (2005) 195–217.

[195] Cf. J. Cheryl Exum, *Plotted, Shot and Painted: Cultural Representations of Biblical Women* (Sheffield 1996) 102.

[196] The violent and sexual humiliation of the female is accorded a strange significance in some of the writing of von Balthasar. I had completed most of this part of my text when I came across ideas that in part harmonized with it in a "scandalous" essay by T. Beattie ("Sex, Death and Melodrama: A Feminist Critique of Hans Urs von Balthasar", *The Way* 44 (October 2005) 160–176). Beattie notes in their radical distinction between male and female a similarity between Balthasar and Luce Irigaray (in *Speculum of the Other Woman* (Eng. trans. Gillian C. Gill, Ithaca, N.Y. 1985)). She is also right (in the "tradition" of Simone de Beauvoir) to detect in Balthasar something of a negative definition of femininity as "other" than masculinity: an idea which, as we have seen, is widely patristic. But she weakens her case by seeming to imply that the alternative to Balthasar's extreme version of separate gender roles is an androgynous (platonizing?) ideal.

Beattie may be right to note that, in his account of Mary becoming the Church from Christ's side as Eve was created from Adam, Balthasar's Mary loses her identity. That seems to be because, as Beattie argues, Balthasar's literalist dependence on Genesis (and other biblical texts) leads him to suppose that femininity "proceeds from" masculinity, and its purpose is *merely* to enable masculinity to complete itself: in other words that Balthasar's "complementarity" is not genuinely reciprocal – a defect I noted in many earlier writers.

Balthasar seems to have a somewhat "Talibanic" idea of the humiliation of man before God as analogous to a supposed humiliation of women by men. Beattie's main concern, however, is that he

something. Male "dominance" and "possession" is an abuse of a generally proper feature of the relationship between the sexes. If we could pursue that further, we might find something of an explanation of why it was so easy for the erroneous notion that woman could not be created in God's image to batten on to ambiguously culture-bound biblical texts.

There is also the mistaken biology of the "one-seed" (or even the "two-seed") theory, the influence of which I have already noticed, and which derives much of its attraction and much of its openness to abuse from the comparison of intercourse to a man sowing a field. A field is passive, however, and this is where the analogy should break down but doesn't. For although, on a modern theory of conception, the woman can still reasonably be said to be "sown", she not only receives the seed by combining it (if she is to be fertile) with her egg (read "female seed"), but she seeks and welcomes male entry in a loving relationship – as distinct from rape or mere duty where she is variously obliged to submit. In her behaviour she both provides a model for the receptive human soul of both male and female in welcoming God's necessary initiative in acts of salvation, and further indicates why Christ has to be represented as the Bridegroom, not as the Bride. That notwithstanding, such receptivity to God, the rightful superior, cannot properly be used to justify a marital superiority which could be of either party, but is more "naturally" assumed of the male who enters, and in the case of a virgin bride perforates, the female. Within a worthy human marriage female receptivity is not submission but a willingly expressed *action* of love.[197]

dwells on the sexual humiliation (real or imagined) of women in constructing theological fantasies. In effect her charge is that Gnosticism (or Manichaeanism) is returning by the back door – though the intruder is more likely to be the "neo-encratite" Gregory of Nyssa than Mani.

I discuss humiliation further below (and in note 197), remarking, as does Beattie, on the influence on Balthasar of that strange woman Adrienne von Speyr.

[197] There is no need to be disturbed (as is Beattie in "Sex, Death and Melodrama" 164) by Irigaray's representation of such acts as "phallocentric"; such language should be taken as descriptive rather than evaluative or normative. The morally ambiguous association of sex and violence which rightly troubles Beattie in Balthasar's use of sexual analogies in theology seems to derive from a tendency to collapse honourable intercourse into rape and consequent humiliation. Balthasar's view (probably derived, as I have observed, from Gregory of Nyssa and cited above in notes 2, 27, 115, 196) that the active deployment of sexuality is not part of the divine image seems also partly dependent on the traditional-seeming and allegedly empirical claim of Adrienne von Speyr that sexual intercourse is always "humiliating" for the woman. That "always" is unacceptable; it should depend on the circumstances and in particular on the "affect" between the spousal couple.

In *Theo-Drama* II (esp. 382) Balthasar leaves the matter of sexual activity in a prelapsarian state open: sexual difference is now part of the original image (Adam is male throughout "right down to each cell . . ." 365), but its physical deployment in intercourse may be a mark only of the fallen state: a corrected version of the position which Gregory (and later Greeks) actually held and the mature Augustine – and later Aquinas – rejected. It should be noted that in refusing Gregory's view we are

In recent treatments of this theme, however, including *Mulieris Dignitatem*, there is a significantly grey area. It can be seen in Scola's "commentary" on John Paul II, where he says that there are three aspects of what he calls "the nuptial mystery": sexual difference, love in its proper sense (relation to the other, gift), and fruitfulness.[198] It is the second of these that needs further examination, for here we meet the central (Platonic) notion of desire for the enjoyment of the other. Scola's account does not omit desire altogether; indeed he reworks a traditional distinction between "pleasure" and "joy" (*gaudium*)[199]as well as the Thomistic distinction between "love of desire" (*amor concupiscentiae*) and love of friendship (*amor amicitiae*).

The core of the problem – to see which will point us towards a clarification of the grey area – is to be found in the fear that a desire to "enjoy", and particularly to enjoy physical pleasure, is egoistic and self-serving. Hence the traditional language of love is widely suspect: not least the phrase – open to abuse as we have seen – that the lover (usually in this context depicted as male) wants to "enjoy" his beloved, to "conquer" her or to "possess" her. Augustine's eventual recognition of the fact that earthly things in general can be properly "enjoyed" only "in the Lord" points the way forward.[200] Though the physical "possession" and enjoyment of a woman often provokes the charge of egoism – and prescinding from the possible fruitfulness of the union – it would not do so if in such "possession" her personal integrity were respected. A woman is possessed egoistically if the man wants her as an object of desire and nothing else, but in mutual human love – symbolized by public commitment – the desire of both parties is mingled with self-giving.[201] Experientially that means that the act is partly egoistic, though not – it is to be hoped – at the other's expense. Sexual acts, like all other acts, are in Christian teaching pervaded by the

---

not obliged to commit ourselves to the contemporary "liberal" idea that "morally good sex" will not regularly display mixed motivations. As a result of the Fall, in sexual acts as elsewhere, good people try to eliminate vicious intentions (such as the wish to dominate or manipulate) but cannot even entirely know how well they have succeeded or how badly they have failed.

    To avoid muddying the waters I deliberately offer no comment on the possibly related question of women's ordination to the priesthood. We are too far from clarity about the complementary natures of men and women to be able to discuss that topic philosophically. For comment see (e.g.) B. Ashley, "Gender and the Priesthood of Christ: A Theological Reflection", *The Thomist* 57 (1993) 343–379.

[198] Scola, *Nuptial Mystery* xxiii.   [199] Scola, *Nuptial Mystery* 123–126, 328–330, 397–399.
[200] Cf. Rist, *Augustine* 162–163.
[201] Hence the Prince's complaint to his confessor about his wife in Tommasi di Lampedusa's *The Leopard* is legitimate: "I have had seven children by her and I have never seen her navel."

effects of original sin; there is no escaping that: it must be admitted with humility.[202]

Scola is right to emphasize that the difference between the sexes, indeed between the sexed individuals as limited individuals, is partial cause of the impossibility of the perfect *gaudium* the lovers may seek. And if they do not recognize that impossibility, they will fail to achieve even the joys available to them. Human love, even between loving marriage-partners, cannot achieve the fullness of joy, because the other party is also only a fallen image of the God who is sole source of a joy that is perfect and permanent. The transitoriness of sexual pleasure is a sign of that inevitable incompleteness.

The recognition of a love of the other *in Deo* marks the permanence of his or her ultimate personal difference, restraining both the temptation to idolize the beloved (that is to place him or her before one's soul's good) or to seek to eliminate that separateness in a dominating form of possession. A proper sexual desire toward the other not only facilitates self-giving but represents a recognition by the lover of the reciprocal and autonomous personality of the other as a personal image of God: joyful because godlike; incomplete because human. At its best *amor concupiscentiae* is to be viewed not as a poor relation of *amor amicitiae* but as the variant of *amor amicitiae* appropriate to marriage – and insofar as it struggles with egoism and remains a source of inspiration as paradigmatic for other friendly relationships.

Catholic tradition, as we have seen, has often tended to find ways to assert either that woman was not created in the image of God (but could gain a more male status) or that though created in the divine image was less fully so created. Sometimes this inequality (or unequal complementarity) gets masked by tendentious translations of traditional texts (as of Aquinas)[203] – making him look contradictory in that the apparent "equality" conflicts with his general representation of women as emotionally inadequate for male decision-making. Modern notions of unequal complementarity might seem a solution that does justice to the tradition, and if merely being in

---

[202] The present comments are necessarily very limited and much of importance has been omitted altogether. A full Christian treatment would require discussion of the *sacrament* of marriage and of virginity/celibacy as of a gift of the still-sexed person as well as of the tendency in any *analysis* to be over-serious, to overlook the specifically human capacity for "fooling around" which is an essential part of a proper sexual relationship. Such overlooking (and the concomitant neglect of original sin) is part explanation of the idolatry of sexual acts as peculiarly perfectible in much current literature.

[203] Thus Finnis writes (*Aquinas* 171–172): "the mind [mens], the intellect and will, which makes us images of the divine – our human kind of soul or spirit – belongs, without distinction or difference to the males and females of the human species; it is found 'as much in man as in woman' [tam in viro quam in muliere]" (*ST* 1 q 93a.4 ad 1 etc.). Here – as noted earlier – Finnis reads *tam ... quam* (usually translated simply as "both ... and") as though Aquinas had written *tantum ... quantum*.

harmony with a supposedly complete tradition were the overriding consideration, that would perhaps have to do. But it is not, and to see why it is not we must recognize how historically being-in-the-image-of-God has been not falsely but incompletely construed.

It would be unrealistic to consider trawling through the whole history of our theme;[204] sufficient to notice that the divine image is very frequently recognized in man's "free choice". In the medieval period such free choice is characterized, in the classical language of Peter Lombard (*Sentences* 2.24.5), as a capacity (*facultas*) of reason and "will". To assert therefore that women are either not created in God's image or are created genuinely but less fully in that image is to assert not that they have some divine characteristics and not others (in a complementary way to the weaknesses and strengths of men), but that they are less well endowed overall with divine characteristics – though worthy enough to merit salvation and indeed of being resurrected in female form. Attempts to misread the history of these matters may be theologically well-meaning, but error needs to be admitted rather than explained away if genuine development is to be achieved.

As we have noticed, and will notice further, there has been much recent concern to revive the traditional "image of God" debate – not least to give an account of man that would allow for the possibility of human rights and human dignity[205] – and if that goal is to be achieved, the question of whether or not woman is created in the divine image becomes immensely important in a contemporary world where other religions deny her equal rights and status. If she is not so created, or only unequally, she may achieve equal glory at the resurrection but will deserve less than equal respect of her rights and dignity here on earth. To aspire to such equal respect she must be able to exert her "free will" in the same manner and to equally good ends as men.

---

[204] Barth's emphasis on relations among human beings and in God's Trinitarian nature is significant, as I have already noted. Man's ability to form relationships is an important part of his nature, and within such relationships that between man and wife (or at least male and female; Adam and Eve in Genesis) is the potentially supreme case (*Church Dogmatics* 3.1). But relationship in itself (as Aristotle knew) depends on the postulated subjects of specific kinds of relationship, so the notion of God's image as relational cannot *replace* the attempt to find specific human characteristics on which such relationships depend. As Gunton puts it in the course of an argument against dualism, "Relations are of the whole person, not of minds or bodies alone ..." ("Trinity, Ontology and Anthropology: Towards a Renewal of the Theology of the Imago Dei," in C. Schwöbel and C. Gunton (eds.), *Persons, Divine and Human* (Edinburgh 1991) 59). But to conclude, with Gunton, that "To be in the image of God therefore means to be conformed on the person of Christ" may be less informative than it sounds, and though perhaps true, appears evasive in regard to female imaging.

[205] For less "official" comment than I have cited above see (e.g.) J. Moltmann, "Christian Faith and Human Rights", in *On Human Dignity* (London 1984) 19–36 and E. Fuchs, "L'homme à l'image de Dieu: L'anthropologie théologique, du point de vue de l'éthique", in P. Bühler (ed.), *Humain à l'image e Dieu* (Geneva 1989) 309–320.

The doctrine of man in the image of God will only be intelligible if "free" is understood not as a "freedom of indifference" – that is as divorced from properly human inclinations to the good – but as a capacity not for choice for its own sake but for the consistent and deliberate choice of good over evil, God over human megalomania. That latter kind of freedom, which must be recovered if man is usefully to be in the image of God, has been largely lost since the Middle Ages and now – perhaps as a result of the patristic revival – seems to be at last being recovered within Christianity.[206] Its loss probably explains in part why the image of God – at least until recently – has also lost its centrality in explicit Christian thought. Its recovery, if it is to benefit females as well as males, must be accompanied by a recognition that men and women, soul in body, body in soul, reflect in their relationships with their fellows the liberty, and the personal relationships, of God – and that they reflect these in partially different but equally valuable ways.

This has been a long and detailed chapter, but the gradual recovery and further development of the notion of "man's" creation in God's image is fundamental for a defensible Catholic view of contemporary psychological and ethical problems – and a study of that development is at the same time a study of one of the essential bases, whether implicit or explicit, of the entire culture of Catholicism. Ultimately Catholic theories of art and of justice, of politics as of ethics, flow from it.

A final note: liberty of indifference *in God* would do nothing for the dignity of either men or women: whatever dignity they might have could then only be a reflection of a "divine" arbitrariness.

---

[206] For interesting comment on the importance of the "modern" liberty of indifference in the four-teenth century and its subversion of both earlier medieval and ancient accounts of freedom see S. Pinckaers, "Le thème de l'image de Dieu en l'homme et l'anthropologie", in Bühler, *Humain à l'image de Dieu* 47–163, esp. 158–163. Pinckaers attributes the fatal change to Ockham.

CHAPTER 2

Divine justice and man's "genetic" flaw

The judgments of God are such as to make the soul shiver.

Augustine

2.1 AUGUSTINE VS JULIAN WITH HINDSIGHT

In the previous chapter I studied the gradual development, within Christianity, of the significance of the biblical teaching that man is created in God's image, and showed how the Church has learned to accept explicitly that both men and women are equally so created. But clearly the hoped-for nature of the image must depend on the nature of the God who is imaged, and I closed the chapter with the implication that a God possessed of the freedom of indifference would have done no good to Christianity's moral reputation.

To approach the question of what kind of God is imaged by man, we need to formulate an account of divine attributes, among which two of the most important, in Christianity, are justice and mercy. Hence the present chapter, in investigating some of the difficulties Christianity has experienced in reconciling these attributes, will at the same time illuminate what we can understand to be the attitude of God to man, and hence of man to God. In the course of the discussion it will become clear how Christianity has with difficulty avoided some of the morally unacceptable accounts of God and his absolute power that monotheism can too easily generate. The struggle that I shall examine in this chapter was not the only occasion in which was raised the possibility in Christianity of an arbitrary God, but it was the most important, and many of the later battles may be looked on as attempts – for better or worse – to reconsider or re-stage it.

In a Christian culture the relationship between man, the image of God, and God himself can be recognized not only in varying accounts of our participation in divine attributes such as goodness or justice, but in a more immediately "moral" contrast between Creator and creature, between divine perfection and human weakness and sinfulness. In preaching its message of redemption, Christianity has always emphasized the obvious facts about human moral frailty, but also needed to assess, in arduous contentions repeated over time, the powers of our moral nature and the degree of help and support that we need if we are to overcome frailty and a tendency to vice. In the first years of Christianity many came to think that the converted could and should avoid all sin after baptism; hence the more practical folk delayed being baptized.

Gradually, however, the expanding Christian culture moved towards a more realistic view of the nature of "fallen" humanity and the role of divine assistance. But that realization contributed to a perception of Christian culture as gloomy, hostile to sexuality and life-fearing – with some justification when the weakness of fallen man seemed to obscure the goodness of God. It therefore remains a prerequisite of any future Catholic culture to retain awareness of human frailty without yielding to pessimism and self-abasement before an omnipotent deity: a balance never easy to strike.

More than any other thinker after New Testament times, Augustine of Hippo developed biblical ideas about the relationship between human nature and God's grace. Some of his variously incoherent and inconsistent ideas in this area were necessarily dropped by the Catholic Church. Some of them were later adapted and adopted in non-Catholic versions of Christianity, and various groups proposed further variants which they then mistakenly attributed to the bishop of Hippo. In the process of acceptance and rejection that generally "Augustinian" ideas provoked, Western Christianity was forced not only to ask just how "fallen" is fallen human nature, but about God's proper judgment of that nature. That entailed reflection on the relationship between his mercy and his justice: as already noted, two questionably compatible attributes. The varying result of this debate was of the greatest importance for the development of the entire Christian culture, for in any religious tradition, as I have already observed, the supposed nature of God cannot be disconnected from ideas about the supposed nature of man and therefore the sort of society for him to live in. It is no accident that Augustine, the "doctor of grace", wrote about the City of God and its possible reflection in human society.

Among claims rejected by the Church but which are mooted in different parts of Augustine's writings are the following: that God accepts some sinners and by active decision (rather than permissively) abandons others to their fate; that God does not wish the salvation of the entire human race; that unbaptized children, as well as adults who are not or cannot be members of the Church, are necessarily condemned since they share in the sin of Adam and have not been cleansed of guilt (normally by baptism). Some of these ideas were developed or proposed by Augustine in significantly more or less harsh versions at different times in his life but were organized into tight and comprehensive systems by both Catholic and non-Catholic successors.

In the controversies that ensued, both groups were able to cite texts from Augustine that suited their own "system". Neither took seriously the words of Augustine himself that his thinking developed, sometimes radically, nor did they notice that genuine inconsistencies can be found in different works of the master written at virtually the same period of his life.[1] For these and other reasons I shall have little to say about the "after-life" of Augustinian theories about grace, predestination and the baptism of infants in the period between the bishop's death and very recent times: not least because the ensuing debates – for reasons that will become apparent – necessarily remained inconclusive.

Few of Augustine's theses, even those later found wanting or incomplete by the Catholic Church, were advanced without due reasoning. Much of that reasoning is on display in the arguments between Augustine and the "Pelagian" bishop Julian of Eclanum, and an examination of their debate against the background of modern Church teaching is particularly rewarding. Since the Church has not always agreed with Augustine, any observer of the development of Catholic doctrine – and hence culture – needs to understand the reasons for those disagreements, and to ask whether Julian had any inkling of them. He can then also ask whether, although Augustine largely prevailed, Julian's concerns were sufficiently serious as to provide evidence about the wider dialectic of Catholic development. And in thinking about that, he may also shed light on a still baffling question: why was Augustine – apparently sensing that all was not yet properly settled – so insistent on returning again and again to the task of battering down a resilient but apparently defeated opponent?

In order to clarify the relevant issues, I shall look first at a number of propositions from the recent *Catechism of the Catholic Church*. These will indicate the present stage of the debate and enable us to see whether, insofar as they indicate a recasting of various views of Augustine, his inadequate positions have been successfully reformulated. Put more bluntly, I am asking: in what particular respects has Augustine's argumentation been found defective, incoherent or incomplete, and why? It may still turn out

---

[1] For comment see Rist, *Augustine* 9–10.

that where Augustine is now held to be wrong – and rightly so – the arguments against him have not always been adequately presented, and if such is the case, we need to know the reason for that too. It may also turn out that there are areas where Julian raised more challenging questions – and got more important things right – than Augustine wanted (or was able) to allow.

I therefore start with the *Catechism*, section 389, where we read:

The doctrine of original sin is, so to speak, the "reverse side" of the Good News that Jesus is the Saviour of all men, that all need salvation and that salvation is offered to all through Christ. The Church, which has the mind of Christ, knows very well that it cannot tamper with the revelation of original sin without undermining the mystery of Christ.

Section 390 (quoting Vatican II's *Gaudium et Spes* 13.1) continues that the Fall "took place at the beginning of the history of man". "Revelation gives us the certainty of faith that the whole of human history is marked by the original fault freely committed by our first parents" (cf. the stance of the Council of Trent: DS 1513).

After discussing the "fall" of the angels, the *Catechism* continues (sections 396–408 on Original Sin) as follows:

1 Man, as a creature, must recognize that he is not a god, that he has "human" limitations;
2 Disobedience has led to sin and death as regular features of human life;
3 "All men are implicated in Adam's sin" (402, note the ambiguity of "implicated"). "As one man's trespass led to condemnation for all men, so one man's righteousness leads to acquittal and life for all men" (Romans 5:12,19).

Section 404 opens by asking, "How did the sin of Adam become the sin of all his descendants?", but though it tells us that "the whole human race is in Adam as one body of one man", it continues by noting that "the transmission of original sin is a mystery that we cannot fully understand", and that "it is a sin which will be transmitted by propagation to all mankind": so far a clearly Augustinian answer.

It is important, however, to notice that when speaking of the "transmission of original sin" the *Catechism* avoids Augustinian phrases like "inherited guilt", preferring to speak of inherited weakness and damage; indeed it goes out of its way to claim that "although it is proper to each individual, original sin does not have the character of a personal fault in any of Adam's descendants". It is only called sin "in an analogical sense": "it is a sin 'contracted', and not 'committed' – a state and not an act". But then (405) we read: "[It] – i.e. human nature – is inclined to sin – an inclination to evil that is called 'concupiscence'.[2] Baptism ... erases [Latin: *delet*] original sin" – that is, apparently, it erases the "original deprivation of holiness"! Apparently we are now "holy" in a special sense, presumably as members of the Christian community, though still inclined to sin, as Adam originally was not.

This, unfortunately, is a muddle; neither Augustine nor, one hopes, many others would want to tell us that the *inclination* to sin is removed by baptism. Augustine held that the *responsibility* for that sinful inclination is removed by baptism; presumably the compilers of the *Catechism* (or most of them?) meant to say that an inclination to sin is not a sin but the *effect* of the sin of Adam, as we read in section 1264, hence that in admitting us to the Christian community baptism recognizes or proclaims that we are not responsible for that effect – a correction of Augustine – and in some sense "turns a man back towards God". I take it that the muddle is the result of the deliberations of a committee anxious to deny Augustine's view that we are personally *guilty* of original sin – as well as the Pelagian view that we are not *affected* by original sin – while at the same time determined to retain the now problematic language which says that baptism "erases" original sin.

Original sin in us has thus been redefined as the effect of the sin of Adam while the necessary corollary of that redefinition, that is, that it is no longer "erased" by baptism – the effect of which is rather to allow us, by grace, formally to enter the Christian community – has been neglected. The text as it stands has the appearance of the work of a labour–management disputes tribunal. The *Catechism* has thus failed to present in coherent form what one may reasonably assume to have been the intended contemporary correction of Augustine's position. Perhaps a more coherent presentation might have looked too close to the position of Julian who, though denying the inherited effects of Adam's sin, certainly regarded baptism as the necessary means of entering the Church and thus obtaining the possibility of salvation.

If we turn to the sections of the *Catechism* on Baptism itself, a very un-Augustinian (indeed largely unpatristic) account of the sacrament is proposed. For while in section 1257 the *Catechism* states that "The Church does not know of any means other than Baptism that assures entry into eternal

---

[2] The concept of *concupiscentia* is basic to Augustine's thought. Unfortunately in Augustine the word is ambiguous, able to refer *both* to an inherited weakness (*imbecillitas*) of the human agent (as in: "I have a weakness for booze") and to an active succumbing to that weakness which would take the form of a *libido*, a lust (as in: "I've gotta have some booze"). In speaking of the effects of the sin of Adam the compilers of the *Catechism* normally refer to the "passive" sense. This is not the place to examine the nature and effects of Augustine's own ambiguous usage.

beatitude," section 1260, glossing Vatican II, notes that "Every man who is ignorant of the Gospel of Christ and of his Church, but seeks the truth and does the will of God in accordance with his understanding of it, can be saved. It may be supposed that such persons would have *desired baptism explicitly* if they had known its necessity." And again we read (1261) that "Jesus' tenderness toward children which caused him to say: 'Let the children come to me, do not hinder them' (Mark 10:14), allows us to hope that there is a way of salvation for children who have died without Baptism": hardly an Augustinian expectation, though his contemporary John Cassian (*Conferences* 13.7.2) – not to speak of the "para-Pelagian" Rufinus of Syria (*De Fide* 41) – would have welcomed it, and indeed quote the parallel passage of Matthew (18:3).

For one of the effects of the so-called Pelagian controversy about grace and human nature in the early fifth century was to highlight serious philosophical and theological problems apparently unsolvable at the time but on which we (as in the *Catechism*) can now claim (or should claim if we are historically responsible) to have introduced clarifications and made a degree of progress: problems about the effects of baptism, the nature of original sin itself and of its possibly inherited guilt, the salvation of the unbaptized and of unbelievers, God's omnipotence. Many earlier assumptions about these problems – as well as their determination in the time of Augustine – have been replaced or corrected, and these replacements or corrections can and must increasingly affect Christian society as well as – one must hope – the perception of that society among non-Christians.

In the present chapter I shall (as normally) only consider the development of specifically Catholic culture and so, as already indicated, I shall have little to say directly about how Augustinian problems about grace and human nature were tackled by Luther, Calvin, Jansen and others, even though so long as they were at the centre of Western thinking – indeed even now when they are largely ignored – the solutions of these later theologians effected radical changes in the intellectual, social and cultural traditions of the West, and eventually in the rest of the Christian world. My reason for neglecting them here, however, is that while they have certainly "concentrated the mind of the Church" since the sixteenth century (both helpfully and unhelpfully), they have – in the longer run and by reaction – contributed more to the appearance and growth of anti-Christian agnosticism and secularism than to a defensible Christian culture. Sometimes, indeed, earlier Catholic notions have had that effect too: which may be at least part of the reason they have been called in question. Some of these problems will re-emerge in chapter 6 in the context of the relationship of the Church to "modernity".

My present approach will be to play over the intellectual brawl between Augustine and Julian of Eclanum, with a view to establishing why, although among his contemporaries and successors Augustine was hailed as winning by a knockout, Julian (whose determined epitaph maintained "Here lies Julian, the Catholic bishop"[3]) has often – and with some reason – been thought to have lost only on points. Yet, not least through pigheadedness, he failed to take advantage of his opponent's theological, philosophical and logical weaknesses and did less than justice to some of his own underlying theological concerns: concerns which later generations have had to take seriously in the hope of avoiding the blind-alleys that Augustine sometimes constructed in evading his unflagging antagonist. Yet even as a biblical interpreter Julian failed to take advantage – again for cultural reasons – of substantial difficulties in Augustine's unsystematic and sometimes arbitrary exegesis; notably, but by no means exclusively, of Paul's epistle to the Romans.

After sketching some of the issues between the antagonists in their historical context, I shall look at what Julian might have done (theoretically, that is) – and what *sub specie aeternitatis* he needed to do – to advance the debate, thus suggesting that Neo-Julian and Neo-Augustine might at least on some points now come to terms where their historical prototypes, both the apparent winner and the anathematized loser, failed to do so. Thus I shall argue that in the Augustine–Julian clash we have an example of a very important debate which at a particular epoch could not properly (as distinct from rhetorically) be resolved: which is not to deny that substantial progress was made, but rather to suggest that new and unpredictable light would have been required for further advance. From that point, I shall as elsewhere raise questions about where we are going now and where we need to go in the future.

2.2 THE OPENING SALVOS IN THE PELAGIAN WAR

Outside theological circles Pelagius is not a household name, yet his impact on the development of Christian and post-Christian culture has been immense. Traditionally his fame is as an arch-heretic, a man who held that we are capable of attaining perfection now, and that we are hell-bound if we fail to attain it. In more recent times he has been hailed as an apostle of human freedom by those who know little of his intransigence and intolerable demands on human nature. His moral thesis was approximately that

[3] See P. Brown, *Augustine of Hippo* (London[2] 2000) 385.

what is morally desirable is morally possible and morally obligatory, though his underlying concern was with salvation. Are we so created, he asked, as to be able to attain perfection and salvation through resolute use of the moral and spiritual capabilities with which God endowed us at birth and at baptism?[4] Is our salvation in Christ to be achieved in virtue of our created willingness and ability to follow God, as Augustine, to his later embarrassment, admitted he too had once been inclined to believe,[5] or are the new "Carthaginians"[6] – as Julian designated the later Augustine and his fellow African bishops – right that in our present and obviously lame and injured condition, itself to be explained as the result of a catastrophic "fall" or apostasy from God, we need the constant support of divine grace even to will to co-operate with Christ the Saviour?

The outbreak of the Pelagian War in North Africa was in large part the result of a number of charges brought in Carthage in 411 against Pelagius' Roman associate Caelestius: not least that he denied the theological claim, especially associated locally with the memory of the martyr-bishop Cyprian, that baptism is administered to infants for the remission of their sins.[7] Such a thesis would only make sense, in Caelestius' view, if there were already sins to forgive in infants: that is, if infants inherit the sin and guilt of Adam:[8] the view accepted by Augustine and the other African bishops long before AD 396 when, replying to his former Milanese mentor Simplicianus, Augustine had formally rejected the thesis that God calls only those whom he *foresees* will respond to his call. According to Caelestius, infants could not have inherited sins since their souls (unlike their bodies) are newly created by God. That "creationism" was the majority view at the time in the East, but also shared by Jerome, Pelagius himself and a number of other Westerners.[9]

---

[4] *Ad Dem.* 2 = *PL* 30, 178. For the origins of the controversy and the date of Pelagius' book *De Natura* (arguably as early as 405–406) see Y.-M. Duval, "La date du 'De Natura', de Pélage", *REA* 36 (1990) 257–283. In any case Pelagian ideas must have preceded Pelagian books.

[5] See *DPS* 3.7, with the comments of J. Lössl, "Augustine on Predestination", *Augustiniana* 52 (2002) 241–272, at 265.

[6] "The philosophical dabbler from Carthage" (*OpImp.* 5.11; cf. 1.6; 6.18, etc.).

[7] For a recent provocative discussion of the complicated series of events of 411 see W. Dunphy, "Pelagius in Carthage, 411–412", *Augustinianum* 45 (2005) 389–466.

[8] *Ad Simp.* 1.2.16: *reatus originalis* first at 1.2.20. At least according to Augustine's final version of the theory, baptized parents also pass on some of the effects of their own "original" sin to their (baptized) children (*OpImp.* 6.21, 23).

[9] On the importance of the soul's origin in the dispute between Julian of Eclanum and Augustine see M. Lamberigts, "Julian and Augustine on the Origin of the Soul", *Augustiniana* 46 (1996) 243–260. Note how an overcoming of the soul–body dichotomy – to which I shall return – would also have been helpful with problems about original sin.

In a letter (166) to Jerome, written in 415, Augustine spells out his objections to such creationism, most particularly that it blocks any serious explanation of original sin. Augustine's growing conviction, perhaps first extensively developed – from roots in Ambrose and Cyprian – in the course of his disputes with the "schismatic" Donatists, and now, he thinks, threatened by creationism, is that, since infants are baptized for the forgiveness of sins, they must have committed sins "in Adam": that is, in what he had come to call our "common" as distinct from our "personal" life.[10] His implicit or explicit arguments for such a life are basically twofold: theological, since the frequent miseries of infants indicate that in a just dispensation they are punished for sins for which they can be held responsible; sociological or psychological in that it seems to be true that no human is born without the certainty of sinning "personally".[11]

All this implies that, Jesus apart, each human being, as such, is deeply flawed not only systemically, by virtue of being born into an inevitably corrupt society (the *saeculum*), but also "genetically" (in being one in Adam). Jesus is genetically protected because Mary, though herself conceived in original sin (that is, by an imperfect act of "genetically flawed" parents), is specially protected before, during and after her own unique impregnation ("not from male seed [with its associated lust] but by the Holy Spirit" (*Incomplete Work* 6.22)). As for the rest of us, Augustine had associated normal human conception with a degree of lustful concupiscence (hence with a certain improper pleasure) at least as early as 394/5 (*83 Questions* 66.6).[12] And our "genetic" disabilities (our now natural ignorance,

---

[10] For further (incomplete) discussion, in the steps of Solignac and O'Connell, see Rist, *Augustine* 121–129.

[11] Normally, as noted in *Conf.* 1.7.11, it does not take long to activate that capacity. The jealousy of babies may be impotent, but the mentality is not innocent. And babies certainly suffer from ignorance.

[12] Augustine does not teach the later doctrine of the Immaculate Conception expressly, though the "protection" he accords to Mary could readily be back-dated to the first moment of her conception. Certainly for Augustine the case of Mary (held by Pelagius to be the star example of achieved sinlessness, hence a demonstration of its possibility) is unique. He says at *DNG* 36.42 that on this question he will not challenge Pelagius "out of honour to the Lord" (cf. *OpImp.* 4.122), while at *OpImp.* 6.22 he repeats to Julian what he had already repeated (for example) in his *Literal Commentary on Genesis* (10.18.32), that Mary was conceived in the carnal concupiscence of her parents (*de carnali concupiscentia parentum*): like the rest of us. The texts are not incompatible: there is nothing in *DNG* to suggest that Mary *could* not inherit the inherent weakness and ignorance of original sin and hence also the apparent certainty of sinning. She was, however, entirely protected by God's grace (see J. M. Rist, "Augustine on Free Will and Predestination", *JTS* 20 (1969) 427) – and since she herself conceived without *carnalis concupiscentia* (since there was no sexual intercourse) she passed on not sinful flesh but "the likeness of sinful flesh" (*OpImp.* 4.60, cf. Romans 8:3 and the discussion of R. Teske, "St Augustine on the Humanity of Christ and Temptation", in *Mélanges offerts à T. J. van Bavel* (*Augustiniana* 2004) 261–277, esp. 273–274). The "likeness of sinful flesh" – though not sinful – is still subject to death.

moral weakness and proneness to evil) remain, he holds, even if baptism washes away inherited and punishable guilt and puts us within reach of other sacramental means of grace.

Our inherited proneness to vice (*concupiscentia*) is in itself a bad thing. In our sexual nature (to which it is not of course limited) it is exhibited in physical manifestations such as unwanted erections and emissions as well as impotency in men (*City of God* 14.16.23–28) – all demonstrating a failure of control over our bodies – and "secret interior feelings in Eve [and in other women[13]] contrary to her will" (*Against Two Letters* 1.16.32). In the argument with Julian Augustine puns on the fact that sexual organs can in common speech be referred to as our "nature": their "behaviour" thus reflects that of our human nature: indecent because disobedient (*On Marriage and Concupiscence* 1.6.7; *Against Julian* 6.7.20). It is our "nature" in Adam which sinned and which is thus "genetically" corrupted.[14] In his earlier writings Augustine sometimes calls this corruption a "general sin" (e.g., *83 Questions* 68.4) and still entertains the (Origenist) possibility that such sin may have occurred before the soul was linked with its body (*On Free Will* 1.12.24) – or more likely before its body was (consequently) degraded so as to be merely "fleshly".[15]

The first stage of the Pelagian controversy (perhaps best represented by Pelagius' treatise *On Nature* and Augustine's reply *On Nature and Grace*) is

---

Augustine was convinced from early in his Christian career that it is sinful sexual *concupiscentia* (an evil used well in marriage) which (necessarily indicated by a morally mixed *delectatio*: so Ambrose (cited at *CJul*. 3.21.48); cf. 2.6.20; 3.14.28) conveys the "genetically based" original sin and guilt from the parents to the children. *Delectatio* in this connection first appears at *83Q*. 66.6 (AD 394/5); so N. Cipriani, "La dottrina del peccato originale negli scritti di S. Agostino fin all' Ad Simplicianum", in L. Alici, R. Piccolomini and A. Pieretti (eds.), *Il mistero del male e la libertà possibile IV* (Rome 1997) 23–48; Rist, *Augustine* 127, note 98. The notion of fallen humanity as a *massa peccati* (the semi-material image suggests mud; cf. Romans 9.21) appears at about the same time (e.g., at *83Q*. 68.4). In his early days Augustine seems to have thought (as in *GenMan*.) that the soul, created immaterial and linked with a "spiritual" body, became after the Fall linked with an "animal" body (2.7), which thus served as the vehicle of the transmitted sin of Adam. The fallen body, however, is weak and destined for death by a just punishment (*DVR* 15.29).

At a much later stage, when Augustine became convinced that the unfallen body of Adam was "animal" – a development discussed in the previous chapter – and still remained "animal" after the Fall, he persisted with some sort of traducianist account of original sin. For what came to worry him, as we shall see, is that if the soul is not transmitted in this quasi-material way, but is created at conception by God, then such "creationism" seems to destroy the doctrine of original sin.

The theme of *massa peccati/damnationis* did not originate with Augustine; it had already been advanced by Ambrosiaster (*CommRom*. 5.12; 9.21; *1Cor*. 15.39); cf. D. Marafioti, "Alle origini del teorema della predestinazione (*Simpl*. 1.2.13–22)", *CIA* (1987) 257–277, at 269.

[13] Cf. *DNC* 2.13.26; *CJul*. 4.13.6; cf. *OpImp*. 5.11.   [14] Already at *83Q*. 68.3; *DVR* 28.51; cf. *CJul*. 3.12.24.
[15] Cf. Rist, *Augustine* 50, note 13; 122, note 89 and esp. 98 with reference to the early *GenMan*. 2.7.9 (388/9) and *DFS* 10.24 (no flesh in heaven, corrected at *Retr*. 1.17).

concerned fundamentally with human nature after the Fall,[16] and the means at our disposal to retrieve that disaster. As such, it has real if restricted parallels with a contemporary "crisis in Neoplatonic ethics" after the death of Plotinus in 270, when the philosophically dominant Neoplatonists lost confidence in our native ability to pull ourselves out of our moral and spiritual chaos by our own bootstraps. Instead we need the help of the gods, via a form of pagan sacramentalism they called theurgy, if we are to attain salvation.[17]

Some believe that Caelestius' views on the effects of baptism may have been at least partly indebted to the hostile comments of Rufinus the Syrian (apparently a monk from Jerome's monastery in Bethlehem) on Augustine's implied defence of the necessity for infant baptism in his replies to Simplicianus' questions about Paul's letter to the Romans in 396.[18] Be that as it may, there is no doubt that it was not Caelestius, but an eventual reading of the treatise of Pelagius himself entitled *On [Human] Nature* – Pelagius seems to have been less concerned with the specific problems of infants – that finally convinced Augustine that he must develop a full-scale refutation, with the naming of names, of what he had come to see as a Pelagian rehash of many of the errors he supposed he had laid to rest in writing to Simplicianus. For then he had worked out an account of grace that he was soon to apply, in the *Confessions*, to his personal history. "Give what you command and command what you will," he wrote in the *Confessions*, and, as he heard later, that incensed Pelagius.[19]

The clearing of Pelagius of charges of heresy by the Synod of Diospolis in Palestine, and the subsequent successful appeal of the African bishops to Rome, produced little immediate change in the nature of the debate. Despite underlying and occasionally surfacing anxieties about the wider theological ramifications of infant baptism where no personal sin has been committed, the key issue is still Augustine's insistence that, without the prevenient grace of an omnipotent God, good works cannot be performed and that perfection is impossible in our present life. Yet those wider concerns gradually became more prominent, recalling the core doctrines of Augustine's reply to Simplicianus and, in pointing away from earth

---

[16] Largely, but not entirely, since the issue of God's justice, so prominent later, is already in the background (e.g., at *PeccMer.* 1.21–31).

[17] See J. M. Rist, "Ps-Dionysius, Neoplatonism and the Problem of Spiritual Weakness", in H. Westra (ed.), *From Athens to Chartres: Festschrift E. Jeauneau* (Leiden 1992) 135–161.

[18] See G. Bonner, "Rufinus of Syria and African Pelagianism", *AS* 1 (1971) 31–47. For hesitations see Dunphy, "Pelagius in Carthage". I am now inclined to date the book of Rufinus, but not the ideas of Rufinus, to after 413.

[19] *Conf.* 10.29.40; cf. *DDP* 20.53.

towards heaven, from man to God, thereby theoretically at least linking Pelagianism with wider problems about divine predestination,[20] and specifically with who is to be saved, who is not and why not. Thus are raised possibly problematic features of God's nature which have cultural as well as theological importance, for a sombre depiction of God is deployed in a sombre religious culture.

2.3 PELAGIANISM, PREDESTINATION AND THE ORIGIN OF THE SOUL

The renewed concern of the aging Augustine with predestination is particularly striking in *Letter* 194 of AD 418 to Sixtus, a prominent Roman priest. In this letter some major themes of his reply to Simplicianus – we need grace even to turn to God; grace is given with no regard for foreseen "merits" – are rehearsed vigorously and unambiguously, and connected with the condemnation of Pelagius and the baptism of infants. We are reminded again that we are the "lump of the condemned", the *massa damnationis*; from that *massa*, by the inscrutable will of God, a select few are redeemed (194.2.4). Which serves to indicate why God's justice soon became a central issue in the Pelagian War.

Nor are arguments about human nature and human capacities now linked only to God's justice. Disagreements about the origin of the soul will also become an integral part of the story. The scholar Jerome, it goes without saying, had never been a Pelagian, but Augustine had long recognized that his attitude to creationism and more generally to the problem of the origin of the soul could give comfort to those who denied original sin. Hence fallen nature, our life "in" Adam, God's justice, predestination and the interpretation of Paul all come together in another letter (190) to Bishop Optatus of Milevis (AD 418 or 419): a letter written, unlike that to Sixtus, with no direct intention of influencing the ongoing and more public debate with Pelagius and his supporters,[21] and all the more informative for that.

---

[20] Not to speak of the accuracy of Augustine's interpretation of Paul's view of such matters. M. Lamberigts, however, is right to observe that "the doctrine of predestination *as such* [my italics] did not play an important role in Augustine's [strictly] anti-Pelagian *oeuvre*" (in "Augustine on Predestination: Some Quaestiones Disputatae Revisited", in *Mélanges offerts à T. J. van Bavel* (Augustiniana 2004) 270–305, at 282ff.). Part of the reason for this is that wider predestinarian problems (such as those about "fate" which later concerned the monks at Hadrumentum) were masked by the agreement of Pelagians and Augustine that baptism is normally essential for salvation.

[21] Augustine clearly has Pelagian concerns in mind, however, and in his next letter to Optatus (202A.2.6 of 420) warns that creationism could lead to Pelagianism (as he had warned Jerome).

Optatus, a creationist whose views on the subject had got him into trouble with some of his older clergy, wanted to know Augustine's present ideas about the origin of the soul. Augustine was willing to tell him, but wanted first to emphasize the connection – perhaps in the minds of Optatus' dissident priests – between that matter and what he held to be the very heart of the Christian faith,[22] the doctrine of original sin and our redemption by Christ, as set out in such texts as Romans 5:12 and 1 Corinthians 15:21. The two dominant theories about the soul are summarized:[23] creationism, supported – among others – by Jerome, and "traducianism": that being one in soul and body in Adam, we have shared in his sin and guilt, and that sin – along with our now personal existence – is transmitted to us by means of the beguilingly pleasurable and residually uncontrollable act by which we are conceived.

From Augustine's point of view, the two theories have merits and demerits; creationism allows us to say that each soul is newly created by the goodness of God, but is hard to square with a notion of inherited sin and a guilt that needs to be washed away in baptism; traducianism explains original sin but at the risk of treating the soul as material, thus leading us into the materialist "madness" (*dementia*, 190.4.14) of Tertullian.[24] As we should expect, in the letter to Optatus the notion of a "common" life in Adam is invoked (190.2.5), not least because the penal state of humanity, including infants, can then be construed as just, and God's justice vindicated.

Yet in this letter it is not only God's justice in punishing infants that is at stake but, as in the reply to Simplicianus (1.2.22), the tension apparent between God's justice and mercy. Augustine is determined to diffuse or disregard the difficulty, insisting that of all humanity only a few are spared, indeed that the great majority are marked down (*praescrivit*) for condemnation (190.3.9), though this is of "no weight with a God who is just" (190.3.12). At this point, we should notice a more general feature of early Christianity, indeed of ancient society: neither Pelagius nor later Julian was

---

[22] So does the *Catechism* (section 389) state that a sound account of Christ cannot be separated from a proper doctrine of original sin.

[23] For present purposes there is no need to say more about other theories discussed earlier by Augustine, as in *De Libero Arbitrio*: such as that pre-existing souls "fell" (or were put) into bodies.

[24] In the period before 396 Augustine was happy to learn from Tertullian when convenient, but from the time of *GenLitt.* 10.24.40–26.50 he is much more cautious: Tertullian is now regularly under attack, held up as a spectre to traducianists: see *AnOr.* 2.5.9. Julian however is not unaware of the original influence of Tertullian on Augustine and claims that it persists (and points towards Mani) (*OpImp.* 2.178). For materialism in African accounts of God and the soul (from which Augustine was converted by Ambrose and the "Platonic books") see Masai, "Les conversions de saint Augustin".

concerned about God's showing no mercy to the guilty while saving the few who are (or are made) righteous. As we shall see, that is because their (and especially Julian's) concern is with the punishment of the innocent, and largely but not exclusively with infants. Like most of his contemporaries, Julian seems to have no complaint about God's apparent reluctance to be generous to the guilty (or more of the guilty). Quoting rather selectively Romans 2:11, he will accuse Augustine's God of favouritism among the innocent (*Incomplete Work* 4.125, 128), without (at least here) indicating wider difficulties about possible favouritism among the guilty. Like his "master", Pelagius, he has no sympathy for those who try (but not hard enough) and fail, nor indeed much for adults who may not have the chance to try – albeit questions about that group were already being raised.

I should ask what assumptions – apart from a hatred of evildoers – Julian (and probably his fellow "Pelagians") shared with Augustine on these issues. I shall also look at the exact significance of Augustinian phrases like "marked down for condemnation", especially during the years between 414 and 423, for they are by no means unique, and we need a careful account of them before we can know what view of God's justice Augustine would (eventually) want to defend. Let us therefore now note an increasingly familiar attitude towards the condemned majority of mankind after 414: they are predestined to punishment (*praedestinata in supplicium*) in the *City of God* (15.1), and Jews are predestined to eternal destruction (*ad sempiternum interitum praedestinatos*) in *Tractate* 48.4 on John (probably 414); however, that is explained in *Tractate* 53.4, as a matter of God's permissive will, and obvious problems are brushed aside with an appeal – habitual after the reply to Simplicianus – to the Pauline *O altitudo*:[25] the unfathomable depth of God's secret judgments. The same explanation is presumably to be supplied for the fate of those "predestined to destruction" in *On the Perfection of Justice* (13.31).

As we have seen, similar ideas are to be found in the letter to Sixtus (194.2.3–4). We hear of those "predestined to eternal death" (*praedestinavit ad aeternam mortem*) in *On the Origin of the Soul* (4.11.16), "to the ultimate penalty" (*iuste nonnullos eorum poenis praedestinavit extremis*) in *Letter* 204.2 to Dulcitius (of 418), "justly predestined to punishment" (*ad eorum*

---

[25] We should recognize that (explicit reference to predestination being still far away) God's justice, which must be enforced if the proper order of the world is to be restored, is discussed in terms of his "most secret judgments" as early as the *De Ordine* (1.1.2) of 386. At *Ad Simp.* 1.2.22 Augustine would be confounded if he knew who were saved as well as who were lost.

damnationem quos iuste praedestinavit) in the *Enchiridion* (26.100 of 421/2) to Dulcitius' brother Laurentius.[26]

Although Augustine would probably always have retained the phrase "marked down for condemnation" *(praescivit)*,[27] he appears later to have eventually abandoned talk of those *"predestined* to punishment" (or "to death"). That may have been in part a correction of sloppy language, but more likely it was a recognition that to predestine should entail God's action rather than his mere permission. Certainly when in 429 Augustine offered a carefully worded definition of predestination (*On the Gift of Perseverance* 14.35), it is in a positive sense as "the foreknowing and preparation of the blessings of God by which those who are freed are most certainly freed". That rules out any "double predestination" of a type whereby God has "before the creation of the world" selected those he will redeem and those whom he has actively destined for hell. Indeed, such a reading even of the *Enchiridion* is ruled out by a repetition in that treatise of the distinction (already made in *Tractate* 53 on the Gospel of John) between God's active and permissive will *(faciendo/sinendo*, 24.95).

However, believers in some version of double predestination are not so easily to be denied. In his account of God, they might argue, Augustine is still in fact committed to a thesis which, while not technically "double predestination", entails consequences not so different from those of the advocates of double predestination in a strict sense. Yet such an argument against Augustine's God was not quite that which Julian and other "Pelagians" presented, and which I shall shortly consider: Julian's charge is that Augustine makes God a punisher of the innocent, while the argument that Augustine needs to face more generally – since he rejects Julian's view that some people are in fact innocent – is that he makes God, in redeeming some, act with a merely merciless, irrational and arbitrary favouritism. In fact, as we shall see, Augustine is prepared to give a very similar reply to the charge of Julian and to the wider challenge; thus in uncovering the rationale of his reply to Julian we are at least beginning to evaluate his more comprehensive position.

Augustine's *Letter* 190 to Optatus, which I have just examined, fell into the hands of a young,[28] self-confident but confused ex-Donatist

---

[26] Notice parallel extreme language at the same period. Thus in 421 Julian is told to speak of a "slave will" (*servo arbitrio*, *CJul.* 2.8.23) and in the *Encheiridion* (9.30) we read that *liberum arbitrium* is lost – where Augustine unusually seems to confuse *liberum arbitrium* with *libertas*. For further comment see Rist, *Augustine* 272, note 43.

[27] Notice the distinction between foreknowledge and predestination at (e.g.) *AnOr.* 3.10.13.

[28] Ibid. 2.3.18; 4.1.1; 4.11.16. As later with Julian, Augustine makes much play of Vincentius' youth and immaturity.

layman, Vincentius Victor, whom it incensed for reasons not entirely dissimilar to those soon to be urged by Julian. Victor seems to have regarded himself as a "new theologian" in respect to arguments about the origin of the soul. An African, he accepted the doctrine of original sin (*On the Soul and Its Origin* 1.11.13; 2.11.15), but rebelled against the dominant local tradition that the soul (which he held to be material[29]) is transmitted through sexual generation: that seemed to attribute excessive guilt to infants. God, Victor insisted, is not unjust; infants, with souls newly created without personal sin but incurring original sin through the contact of their souls with infected bodies, could be pardoned by God even if not baptized.[30]

Augustine had little difficulty in pointing out the problems with Victor's view that the guilt of original sin is "caught" by the soul from the body (1.6.6; 1.6.7). He insists that it is the soul that sins and involves the body in sin. Nor do we need to linger over his objections to Victor's acceptance of the "crazy" theory of Tertullian that the soul itself is material (2.5.9). More immediately important is his reaction to Victor's view that original sin can be pardoned without benefit of baptism – which Victor regards as an essential step on the road to Christian perfection for those not dying in infancy.

The Pelagian compromise, condemned by Canon 3 of the Council of Carthage (AD 418), was that, although infants dying before baptism could enter paradise, they are excluded from the kingdom of heaven. Victor wanted no such distinctions: such infants are pardoned by a merciful God – a view more like that of the modern *Catechism*: Augustine in his turn was incensed. Since such infants are sinful, and since only baptism (or martyrdom) can wash away their guilt, they are beyond redemption. Augustine constantly appeals to Scripture, especially to John 3.5: "Unless someone is born from water and the Holy Spirit, he cannot enter the kingdom of God." And he is unambiguous: "Heaven forbid that I should say that even without baptism original sins are removed and that the kingdom of heaven is in the end given even to the unbaptized" (4.11.16).[31]

Augustine thinks of circumcision as a "sacrament" for Jews analogous to baptism and tells those impressed by Victor's arguments that, just as it would have been vain for the Maccabees to pray for the dead if they were not circumcised (so 2 Maccabees 12:43), so, "If you want to be a Catholic", you

---

[29] Ibid. 1.5.5; 1.6.6; 4.12.18. Victor does not, however, follow Tertullian in also making God a body.
[30] Cf. ibid. 1.11.13.   [31] Cf. 2.11.15; 2.15.21.

will maintain that sacrifice cannot be offered for the dead if they are unbaptized.[32]

Vincentius Victor had appealed to Luke's Gospel (23:43), where Christ tells the penitent "thief", "To-day you will be with me in paradise": a text on which Augustine had reflected before. In his work *On Baptism* (4.22.29: *c*. 405), perhaps at a more generous stage of his career, he says that Christ's words refer to the "thief" in that, though not baptized, he had experienced in his "martyrdom" a heartfelt conversion (*fidem conversionemque cordis*). But now, considering the claims of Victor, he hesitates even more (1.9.11; 2.10.14 and 16; 3.9.12): perhaps the "thief" was baptized by water from Christ's side; perhaps he had been baptized in prison, or even before, perhaps even before a later but now repented reversion to crime.[33] Augustine seems particularly concerned, whereas Cyprian had not been (*Letter* 73.22), with the thief's not being condemned to death for being a Christian, but becoming a Christian in the course of his death. We do not know the whole story, Augustine concludes; thereby demonstrating how inconceivable he found it that without baptism or explicitly Christian martyrdom (1.9.10) anyone could attain salvation. Vincentius Victor was evidently convinced, for we read in the *Reconsiderations* (2.56.83) that he withdrew his objection.

It has been suggested that earlier in his life and facing different problems, Augustine had been slightly less rigorist. In 402, he wrote *Letter* 102 to Deogratias, answering various questions posed by pagans about Christianity. With reference to the question why God had waited so long before sending the Redeemer and had apparently shown no interest in earlier generations, Augustine noted that the holy men among the Jews from the time of Abraham have been saved, and that this would include even earlier figures (such as Noah) who in some sense kept the commandments, perhaps in

---

[32] 2.12.17; cf. 1.11.13; 4.24.38. Analogously, newborn and hence uncircumcised Jewish boys are beyond the salvational pale till circumcision (*OpImp.* 2.73).

One cannot but wonder what Augustine would have said about Jewish women, who would presumably have been regarded as of the same "tribe" as their circumcised men and might also be recognized as Jewish by their various customs: such as by the *mikvah* and their observance of dietary regulations, perhaps also considered by Augustine as sacramental acts.

The question of how one might have recognized members of the "other half of the population" (or even males outside the baths and gymnasia) as Jewish is raised by L. A. Unterseher, "The Mark of Cain and the Jews: Augustine's Theology of Jews", *AS* 33 (2002) 99–121 at 118. Unterseher cites S. J. D. Cohen, "'Those who say they are Jews and are not': How do you know a Jew in antiquity when you see one?", in S. J. D. Cohen and E. S. Frerichs (eds.), *Diasporas in Antiquity* (Atlanta 1993) 1–45.

[33] Augustine restates his doubts at *Retr.* 2.18. Interestingly in this case he never considers the "sacrament" of circumcision (which the thief had presumably undergone) to be adequate.

virtue of a sacrament in effect before circumcision, as he will later tell Julian (*Against Julian* 5.11.45).

That appears to limit the saved before the time of Christ to Old Testament figures (normally those who had received the "sacrament" of circumcision) and gives no warrant for the belief that Augustine (like Justin Martyr who thought that Socrates and other sages who followed the Logos could be described as Christians (*First Apology* 46.1–3)) held that the saved, even before Christ, might include a wider spectrum of men of good will, let alone that it supports the assertion that contemporary theologians know "that Augustine affirms that believers other than Christians and Jews have been saved".[34] The most that can be drawn from *Letter* 102 – a letter itself, as we shall see, that will be significantly corrected – is that if there are pagans who are saved, it is through Christ. But there is little reason to think that Augustine believed that possibility to have been realized.[35]

In his *Reconsiderations* (2.31) Augustine returned to his reply to Deogratias, blaming his earlier self for saying that some were worthy of salvation, thus explaining again that no worth but only God's hidden judgment counts in this regard. The effect of that comment is to emphasize that even among those who lived before Christ no merit, only circumcision or a special dispensation, could be salvific. In one of the sermons recently discovered by Dolbeau, however, some have seen evidence of such a dispensation. For in *Sermon* 26.36 (of AD 404, thus not too far in date from *Letter* 102) Augustine says that, although most of the pre-Christian philosophers were guilty of pride and the worship of idols, Pythagoras and others may have been innocent on both counts – there is a sense in which Pythagoras' humility is particularly significant (26.38), as we shall see – and so may have received a special revelation: "Perhaps the Saviour, without whom no-one can be saved, revealed himself to them in some way or another."[36]

---

[34] R. Dodaro, "The Secret Justice of God and the Gift of Humility", *AS* 34 (2003) 83–96, at 84.

[35] J. Tch'ang Tche Wang, *Saint Augustin et les virtus des paiens* (Paris 1938) implies that Augustine's view is to be read "generously": it is likely that pagans were (and are) in fact saved. Despite an interesting new piece of evidence (see below), I find no need to modify my view that this is anachronistic wishful thinking (Rist, *Augustine* 172, note 32). It may be good theology, but it is bad historical interpretation. For the period *after* Christ – in view of Augustine's frequently expressed emphasis on the absolute necessity of baptism or holy martyrdom – it is out of the question. There may have been a problem about unbaptized infants in the mind of a few Christians in antiquity, but the general consensus was with Augustine: few human beings are saved – not least because few meet the minimum requirement: that is, of being baptized members of the Church. For Old Testament figures see for example *Perflust.* 19.42; *Ench.* 31.118.

[36] See Brown, *Augustine of Hippo* 458; Dodaro, "Secret Justice"; A. Solignac, "Le salut des paiens d'après la prédication de saint Augustin", in G. Madec (ed.), *Augustin prédicateur (395–411)* (Paris 1998) 419–428.

This is the best evidence in Augustine for the possible salvation of pagans (at least for a few before the time of Christ),[37] and the text looks as though Augustine was prepared to take the matter seriously. But note its date, before the Pelagian controversy. After 411 it seems highly unlikely that Augustine would have thought even Pythagoras free of original sin. As we have seen, he was not prepared fully to commit himself that far even in the case of Mary, nor the patriarchs of the Old Testament,[38] and he held that the followers of both Plato and Pythagoras displayed inauthentic virtues (*Against Julian* 4.3.17). *Letter* 102, indeed, shows that Augustine was capable in a moment of inattention of forgetting the full import of his reply to Simplicianus on Paul's letter to the Romans,[39] and in the Dolbeau *Sermon* 26.38 he allows himself to speak of those "worthy" (presumably because of their humility) of a special revelation. At least after the Pelagian War had begun, such language could only refer to the presumption that our "nature" has a certain residual goodness (*Against Julian* 4.3.16),[40] though not, as we shall see, enough for salvation. I conclude that even if Dolbeau *Sermon* 26 shows that Augustine was at times prepared to allow for the possible salvation of a few pre-Christian pagans – though he speaks only of revelation to them, not of salvation – he soon abandoned that possibility, for what must have seemed excellent reasons.

---

[37] Solignac ("Le salut des paiens" 420–425) sees similar evidence in Serm.Dolbeau 25 and a few other texts. None of them is plausibly interpreted in a more "generous" sense, with the possible exception of *Sermons* 202 and 374 [= Dolbeau 23] on the "humble" Magi. But these can hardly be regarded as treating typical examples of the humble unbaptized and do not justify Solignac's cheerfully unhistorical conclusion that Augustine has generously modified ancient readings of *Extra ecclesiam nulla salus* (p. 428). If anything the reverse is the case, as I observed in the Introduction.

[38] Hunter observes that, especially when reflecting on his mature theory of grace during his anti-Pelagian period, Augustine insists that the patriarchs and even Abraham suffered from sexual concupiscence, though, thanks to his "faith in the future humility of Christ revealed to him through the Spirit" (that is, by the *sacramentum* of the Son of God: cf. *CatRud.* 19.33), he was able to overcome it and thus (like other Old Testament "adulterers" and "polygamists") to have sex only for procreative purposes (cf. D. G. Hunter, "Reclaiming Biblical Morality: Sex and Salvation History in Augustine's Treatment of the Hebrew Saints", in P. Blowers et al. (eds.), *In Domenico Eloquio* (FS Wilken) (Grand Rapids 2002) 317–335).

[39] Speaking of the conversion of Cornelius at *Ad Simp.* 1.2.2, Augustine notes that a man receives grace from the moment he begins to believe in God, but that does not entail that he is yet saved. Cornelius, of course, was later baptized. And Augustine continues by saying that the fullness and evidentness of the infusion of grace depends on sacramental rites. So Cornelius himself could not be saved until he participated in the sacraments: that is, at the least, until he was baptized. Augustine follows up his comments on Cornelius with a reference to John 3:5: an anticipation of the use of John in reply to Vincentius Victor and others.

[40] *Qua . . . imago dei est, meretur hanc gratiam.* Very occasionally Augustine suggests that after the Fall the image is lost, but this is certainly hyperbole, not his considered position. His normal view is that *extrema vestigia* remain; cf Rist, *Augustine* 272, note 43; G. Bonner, "Augustine's Doctrine of Man: Image of God and Sinner", *Augustinianum* 24 (1984) 495–514, esp. 504–505.

In all his anti-Pelagian writings Augustine only twice cites Romans 2.14–15, where – to the delight of later commentators – Paul speaks of the Gentiles having the natural law inscribed on their hearts. Pelagius had appealed to it,[41] apparently talking about a "natural sanctity" and the "integrity of our nature", and Julian followed him. Though earlier less dismissive, Augustine was now concerned to explain the text away, offering two alternatives: either the Gentiles who had the law inscribed on their hearts are converts to Christianity (*Spirit and Letter* 26.43–27.48; *Against Julian* 4.3.23–25) or Paul refers to the spark of goodness which remains in the fallen human image of God and allows us to do some good too feeble to merit salvation, but ensuring less punishment. How different from Abraham, who was imbued with faith in the Incarnation (*Grace and Original Sin* 2.26.30)!

In this same context we must set Augustine's view – to which I have already alluded – that pagan "virtues" are not strictly virtues, though they may be better than plain vices. Augustine tells Julian (*Against Julian* 4.3.21), as he had told Pelagius (*Spirit and Letter* 27.48), that we should judge not acts but their motivation. Unless an act is done *explicitly* for love of God, it is not virtuous: the courage of Regulus indeed seems heroic (*Against Julian* 4.3.17; *City of God* 1.15), and as with other pagan behaviour may have a certain uprightness of its own (*Letter* 138.3.17), but Regulus is far from grace (*Letter* 125.3) and being without faith inevitably lacks humility (*Against Julian* 4.3.17). The "virtues" of pagans are vices *rather* than virtues (*City of God* 19.25; *Against Julian* 4.3.18), though in looking like their true counterparts (*Against Julian* 4.3.20) they may exhibit a certain "human love" (*Sermon* 349). The chastity of pagan spouses, however (as the courage of Donatist "martyrs") is significantly a sham (*Marriage and Concupiscence* 1.3.4; *Against Julian* 4.3.4–23).[42] In all this we must allow for Augustine's ultimately untenable and unnecessary view – which I shall soon consider in detail – that God's justice is wholly incomprehensible. We should also recognize that, insofar as Augustine's view of the destiny of pagans has been superseded, his theory of baptism has also required and received development. It thus represents not the future of Catholic culture but what that culture has been offered and rejected.

---

[41] *Ad Dem.* 5; *Comm. Rom.* (*PL* 30; p. 73 De Bruyn).

[42] In such attitudes we can recognize a Christianization both of the Platonic distinction between knowledge and "true opinion" ("fine" behaviour based on true opinion is specious and will not be maintained under pressure) and of the Stoic idea that only the sage is virtuous while the rest (though some are "progressing" towards virtue more than others) are wholly vicious (though unequally guilty; cf. *CJul.* 4.3.25 on *numeri*).

2.4 JULIAN: MARRIAGE, MANI AND ARISTOTLE

Pelagius and Caelestius were condemned in Rome in 418, their theories of human nature demolished in Augustine's *Nature and Grace*, their insistence that obedience to strict and specifiable laws of morality could form the basis of a perfect Christian life long since dismissed in *Spirit and Letter* (412) as little more than a revised version of the pharisaism condemned by Paul. It might have seemed as though the "new heretics" were finished. That this was far from the case was due almost entirely to the efforts of Bishop Julian of Eclanum, who first began to write in 419, shortly after the condemnation of his friend Caelestius.

Julian's strength lay in an appeal to the first principles of philosophical theology, principles not invoked now for the first time in the "Pelagian" controversy, and present also to the mind of non-Pelagians such as Vincentius Victor. These principles underlay the original claims of Pelagius about the nature of man, as well as the difficulties about baptism and original sin, though Julian denied the latter and claimed he had a more traditional understanding of the former. Nor did they immediately involve predestination, though, as Augustine knew, they were far from irrelevant to disputes about the implications of predestination which were soon to trouble Catholic monks with no wish to be lumped together with Pelagius.[43]

Julian's most serious appeal to his readers past and present is that they consider before all the nature and power of God, of the *Deus Christianorum* (*Incomplete Work* 5.64), but, unlike Pelagius himself, he determined to go on the offensive, focussing on what he hoped would be a particularly damaging accusation, namely that Augustine remained a closet Manichaean whose heresy was recognizable in his view that marriage is essentially diabolical. Among Julian's contemporaries such a charge could not be made to stick, and though Julian has had greater success with less well-informed generations, Augustine had little difficulty in showing that, although both he and the Manichaeans were concerned with the problem of evil – as all theists should be – their respective solutions in general and in particular their views of marriage were quite distinct.

In dealing with marriage and related questions, Julian ignored many very precise details of Augustine's argument while failing to attack the genuine weaknesses of his opponent's position: not least Augustine's inadequate

---

[43] It is worth observing – with an eye to the Reformation – that extreme doctrines of predestination have always implied (or seemed to imply) hostility to monasticism.

account of pleasure, his explanation of the goodness of sexual intercourse solely in terms of the continuance of the human race, and his consequent inability to relate genital activity to the development of marital trust and affection. On such subjects Julian shared many of Augustine's cultural prejudices, while he underestimated the "Carthaginian's" gift for psychological observation. That latter failing might be explained by what some have seen as his "Aristotelian" and value-neutral approach to sexual phenomenology and to human nature more generally.

Needing biblical examples to back up his account of fallen sexuality, Augustine drew Julian's attention to the behaviour of Potiphar's wife, for Julian denied female *libido*, though not female pleasure, and had scant idea of the significance of erogenous zones of the body,[44] let alone of the erotic more generally.[45] The first of these mistakes may be little more than characteristic Roman prejudice: since *libido* is not required for conception, decent *matronae* do not need it; for them duty is enough – as Julian could have learned fron Lucretius – and carries a pleasurable reward.

Julian's wider philistinism and reductionism about sexuality are probably to be connected with his claim that sexual arousal in males is in itself morally neutral. But the significance of eroticism is that sexual desire and activity are never morally (or spiritually) neutral. Julian considered *libido* a simple bodily reflex and marriage a mere union of bodies (*Against Julian* 5.16.62). Not least perhaps because of such beliefs, and despite his attack on Augustine's view of original sin, Julian failed to challenge the shaky assumptions on which Augustine's account of marriage (as of the origin of the soul) depends: assumptions connected with his failure (noted in the previous chapter and characteristic of Christian antiquity generally) adequately to explain the ontological relationship between soul and body.

Instead of opposing such serious lacunae in his opponent's position, Julian gave way to journalistic impulse and the attraction of a sexy charge of Manichaeism, with which he might hope to win an easy victory. He thus lost the chance of securing a theoretical triumph which might seem to have been within his grasp.

But was such an opportunity in fact available to him? If he was the Aristotelian he is often said to have been, the answer must be Yes. Certainly Augustine regularly accuses him of Aristotelianism and of appealing to a

---

[44] See P. Brown, "Sexuality and Society in the Fifth Century A.D.: Augustine and Julian of Eclanum", in E. Gabba (ed.), *Tria corda: Scritti in onore di Arnaldo Momigliano* (Como 1983) 49–70, esp. 56.

[45] P. Fredriksen, "Beyond the Body/Soul Dichotomy: Augustine on Paul against the Manichees and the Pelagians", *REA* 23 (1988) 87–114, at 112.

"Council of Aristotelians" (*Against Julian* 2.10.36), though to judge by the efforts of Basil, Gregory of Nyssa and Eunomius (not to speak of Julian himself) that was a standard ploy in the ecclesiastical polemics of the day, marked by the anti-intellectualism to which religious belief is often tempted.

For all the efforts of modern scholars to demonstrate the contrary,[46] Julian's direct acquaintance with Aristotle, like Augustine's, was probably limited to the *Categories* (read with Porphyry's *Introduction*).[47] There is little "Aristotelian" material in Julian that cannot be found either in the *Categories* or in the philosophical writings of Cicero, particularly the *Tusculan Disputations* (known also to Augustine), or in gynaecological treatises with which Augustine again shares a certain familiarity, in part via Tertullian. The Latin background-reading of Julian and Augustine was probably rather similar (though Julian knew more Greek), as one would expect of those who had benefited from a traditional education: above all they knew Virgil and Cicero.[48]

The "Pelagians" had always appealed to what might seem at first sight to be an Aristotelian view of human nature, especially human sexual nature: the view that one can give value-free descriptions of human nature whereby such controverted phenomena as arousal can be "scientifically" presented. But had Julian (or indeed Pelagius) had any serious understanding of Aristotelian physics, of which biology is a part, he would have known that for Aristotle bodily sexual differences are reflected in differences in the male and female psyche: indeed that the weakness in female deliberative power is directly related to her physiological inferiority. But Julian knows nothing of

---

[46] Julian's Aristotelianism has been widely accepted since F. Refoulé, "Julien d'Eclane, théologien et philosophe", *RSR* 52 (1964) 42–84, 233–247, though usually in the more restrained version proposed by F.-J. Thonnard, "L'aristotélisme de Julien d'Eclane et saint Augustin", *REA* 12 (1965) 296–304. Among those who accept it are Brown, *Augustine of Hippo* 389; N. Cipriani, "Echi antiapollinaristici e aristotelismo nella polemica di Giuliano d'Eclano, *Augustinianum* 21 (1981) 373–389 (Cipriani seeks its source in Theodore of Mopsuestia, with whom Julian spent time in exile); Teske, "St Augustine on the Humanity of Christ" 271.

[47] For the *Isagoge* see *OpImp.* 5.24; for the *Categories* (where both parties claim knowledge) *OpImp.* 2.51; *CJul.* 1.4.12; cf. 2.10.34; 3.7.14; for Julian's (un-Christian) teachers being Aristotle and Chrysippus, *OpImp.* 5.23. Julian refers to Augustine (sarcastically) as the "Aristotle of the Carthaginians" (*OpImp.* 3.199).

[48] Julian quotes Virgil's *Georgics* at *OpImp.* 4.38 and 5.11 (cf. *CJul.* 2.6.20; 6.5.12), the *Aeneid* at 2.99 and 6.15, the *Eclogues* at 4.116, Terence at 4.87, Plautus at 6.17 and 21, Lucan at *CJul.* 5.9.40, Juvenal, *Satires* 1.5 and 1.19 at *OpImp.* 6.29; for Horace see *CJul.* 4.3.17. Among prose writers he also cites Nepos (on Crates and Hipparchia) at 4.43, and Cicero, *DeOff.* at *OpImp.* 1.78 and 4.43 (cf. *CJul.* 2.10.36), *DeFin.* at 1.64, *DispTusc.* at 1.64, 2.5 and 4.45, *InCat.* at 1.22. Some of this learning may be mediated through Lactantius: so for *DispTusc.* 4.45 cf. *InstDiv.* 3.7. In the latter books of *CJul.* where Augustine notes Julian's liking to quote "secular authors", Cicero's works, especially the *Hortensius* (at 5.7.29; 5.10.42), are frequently cited (*ParaSt.* at 3.2.8; *De Nat. Deorum* at 4.12.58; *DeRep.* at 4.12.61).

this; his sources for value-free descriptions of human sexuality are not Aristotle but medical writers like Soranus (also named by Augustine at *Reconsiderations* 2.62.68) who provide him with the physiological accounts of sexual phenomena on which he relies and which Augustine knows to be "morally" incomplete.

Apparently unlike Augustine, whom he mocks as a "newfangled scientist" (*Incomplete Work* 5.11), Julian holds to a two-seed theory of human reproduction which is not Aristotelian.[49] He thinks that at the moment of conception male and female seeds are "pleasurably mingled" in a woman's womb (*utriusque sexus semina in muliebri utero cum voluptate misceantur*) (*Marriage and Concupiscence* 2.13.26; *Incomplete Work* 5.11).[50] Augustine declines to comment on the details of female experience, but casually accepts Julian's general thesis about conception. That was a mistake, because part of his reply to Julian about the "non-natural" – indeed indecent because disobedient – aspects of erection and ejaculation depends on the claim that the male (and sole) seed, if it alone transmits original sin, as it must, contains or is somehow accompanied by a human soul. That too is un-Aristotelian, though remaining nearer to Aristotle than does the two-seed theory of Julian. It is more Aristotelian, however, not because Augustine knows Aristotle's *Generation of Animals* but, as we have seen, because such ideas were commonly to be found in medical textbooks.

Augustine might have raised with Julian the dilemma that he had already laid before Optatus (*Letter* 190.4.15): in cases when ejaculation does not lead to conception, what happens to the soul? Does it instantly return to the male? Or does it perish, thus showing itself to be material and not immortal? But such an approach, whether or not persuasive with Optatus, does not touch Julian's "creationism" at the physiological level. Fore-armed with a two-seed theory, Julian can reject any such options: God only creates the new soul when conception actually takes place. If Julian had accepted

---

[49] For Julian also *OpImp.* 2.41; 2.138; *DNC* 2.13.26; for Augustine, *OpImp.* 2.5; 6.22.

[50] Perhaps in virtue of the two-seed theory Julian claimed to have shown in his *Ad Turbantium* that if there were original sin, Christ would have contracted it from the flesh of Mary (*OpImp.* 4.51). Certainly his denial of original sin is connected with his denial of female *libido*, for on his view Mary was not only not afflicted by original sin, but like women generally did not experience that *libido* which original sin was in part intended to explain. For his part Augustine denied that original sin was caught from the flesh, holding that it is located in the mentality of the act. As with material diseases such as gout, however, demons might be involved, perhaps damaging the seeds (*OpImp.* 2.177; 4.75; cf. *CJul.* 6.9.24); or the effects of the ancient sin might be understood by analogy with those caused in a woman told by her husband "Dionysius" to look at a picture of a handsome man during intercourse: that would improve her chances of conceiving a handsome child (*CJul.* 5.14.51). (At *Retr.* 2.62.88 Augustine notes that Soranus is the source of this information and that the husband was in fact a king of Cyprus.)

original sin, he might still have wanted to say that it is transmitted through the union of bodies (which Augustine would correct to avoid the materialism); that aside, Augustine fails to recognize that his opponent's account of conception disposes of some at least of the problems about the soul's origin that a one-seed theory incurs. Nonetheless, it is not Aristotelian, which leaves us better able to understand why Julian fails to come to grips with the weaknesses of Augustine's more general account of the relationship between soul and body, by suggesting that he lacked the conceptual resources to do better.[51]

The most interesting claim made by those who want to see a wider Aristotelian influence on Julian is that it can be recognized in his attempt to distinguish between human nature and human will. This in turn is part of his attempt to show that Adam's evil will damaged his prospects, indeed condemned him to death, but could not affect human nature as such (whereas Augustine, holding that we are "in" Adam, believed that our nature as such has been damaged). Here Julian's case depends on an argument that being can be separated from (at least some of) the qualities that inhere in it, or, in more specific and Aristotelian terms, that our willed activities do not affect our essence. We are dealing, that is, with the relationship between what Aristotle's *Categories* treats as the essential or non-essential qualities of a (secondary) substance, in this case of human nature.

But Aristotle in the *Categories* distinguishes clearly between qualities and qualitative but impermanent states, like blushing. So the argument between Julian and Augustine at this point is whether the effects of Adam's sin on human nature are so serious that that nature is radically changed (and so can be described in terms of Aristotelian essential qualities rather than in terms of merely transitory or localized characteristics). That is why both Augustine and Julian have recourse to the *Categories* (and the *Introduction*). They allude to no other Aristotelian texts and would have had no need to do so even if they had been readily available.

---

[51] Pelagius, we recall, held that Mary, free from original sin, was able to live a sinless life. Augustine thinks that though theoretically inheriting the effects of original sin from the intercourse of her parents, she was permanently shielded from sin by God. Julian's two-seed theory might have given him the opportunity to explain both how the soul of each newly conceived being is a new creation, yet at the same time how its "genetic" components could pass on, from both parents, the effects of Adam's sin. But he had no wish to defend original sin, hence made no attempt to develop his ideas in that direction. Had he done so, however, he might ironically have offered Augustine a way to combine creationism about the soul with a "traducianist" account of original sin, without recourse to so difficult an idea as our "common life" in Adam. It remains doubtful, however, whether he would have found such "genetic" responsibility adequate for his theological purposes; which may indicate one reason why those purposes still need revision.

Aristotle, we conclude, has rather limited relevance to the dispute between Augustine and Julian; Julian could have little recourse to Aristotelianism in developing a critique of Augustine's account of human nature. Julian's clinical account of marriage and his inability to improve on Augustine's account of the relationship between body and soul, combined with his unwillingness to listen to Augustine's clear explanation of how his view of marriage differs radically from that of Mani, entailed that his attempt to show that Augustine's view of marriage is Manichaean was doomed. He is on more promising ground, however, when he turns from problems about human sexuality to wider and more enduring questions about the nature and actions of God – and he could have been on even firmer ground had he developed his arguments with more skill, less tunnel-vision and less rhetorical flourish before dismissing his opponent as "the boss of donkeys": *patronus asinorum* (*Incomplete Work* 4.46).

2.5 JULIAN'S OPTIONS AFTER 419

Though by 419 Julian had a number of potentially powerful lines of attack, in his time and place he was able to make only limited use of them. Nevertheless, to consider some of his theoretical options will help in understanding the gradual emergence of "Catholic" ideas as well as the dialectics of the ten-year theological debate that ensued.

2.5.1 Biology

If Julian could have developed his biological theories, it might have enabled him to argue more effectively that Augustine's theology of original sin entails only a flawed, not a guilty, humanity.

According to Augustine's one-seed biology, and assuming that creationism is ruled out, the soul (the bearer of moral sin and guilt) must be present in the newborn as a result of specifically male *concupiscentia*; thus the new soul must be complete in the father. For Julian that would be impossible; the soul, at least as a finished "product", must be created in or with the fusion of male and female seeds: which might seem to add yet another material aspect to its nature. Julian could have argued that the two-seed theory demands either that genetic flaws (but not the guilty "person") derive from both parents or (as he would have preferred) that creationism is more plausible. The latter option, however, would not have satisfied Augustine since the soul would still be a good creation of God which, if original sin is to be maintained, could only be infected by the body: an explanation which, as we have seen, he finds unacceptable. Which would leave anyone who subscribed to something more like Julian's two-seed theory as well as to a doctrine of original sin the option of the newborn person being flawed from his genetic inheritance on each side: we would have original sin in the sense of weakness but no guilt on the part of the new individual. Julian would thus be nearer the *Catechism*.

Julian's better biology allows that genetic flaws could be handed down but not that the soul itself existed in Adam. The corollary of that is that we might suffer from inherited weakness but not incur inherited guilt. As noted earlier in this chapter, the recent *Catechism* avoids the phrase "inherited guilt" and in speaking of original sin uses the conveniently imprecise phrase that we are "implicated" in Adam's sin since "the whole human race is in Adam". Hence Julian would be happy to read in the *Catechism* that "original sin does not have the character of a personal fault in any of Adam's descendants".

Although there is nothing in the *Catechism* that would give comfort to Julian in his denial of inherited weakness (and that would therefore help his "creationism"), he could derive a certain satisfaction from the fact that section 1261 (as we have seen) "allows us to hope that there is a way of salvation for children who have died without Baptism". He would also be happy to notice that, although the *Catechism* still speaks of original *sin*, the only actual sin involved is that of Adam (and Eve). To the rest of us the phrase "original sin" still applies, and we are still "implicated" in it, but the substance of the phrase – now referring not to an act but to a state – has become far less Augustinian.

As we have seen, this is not the only instance of the Church retaining traditional language but revising much of the content of the doctrine denoted. That, perhaps, is part of a broader problem: an unwillingness to acknowledge doctrinal *improvement* as a essential part of doctrinal development and reformulation. In the particular case of Julian's "biology" we may also recognize a primitive example of a now more obvious difficulty which will be treated later in the present study: how should theology (and the Catholic culture that ultimately depends on it) react – as it will eventually be compelled to react – to the challenge of new and rapidly advancing science? In our time it is much less easy than in that of Julian to sweep inadequacies of teaching brought to light by scientific investigation under the theological (or rhetorical) rug.

2.5.2 Baptism

I have connected some of my remarks on Julian's biology with ancient and modern views of baptism. Theoretically, Julian might have argued that major theological difficulties would be avoided if Augustine's view of the necessity of baptism were to be revised. Why then did he not move further in that direction? Because, for all his polemic against Augustine, he shared many of his rival's assumptions. Although Julian worried about the condemnation of "innocent" unbaptized infants, he accepted Augustine's view (as did most of his contemporaries) that many (or most) of humanity would fetch up in hell. Clearly there were many reasons for this pessimism, ranging from the purely theological (as in the apparent insistence in John's Gospel that baptism is necessary for salvation) to the empirical: most Christians (especially in the penal times but also later) supposed that most of their contemporaries lived wicked and died wicked; hence, as a matter of mere justice, they must be condemned.

Like Augustine himself, these contemporaries would have recognized that they could not read the human heart, and might be mistaken about apparently hell-bound individuals; yet, relying on the necessity of baptism (or martyrdom) for salvation, they could only conclude that, while there might be bad apples among the baptized, among the non-baptized there could be no good ones! This worried Julian in the case of apparently innocent children, but he worried no more than Augustine about unbaptized adults and clearly did not raise difficulties about this because, like Augustine, he assumed that God had good reasons to condemn the vast majority of the human race. Scripture told him that, as it had told Augustine; moreover, as a Pelagian who believed that the baptized are given sufficient aid in their birth and baptism to be saved – baptism opening up the other sacraments, especially the eucharist – he plausibly would be even harsher than Augustine on the baptized.

When Justin Martyr held Socrates to have been a *de facto* Christian, he was clearly little concerned that he had not been baptized. If we look back from the prospective of the modern Catholic Church, we can see that a misplaced literalness about biblical accounts of baptism provoked Augustine to error and prevented Julian from making the best use of his opportunity to point the error out! We should recognize, however, that the Pelagians generally allowed, as Augustine did not, that I Corinthians 7:14 at least *supports* the thesis that the children of baptized *Christians* do not need *infant* baptism for the forgiveness of past sins. Augustine never seriously responded to the challenge of that text.

2.5.3 God's justice

From science and baptism we pass to the fundamental issue underlying, as we have seen, the Pelagian quarrel from the beginning: the nature, acts and will of the Christian God. Julian could have argued that problems about God's justice arising from Augustine's attempt to defend the condemnation of infants are part of a wider difficulty that affects not simply infants but all who are condemned, thus linking his concerns with those of the Massilian monks who argued in effect that, given predestination, their choice of life was vain. (Augustine himself, in his letter to Sixtus, had recognized the connection between the wider and the narrower issue.)

Julian could also have associated problems about God's justice with difficulties about omnipotence, as did John Cassian, and issued the philosophical challenge that, if Augustine's account of God's justice is correct, we can have no notion of the nature of human justice, or at least of how it relates to its divine examplar.

Let us follow Augustine's argument about divine justice step by step. I start with a passage from his first reply to Julian (*Against Julian* 4.8.45, in Teske's translation):

If at this point you say to me, "Why then does he [God] not transform the wills of all who are unwilling" [*scil.* to reform], I shall answer, "Why does he not by the bath of rebirth adopt all who are going to die as infants, since as yet they have no will and hence no contrary will ... Why in the case of adults and in the case of children [does] God [will] to come to the aid of one and not to the aid of another. And yet we hold it as certain that there is no injustice in God by which he condemns anyone who has not deserved it ..."

Again: "In those he condemns he shows what all deserve so that those he sets free may learn from this the punishment they deserve ..." That is: from the condemnation of unbaptized infants we can infer that the same justice is to be recognized in the condemnation not only of all the unbaptized, but (the point is made elsewhere) at least normally of those who though baptized do not share the Lord's body and blood.[52] From seeing the fate of the condemned the rest can be grateful not to be suffering what they too deserve.[53]

Clearly this argument depends on the premiss that the unbaptized (in the case of pre-Christian Jews the uncircumcised) are condemned. If there is already a problem with that, it lies, as we have seen, in part with Augustine's account of baptism. Now Julian denies that those who die unbaptized as infants are condemned, but agrees with Augustine that those who are not baptized later in life (and partake of the eucharist) *are* condemned for their personal sins. In other words, Augustine and Julian agree that – infants

---

[52] Cf. *CJul.* 1.4.13; 3.1.4; 3.12.25, citing John 6.54. For baptism John 3.5 is normally cited.
[53] Cf. *Ad Simp.* 1.2.18; *CJul.* 5.4.14; *DPS* 8.16.

apart – the unbaptized are condemned. As we have seen, this is important, because it debars Julian from launching a full-scale attack on the apparent injustice of Augustine's God in not offering salvation to all.

Notice however that, despite Augustine's apparent movement towards double predestination in texts written between 414 and 423, he does not commit himself to that position in *Against Julian*, nor anywhere else in his replies to Julian, but on several occasions goes out of his way to emphasize the distinction made in the *Enchiridion* between God's active and permissive will. Denying Julian's claim that his God *deliberately* makes people sin, he concludes (*Against Julian* 5.3.8): "If it [the blindness of evildoers] is not the punishment of sin, it is surely an unjust punishment, and you make God either unjust since he commands or permits it, or weak since it is inflicted on the innocent without his turning it aside."[54]

It may be helpful to offer a rather more formal presentation of Augustine's argument, because he himself, in default of an appeal to God's inscrutable judgments, will sometimes be prepared to tell Julian merely that original sin "is not easily defended" (*Against Julian* 6.5.11). The difficulty lies not least in the "one in Adam" thesis itself.

Augustine's argument might be set up as follows:

1 Unbaptized infants may suffer horribly in this life.
2 A just God would not permit that unless they are guilty.
3 Since they have no personal sins, they must derive their sins and guilt from Adam.

However, as stated, the second premiss is tendentious, for Augustine regularly allows that the God of the Old Testament permits (even promotes) evils,[55] including the visiting of the sins of the fathers on the children,[56] and such personal ills as the sorrows of the women of Abimelech.[57] Augustine does not think that in these cases people are punished as guilty of *original* sin, but rather for the unoriginal sin of some other descendant of Adam. Hence the third move in the argument I have constructed for Augustine also is invalid.

What this conclusion shows is that I have set the argument up incorrectly. Augustine would introduce at least two further biblical premisses. The first is that we are baptized for the forgiveness of sins; he assumes that this is applied to all the baptized. Why? Because he assumes (e.g., at *Against*

---

[54] Cf. *CJul.* 5.3.10 (an *O Altitudo* passage).   [55] Note the case of Ahab at *CJul.* 5.3.13.
[56] Note the emphasis on the suffering for another's (personal) sin (*CJul.* 2.12.27; cf. 1.3.6; 6.26.83; *OpImp.* 1.48).
[57] *CJul.* 2.15.30; 3.19.37.

Julian 2.6.18) that John 3.5 entails that without baptism we are condemned. And we are justly condemned because we are (after all) all guilty; and in the case of infants that guilt can only have been incurred in Adam. To avoid this conclusion one would have to admit that Augustine's theory of baptism is incorrect or incomplete. But it would seem that objections to his defence of the workings of divine vengeance in the Old Testament can be discounted as irrelevant in the present case.

Let us then grant – *etsi non daretur* – that baptism (or its equivalent) is essential because all have sinned in Adam. The second difficulty, which, as we have seen, Augustine himself brings up, despite his comparative neglect of broader problems of predestination in debating with the Pelagians, is why some get the chance to be baptized while others, either because they are infants or because they have never heard of Christ, do not. I rule out double predestination in its Calvinist or Jansenist form as a genuinely Augustinian answer to this. His regular answer is that God declines to show mercy to most of us, thus leaving us justly condemned. And in reply to the objection that it is incomprehensible why some are offered grace – either grace should be offered to all or to none – Augustine regularly appeals to God's inscrutable wisdom and judgment.

The thinking here is that if God wanted to offer grace to all, he would have done so, and if such grace were offered in the appropriate gracious way (*congruenter*) it would be accepted, at least adequately for eventual perseverance.[58] Hence, notoriously, Augustine inferred that God did not want all men to be saved;[59] or perhaps thought that God *could not* want all men to be saved; for not to punish the wrongdoer is unjust,[60] and God is certainly not unjust.

As I have argued elsewhere, no small part of the difficulty is rooted in Augustine's account of omnipotence.[61] He will not allow the (logical) possibility that – in the interest of preserving a scintilla of the freedom[62] and worthiness of our original state as created in the image of God[63] – salvific

---

[58] N. Cipriani points out (in his splendidly accurate "*L'altro Agostino* di G. Lettieri", *REA* 48 (2002) 259) that even the saints are liable to sin, indeed do sin at least venially – which is still contrary to the active, though not to the permissive, will of God. In this limited respect Augustine does allow that God's will is thwarted, but that does not resolve the problem of cases where grace is not offered at all and mere justice is done to sinners.

[59] On Augustine's misuse of 1 Tim. 2:4 see *CJul.* 4.8.42, *DPS* 10.19, *OpImp.* 2.135–136, 147–148, 175, *Ep.* 217.6.19. Cf. Rist, *Augustine* 270 on *Ench.* 27.103 and elsewhere; cf. *DCG* 15.44; 22.1; *CD* 22.1.2.

[60] Cf. *DLA* 3.9.26; 3.15.44; *DNB* 9.20; *DeCont.* 6.15; *CD* 12.3.

[61] Rist, *Augustine* 269–278.

[62] I hesitate over the word "freedom", but the theme is important: if the original image were entirely destroyed and our "nature" wholly corrupted in Adam, we would have to be reborn *as different people*, not merely spiritually but ontologically, at baptism or at the very least (for the lucky ones) in heaven.

[63] For "worth" note again the striking passage at *CJul.* 4.3.16 (*Qua . . . imago dei est, meretur hanc gratiam*).

grace could eventually be rejected: that would be to deny God's omnipotence (*Reply to Simplicianus* 1.2.13). The price he pays for that is that, unless they are freed by grace so as to be able to persevere to the end, men are impotent puppets abiding God's tug on the strings.

There have been a number of attempts to alleviate Augustine's difficulties about justice and mercy. The most recent is a more theologically sophisticated revival of earlier versions.[64] According to Dodaro,[65] we are saved by the recognition of Christ's humility. That is true, but does not help Augustine's case, not least because to recognize such humility we have to know about Christ and submit to baptism (or if a Jew – at least in Old Testament times – to circumcision or its forerunner). Dodaro, modifying Solignac,[66] has to rely on faulty claims about a wider availability not merely of humility, salvation's *sine qua non*, but of salvation itself to pagans – which I have already discounted.

An apparently more promising recent attempt to defend Augustine has been made by Rigby,[67] who tries to put a more positive spin on Studer's view that we cannot expect to understand how the determinations of God are just:[68] they are beyond human capacity. There is logical power in this suggestion: certainly there is no reason to assume that everything intelligible is intelligible to the human mind. Rigby points out that God's wisdom mediates between his justice and his mercy, and he is right that, when Augustine uses the Pauline invocation *O Altitudo* to silence those who challenge his version of God's justice, his appeal is not merely to a hidden equity of God that cannot be measured by human standards (*Reply to Simplicianus* 1.2.16) but to God's hidden wisdom.

---

[64] Cf. D. J. McQueen, "Augustine on Freewill and Predestination: A Critique of J. M. Rist", *Museum: West African Journal of Theology* (1974) 17–28. Like Dodaro, McQueen introduces humility as the way out of Augustine's difficulties, but humility is itself a gift of God, so we are no further on. In replying to McQueen (*Augustine* 133, note 109), however, I gave too restricted an account of Augustine's humility, understanding it largely at an ontological level, inadequately as a recognition of sinfulness. I wrote (misleadingly) that the kind of humility that is "the mere recognition of our moral inadequacy" might have helped Augustine forward. Dodaro [see note 34 above and in more detail in his *Christ and the Just Society in the Thought of Augustine* (Cambridge 2004)] explains how Augustine's concept of humility does indeed have such moral aspects, but my objection to his position on salvation still remains. Humility, of whatever sort, is a gift of God, not least since, as Dodaro shows, it is tied to Augustine's view that we need a specific recognition of the humility of *Christ* as (but only as) the *sine qua non* of further progress. For further comment on Dodaro see below.

[65] Dodaro, "The Secret Justice of God" 83–96.   [66] Solignac, "Le salut des paiens".

[67] P. Rigby, "The Role of God's 'Inscrutable Judgments' in Augustine's Doctrine of Predestination", *AS* 33 (2002) 213–222.

[68] B. Studer, *The Grace of Christ and the Grace of God in Augustine of Hippo: Christocentrism or Theocentrism?* (Collegeville 1997) 102.

But very serious objections have been made to moves of this sort, and in specifically Augustinian terms;[69] I have already alluded to them. For although there may be a logically legitimate appeal to man's mental inadequacy, Augustine is not entitled to avail himself of it. As a Platonist he holds that human justice is operated and recognized as participation in divine justice.[70] If the judgments of God are inscrutable, it must be that we have no reliable understanding of justice at all – and so all human relations are undermined.[71] Rigby is probably right that Augustine saw God's wisdom as the mediation between his justice and his mercy, but appears not to recognize that such mediation could only save divine justice (and divine mercy) at the price of rendering human justice and mercy unsupported if not unintelligible.

Thonnard's earlier paper had offered an argument not dissimilar to Rigby's. Thonnard admits that Augustine says repeatedly that God forbids us to do what he does himself: not least in punishing the children for the sins of their parents (*Incomplete Work* 3.12; 3.15; 3.244.128). Clearly this is partly driven by Augustine's desire to defend all acts supposed by Old Testament writers to have been ordered by God – which include genocide in the case of the Canaanites – but he also claims that, since only God understands the human heart, he can properly forbid us to act where we do not properly understand the facts of the case. Although Thonnard wants to leave Augustine with some kind of account by analogy of the relationship between God's justice and ours, he is effectively reduced to saying that we must do what we are told when God gives us directions about living justly. That is to give up on an explanation of justice and makes Thonnard's talk of participation meaningless. He is in effect left with the one option – which he will not admit – to attribute a simple divine-command ethic to Augustine. In support of such an attribution might be the fact that in his anti-Pelagian writings Augustine evades the "natural law" text of Romans 2:14–15. But Augustine's continuing Platonism (recognized by Thonnard)

---

[69] As, for example, by K. Flasch, *Die Logik des Schreckens: Augustinus von Hippo, Die Gnadenlehre von 397* (Mainz 1990) 65–71. Studer too is worried that justice and human freedom might wholly disappear from view if God's will really is irresistible and absolute or if (more precisely) when we receive grace our will can irresistibly attain its goal.

[70] F. J. Thonnard ("Justice de Dieu et justice humaine selon saint Augustin", *Augustinus* 12 (1967) 387–402) is one of the few who have tried to explain how human justice can be related to divine justice as Augustine understands it. For participation he cites *Ep.* 120.4.19.

[71] For the idea that when our soul ascends it can recognize justice and wisdom see *IoEv.* 19.5.12. Augustine's position on inscrutable judgments would seem to entail that only the saved could do this (which he apparently would not wish to profess) or, if others can, that they see justice but not divine justice. But he never seems to want such a distinction, and reasonably so, since it leaves us all with no notion at all of what justice is!

cannot be squared with a radical divine-command ethic;[72] so the difficulty remains.

The problem with Augustine's account of the withholding of God's mercy from unbaptized infants and most others apart from (some) baptized Christians is not so much that it is inscrutable, but that it seems morally offensive and irrational. That is exactly how Julian saw it in the case of infants; according to him Augustine's God behaves like a criminal.[73] This is clearly not what Augustine intended, so what (problems about baptism apart) has gone wrong? Both Julian and Augustine recognize that the dispute turns on God's omnipotence (cf. *Incomplete Work* 1.49), in which, of course, both believe. Thus, despite Augustine's readiness to distinguish between God's active and permissive will, he remains troubled by the apparent truth that if God wanted all men to be saved, all men would be saved.

That, as we shall see, drives Augustine to strange readings of Scripture, yet also to the conclusion that since unbaptized infants (not to speak of others) cannot be saved, God cannot actively want them to be saved. Interestingly his contemporary John Cassian (before 426) took a very different view on a similar issue: "If God does not will that one of his little ones shall perish (Matthew 18:14), how can we imagine, without the greatest blasphemy, that he does not wish all men, but only some in place of all, to be saved? Therefore those who perish, whoever they may be, perish against his will."[74] Even if, as is widely believed, Cassian's remarks were aimed at Pelagius rather than Augustine, they show that such problems were very much in the air. Yet Augustine's victory over Julian tells us that the age was not yet prepared to see what Cassian's wiser advice entails not only for baptism but for an account of God's omnipotence, and beyond that of his justice. It is a thesis of the present book that theological advances are impossible until the ground has been properly prepared. In matters relating to the nature of omnipotence, that was certainly not the case in the early years of the fifth century.

Cassian and Augustine are agreed that God's will is not always achieved, but explain it differently. Cassian is prepared to allow that what God promotes can be thwarted by the vices of free agents; Augustine will not go so far. He is prepared to allow that, although God wished Adam to live a

---

[72] It is Augustine's maintenance of "participation" that saves him. An abandonment of participation in the interest of preserving God's transcendence must always lead to a divine-command ethics, if not also (as in Islam) to a rejection of the *imago Dei* – as it did in the later Middle Ages.

[73] Cf. *OpImp.* 1.49–50; 1.122; 3.2; 3.6, etc.   [74] *Conl.* 13.7.2 = *CSEL* 13, 369.13–16.

blessed life, Adam chose otherwise; he is prepared to allow that even the saints are liable to sin, indeed do sin, though God does not wish this. What he is not prepared to allow is that God's omnipotence is compatible with the choice of a man, predestined in grace for salvation, ultimately to refuse that salvation. Hence it follows that those who are to be saved are saved according to his omnipotent will and those who are not saved (though they cannot be acting "contrary" to his active will since that is impossible) must be let go because God does not "elect" to bring them to salvation.

Cassian's notion of God's omnipotence takes account of God's allowing his active will to be thwarted in the interest of preserving human free will and (in the case of infants and of those who could not know Christ) enables him to see an intelligible theory of God's justice. In this respect Cassian, relying on his instincts and on straightforward exegesis rather than analysis, is nearer to the *Catechism*, Julian comes in second and Augustine – prepared in this instance to drive apparent logic and particular scriptural texts rough-shod over others – a puzzled third. Had his account of omnipotence been better, he would have had less reason to mishandle Scripture. And his problems about omnipotence (at least in this sort of instance) were eventually to be clarified by Maximus the Confessor who, "formalizing" the approach of Cassian, distinguished between God's "antecedent" and "consequent" will (*Ambigua* 7, 1069A11–1102C4); John Damascene and Aquinas followed Maximus' lead.[75]

2.5.4 *Scriptural interpretation*

Julian could have pointed out that Augustine's accounts of our mutilated condition after the Fall (assuming there is a fall of the human race rather than just a fall of Adam) and of the predestinationism (including possibly double predestination) that follows from it depend on a misapplication of scriptural texts.

This is not the place to enter upon a full-scale discussion of Augustine's methods of exegesis, but from a modern point of view his approach suffers from at least two serious defects. In the first place, he – and many others of his time and in later centuries – have to defend all the acts attributed to God or to God's will in the Old Testament, regardless of whether they may in

---

[75] Cf. B. Daley, "Apocatastasis and the 'Honourable' Silence in the Eschatology of Maximus the Confessor", in T. Heinzer and C. Schönborn (eds.), *Maximus the Confessor* (Fribourg 1982) 309–333. For contemporary comment cf. T. J. White, "Von Balthasar and Journet on Grace and Freedom", *Nova et Vetera* 4 (2006) 633–665.

fact represent a historically determined but limited vision of God then current: hence, for example, the problems about the sacrifice of Isaac which seems to destroy confidence in the prohibition against killing the innocent.[76] In the second place he follows the common patristic path of relying too much on individual proof texts. On some occasions this does no harm, since his doctrine is fully worked out before he comes to rely on a particular text in reference to it.[77] On other occasions his "ideological" presuppositions may too readily be deployed in the selection of one or two biblical passages to the exclusion of some inconvenient others.

We have already noticed two striking examples of this: his latter-day neglect, despite the challenge of Pelagius, of the "natural law text" in Romans 2:14–15; and his notorious re-writing of 1 Timothy 2:4 on God's wish to save all mankind. Even more striking, and particularly relevant to the debate with Julian, is his treatment of Paul's epistle to the Romans almost entirely as a vehicle for his account of God's justice and mercy – not least those sections of the letter dealing with God's inscrutable judgments.

Augustine's dilemma, caused in no small part, as we have seen, by his account of omnipotence, is clear: he feels obliged to say that we simply cannot understand why God seems so inadequately merciful. Let us, however, look briefly at the *O Altitudo* passage in Romans itself. It is clear that Paul's purpose is very different from Augustine's, and does not license Augustine to use his text to evade difficulties about God's arbitrary mercilessness.

Paul's primary thesis is that, extraordinarily, God has not limited salvation to the Jews. Only the prophets realized that he would extend his mercy (3:21), and is far more generous than the history of Israel apparently might lead us to suppose. What is incomprehensible for Paul is God's generosity in offering salvation to the Gentiles. Perhaps, Augustine might claim, Paul would have gone further in explaining the terms of that generous offer in Augustinian fashion, but in fact, in speaking of Gentiles who have the natural law written in their hearts (2:11–16), he comes much nearer than does Augustine (and most other early Christians) to allowing the possibility of salvation for non-Christians.

But what about Paul's view of the Jews? The hearts of many of them are hardened; only a remnant are saved by grace (11.5). But God does not go back on his promises; eventually the Jews too will be saved. God has

---

[76] For comment see Rist, *Augustine* 296–297.
[77] An example is Augustine's use of a (faulty) translation of Romans 5:12. See Rist, *Augustine* 124, note 93.

imprisoned all men in disbelief in order that he may show mercy to them all (11.35): none too Augustinian a text!

It is immediately after this that Paul cries out *O Altitudo* in wonder at the wisdom of God's generosity. Augustine, however, cites it, against a background of his account of baptism and omnipotence, to explain God's *lack* – in human terms – of generosity and to protect God's justice (e.g., *Against Julian* 3.19.37): that is, to defend an account of divine justice that makes human justice unintelligible and must also raise severe problems for an understanding of humility and other human virtues.

Unfortunately, although the Pelagians did better on the natural law texts, Julian was unable to capitalize on Augustine's treatment of Romans as a whole. Indeed, if Augustine is to be believed (*Against Julian* 5.9.35), Julian's reading of *O Altitudo* could be more bizarre than his own. According to Augustine, *O Altitudo* was Julian's response to God's extraordinary wisdom in creating for purposes of procreation the *calor genitalis* – in Augustine's version the sexual lust – leading to the "natural" erection of men's sexual organs.

There is, however, a further defective feature of much of Augustine's argumentation which Julian failed to turn to his own advantage, not least because he himself is often guilty of the same mischievous mode of proceeding. Ancient debates, both philosophical and theological, are regularly driven by two ambitions: to get the right answer and to destroy the view – and the reputation – of an opponent. Unfortunately these objectives may be in conflict with one another, leading to the use of *ad hominem* procedures that win arguments at the expense of truth. Thus (for example) in his *De Fide* (40) Rufinus of Syria draws attention to Paul's apparent teaching in 1 Corinthians (7:14) that the children of baptized couples – indeed of couples only one member of which is baptized – are already holy. According to Rufinus this is an argument against the infant baptism of Christian children. Caelestius apparently used the same passage, but when Augustine got into the debate (as in *On the Deserts of Sinners* (2.25.41)), he evades the difficulty caused by the clear sense of the Pauline text and tries to distract the reader's attention by raising related, but ultimately irrelevant, issues.

2.6 AUGUSTINE VS JULIAN: CULTURAL EFFECTS
AND UNFINISHED BUSINESS

I have listed four opportunities theoretically available to Julian in his war with the "Carthaginians". They are interconnected, but Julian failed to see the connections (not to speak of his related failure to develop the individual themes). He sensed that Augustine's theology, Manichaean or not, needed some radical correction, but he could not put his finger firmly on what was required. It was problems in his own theology, not merely in that of Augustine, that caused the trouble, and when we recognize that, we realize the necessarily ongoing character of Christian thought: that even in the case of a theologian of Augustine's surpassing calibre, facing an able and persistent challenger, there are problems insoluble in their own times and terms, and indeed then only dimly identifiable. From Augustine's response to what Julian did and might have done, and from the successes and failures of that response, we recognize something of the slow construction, through trial and error over historical time, of an ever more coherent but always incomplete Christian world-view.

Augustine's treatment of divine justice and human weakness has left an enduring cultural legacy. He contributed with unflinching honesty to the debate about the limits of our capacity to achieve the good life and argued that such frailty can only be overcome by humility: that is, by an unambiguous recognition of our dependence as created moral – and constantly immoral – animals on our Creator. Yet with his mainly unavoidable mistakes about baptism, with his uncritical acceptance of biological stereotypes and understandable inability to question and transcend what seemed the scientific truths in his day, with his over-confident use of biblical data without sufficient respect for context, and finally with his inadequate logic of omnipotence, he pointed towards an arbitrary divine-command morality in which he did not believe and which Julian mercilessly exposed.

In their rightful insistence on the overwhelming ontological superiority of the Creator over his creatures, all the "Abrahamic" religions are open to the false conclusion that the arbitrary power of God is his supreme attribute. All are liable, in effect, to a divinized version of emperor-worship, to that pagan worship, to which I have several times alluded, of self-abasement before raw power. All have at times succumbed to that temptation. There can be no doubt that in Christianity an arbitrary divine absolutism is contrary to the basic doctrines of the *love* of God and his creation of man in his image and therefore in some sense as a free agent. Paul may be justified in using ontologically the image of the pots in the hand of the potter, but that image is not to be pressed so that we forget that God in his ("inscrutable" but "natural") wisdom has created us in his image, has made a covenant of love with us and does not forget his promises.

Augustine knew all this well and in much of his writing, perhaps especially in his comments on John's Gospel and Epistle, presents it with striking clarity. Yet in determining that he must find a solution to the problems of predestination and the justice of God, he can also become one-sided, as Julian (and implicitly Cassian) realized. As a result, it is a negative part of the legacy of Augustine (further "developed" by Calvinists and Jansenists) to have contributed, against his intention, to the fear and even loathing from which the cultural image of Christianity now suffers in the West.

It is not least his dominance as a theologian that has made Augustine in this respect a tragic (perhaps one might say an "Augustinian") figure. Theology, in a Christian context, is a dangerous business; mistakes can have catastrophic effects, yet it is humanly impossible to avoid making them. We can, however, learn from them. While we can with justice admire Augustine's unflinching analysis of human nature, we should not allow deference to prevent us from recognizing the largely unavoidable but often tragic limitations of genius. As theology should not be confused with the history of theology, nor should it be debased as hagiography. The story of Augustine's war with Julian and of its aftermath – especially over divine justice and mercy – is an example of how the theological limitations imposed by a particular age and a particular personality, for all their unavoidably disastrous consequences in the medium term, can be, need to be and are overcome over the succeeding centuries. That, in this "darkness of social life", is the nature of theological and hence cultural development in the Catholic Church.

The history of later Catholic thought, about the interpretation of Scripture, about the metaphysics of God's attributes, about the relationship between religion and science, and more broadly about the recognized need for a constant expansion of Catholic theology, shows how a ghetto of ignorance and of theocratic savagery tempered by sentimentality was eventually and providentially avoided. We can point to Augustine as perhaps the major contributor to the growth of later Catholic theology and Catholic culture, yet at the same time as a reminder of what more needed (and needs) to be done and of the cultural disasters that may attend upon error. Yet while his analysis of God's justice – brilliant though it was – remains in many respects a failure, in the next chapter I shall argue that much of his analysis of beauty, and its relationship to love both human and divine, marked a stupendous and enriching development – part "pagan-inspired" – of Christian accounts of divine attributes: hence of the nature of the good life for man who is created in God's image and of the value and role of human art properly understood. For we must ever bear it in mind that in religions, as is the nature of their God or gods, so will be the nature – instantiated and desiderate – of man. If Augustine's account of God's justice pointed too much to a Christianity of fear, the same thinker's account of God's beauty pointed to an improved account of a God not merely of power but of love.

CHAPTER 3

Divine beauty: Nature, art and humanity

For without a doubt no-one has succeeded in escaping *eros* nor will anyone in the future, so long as beauty (*kallos*) exists and there are eyes to see.

Longus, Daphnis and Chloe (Preface)

It is the enthusiastic imposition on us by the Roman Emperors and their successive governments of one form or another of an intolerant Abrahamic exclusive monotheism which has at last brought largely justified revolt and led most people to see "religion" as a dull, ugly, quarrelsome sub-department of life rather than the waking to the love of Beauty and its source, which can demand greater sacrifices than the fashionable cult of money and success.

A. H. Armstrong.[1]

3.1 ETHICS AND AESTHETICS

The most casual reflection on the history of European culture will indicate the enormous influence of Christianity – for at least the first sixteen centuries of our era primarily Catholic Christianity – in literature, music, architecture, painting and sculpture. That is not something one could easily deduce or expect from reading the Bible or the writings of the earliest Christians. Yet Western European culture has been Christian, and if it is genuinely Christian, it can only be justified as such in terms of the developing nature of Christianity itself. That justification, I shall argue, will also afford Catholic thinkers an intelligible account of authentic, albeit varying, artistic forms which is largely passing out of the reach of secular investigators – in particular a means of determining the difference in the arts between what is good and admirable and what is not.

---

[1] "Plotinus on the Origin and Place of Beauty in Thought about the World", in R. Baine Harris (ed.), *Neoplatonism and Contemporary Thought* (part 2) (Albany 2002) 227.

Since the work of Baumgarten in the early eighteenth century, we have agreed to call the study of art in its various forms aesthetics.[2] One of the basic problems of that branch of philosophy has an apparent analogue in ethics: is it possible or reasonable to avoid subjectivism, or, ultimately, nihilism? The problem is more difficult in aesthetics because it seems safer to accept the cliché that beauty lies in the eye of the beholder, in other words that it is all a matter of taste. Beneath that immediate problem, however, lies that of the proper relationship between aesthetics and ethics as such.

Catholic reflection on the arts has also been indebted to Platonism, and the Platonic tradition has always aimed to overcome subjectivism in aesthetics as in ethics, and in doing so to provide, in its pagan and later its Christian form, *justification* for aesthetic assertions, a claim that there is a sense in which, like ethical assertions, they can be right or wrong. The key to that justification lies not merely in the scriptural notion that the world reveals something of the splendour of God, but in an argument as to how it can be understood as doing so: the argument that created beauty (both of nature and of human beings), as well as moral "beauty", can only intelligibly be *beautiful* insofar as it indicates the beauty – and not merely the power, the glory or even the goodness – of the God of Truth.

We need first, however, a preliminary note on the concept of beauty itself, in particular of the beauty of physical objects. A recent attempt to defend an "objectivism" in aesthetic judgments indicates the problem. According to Mary Mothersill,[3] "Any individual is beautiful if and only if it is such as to be a cause of pleasure in virtue of its aesthetic properties." That invites the question of the nature of the person who feels the aesthetic pleasure, and I shall suggest that there are those who feel aesthetic pleasure where the "good aesthete" would not. More importantly, the Platonic tradition that I want to discuss, while agreeing that beauty causes pleasure (also, one might add, that the beautiful object is "sublime"), puts particular emphasis on the *inspirational* aspect of the aesthetic sensations and imaginings provoked by physical beauty as well as on the inspiration of non-sensible objects of beauty.

[2] A. Baumgarten, *Reflections on Poetry* (Halle 1735). For discussion of Baumgarten's predecessors (Shaftesbury, Hutcheson, Du Bos, Addison) see P. Guyer, *Values of Beauty: Historical Essays in Aesthetics* (Cambridge 2005) 3–36.
[3] M. Mothersill, *Beauty Restored* (Oxford 1984) 347. For a development of Mothersill's views see Guyer, *Values of Beauty* 326–344.

3.2 BIBLICAL BEAUTY

In the Old Testament the concept of beauty appears principally in derivative connection with the "formless" splendour and glory (*kabod*, Greek: *doxa*) of God. Beauty is the luminous revelation of that glory and majesty: "I will make my beauty pass before you" (Exodus 33:19; cf. 28:18). Yet God's own beauty is a rare theme in the Old Testament. God himself is not identified as Beauty; rather, he is shown *in* beauty and that beauty is thought of as "splendour", the revelation of his majesty and power, rather than more "aesthetically". At the earthly level the beauty of the damsel Jerusalem was perfected by God's splendour (*Ezechiel* 16:14) but corrupted by human sinfulness; and in general physical beauty can be recognized in the beauty of a natural world that points us to God (Psalm 8).

This theme is particularly evident in the Greek books (Wisdom 13:5; Sirach 43: 9–11) and in the Psalms, while the beauty of the human figure, especially the female figure, is emphasized in Psalm 44 (45) and above all in the Song of Songs – to which there is no need to attach an early allegorical understanding:[4] the tradition of Adam's delight in his new helpmeet is sufficient religious "justification" for this explicitly erotic, probably marital and perhaps courtly poetry. All these texts certainly reaffirm a traditional emphasis on the desire of love, both for God and for woman,[5] yet generally and increasingly (despite the beauty of many of the matriarchs and of Lady Wisdom (Wisdom 7:26; 8:2[6])), as we move into Hellenistic Judaism (Proverbs 6:25; 11:22; 31:30) – we shall see it sharply in Philo – female beauty is a snare and a delusion, liable to induce false worship: a theme to which the older language of Jerusalem as a harlot "whoring after false gods" (Jeremiah 3.3, etc.) certainly contributed.

In the New Testament there are a limited number of references to beauty, but again normally revealed as "glory": in the account of the Transfiguration, in Hebrews 1:3 (Christ is the splendour of God's glory) and in Revelation 21:11.[7] In such cases glory promotes awe, but awe overwhelming rather than inspirational. Gradually Christians came to pay beauty more attention, but in the "philosophical theology" of the early centuries of the Christian era beauty (especially the beauty of the human figure) was far more important among pagans, especially Platonists, than

---

[4] The first allegorical interpretation known to us is that of Rabbi Aqiba in the early second century AD.
[5] See G. Strola, *Il desiderio di Dio. Studio dei salmi 42–43* (Assisi 2003).
[6] OT males are rarely described as beautiful: David is one of the few exceptions (1 Sam. 16:18).
[7] See the comments of E. F. Osborn, *Irenaeus of Lyons* (Cambridge 2001) 200.

among Christians who inherited something of the Jewish suspicion of images – not to speak of fear rather than love being often the beginning of wisdom.

Clearly the earliest Christians regarded images of pagan gods as objects of idolatrous worship and they probably evinced a more generalized concern that any physical beauty could lead to the worship of created objects, including the human form and the universe itself: a problem already foreshadowed in the Wisdom literature (*Wisdom* 13:3; 13:7). The earliest Christian art, as in the Roman catacombs, seems to reflect neither canons of beauty nor even theological claims about glory. It is strictly "religious" and normally funerary, part of a personal and simple prayer for salvation: "Save me as you saved Daniel or Susannah".[8]

3.3 THE ORIGIN OF AESTHETIC PROBLEMS IN ANCIENT CHRISTIANITY

The pagan background (not to speak of the related sexual overtones) of ancient art helps to explain a morally and religiously based ambivalence about beauty among many of the Fathers. Indeed, from time to time throughout the history of Christianity preachers have sought to dismiss earthly beauty as at best irrelevant to religion, at worst a source of irreligion and immorality (which, as Plato already knew, it often is!).[9] I shall consider the reasons for ongoing Christian suspicions of art in somewhat more detail, and with reference to a few specific historical circumstances. First, however, I want to examine the strong "pagan" encouragement active on those early Christians who began to understand the religious importance of beauty and "aesthetic" considerations more generally: a development recognized both by those who exult in the growth of platonizing Christian concepts of beauty and those who decry it as a corruption of Christianity. I shall be able to catalogue developing ideas of beauty arising in the primitive Christian tradition as it appropriated and – as it believed – replaced the Judaic past.

The religion of the New Testament can be read as a culmination of ongoing developments in the Old: as when we watch the religious consciousness of the Jews developing from a belief in Jahwe as a superior God

---

[8] P. Prigent, *L'art des premiers chrétiens* (Paris 1995) 243–249; Murray, "Art and the Early Church", Jensen, *Face to Face*; cf. F. A. Murphy, *Christ the Form of Beauty* (Edinburgh 1995).

[9] H.-G. Gadamer is right to point out that "the rejection of iconoclasm . . . was a decision of incalculable significance". For discussion see *The Relevance of the Beautiful and Other Essays* (Cambridge 1986) 1–53.

among other gods to a strict and exclusive monotheism; or as we see a development from the belief (common among ancient Semitic peoples) that God requires a human sacrifice, normally of the first-born, via Abraham's realization that such sacrifice is not demanded and the offering of animals can adequately indicate the submission of man to God, to the thesis of Isaiah that God wants no blood offerings but the sacrifice of a pure heart. Similarly among Platonists or "platonizers" we can observe a development in "aesthetic" reflection from its first appearance in Plato through its Plotinian avatar to its Christian transformation where Christ (and ultimately the Trinity) is revealed as the Beauty of God (or as God the Beautiful), and hence ultimately beauty becomes some sort of "transcendental": a divine attribute along with being, goodness and truth. Whether such a transformation is intelligible and finally solves longstanding problems – not to speak of problems to come – or whether it offers merely apparent, even merely verbal, solutions to genuine and recognized difficulties in pagan traditions, remains for us to see.

3.4 PLATO'S ORIGINAL PROPOSALS

Socrates, by universal consent of his contemporaries, was a "lover", an *erōtikos* engaged in a passionate search for truth. But he made the important connection of truth and the love of truth with beauty and the love of beauty – in the first instance (at least in his own society) with the beauty of the human body. As Plato expressed it in the *Phaedrus*, of all the transcendent Forms, Beauty is the most accessible because presented to our sight, the keenest and most perceptive of our senses. The shining splendour of beauty is the clearest link between the sensible and non-sensible worlds: it is "reality" in visible form. In the *Symposium*, in a series of eulogies and analogies of love (*eros*), Beauty is the only Form discussed; in the *Republic* it is the first to be introduced (476B6). However, in Plato's interpretation of the Socratic ascent of the soul, in the *Symposium* and the *Phaedrus*, the natural search for the sight and enjoyment of physical beauty leads in finer minds to a recognition that earthly beauties share in a higher transcendental beauty in comparison with which they pale into insignificance (though what degree of insignificance will remain debatable). What then is that higher Beauty to which alone the self-predicating epithet "beautiful" can properly be attached?

The Platonic Socrates is a lover of Beauty (*to kalon*), but in the *Republic* Plato expands his ambitions, showing Socrates hardly distinguishing between his love of Beauty and his concern with Goodness – except insofar as he sometimes suggests that to speak of "Goodness" is to introduce ideas about the benefit or advantage accruing to those who know it; or perhaps that Beauty should be seen as a feature of Goodness and a way to Goodness – as at *Philebus* 65A where its other features are proportion and truth. In Greek, "X is good" can mean that X is good for something, or good at something; the word "good" can be followed by an epexegetic or explanatory infinitive. "Beautiful" (*kalon*), however, is absolute; what is *kalon* is simply beautiful, an object of admiration and desire and a source of some kind of inspiration.

Broadly conceived, beauty is the inspirational object and goal of (erotic) desire as such. Like "good", "beautiful" may have considerable "moral" significance, but its reference is much wider than morality. "Good" may also, perhaps originally, indicate a skill, as that of a good thief;[10] "beautiful" will invite love and desire, also not necessarily of a "moral" sort. "Beautiful" indicates what is good (or supposedly good) viewed under a particular aspect and description; the good shows itself as beautiful. For Plato, if we understand what it is to be beautiful, we shall have advanced towards understanding what it is to be good, and vice versa. We too might say of the work of a good thief, "That was a beautiful job" – as Macchiavelli suggests at least that political murders by Cesare Borgia were beautifully done.

Looking into Plato's view of the relationship between goodness and beauty, we find ourselves in a strange but not unfamiliar world. We normally distinguish between ethics and aesthetics, but Plato would question that distinction. For him the first principles of morality and of a proper "aesthetics" must be identical – but in specifying a "proper" aesthetics we reach an apparently fundamental difference between beauty and goodness: no-one would be content with what only *appears* good rather than really is good; the measure of a good man is not that he appears to be honest but that he *is* honest. So also justice must be seen to be done, not seem to be done. On the other hand, Plato says in the last book of the *Republic* that Homer really is a good poet, in that he writes beautiful poems, but that there is a powerful case to be made that in an ideal society such poems would be banned as immoral. They appeal to us as beautiful but they are not good for us or for most of us. Thus there is a sense in which they seem more beautiful than they are, and that what seems more beautiful than it is is beautiful in itself and harmful in its effects.

Perhaps that means that such things are not really beautiful; they merely seem so. Or is it that Plato would like to say – but lacks the linguistic and

[10] Cf. *Rep.* 1.334A5ff.

conceptual tools to say directly – that they are aesthetically beautiful but morally dangerous or even ugly? In challenging Homer, *the* educator of the Greeks, he raises in the sharpest possible form a dilemma that will eventually face Christians: namely, how to square "moral" with "aesthetic" goods, and what to do about the aesthetic goods if (or when) they seem unsquarable with morality. For in appearing beautiful they will also be inspiring: presumably open to vice.

Before facing this directly, I must enquire whether Plato might have lacked such conceptual tools. Why can he not formulate the concept of the simply "aesthetic", and why does he apparently always seek to identify the aesthetic with the moral, or at least moral language with aesthetic language, only to be pulled up short when he finds them apparently discordant? To answer this, I would need to know what, according to Plato, makes something beautiful (and therefore the target of *eros*) and what makes something good. But it will emerge that the principles of beauty and of goodness are closely related. Hence I shall have to turn (in the case of beauty) not merely to whether something is or seems to be beautiful but also to the effects its beauty has on those who recognize it. For what is somehow beautiful may be harmful to me (perhaps because of some fault or weakness in myself), while what is genuinely good can only be beneficial. And would this distinction be relevant to the "problematic" beauty of the human body, the prime "target" of *eros*?

Plato is, of course, aware that beauty is seductive and may induce possessiveness and erratic judgment, so the underlying difficulty is why he is inclined to think that *qua* beautiful the genuinely beautiful will also be genuinely good – whatever immediately unfortunate effects it may have in individual cases. Part of the explanation, as I have noted, is that the metaphysical principles of goodness and beauty are closely linked. For goodness is intimately linked with unity (a perfect X is exactly X, with nothing fuzzy round the edges!) while beauty is intimately bound up with proportion and symmetry, with being, mathematically or otherwise, just right. But to say that something good is exactly what it is obviously is not to provide a full account of it – otherwise perfect justice would be identical to perfect courage, or a good man identical to a good horse – and the proposition that beauty is *just* symmetry or *just* proportion is questionable. Otherwise a perfectly symmetrical X would, *qua* beautiful, be equivalent to a perfectly symmetrical Y, and any intelligible theory of *grades* of beauty such as Plato himself offers in the *Symposium* ("The beautiful soul is more beautiful than the beautiful body") would be ruled out. None of which prevents unity and symmetry being necessary features of the beautiful (and therefore part of its attractiveness and inspirational force), as – somehow – of the good.

An awareness that the beautiful may distract from the good is part of the rationale for Plato's ladder of ascent to the Beautiful itself. Particulars cannot be perfectly symmetrical – not least if (platonically) to be perfectly symmetrical entails *always* to be symmetrical and in no way to appear asymmetrical. But that is not the only disturbing feature of a Platonic particular: particular beauties may distract not only from the good but from what is "more beautiful". Hence the first and basic distinction Plato draws in the *Symposium* is between "demotic" and "heavenly" desire and between "demotic" and "heavenly" beauty. "Demotic" beauty and desire are concerned exclusively with the material body; "heavenly" *eros* is directed primarily toward (the good of) an immaterial soul. Love for a beautiful body – which is certainly beautiful, albeit with only a passing beauty – can distract from love of the soul; that is the star instance of a possible separation of beauty from goodness. But how exactly do we enjoy a beautiful soul? Answering that should help us know the right way to enjoy a beautiful body.

If we briefly take our eyes off Plato himself to look at his influence – for example on art, on evaluations of material beauty and above all of the beauty of the human body – we recognize that, whereas he apparently thought rather differently on similar themes at different times of his life, and many of his explanations are admitted to be incomplete, thus allowing differing completions to be revealed in differing philosophical contexts, Platonists in later antiquity, not least those known to early Christian thinkers, normally supposed that a single systematic philosophy can be identified in the whole and in any individual part of his writings. Thus if later Platonists notice what *prima facie* seem to be differing theories in different Platonic texts, they assume that Plato himself could have reconciled them, and hence often impose on him a synthesis that he would have found unacceptable at any point in his philosophical career. A number of examples of this phenomenon deserve attention, if only to show that a better awareness of the unfolding of Plato's views might have helped the Christians to develop a more coherent, more "catholic" account of beauty than they readily achieved. Too often views that Plato himself discarded had greater immediate influence on the Christian tradition than those he came to prefer.

Some of the most dramatic variations in Plato's views concern the nature of artistic activity, the relationship between beauty and goodness, and above all the relationship between the body and the soul and in consequence the soul's very nature. Even within the pages of the *Republic*, we find two *prima facie* incompatible accounts of the nature of painting: speaking briefly and perhaps with less ethical and metaphysical concerns in his mind, Socrates suggests in books 5 and 6 (472D4ff.; 484C8) that when a painter creates a picture he thinks both of the relevant perfection – the idealization of much classical art – and of the particular form of an actual model. In book 10, however – and far more influentually – he describes painting as being (more like photography) the creation of an image of an image, thus establishing a tradition which not only condemns art as frequently immoral in its emotional effects, but which seems to explain that immorality by arguing that painting can never produce even "natural" realities but only copies of realities that are themselves copies of the immaterial Forms. One of the effects of such an approach is to downplay human artistic creation in comparison with the beauties of nature – though Plato would instance the starry heavens rather than a mere landscape as depicted by Constable or Cézanne.

Although Beauty is the only Form introduced in the *Symposium* and the first to be given close attention in the *Republic*, in the latter dialogue it is subordinate to the Good on which the whole work is centred. That is because in the *Republic*, where society as a whole as well as its individual members is in question, Plato's primary concern about physical beauty is that it shall not distract us from the eternal or prevent us seeing the eternal through the time-bound. A few beautiful artefacts are to be allowed into the Ideal State, but their admission is to depend on their effects on the moral nature of the souls of the citizens; the purely aesthetic is to be strictly subordinated to the moral. Only "real", that is, enduring and morally beneficial, beauties are to be accepted. The Form of Beauty will, as it were, not tolerate its own morally dangerous instantiations. No possibility is envisaged of a morally ambiguous or risky artefact being, though dangerous, capable of enriching the minds and lives of the citizens.

Of prime importance is the fact that *real* beauty is immaterial; physical beauties only participate in that higher beauty. But how do we know that that higher beauty is beautiful in any sense of the word we can recognize? First, because it can stimulate a love (*eros*) that is the motive force for all honest philosophical and political activity. Hence the moral virtue of *eros* in any given individual can be determined; it varies with its objects, but it is the only way we have to experience the vast range of beauties both material and immaterial.

Yet Plato has generated a serious difficulty. Though the Forms, as beautiful, are the objects of our highest desire, they are impersonal, and in the *Symposium* the lover, when he has passed from bodies to souls, moves on

to impersonal objects of love, namely laws and institutions, before reaching
the impersonal Form of Beauty itself. So Plato has produced an "order of
love" which holds the "person" comparatively low in its hierarchy. It is as
though he were saying that *qua* beautiful the play, *Hamlet*, is more lovable
than the author, Shakespeare. Whose valuation could this be? Presumably
that of the wise man, the philosopher. Though many might agree with this
valuation, it cannot be acceptable to Christians. Ancient Platonists were
inclined to think that Christians give human beings too important a place in
the cosmos, for what the *Symposium* suggests is that, in the search for the
highest immaterial goods, human love is merely a means to an end.
Surprisingly, in correcting that view – to which some of them were nonetheless certainly attracted – Christian thinkers made moves that helped
provide a uniquely "providentialist" justification of art and beauty.

Plato himself substantially corrects the *Symposium* in the *Phaedrus*,
normally regarded in antiquity as the more influential and philosophically
dominant of the two dialogues.[11] In later antiquity the two dialogues are
normally "reconciled"; we do not hear of the *Symposium*'s being corrected.
Hence, if there is conflict between them, that conflict will be reflected in
philosophical ambiguities in their interpreters, whether Christian or pagan.
Of course the centrality of beauty and of *eros* in the good life stands in the
Phaedrus, and *eros* is still ambivalent, its quality depending on that of its
(preferably impersonal) ultimate object. But in the *Phaedrus* there is no
suggestion that that love between individuals that leads to the divine madness in which state we recognize Beauty and the other Forms is superseded.
There is mutuality (with a responsive *eros*, an *anteros*) between lover and
beloved. Love of beauty is more firmly attached – though not yet firmly
enough – to love of persons.[12]

The most influential instance of misinterpretation of Plato by Platonists –
deriving from an over-systematic re-working of the Master's thought – is
due in no small part to the fame of the account of Socrates' death in the
Phaedo. In this dialogue Plato discusses virtue and vice in terms of a radical
differentiation between soul and body, and argues that the evils of mankind
derive from the desires of the body prevailing over those of the soul. Yet
although Plato developed this dualism to great effect not only in the *Phaedo*
but in his account of the search for beauty in the nearly contemporary

---

[11] See J. M. Rist, "Plutarch's *Amatorius*: A Commentary on Plato's Theories of Love?", *CQ* 51 (2001)
557–575.
[12] The increasing emphasis on the interpersonal is probably to be connected with Plato's apparently
growing conviction (to be exploited by the Neoplatonists) that the Good and the gods must somehow
be brought closer together. This is not the place to consider that wider theme.

Symposium, by the time he came to write the *Republic* and the *Phaedrus* he had radically modified it. Though he still maintained that we can indeed be seduced by bodily desires, he seems to have come to the manifestly reasonable conclusion that, if the soul is so easily seduced, it must have significant weaknesses of its own; it needs, that is, to be disciplined, to be subject to ascesis. Hence the theory of the so-called tripartite soul.[13]

The soul–body dualism of the *Phaedo* proved attractive to moralists both Christian and pagan – Christians, as we have seen, being wrongly inclined to assimilate it to Paul's distinction between "spirit" and "flesh" – while the more sophisticated tripartite theory was often neglected or misread. Plotinus, for example, hardly uses it all, preferring a dualistic thesis when treating of morality and something closer to Aristotle's faculty theory when doing psychology.[14] The "Platonic" tendency to denigrate the body permeated much Christian thought as well, though in their better (and often less philosophical) moments Christians were compelled to recognize that the bodily Incarnation of Jesus and the Resurrection were fundamentals of their belief not to be compromised by distaste for the body whether supposedly Platonic or Pauline. Yet the dualism of the *Phaedo* remained attractive – we note Porphyry's "all body is to be avoided"[15] – and with it a tendency to denigrate physical beauty, be it of that human body which to the Greeks was the highest examplar of physical beauty – the bodies of the gods were seen as examples of human beauty raised to the highest degree – or the beauty of the physical cosmos in general.

In both cases Plato offered a corrective; Neoplatonists and Christian Platonists were able to appeal to the *Timaeus* as indicating beauty in God's creation or craftsmanship of the physical world. But Plato's emphasis in the *Phaedrus* on the continuing mutual attraction of lovers, even though preferably without bodily consummation, remained widely unacceptable: the "classical" evaluation of the human body's beauty, even transposed to a heterosexual context, faced an upward battle in Christianity, whose thinkers preferred to introduce physical beauty at the divine level of the physical beauty of the Transfigured Jesus. Erotic writing might be defused allegorically, but it generally seemed safer to defer admiration of the human body until the Resurrection. However, Plato's claim that material beauty is beautiful by participation in immaterial beauty was left on the table, since

---

[13] The phrase itself is un-Platonic, and is used only once by Aristotle (*Top.* 133A31, but cf. *De An.* 3.432B6).

[14] See H. J. Blumenthal, *Plotinus' Psychology* (The Hague 1971) 21–25.

[15] *Omne corpus est fugiendum* (*Ad Marcellam* 8.32.34). Note Augustine's self-condemnation in the *Retractationes* (1.4.3) for getting too close to this idea in *Soliloquies* 1.14.24.

the only alternative to it was to reject the beauty of physical bodies altogether as spurious.

Plato set the stage for all ancient discussions of beauty, as of its correlate *eros*. But he never reached late antiquity in a pure form; always there were Platonist and other intermediaries, so that by the fourth century (before which, as we shall see, there was rather little attention to *platonizing* accounts of beauty among orthodox Christians) his own views – though at times read directly – were seen against a wider background of thought both platonizing and anti-Platonist. In particular, the opinions of the Stoics and of Plotinus deserve attention, for they formed part of the intellectual air breathed by those Christians of late antiquity who came to believe that they needed a Christian "account" of Beauty. Such opinions could easily be mistaken for those of "Plato" himself, or for legitimate expansions of his thought.

3.5 EPICURUS AND THE STOICS[16]

Epicurus subordinated "beauty", whether aesthetic or moral, to pleasure: "I spit on 'the beautiful' unless it gives me pleasure" (Athenaeus, *Sophists at Dinner* 12.546–547). So although there are Epicurean poets – Lucretius is the star instance – they at least claim that their motivation is didactic, since helping people out of their religious and moral difficulties might be supposed (idiosyncratically) to give them pleasure. Not surprisingly Epicurean influence on Christian theories of beauty was negligible.

For very different reasons there is no need to spend much time on the Stoics either, but not because their theories of art were uninfluential; they were known and influential not only on Plotinus, who reacted against them, but on Christian writers such as Clement and Augustine, as well as on Philo, a major source for Christianity here as elsewhere.

The formal Stoic account of beauty, in some respects a development of Platonic as well as of Pythagorean and more popular ideas, is clear: beauty, whether of the body, of the soul, or of anything else, is a symmetry of limbs or parts and an appropriateness of part to part and part to whole, coupled with a certain "sweetness" of colour if the beauty is physical.[17] Beauty – again traditionally enough – when impressed on the soul induces *eros*,[18] which if

---

[16] The only recent full-length study of Stoic theories of art is M.-A. Zagdoun, *La philosophie stoicienne de l'art* (Paris 2000).

[17] *SVF* 3.278 (Stobaeus); 279 (Cicero, *Disp Tusc.*); 471–472 (Galen on Chrysippus); 592 (Philo).

[18] *SVF* 3.719 (Plutarch).

passionate (that is, considered as Platonic madness) is undesirable, since it disturbs the human equilibrium and the "smooth flow of life". Proper *eros*, however, is an *epibolē* (an "impulse before an impulse"), not a pathological condition; it is found only in the wise man who is worthy of it.[19] He will be a "lover", for at its rational best *eros* is an impetus to friendship mediated by the beauty of the young in their prime if they are noble and handsome.[20] All this caused opponents of Stoicism to ask whether such a cold-blooded affect should properly be described as *eros* at all![21]

3.6 PLOTINUS: ADVANCES AND AMBIGUITIES IN "PLATONIC" THEORY[22]

Plotinus' account of beauty is basically Platonic, but it is modified by pressing contemporary considerations and presented in systematic form. Thus he treats of the moral ambiguity of *eros* in the figure of the soul as an amphibian moving through different worlds, arguing that it can be a god, a *daimon* or a *pathos* (a Stoic-sounding "unnatural" sickness of the soul).[23] As a divine "hypostasis" it is generated when a lower level of reality dimly grasps a higher (and beautiful) reality, being thus at the same time a strong natural and proper desire and astonishment or admiration. More generally, since Plotinus' "aesthetic" is Platonic, its first principles are metaphysical. The intelligibility of "aesthetics" in the strict sense, that is, an account of the nature of a beauty recognizable through the senses, depends on related metaphysical and ethical claims about the existence of a transcendent world of Forms, of Beauty and of Goodness. "Aesthetic" claims and values are thus set in the context of the moral and "spiritual" life and capabilities of the soul.

But considerations peculiar to his time and place affect both the substance and the emphases of Plotinus' position. Plato's original aim had been

---

[19] *SVF* 3.598 (Sextus).   [20] *SVF* 3.650 (Stobaeus).

[21] M. Schofield, *The Stoic Idea of the City* (Chicago 1999) 34, 45–46, is wrong about both Plato and the Stoics when he identifies Stoic *eros* with "a sublimated Platonic form of love"; see Gaça, *Making of Fornication* 63–65, though Gaça exaggerates early Stoic antinomianism (81): the Stoic concern was to vindicate the wise man's capacity to abandon normal conventions when appropriate. B. Inwood is right ("Why Do Fools Fall in Love?", in R. Sorabji (ed.), *Aristotle and After* (London 1997) 55–69) to compare (but not to identify) the early Stoic view with that of Pausanias in Plato's *Symposium*.

[22] For fuller accounts of Plotinus' theory of beauty and art see E. de Keyser, *La signification de l'art dans les Ennéades de Plotin* (Louvain 1955); J. M. Rist, *Plotinus: The Road to Reality* (Cambridge 1967) 53–65; L. P. Gerson, *Plotinus* (London/New York 1994) 212–218; J.-M. Narbonne, "Action, Contemplation and Interiority in the Thinking of Beauty in Plotinus", in A. Alexandrakis (ed.), *Neoplatonism and Western Aesthetics* (Albany 2002) 3–18; P. Mathias, *Plotin. Du Beau, Ennéades 1.6 et 5.8* (Paris 1991).

[23] *Enn.* 3.5.7.9. See J. C. Kanyaroro, "Les richesses intérieures de l'âme selon Plotin", *LTP* 59 (2003) 235–256, esp. 251.

twofold: to identify love of beauty and goodness as the necessary motor of the good life, and to devalue beauty of the body in comparison with beauty of the soul. At this point we should recall that, although we ourselves might distinguish three types of beauty (of art, nature and intelligible reality), our views of the relationships between these groups are not Plato's, nor those of Greeks of the classical age in general. As I have already observed, for the Greeks the most important of the natural beauties is that of the human (or divine) figure. The beauty of landscape and of details of nature is hardly considered,[24] and where it is, it is usually in the context of the success of the gods or of the Platonic Demiurge in bringing order and proportion to the ugliness and shapelessness of unformed matter. Artists certainly depicted natural beauties, as in Nilotic scenes, but such representations were not "high art"; as were the Zeus of Pheidias or (later) the Aphrodite of Praxiteles who rated such prestige body and soul, if I may so express it.

Plotinus too distinguished beauties of nature from the beauties of art, and the beauty of the human body as pre-eminent among natural beauties – what else could be the primary target of *eros*? – but he had reasons for being more concerned than was Plato with the beauty of the natural world. Chief among these was a hostility (which he shared with Christians) to Gnosticism. Several of the Gnostic groups claimed affinity with Plato – a modern scholar has referred to Gnosticism as a "Platonic underworld"[25] – though Plotinus furiously rejected all such claims and held that the Gnostics had betrayed the spirit of Hellenism.

Plotinus' major anti-Gnostic tract (*Ennead* 2.9) was reasonably subtitled by Porphyry as "Against those who think the maker of the universe and the universe are evil", and he was particularly concerned to argue that since the maker of the universe (as presented in Plato's *Timaeus*) is good, his products must all be good and beautiful. Hence, as Plato had claimed in the *Phaedrus*, the Form of Beauty is specially clear to mankind because beautiful objects in the material world are visible. Obviously Plotinus agrees with Plato that physical beauty can distract from higher beauties, but his immediate polemical concerns frequently lead him to a different emphasis.

Plotinus did more than place his emphases differently; he *developed* Platonic metaphysics. As we have observed, he always claimed simply to be following his master, who must have got things right, but however that claim should be understood there is no doubt that – at least for most of his

---

[24] Cf. J. M. Rist, "Why Greek Philosophers Might Have Been concerned about the Environment", in L. Westra and T. M. Robinson (eds.), *The Greeks and the Environment* (Lanham 1997) 19–32.

[25] Dillon, *The Middle Platonists* 384.

life – Plato described the relationship between forms and the souls and minds characterized by them differently from his "Neoplatonic" successor. Porphyry records a famous argument between Plotinus and a more "orthodox" contemporary Platonist, Longinus, Porphyry's former teacher. Plotinus held that "The forms are not outside the intellect"; Longinus took this to be un-Platonic, arguing for a separation of form and soul. Historically, Longinus was right; Plotinus' view is Aristotelian inasmuch as he held that the notion that there is a pure object of thought which is not thought eternally is unintelligible – therefore Plato could not have believed it!

Contemporary problems in "aesthetics" revolve around the attraction of sense-perceptible "objects" or "targets". Properly Platonic theories all start from the premiss that the beauty of the sensible world exists in some sort of dependence on a "real" beauty which exists in the intelligible and immaterial world; otherwise true propositions in aesthetics, as in ethics, could not be upheld: choice, taste or mere dictates of will would prevail. For Plotinus, as for Plato, sensible beauties are beautiful by participation or "imitation" of beauty itself. Material objects cannot strictly be called beautiful, but they can be understood as "beautiful" in virtue of this participation. Among material beauties we must distinguish between the beauty of natural objects – above all the human form – and the beauties of human artefacts or "works of art". In principle all material beauties can be evaluated and prioritized with reference to immaterial beauty.

Hence arise a number of typical problems:

1 How can we rate the beauty of physical objects?
2 Of what use is physical beauty?
3 If matter is not of the essence of beauty, what *are* beauty's essential elements?
4 In the universe of Plotinus (and of "Neoplatonists" in general) what is the relationship between the Form of Beauty – and more generally the beauty of the intelligible world of immaterial Forms – and the One or Good: in what sense is the One beautiful?

Questions 1 and 2 are comparatively straightforward. Physical beauty – as the *Symposium* and the whole tradition has it – is rated by its approximation to immaterial beauty and its capacity to lead the soul beyond itself. It arouses love and has something to teach us about love's nature, for love cannot come about without a beautiful object. Its value is obvious, but since there are higher loves than those of the physical world and the human figure, physical love, unless ordered, is also risky and may resolve itself into a mere *pathos*, a sick and distracting obsession. The Stoics were right, Plotinus thinks, to point out that some "loves" may be *pathē* (sicknesses of the soul) but dreadfully wrong to put them all into that class and to debase *eros* itself.

For Plotinus, the most beautiful physical object will presumably be that which properly attracts the soul without at the same time distracting it from higher goals: which, acting in Plato's language as a stepping-stone,[26] encourages the lover to transcend his immediate quest. If lower loves are not treated as stepping-stones, it may happen that a lover, through misuse of beauty, will fall into ugliness (3.5.1.63). Which reopens the question (implicit in the *Symposium*) of whether physical loves are mere *means* to something higher – which is not a question whether physical things are properly described as beautiful, which they are by reference to the Form, but of the attitude we should adopt towards them.

That question becomes the more pressing when we think not of the impersonal beauties of nature – though for Plotinus these are not strictly impersonal, being manifestations of the World Soul – but of human beauty. Perhaps, as in the *Symposium*, and encouraged by his vitalist account of nature, Plotinus gives too little attention to whether the love and erotic arousal caused by the beauty of human beings may not demand special treatment (as it receives in the *Phaedrus*) – though when he discounts mere detachment from our fellows, citing as axiomatic that one cannot claim to love the father if one does not also love the children, he seems at least to question extremes of Stoic, let alone Cynic, insensitivity and invulnerability.[27]

At this point we should consider the specifically Plotinian *analysis* of physical beauty, and from that feel our way towards the essential features of beauty in its highest form. Without wholly rejecting the popular Stoic claim that beauty resides in some sort of symmetry of parts, with the addition of a good colouring (1.6.1.21ff.; 6.7.22.25),[28] Plotinus argues that it is insufficient. If beauty can only exist in composites, how can we explain the beauty of simple phenomena such as sunlight or a flash of lightning or the "simple beauty of colour" (1.6.1.31; 1.6.3.17) – or the more or less beautiful appearance of a similarly symmetrical face (1.6.1.37; 6.7.22.27)? Rather than mere symmetry, the source of physical beauty is to be sought (as the *Phaedrus* had begun to suggest) in the splendour of life-giving light. Unless such "grace" plays on the symmetry of physical objects, we have a merely death-like symmetry (6.7.22.22; cf. 5.8.1.32ff.). Thus in the case of a work of art beauty resides less in the constituted object (though it is there too) than in the active mind of the artist, just as the beauty of the natural world lies to a higher degree in its spiritual maker, the World Soul and beyond that in the

---

[26] *Symp.* 211C3; cf. Plot., *Enn.* 1.6.1.20.   [27] For further comment see Rist, *Plotinus* 161–168.
[28] Cf. Cic., *Tusc.Disp.* 4.31: a well-known source probably cited, for example, by Augustine, *CD* 22.19.

living form of Beauty itself. The beauty of the cause is always more inspirational than that of the effect.

In such ideas much modern "aesthetics" is transcended. Beauty is now to be evaluated not, of course, by a mere moralism measuring only short-term effects but in terms of its power to inspire to those purifications necessary if the "beautiful" soul is to pass through and beyond the world of sense to the world of the living Forms, then to the One, itself somehow both beautiful and the source of beauty. A beauty beyond that of physical objects but also the cause of their beauty is to be found first in the mind of the artist, who at his best – as Pheidias in sculpting his statue of Zeus – is aware not just of models available to the senses but of "what Zeus would be like if he wanted to make himself visible" (5.8.1.32–40). So Beethoven's Ninth Symphony, when performed, is beautiful, but its aural beauty (insofar as it is genuine) is grounded in the composer's beautiful mind. Living spiritual beauty is the source of physical beauty, whose nature can be neither understood nor justified without reference to it.

Our love is properly and ultimately directed at the One, but by way of the Forms, and Plotinus wants to locate true beauty in the formal realm of perfect types. But forms are formless in the sense that they have no physicality (6.7.32.6–9). Each is a perfect intelligible unity, but insofar as they are discrete, they cannot satisfy our love for unity and completeness; indeed, just as physical beauties may distract us from intelligible beauties, so even the form of beauty itself may distract the ignorant from its superior and source, the One or Good (5.5.12.38ff.).

The One or Good is unbounded (as is the "boundless and immeasurable" love it evokes, 6.7.32.26–29); it is – I shall return to the phrase – a "beauty above beauty". It alone is available to all its lovers, those who "love it entire", that is, bounded by the limitations neither of the world of particulars – where the lover can merely stand at the door[29] – nor even of the intelligible world, the "one-many" (6.5.10.8). But if the One is itself the object of the highest love, it must itself be in some extended (or primal) sense Beauty. And here Plotinus (in the tradition of Plato) has a "counter-intuitive" difficulty: not only is "aesthetics", understood as the study and achievement of physical beauty, transcended in the beauty of the soul of the artist, the World Soul and beyond that the Divine Intellect, but even that unified and simple beauty – Beauty is nothing but beauty – is transcended in this higher love of something now two removes from beauty as it is normally

[29] *Symp.* 203C3–D2; *Enn.* 6.5.10.3ff.; cf Aug., *Solil.* 1.13.22; *DLA* 2.12.33–14.37, with R. J. O'Connell, *Saint Augustine's Early Theory of Man, AD 386–391* (Cambridge, Mass. 1968) 53ff.; *EnPs.* 2.6.

understood. We are back to the problem, seemingly unresolved in Plato, of the relationship between the first principle, called the Good and later the One – but also, at least in the *Symposium*, apparently the Beautiful – and Beauty as a Form.

Recall again the position of Plato, for whom, in the *Symposium*, the object of the soul's quest is the Form of Beauty, and it has proved easy both for the ancients and for modern scholars to identify that Form with the Good of the *Republic*. But the reality is more complex. The *Symposium* is probably the first dialogue to introduce a transcendent Form, yet, though it is presumed to be more or less contemporaneous with the *Phaedo* where a great variety of such Forms appear, there is only one Form in the *Symposium*, the Form of Beauty. Since in the more detailed introduction of Forms in book 6 of the *Republic* that Form is the first to be discussed, it is plausible to conclude either that it was the first Form Plato came to identify or that it was the Form whose exposition best served his philosophical purposes, one of which was how to introduce the Forms to a sceptical public.

There is a sense, therefore, in which in the *Symposium* the ascent to beauty represents the ascent to the intelligible world in general, not least because such ascent can most plausibly be presented as driven by *eros* – which we all think we know about. By the time he wrote the *Republic*, however, Plato not only wanted to introduce a whole panoply of Forms but to identify not beauty but the Good as the superior reality of the intelligible world and only claimant to the title, "beyond being" (509B6). But, with "the Good" (and later apparently "the One") as the preferred denotation of the highest of the Forms, Plato cannot evade the question of the relationship between that Good and Beauty, the most typical and informative of the Forms as well as the most natural target of *eros*. Nevertheless, he gives little further hint of his intentions, except to say mysteriously in the *Philebus* – as we have seen – that if we want to "track down" the Form of the Good we can work with three concepts: beauty, proportion and truth (65A): a text that shows an unwillingness to identify beauty and symmetry and a clear confirmation that the Good enjoys superiority.

Plotinus thinks of Plato as the Master, so that where he is obscure, or appears to contradict himself from one dialogue to another, it is the duty of the Platonist to find a reconciliation. Plotinus' treatment of the relationship between the Good (or more normally the One) and beauty is a fine example of this. He knows that in the ascent passages of the *Symposium*, which provide him with guidance for his account of the return of the soul to the One (not least in 1.6), it is beauty which is the object of the lover's quest, and therefore that it is beauty which is the object of love. (Contrariwise, the soul is repelled by ugliness (1.6.2.5–6), by the "mark of the shapeless" (2.4.10.23).)

Hence Plotinus' "Neoplatonic" reconciliation: there is a sense in which we can identify the One as a special kind of beauty: a Beauty (*kallos*) above Beauty – as we have seen – or a Beauty in another mode (6.7.32.26–29). Or he may use another, rarer word: *kallonē* (1.6.6.25; 6.2.18.1), or the archaic *aglaia*, a word which means "splendour" (6.9.4.18), and is the name of one of the Graces. *Aglaia* is also applied to *Nous* and to the soul and seemingly indicates the One as seen by the aspirant to unity, showing itself *as* splendour (in the spirit of the *Phaedrus*), in being the "source" and maker of Beauty (*kallopoion*, 6.7.32). This is not the "splendour" of the Old Testament; it is what Plotinus, and other Neoplatonists who follow him, rather oddly call the "flower of Beauty" to mark an ontological superiority.[30] Finally, the effect of the beauty of the One on its lovers is to make them beautiful and lovable (1.6.7). Inspirational love of the One shows us how lesser loves can be explained both as inspirational and as *less* inspirational.

Perhaps Plotinus has deluded himself into thinking that he has explained the relationship between Beauty and the One. He seems to say that the One is somehow revealed *as* Beauty, yet the relationship between the One *as* Beauty and the Form of Beauty is far from clear, especially as the two exist at different ontological levels. But what if they were to be identified as at the same ontological level? What if God's goodness is beauty or his beauty goodness, such that, although at a level below the Good love of beauty will not always be identified with love of goodness, nonetheless at its highest it will be so identified? Here we recognize an option available to Christians after the Council of Nicaea: Beauty as revelatory of the "first" God – to use the antique language – but in no way inferior to it.

There is scope for other development too. Plato's "counter-intuitive" position from the beginning was that the supreme beauty is non-physical, being above the works of nature and of human art. These latter beauties are indicators of the spiritual "beauty" of their immaterial makers, but above even these makers – in Plotinian terms above the beauteous intelligible world – is that special beauty of completeness which can only be grasped, via the beauty of the Forms, by the sage who can "see it whole" (6.7.35).

---

[30] By analogy "flower" may perhaps also suggest a perpetually unreachable virginity, as the target of "erotic" *nous* (6.7.35.19ff.); in general see J. M. Rist, "Mysticism and Transcendence in Later Neoplatonism", *Hermes* 92 (1964) 215–217.

Philosophically, a fundamental problem remains. Traditional Platonic aesthetics explains the nature of the beauties of the world, including and especially that of the human figure, in terms of the intelligible beauty of finite perfection recognized by intuitive thought. But in what sense – other than by a play on words – can the One's "splendour" properly be called "beauty" at all? (And what is meant by the "beauty" of moral forms, like Justice?) Plotinus' answer is that the maker of beauty must in some sense be beautiful. But that still leaves it open as to what this beauty is. Plotinus knows that we recognize the One *as* beautiful; he says more than once that when we see it we know that it is beautiful (1.6.7.2ff.; 6.9.9.47). But he says little to explain why it is appropriate that the One is called beautiful beyond the principle that an effect is better recognized in its cause.

Although a "higher" beauty is basic to Neoplatonic metaphysics, in that without it a return to the One would be impossible, and although the Form of Beauty is the supreme cause of the "lower" kinds of beauty, physical and intelligible, its status remains ambiguous and incomplete. When Christians began to consider Neoplatonic notions of beauty, they were not confronted with a coherent canvas and they could thus more easily pick and choose. Told that the One is Beauty, or is revealed as Beauty, they may be pardoned if they are puzzled as to the nature of that highest beauty to which they are urged to aspire. What they do know is that it is available to all, and that it makes beautiful what would otherwise be un-beautiful.

It has always being puzzling how, especially in the *Symposium*, Plato moves the objects of *eros* so easily from the personal to the impersonal domain. If (but only if) the Form of the Good is never identified with any kind of mind, that problem remained unconsidered by him. If, however, as I have argued elsewhere, he eventually moved towards an identification of God and the Good,[31] the problem is considerably diminished, insofar as the highest object of love is now somehow "personalized".

Hesitancy between a personal and an impersonal first principle persists in Plotinus, for although, in adopting pieces of Aristotle's account of the identity of knower and known, he is able to overcome the normal Platonic separation of the "personal" God and the impersonal Form, yet that solution itself both is and is not transcended in the "semi-personal" account he seems to give of the One, which he is able to discuss now in personal, now in impersonal terms. Until this ambiguity is resolved in favour of the "personal", we still wonder how the One (or its equivalent) can be a legitimate target for anything properly recognizable as inspired *eros*.

---

[31] Rist, *The Mind of Aristotle* 197–205.

To put it differently, do Plato and Plotinus allow their theory of *eros* to outrun their theory of the One? And of Form itself? Curiously (though, as we shall see, not uniquely), in Plotinus the "natural" connection between *eros* and beauty is at times almost broken. While there is no doubt that *eros* will be satisfied with nothing less than the One, beauty, seen as the splendour *of* (or from) the One and its creative contemplation, is *par excellence* a mark not so much of the One itself as of its product (almost of its incidental product) *Nous*, the "Divine Mind", the second level of reality.

Plotinus has moved in the direction of personalizing the highest object of love, but he has failed to notice Plato's partial self-correction over another aspect of the "personalism" problem in the *Phaedrus*. In Neoplatonism mutuality between human lovers almost disappears (though a more personal relationship with the One seems to be achieved). Plotinus, I have suggested, was so over-impressed by the dualism of the *Phaedo* as to overlook Plato's less disembodied account of even superior forms of human love in the *Phaedrus*.

At least he never overlooked the more physical aspects of beauty altogether; never lost sight of a bodily beauty for all its "seductiveness" still partaking of the divine. Nor did he neglect another basic principle of Platonism: that all beauty (even seductive beauty) can be inspirational – not merely arousing – and that without beauty there is no honest inspiration, though there may be awe. That axiom, whether they liked it or not, was to be of inestimable value to Christians.

3.7 CHRISTIANITY BEFORE ORIGEN

Long before Plotinus a strange and disconcerting cloud had appeared on the Christian horizon: Philo of Alexandria – whom we have already heard on *apatheia* and the inadequacy of females – was to have enormous influence on many of his Christian successors. As with *apatheia* so with beauty, that influence was mixed.[32] Philo accepted the most "dualist" features of the Platonism of the *Phaedo* and blended them with an adaptation of the *Timaeus* (which enabled him to speak of the creation in general as God's good and beautiful work), and with Stoicizing accounts of virtue and an allegorical reading of the Hebrew Bible. As we have seen, he associated the female with sensuality and the pleasure necessary, alas, for promoting

---

[32] For the best account of beauty in Philo see now M. B. Zorzi, *Desiderio della bellezza* (Rome 2007) 181–200.

reproductive acts (*Allegories of the Laws* 2.8). Strictly speaking the serpent is pleasure (*On Creation* 158), the irresistible attraction of a "pretty woman" or prostitute (*On Sacrifice* 29; *On Creation* 166). His normal view of beauty is on similar lines; abandoned was the classical idea that, despite its possible dangers, the beauty of the human body partakes of divine beauty along with the rest of creation.

Philo abhorred homosexuality, and condemned Plato's *Symposium* thoughtlessly and in the harshest terms (*The Contemplative Life* 57–63). His view of female "seductiveness" was no less severe, and he proposed a sharp distinction between love of the bogus or shadowlike beauty of the human body (*Posterity of Cain* 112) and the "divine madness" (adapted from the *Phaedrus*) that leads men and "masculine" women to love of God and truth. He is willing to speak of the philosopher as a lover of God, and of the grace of God which arouses an untameable yearning for beauty (*Abraham's Migration* 132, cf. *Allegories of the Laws* 137), but that love of virtue has no physical counterpart, for the wise reject sensation (*Cherubim* 41). Although Philo's God is personal, he is only rarely willing to think of beauty as a divine attribute – though only God is beautiful (*Posterity* 182, cf. 92; *Drunkenness* 137–138; *Who is the Heir?* 65). In effect virtue – as normally the love of virtue, truth and God – is separate from the love of beauty. The beauty of the cosmos which marks God's handiwork is other than the physical "beauty" of mankind. Angels, being incorporeal, are at no erotic risk (*Cherubim* 20), but human *eros* should be directed to virtue (or an equivalent),[33] as the Stoics held (*Dreams* 2.132; *Abraham* 224), rather than to (divine) beauty. Yet a certain reciprocity of love between incorporeals can be achieved: that is, between man's true self and an immaterial God (*Posterity* 12.6–13).

Similarly suspect as a source of sexual laxity, if not homosexual perversion and idolatry, beauty seems far from central among the earliest Christians, whose attitudes on the matter were largely derived from the Old Testament. That the suffering servant was without beauty (Isaiah 53) they applied to Jesus. So regularly Justin (*Dialogus* 14.8; 49.2; 88.8) who has nothing to say of beauty even when speaking of the "glory" of Christ's second coming; and he recycles the old myth of the choice of Heracles (pleasure as a beautiful woman, virtue as plain and straightlaced) to point a puritanical contrast (*Second Apology* 11.4–5). Tertullian (perhaps surprisingly) is less austere; certainly Jesus was ugly, as is appropriate for life in the flesh (*On the Flesh of Christ* 8), with no beauty or splendour (15), but it will be very different at

---

[33] Wisdom (*De Opif.* 70), knowledge (*Cher.* 19), truth (*SpecLeg.* 1.59), etc.

the second coming (*Against the Jews* 14), and we recognize, with Psalm 44, the beauty and glory of his spiritual grace (*Against Marcion* 3.17).

Clement, often more platonizing, is not very different. The beauty of both soul and body is genuine, so long as one does not mistake the beauty of the body for the "deceitful beauty of the [earthly] flesh": a "Philonic" separation of bodily and spiritual beauty too extreme for Plato after the *Phaedo*. More generally Clement is concerned to emphasize the true beauty of the soul (*Miscellanies* 2.5.21.1). The Saviour has a "dishonoured, despised" exterior (*Protrepticus.* 10.110.1; *Miscellanies* 3.17.103.3); there is no "redeeming" physical beauty before the resurrection.

Clement's account of beauty is largely Stoic; physical beauty is the traditional harmony of limbs and parts with good colouring (*Paedagogus* 3.11.64.2). Like the Stoics, whose theories of "impassibility" he also largely accepted, as we have seen, he has no wish to invoke the Platonic (or even the Philonic) "madness" of love for spiritual (let alone physical) beauty. Fear of physical beauty keeps him, on this point, well outside the Platonic fold; his Jesus, like Socrates, has an ugly exterior but a beautiful soul. The most Clement will allow himself to say – rarely – is that "divine" *eros* is present when "real beauty" shines out in the soul (*Protrepticus* 11.117.2).

3.8 THE TRUTH ABOUT IRENAEUS

We must go back a little in time. Among Christian thinkers before the Alexandrians, though Jesus has a beautiful soul, beauty is hardly a divine attribute and love of God is normally disconnected from the Greek notion that erotic love (however explained) is of the physically beautiful.

According to Balthasar, however, although Irenaeus, the second-century bishop of Lyon, also applies Isaiah 53 to the appearance of Jesus in the Passion, a Christian aesthetic can be recognized in his writings.[34] This claim, if true, would be surprising and significant, since Irenaeus is largely innocent of those Platonic influences which promoted a more serious concern with beauty among the Alexandrians and Cappadocians and in Augustine. According to Balthasar, Irenaeus' "theological aesthetic", which concerns itself not only with the glory of God but with the splendour of his creation, was developed as part of his reply to the myth-making fantasies of the Gnostics. Irenaeus' approach, in fact, largely derives from the seeming historical realism of the Old Testament, yet perhaps a parallel with Plotinus

---

[34] Balthasar, *The Glory of the Lord* II (Edinburgh 1984) 64ff.

can also be discerned and I have argued that in Plotinus the One's splendour (*aglaia*) is recognizable as beauty.

According to Balthasar, whereas Plato developed philosophy from myth, Gnostic teachers such as Valentinus and his successors proposed a mythical replacement of both philosophy and history, substituting "idealist" products of their own imaginations for the given facts of biblical theology and history. In replacing God's historical dealings with mankind with projections of their own psychological states, they created a fantasy universe which was to prove, in revised versions and usually in Christian or ex-Christian dress, a fatal attraction to such influential "romantic" figures as Blake, Shelley and Wagner.

Balthasar's account of Irenaeus, however, is typically modern, and part of a vast and questionable prioritizing of an aesthetic over a conceptually based theology – a design arguably nearer to that of Irenaeus' Gnostic opponents than to Irenaeus himself.[35] Certainly Irenaeus takes over the account in the Old Testament (and in Hebrews) of the universe as the revelation of God's splendour, and adds his own theology of the "recapitulation" of all things in Christ who makes that splendour manifest. Yet there is little suggestion of an erotic path from the universe to God, either by way of wonder at the marvels of God's handiwork or by any recognition of a special *beauty* in humanity – though Irenaeus regards not just the soul but the whole human being as God's image (*Against Heresies* 5.16.1).

Recognizing the skill and splendour of God as Creator, Irenaeus shows little awareness of any innate power which (by God's grace) may lead the universe, or even the human being, back to its maker. In explaining man's relationship as image to his divine Archetype he does not emphasize the eroticism of the Song of Songs or other Old Testament texts. Thus, whatever resources in the biblical tradition might harness *eros* and the love of beauty to Christianity, Irenaeus makes little use of them. Despite "recapitulation", his appreciation of God's achievement is metaphysically declarative but psychologically static. Man is to "embrace" God, through the power of God's love and his own (unanalysed) "freedom", but the human capacity for such embracing is merely assumed. There is mention of physical beauty, but the psychological impact of that (or any other) beauty is hardly investigated.

---

[35] Criticism of Balthasar's account of Irenaeus is not necessarily criticism of his entire project, nor is it my concern to discuss the strengths and weaknesses of the latter. For an introduction to some of Balthasar's more interesting epistemological ideas (with a certain discussion of beauty) see D. C. Schindler, "Reason in Mystery. Gestalt: Knowledge and Aesthetic Experience in Balthasar and Augustine", *Second Spring* 6 (2004) 23–33.

There are metaphysical as well as psychological difficulties. In his analysis of Irenaeus Balthasar assumes God's glory to God's beauty, the requisite for a genuine "aesthetic". Balthasar follows Irenaeus in identifying beauty with what is fitting, with measure and order, in language which is largely that of popular Stoicism. God creates through his "artistic logos" (*Demonstration* 38); his creation is "in measure and order" (*Against Heresies* 4.6); nothing lacks proportion because nothing is without number. Thus creation shows the "glory" of God who drew from himself – a curious if unexplained phrase – the "beautiful form" of created things and the "beautiful ordering" of the world (2.6.3). Lacking is any justification of the claim that we can move from God's glory not merely to the *order* of the world and its revelation of God's majesty but specifically to its *beauty*: that is, unless beauty simply *is* order, or what is fitting (*Demonstration* 2), as the Stoics supposed. It has been widely recognized that Irenaeus tends to argue that if X is fitting and also possible, it is the case. Though this may be accepted as a working hypothesis, it requires the further assumption that what is produced is beautiful. But in what sense?

For Irenaeus the physical beauty (i.e., the proportion and appropriateness) of the world is an aspect of the glory of the Creator; but an argument from the order of the world is an argument not for God's beauty but for his power to get things right. In reading the Old Testament we find such power and splendour as awesome, but not as erotically inspirational. There may be here precursor of an "aesthetic", but certainly there is no notion of beauty itself, only acceptance of the popular and Stoic notion that proportion and order themselves constitute beauty. Nor is there any "Plotinian" claim that God is beautiful. The appropriate and the fitting may indeed be aspects of beauty; certainly they are aspects of art that the artist can produce – though he may also skilfully produce a certain (apparent) ugliness and inappropriateness.

It is fair to conclude that Irenaeus has no broadly theistic (in effect "platonizing") view of the power of beauty in physical objects to lead by inspiration to Beauty itself; rather, since "the glory of God is a living man" (*Against Heresies* 4.20.7), he finds the splendour of God is specifically, immediately and uniquely in Christ and *Christian* theism. This certainly leaves open the possibility that a more "platonizing" position can be developed and that Christ be seen and desired as a fully personal beauty, yet Irenaeus gives no hint that all beauty is somehow metaphysically associated with the beauty of Christ. The furthest he will go is to say that goodness must be among our natural endowments, otherwise we would not be able to recognize how attractive and beautiful it is; this amounts to little more than saying what a fine thing goodness is.

Irenaeus overcomes the Gnostics less by an aesthetic theology than by a hard-headed appeal to evident fact and resolute eschewing of theosophical fantasies. He should be seen against the general background of the earliest Christian art with its simple symbols of salvation: its Good Shepherds and Susannas. His "aesthetic" is a declarative and kerygmatic revelation of God's glory and majesty, with no appeal to the psychological and emotional "pull" and inspiration of beauty itself as ordinarily understood. Hence little fresh attempt to explain why what is beautiful is beautiful; it is simply beautiful in its appropriate form – "appropriate" being persuasively defined (or rather left undefined) – as revealing of the splendour of God. Glory may be a divine attribute, but it is not to be identified with beauty, personal or impersonal. Irenaeus has not grasped the need to enrich the Christian account of God's majesty – with its traditional accompaniment of the fear of the Lord – with a Christian account of God's beauty, the object of human desire.

3.9 ORIGEN ON GOD'S BEAUTY

Origen's *Commentary* (and *Homilies*) on the Song of Songs mark a major advance in Christian sensibility. Although "carnal" love is certainly "from Satan" (*Homily* 1), Origen's likening of all human souls to the Bride in her relationship with the divine Spouse is an unambiguous attempt to argue that the language of erotic love (indeed erotic love of a female) is an appropriate vehicle for describing progression in Christian holiness, and his confidence, even recklessness, in the matter is evidenced in his insistence – in contrast to Clement's tentativeness – that for such love the word *eros* is appropriate. For Origen the soul, in seeking God, must become "beautiful" and female (*formosa, Homily* 1.3); that is, receptive (but not passive). God's Word, too, the object of the soul's love, is beautiful: *pulchritudine et decore* (*Prologue to Commentary on Song of Songs* 2.17).

The Word is the image and *splendour* of God, but this *splendour* is now to be understood *not only* as glory but as spiritual beauty; that is why *eros–amor* is the appropriate word to express the soul's love of Christ (2.20). The soul, as Wisdom 8.2. puts it, is a "lover of his form" (*decus*); there is nothing "indecorous" about the love of higher things, and they are beautiful. In language Plato might have used Origen says that Divine Wisdom is a beauty that arouses to love those who understand in depth the divine and heavenly beauty (*Commentary on John* 1.55).

By reducing the love of physical beauty to allegory, and thus apparently neutralizing it, Origen is able to speak of the soul's love not merely of God but of the beauty of God; and – again in contrast to the (late) Stoic qualms of Clement – in using the "e-word" (*eros*) for that love, he has unwittingly paved part of the way for the love of physical beauty not from Satan but in Christ. Jesus' Transfiguration, an "anticipation" of the Resurrection, shows us that he is both ugly and beautiful, representing stages in our advance toward likeness to God. While Isaiah 53 indicates his ugliness, Psalm 44 indicates his spiritual beauty (cf. *Against Celsus* 6.76).[36] Christ is not only *splendor*, the revealed majesty of God, but specifically both Beauty itself (*pulchritudo, decus*) and the source of all other beauty, hence of the highest inspiration. Here Beauty is clearly and philosophically identified as a divine attribute without reduction to the ambiguous – if not indeed distinct – "glory". Origen's claim, in effect, is that there is a specifically Christian, therefore correct, account of beauty, so that, in more modern parlance, a Christian aesthetic becomes possible – and therefore that any serious aesthetic must be Christian.

That Origen could not have written such an account of his own achievement should cause no surprise; it is an axiom of the history of ideas that new concepts arise often long before they are recognized. No-one in antiquity talked about "aesthetics"; indeed, as I have noted, the concept was not in use until comparatively recent times. In antiquity "aesthetics" was a part of ethics, and in claiming that Christ is beautiful, and as such an object of desire, Origen is implying (but not asserting) – as were the Platonists – that moral or spiritual beauty is *the* reference point and cause of all forms of beauty, physical or spiritual. He can do that because he has accepted the platonizing claim that Beauty it is that inspires us: that is, that it is the Good in its affective aspect. We love the Good as beautiful – hence as the spur to creative action – while we recognize it as good.

"Erotic" love is a form of directed (or "intentional") desire: specifically desire for the beautiful. It is not mere feeling but a drive, in Greek a *daimon*. The problem, as Plato and Plotinus had realized, is how to distinguish what is "really" beautiful from what is less beautiful and what merely seems beautiful. On that discernment depends the action inspired. If it is true, as I have argued elsewhere,[37] in explanation of another Platonic thesis, that we are multiple selves, at best moving in hope towards a simple and completed "soul", then so long as we are divided we shall have divided and diverse loves, because we shall find different and diverse things, often perversely, beautiful. Just as we have

---

[36] Cf. J. McGuckin, "The Changing Forms of Jesus", in L. Lies (ed.) *Origeniana Quarta* (Vienna 1987) 215–222.

[37] J. M. Rist, *Real Ethics* (Cambridge 2002).

many "goods", so we shall strive for many "beauties", and since some of these "beauties" are ugly to the good man, we shall find ourselves with disordered desires not only for sex but for other attractions ("Money, lovely money"), as Plato had already pointed out in the *Republic*.

Even apart from obviously ugly "beauties", we shall have problems over choice: we shall have to prefer some beauties to others either because they are more beautiful, or because the others are for various good reasons "not for me". We cannot hope to make such choices if we have no standard, and Origen offers the standard of Christ. Nor perhaps can we determine in advance what choices are to be made – though rules of thumb are available.

Unsurprisingly, Origen's version of all this is far from perfect, not least because he is a substance dualist and hence (in the steps of Philo and Clement) inclined to set the goods and the beauties of the separate soul too radically against the goods and beauties of the body – even of the "spiritual" resurrection body. Here indeed we see something of the root of what is at times unreasonably denied: that Christians in antiquity were often properly accused as dreary enemies of the beautiful. There are times in antiquity, as later, when this charge looks absurd, but it is a historical irony that Christians have produced masterpieces of art – albeit often within a limited repertoire – while inclining to anathematize physical beauties in their more theoretical writings. The Renaissance corrected this ancient inheritance, but, unfortunately but predictably, swung the balance too far the other way, leaving the road open to the modern vision of the artist (and even of the "celebrity") as a kind of god, or as the nearest thing to a god there is. I shall return to that road in due course.

As for Origen, there is the further caveat that he is a theological subordinationist, putting Christ on a lower ontological level than God the Father. We see repercussions of this in his attitude to beauty – which in this respect is more easily harmonized with the Old Testament. It is Christ, not the Father, who is beautiful; hence, if we put Origen's Christology and "aesthetics" together, we have to conclude that – for all the progress he made – he still manages to attach beauty to the strictly less divine. And although he follows a platonizing schema in allowing physical beauty to be beautiful by participation in a divine Beauty, his fear of "carnal" *eros* inhibits a fully comprehensive Christian account both of art and of physical beauty.

3.10 METHODIUS AND THE FOURTH-CENTURY REVOLUTION

Although Origen laid much of the groundwork for a Christian – and platonizing – "aesthetics" which would go beyond the mere assertion that our universe is an image of God's glory, and for a Christian vision of

physical beauty, especially the beauty of the human body, the full significance of his work – however historically transmitted – only became apparent in the next century, in both East and West. The new situation is
recognized (though its novelty is rarely appreciated) in the works of Gregory
of Nyssa and of Augustine. The role of an earlier figure, Methodius of
Olympus, both follower and opponent of Origen, is usually neglected.

Before looking briefly at Methodius, we should notice an effect on the
mentality of Christianity in this period of its increasing distance from
Judaism. Whereas for Justin and Irenaeus the Old Testament is at the
centre of their faith – not least in that the Hebrew Bible has to be defended
against variant interpretations by Jews and Gnostics – and in Justin's time
readings in church were normally from the Hebrew not the Christian Bible,
by the fourth century, though Gnosticism especially in its later Manichaean
manifestation was still very much alive, there was no great difficulty about
insisting on the continuing importance of the Old Testament against the
Manichaeans, while contemporary Jews were rather ignored than refuted.
Already in the third century the New Testament had a centrality which in
earlier days of Christianity it had yet to acquire in written form, and the Old
Testament was read ever more widely in terms of the New.

Where Irenaeus and Justin had inherited from the Old Testament a
limited set of attitudes to beauty as God's splendour, by the fourth century
much of the original context of that sense of beauty had receded. For
Christian intellectuals in particular, concern with beauty was to be found
primarily in the writings not of Jews but of Platonic philosophers. For
although, as I have observed, early Christians seem generally to have been
less affected by the Jewish hostility to images than is sometimes supposed,[38]
the prospect of an aniconic Christianity remained alluring and Christians
remained exceedingly wary of statues out of fear of idolatry. Hence, despite
Plato's anxiety about artistic representation in the *Republic*[39] – echoed by
Plotinus who, according to Porphyry (*Life of Plotinus* 1), refused to have his
portrait painted – the Platonic tradition was to remain, after Origen, the
primary source of what was to develop into consciously Christian accounts
of beauty. Gregory of Nyssa and Augustine, in particular, were to use
Plotinus' treatise *On Beauty* (*Ennead* 1.6) to transform the old (Philonic)
notion of *eros* for God into a concept of *eros* for God as beauty.

---

[38] Cf. also J. Elsner, "Late Antique Art: The Problem of the Concept and the Cumulative Aesthetic", in
S. Swain and M. Edwards (eds.), *Approaching Late Antiquity* (Oxford 2004) 271–309.

[39] C. Osborne, "The Repudiation of Representation in Plato's *Republic* and Its Repercussions", *PCPS* 33
(1987) 53–73.

Turning then to Methodius, and in particular to his treatise titled *Symposium*, with its obvious Platonic echoes – and subtitled *On Chastity*, with an equally obvious Christian reference – we see Origen's Platonism and Christianity further developed into a uniquely Christian mix. That mix would be often neglected in centuries to come as more "encratite" versions of Christian asceticism which Methodius would probably have disliked – marked by treatises not on chastity but more specifically on virginity – tended to prevail. Nevertheless, Methodius' representation of God the Father as beauty (an advance on Origen: 6.1) and the source of beauty (6.2.1ff.), and of Christ as beauty and lover of beauty (7.1), marks a strikingly powerful and coherent development.[40]

Following Origen, Methodius wrote a commentary on the Song of Songs which unfortunately is lost, but we can identify some of his basic attitudes from his *Symposium*. Like Origen he refers the bride of the Song both to the soul and to the Church; like Origen he has no hesitation about the Platonic language of *eros*. Indeed, as is becoming increasingly recognized, the very title *Symposium* indicates a wish not merely to use Platonic themes, but to appropriate and develop those themes in a Christian sense: for Methodius the highest form of *eros* for God as beauty resides in chastity (*hagneia*; 10.1.15; cf. 6.2.6), of which virginity is the dominant but not the exclusive form.

Methodius' purpose, made clear in his defence of marriage and procreation in a Christian but "erotic" world, and especially in his conclusion, is not only to appropriate Platonism (apparently not yet Neoplatonism) in the service of Christianity, but to target "encratite" aberrations. In effect he uses Origenist ideas and exegesis in an attack on an Origenist ideology of perfection. As for beauty, the object of eros-chastity, Methodius' Christ, lover of beauty (7.1.30–31; 7.1.39), is modelled in part on the charioteer of Plato's *Phaedrus*,[41] while the soul as virgin must be a lover of things beautiful: that is, of Christ himself.

There is little specific discussion in the *Symposium* about the relationship between the beauty of Christ and the physical beauties of the world, but the whole setting of the dialogue is redolent of that theme. Fully present is the Platonic thesis that physical beauties partake of the beauty of the divine, the basis for any Christian aesthetics. Yet it is remarkable that Methodius offers his reading of Platonic and Christian beauty with no apparent reference to

---

[40] The best account of Methodius on *eros* and beauty is M. B. Zorzi, "La reinterpretazione dell' eros platonico nel *Simposio* di Metodio d'Olimpo", *Adamantius* 9 (2003) 102–127. Zorzi makes good use of principles developed by E. Prinzivalli, *L'esegesi di Metodio d'Olimpo* (Rome 1984).

[41] See Zorzi, "L'eros platonico", esp. 118–119.

the specifically beauty-driven version of Platonism which helped mark off the philosophy of Plotinus from that of his Middle Platonic predecessors and which undoubtedly enriched the views of beauty of the two Fathers who set the tone for later Christian aesthetics in both East and West: Gregory of Nyssa and Augustine.

Could the explanation be that Methodius differs from the Neoplatonists (and from Origen) in offering a more "holistic" account of man? We are a soul-and-body, both to be renewed in the resurrection. As is normal in Christian antiquity, Methodius lacks the ontology to explain this, but certainly believes it to be the case. Christ is thus the lover of the beauty of the whole person, though it is the soul in the body (with nothing "carnal" about it) that he loves (7.1.57–58). Yet one of the reasons for Methodius' concern with virginity is that he believes it to be an "uncorrupted" state of body as well as of soul which foreshadows (and "promotes") the resurrection (cf. 6.2; 10.3.19).

3.II GREGORY OF NYSSA: DEVELOPMENT IN THE EAST

Methodius' treatment of human and divine beauty foreshadows what was to come when Neoplatonic accounts of beauty were more fully appropriated by Christian thinkers in the fourth and early fifth centuries. I shall consider first Gregory of Nyssa, then Augustine. There are many differences between them, but also striking similarities, of which the most important and surprising is their *assumption* that beauty, with many of its Neoplatonic characteristics, is a divine attribute, and that this does not require argument. In briefly discussing each of them I shall examine a common love of beauty which underlies their divergent accounts of human nature and of the love of man for God. In particular I want to draw attention to the *development* of their thought along parallel but independent lines.

Whereas modern writers are normally aware of development in Augustine – though they may disagree about the details – recognition of similar development in Gregory is a recent scholarly phenomenon.[42] At least

---

[42] Since his "discovery" by Balthasar and Daniélou, Gregory's "mysticism" has been the subject of much profitable scholarly work. Among the more useful contributions on beauty and Gregory's development are the following: J. Daniélou, "La chronologie des oeuvres de Grégoire de Nysse", *Studia Patristica* 7, TU 92 (1966) 159–169; G. May, "Die Chronologie des Lebens und der Werke des Gregor von Nyssa", in *Ecriture et culture philosophique dans la pensée de Grégoire de Nysse* (Leiden 1971) 51–67; A. A. Mosshammer, "The Created and the Uncreated in Gregory of Nyssa "Contra Eunomium I", in L. F. Mateo-Seco and J. Bastero (eds.), *El "Contra Eunomium I" en la producción literaria de Gregorio de Nisa* (Pamplona 1988) 353–379; C. De Salvo, *L'oltre nel presente* (Milan 1996); Osborne, *Eros Unveiled*; A. Capboscq, *Schönheit Gottes und des Menschen: Theologische Untersuchung des Werkes "In Canticum Canticorum" von Gregor von Nyssa aus der Perspektive des Schönen und des Guten* (Frankfurt 2000).

part of the explanation of this is that Augustine, being more of a theological loner (especially in his early days), makes no secret of his intellectual debts to paganism, and is thus able to argue openly with the pagans, whereas Gregory, operating within a well-established Greek Christian theological tradition, thinks primarily in terms of the continuity of that tradition even when he makes (unacknowledged) use of non-Christian sources.

Gregory's work is roughly divided into three stages, the first, and most obviously Plotinian, represented especially by *On Virginity*, where Gregory is already unambiguous in his opinion. Not only is Christ, as Wisdom and Logos, beautiful, the expression of divine beauty, the source of beauty, and lover of the beauty of the human soul, but (contrary to the view of Origen) God the Father too is appropriately to be called "beautiful" and the object of an *eros* by which he draws all to himself.

For Gregory the "divine nature" of the whole Trinity is beautiful,[43] because his is a post-Nicene picture.[44] In Plotinus the first hypostasis is the *source* of beauty or is beauty in some special sense, while the *Form* of Beauty is associated with *Nous* at a lower ontological level. For Gregory, as a "neo-Nicene", that would be impossible; any divine attribute (other than those of Fatherhood and Sonship) appropriate to Christ must also be appropriate to the Father.

In both the early and middle phases of Gregory's theology,[45] our love for God is still understood in "Origenist" fashion as the love of a finite perfection and therefore completed in our achieving perfection in him. Furthermore, in the early Gregory, such love is "semi-Pelagian" in that God responds to the love and prayer we choose to direct to him.

The second stage of Gregory's writing (represented typically by the *Creation of Man, Against Eunomius* I and *On the Soul and the Resurrection*) is marked by two major and "typically" Gregorian developments. First the emphasis on the *diastēma* or gap between the Creator and the entire created universe comes to pre-empt, though not to replace, the standard platonizing distinction between the intelligible and the sensible, enabling Gregory to recognize that God is the Creator (*ex nihilo*) of "things invisible" as well as visible. The second emphasis is on God's infinity,[46] probably worked out in

---

[43] *De Virg.* II; cf. *De an. et resurr.* (*PG* 46, col. 92).

[44] *De Virg.* II; cf. *De Perf. Chr.* 8.1. More generally see F. Ricken, "Nikaia als Krisis des altchristlichen Platonismus", *Theologie und Philosophie* 44 (1969) 321–341.

[45] Cf. *De an et resurr.* (*PG* 46, 89).

[46] See E. Mühlenberg, *Die Unendlichkeit Gottes bei Gregor von Nyssa* (Göttingen 1966); C. Kannengiesser, "L'infinité divine chez Grégoire de Nysse", *RSR* 55 (1967) 55–65; A. Lévy, "Aux confines du créé et de l'incréé: Les dimensions de l'épectase chez Grégoire de Nysse", *RSPT* 84 (2000) 247–274.

opposition to the claim of the "neo-Arian" Eunomius that the only attribute appropriate to God the Father is "Ingenerate". Gregory's notion of God's infinity is parallel to ideas in Plotinus, and seems to have found support in that pagan source, but he probably first developed the idea independently of the *Enneads*.

The combination of these two more or less "un-Plotinian" themes enables Gregory, in the third and last stage of his thought – represented by the *Life of Moses* and the *Commentary on the Song of Songs* – to propose his famous thesis that our love for God is never completed: that we are ever able to deepen our "likeness" to God through an expanding love which suffers neither from satiety nor neediness: an endlessly continuing desire without the possibly endless inadequacy of a love desperate for "completion".

Together with this doctrine of "continual progress" (*epektasis*) comes Gregory's "Augustinian" and "non-Pelagian" development, in that he now recognizes that our love for God's beauty originates in God's compassion for our ugliness, and we should pray for that (*Life of Moses* 230; *Commentary on the Song of Songs* 59). God's beauty first makes the soul beautiful, and so, with the aid of Christ the Logos, "lovable".[47] Curiously, though Gregory follows Origen in his *Commentary on the Song of Songs* in making the soul as bride in love with Christ the bridegroom – that love being reciprocal,[48] as at times in Methodius – yet sometimes, in the spirit of texts about the suitors of Lady Philosophy from Plato's *Republic*, he also thinks (as in his *Commentary on Proverbs*) of Christ-Wisdom as the female object of the love of the purified soul.

But Gregory, as we have seen, is still in the "Alexandrian" tradition in treating of man's creation in God's image. His account of God's beauty, God's love of beauty and God's creation of the beauties of the universe forms the basis for a specifically Christian "aesthetic". In the steps of Origen he holds that the soul is in love with God in Christ, who is eminently beautiful. But fear of the body is if anything stronger in Gregory even than in Origen, for the body is marked by sexuality, and God's original design for the human race was for non-sexualized beings. Reproduction would not have been sexual and the human body, as presently functioning and constructed, is, in the tradition of Philo (and of the extreme Platonism of the *Phaedo*[49]) downplayed as carnal and therefore no object of God's love.

---

[47] *GNO* VI (*CCt.* 1.5) 46, 8–9; VI 49, 17–18.

[48] *GNO* VI (*CCt.* 4.10) 264, 3–5; cf. F. Dünzl, *Braut und Bräutigam: Die Auslegung des Canticum durch Gregor von Nyssa* (Tübingen 1993) 341–347.

[49] Gregory also follows Philo, against Origen as well as the Platonists, in his account of the Divine Darkness.

Hence in Gregory, as in Origen, the doctrine of the resurrection of the body is fudged: it is only the "spiritual", non-genital body – as supposedly of Adam before the Fall – which is resurrected. This position Augustine was to reject, abandoning the notion of a "spiritual", non-sexual reproduction in Eden, and arguing that our final state, with a more physical version of the resurrected "spiritual" body, is higher than that of unfallen Adam and Eve.

What sort of "aesthetic" could Gregory have achieved? God is beautiful, the source of all beauty and Creator of the beauties of the universe. Thus spiritual and moral beauties are higher than physical beauty, though physical beauty, platonically, partakes of higher beauty, and points the way to the beauty of God and the soul. An essential aspect of a physical object, *qua* beautiful, is that it indicates the beauty of its maker. The natural world, *qua* beautiful, shows the beauty of God; the world of art, *qua* beautiful, shows the beauty of man its maker, created in God's image and as creator of beauties in his turn.

There is no place, however, for human sexualized beauty,[50] which is the "beauty" not of beautiful unfallen man, but of the sexualized post-lapsarian version. Indeed, what Gregory describes as human is not a man, but a kind of angel. Hence, while he has the opportunity to sketch an account of all beauty, divine and human, moral and physical, Gregory fails in the crucial case of the beauty of the human body, let alone of the beauty of artistic representations of the human body. As in ethics, so in aesthetics, his defective "anthropology" is at the root of his ultimate failure to construct a complete and intelligible account of physical beauty.

Yet it must be allowed that Gregory is aware of the problem: there is an "unbreakable bond" between the mind and the body.[51] It is not clear whether Gregory knew the work of Nemesius of Emesa;[52] it is at least certain that he made no significant use of it. Had he done so, he might have discovered in Nemesius' unusual sympathy for Aristotelianism a way out of the moral and "aesthetic" cul-de-sac of his "angelism".

3.12 AUGUSTINE: DEVELOPMENT IN THE WEST[53]

In 1918 P. Alfaric published a controversial book in which he claimed that the original conversion of Augustine in Milan was not to Christianity but to

---

[50] Cf. *De Virg.* 12.2.48–50 (Aubineau).   [51] *HomOpif.* 72 (*PG* 44, 177 BC).
[52] See Motta, *La mediazione estrema.*
[53] Studies of Augustine's "aesthetics" include K. Svoboda, *L'Esthétique de saint Augustin et ses sources* (Brno 1933); R. J. O'Connell, *Art and the Christian Intelligence in Saint Augustine* (Cambridge, Mass. 1978); Balthasar, *The Glory of the Lord* II; C. Harrison, *Beauty and Revelation in the Thought of Saint Augustine* (Oxford 1992).

the Neoplatonism of Plotinus. As stated, such a disjunction is seriously misleading and has been generally rejected. The truth is not that Augustine was converted first to Neoplatonism and then to Christianity but that he was converted to the "spiritualizing" form of Christianity originating in Alexandria in which first Platonic, then Neoplatonic ideas were used to provide a philosophical explanation of Christianity and to attempt a certain assimilation of Christianity and Neoplatonism insofar as they might be able to be read as compatible.

Nowhere is this clearer than in the realm of "aesthetics". As we have seen in the case of Irenaeus, it was possible in the early days of Christianity to talk about the splendour of God, or to see Christ as the splendour of God, and then to identify the effects of that splendour in the material cosmos. What was not available was any philosophical attempt to understand what it is about the beauty of physical objects – and not simply in our awe before their maker – that enables them to be recognized as the splendour of God. One could talk about beauty as splendour, but the material for a substantive theory of aesthetics was lacking.

Clement of Alexandria began to improve this situation by adapting a certain amount of theory from the Stoics, while Origen's use of the Song of Songs opened up much wider possibilities. Gregory carried Origen's work further, aided by the semi-personalized account of beauty in the *Enneads*. Augustine, for his part, had the opportunity to develop ideas gleaned from the philosophical writings of Cicero, then from the Platonists: not least in availing himself of Plotinus' view that God himself is inspirational Beauty and the source of Beauty: beauty, not simply splendour; inspiration, not simply awe. At last we find the possibility of a comprehensive Christian understanding of beauty in all its manifestations.

Among many ancient Christians, including Augustine, it is Christ himself, the perfect image of the Father, who is recognized as divine beauty (*species Dei, On Music* 6.11.29–30). But moving beyond the uncertainties of some of his Latin predecessors – not least of Ambrose – Augustine was always convinced that not only Christ but also man is created not simply "according to the image of God" but *as* the image of God, and for most of his life he held that man is the image of the whole Trinity: not a perfect but an unequal image (*impar imago*).[54]

In a highly enhanced version of Alexandrian theology, Augustine dilates time and again on the beauty of God (*Soliloquies* 1.1.3) who is "most just,

---

[54] For further discussion see especially Markus, "'Imago' and 'Similitudo'"; more generally T. Camelot, "La théologie de l'image de Dieu", *RSPT* 40 (1956) 443–471.

most beautiful" (*Magnitude of the Soul* 36.80), and on the beauty of Christ who is the supreme form and beauty of God (*On Music* 6.17.56, etc.). Especially in the *Confessions* he insists that it is this beauty, so ancient and so new (*Confessions* 10.27.38; cf. 7.17.23), that he has come to *love*, this beauty of "form" which gives us *delight*, for, as he tells us in Plotinian fashion, we can love only what is beautiful and delightful (*On Music* 6.11.29–30; 6.13.38).[55] The highest beauty is a divine (and therefore necessary) attribute; God is simply beautiful because he exists: by nature, that is, not by creation (*On True Religion* 18.35–36). His existence, goodness and beauty are one.

It was an essential part of Augustine's conversion to Christianity that he was converted to belief in an *immaterial* God; hence for Augustine the highest beauty is immaterial. This – despite claims that Jahwe is somehow "spiritual" – is no necessary part of Old Testament and early Christian theology, so Augustine must offer a Christian version of how one can speak both of the "beauty" of an immaterial object – that is, of God – and also of the beauties of the material world, whether natural objects or human constructs. He is in a rather Platonic dilemma and the truth behind Alfaric's exaggerations is that Augustine is committed to a version of Christianity that requires (*inter alia*) some specifically Platonic philosophizing about beauty.

In his account of physical beauty, Augustine offers us a thesis that is a curious blend of Stoicism (largely derived from Cicero) and the anti-Stoicism of Plotinus. The Stoics, as we have seen, accounted for beauty in terms of symmetry and proportion, and Augustine (whose first – now lost – work was on *The Beautiful and the Fitting* (*Confessions* 4.13.20; 4.15.24–27)) allows this more weight than might be expected from an enthusiast for Plotinus: in his *On Order* beauty is to be found in the appropriateness of the parts (*congruentia partium*, 2.11.33). Plotinus, as we have seen, finds that the Stoic account is incomplete, since symmetry and proportion fail to account for all the beauties of the physical world. He argues that beauty, the mark of the intelligible world, shines on harmonious objects, colouring them with *life*, for life, beauty and the fullness of existence go together. Insofar as the material participates in the beauty of the immaterial, it can reveal something of living beauty as well as of its own material perfection.

Augustine ignores some of the more pertinent criticism by Plotinus of Stoic symmetry. Retaining the Stoic language of symmetry and proportion, he reads it with platonizing eyes. It is the form of the intelligible that reveals

---

[55] Cf. *Serm.* 159.3; *EnPs.* 118.10.6. As we have seen, the idea that only the truly beautiful can be loved is Stoic as well as Platonic; cf. *SVF* 3.598: that which is worthy of love is *kalos*.

beauty, through mathematical structures, in the physical world.[56] The physical beauty of an object is indeed indicated by the proportion of its parts and a certain sweetness of colour (*City of God* 22.19.2; *Letter* 3.4). But then comes the platonizing twist: the form of each thing is indicated by its unity, and every beautiful thing, insofar as it exists and is formed, possesses a vestige of the divine unity.[57]

Plotinus adheres to the Platonic dictum that we love what is lovable: that is, beautiful. Augustine (like Gregory) expands the more "pagan" Platonism, not in a wholly new direction but certainly with new emphasis. Beauty is recognized not in a Plotinian world of impersonal (if living) realities, namely the beauteous Forms, but in the living *person* of Christ himself.

We have seen how Plotinus, by linking Forms and the "Divine Mind", avoids Plato's original problems, in the *Symposium*, about an ardent love for what is impersonal, and therefore necessarily non-reciprocating, but neglects the reciprocity of love in the *Phaedrus*. In Plotinus the world of Forms is living, but unable to reciprocate because neither it nor the One is personal *enough*. Augustine, like Gregory, is able to draw on the resources of Christianity to develop an account of the personal character of true beauty: it is from the personal beauty of God in Christ that lesser beauties, especially those of God's image, man, are to be explained.

Augustine can further maintain the Platonic and Plotinian emphasis on the delight that both seeks and results from what is beautiful.[58] He cites the Platonic maxim, "We cannot love anything unless it is beautiful" (*On Music* 6.13.38), but already with oddities: in *Catechizing the Simple* (4.7) we read, "There is no greater invitation to love than prevenient love," and in the *Confessions* (10.29.40) the phrase that incensed Pelagius: "Love, who are always ablaze . . . enkindle me. Give what you command and command what you will." Thus we see God as the creator and sustainer of love in the human lover. Elsewhere, both in the relation of Adam to Eve before the Fall – Adam makes Eve beautiful by loving her (*On Psalms* 132.10) – and in his sermons on John's first epistle under the general rubric that God is love and love is God, Augustine argues at length that it is the special virtue of the highest love that it makes the less-than-beautiful beautiful and thus lovable (*On John's Epistle* 9.9).[59] Where Plotinus was already saying that the *effect* of

---

[56] *De Ord.* 2.15.42–43; *DLA* 2.16.41–44; *De Mus.* 6.13.38 (Beauty is *aequalitas numerosa*); *DVR* 32.59; 42.79.
[57] *GenMan.* 1.12.18; *De Trin.* 6.10.11; *DVR* 32.59–60; 42.79.
[58] *De Mus.* 6.11.29–30; *Conf.* 4.13.20; *Ad Simp.* 1.2.22.
[59] See T. J. van Bavel, "The Double Face of Love in St. Augustine. The Daring Inversion: Love is God", *CIA* III (Rome 1987) 69–80 and especially D. Dideberg, *Saint Augustin et la première epître de saint*

the One on its lovers is to make them beautiful and lovable, Augustine (like
Gregory) goes further and in a different mode. It is the *direct and personal* act,
not merely the effect, of God through the Spirit to make those who love him
beautiful, for love (which is God) is the beauty of the soul.

Here we have a marked development of the view going back to the
Symposium that love (*eros*) is a kind of need of the beautiful. In its incomplete form, that is in human beings, need for the beauty of God is ever an
element in *eros*. In its perfect form of love identified with the Holy Spirit,
there is in God both a love of the lovable and a creation of the lovable, not
from need but from the divine goodness. Both in Plato, and – more
strangely since love operates at a cosmic level – in Plotinus, love is creative,
yet almost incidentally so, as is particularly obvious in Plotinus, where
emanation is not a deliberate act but an effect (almost a description) of
God's being. Despite Plotinus' unusual remarks about God's will in 6.8, the
One is only minimally a directly efficient cause.

Referring back to the *Symposium*, Platonists always held that in seeing the
beautiful the lover would want to create in the beautiful. Augustine looks at
the theme from the other end, from the point of view of the perfect lover
and of Beauty itself, that is, from the point of view of God. Plato had always
urged, both in the *Symposium* and especially in the *Phaedrus*, that the lover
will "work on" the beloved and try to make him better, more virtuous. But,
lacking a contrast between creator and creature, he is unable to portray the
perfect lover creating what is lovable, but only a good man recognizing what
is lovable – that is, beautiful – and improving it. Augustine developed that
theme as love in God identified with the Holy Spirit.[60] Augustine's more
developed theism enabled him to go where Plato would seem to have
wished, had he not lacked the metaphysical underpinnings.

If Love is God, Augustine's portrait of himself at Carthage as "in love
with love" is not wholly vicious (*Confessions* 3.1.1); rather, he did not
recognize Who Love is. Eventually he was entranced by God's beauty
(*Confessions* 7.17.23), for love is beautiful (*Sermon* 365.1), and God is the
Beauty of every beauty (*Confessions* 4.13.20), the "measure without measure,
the number without number, the weight without weight" (*Literal
Commentary* 4.3.8).

Jean: Une théologie de l'amour (Paris 1975). Following Hultgren, Dideberg (143–236) shows how
   Augustine's thought on the identification of Love with God develops from *De Fide et Symbolo* (AD 393)
   through the *Tractatus in Epistolam Ioannis* (407) to *Ep.* 186 and *Serm.* 34 (of 418).
[60] For more detail see J. M. Rist, "Augustine: Freedom, Love and Intention", in L. Alici, R. Piccolomini
   and A. Pieretti (eds.), *Il mistero del male e la libertà possibile (IV): Ripensare Agostino* (Rome 1997) 17,
   and "Love and Will: Around *De Trinitate* XV 20, 38", in J. Brachtendorf (ed.), *Gott und Sein Bild*
   (Paderborn 2000) 205–216.

Augustine's position is sometimes un-Platonic where it is startlingly Christian. Plato's lover does not need to make the beloved lovely, because he is not *so* unlovely. Augustine's position must satisfy and "overcome" his own doctrine of the Fall and the more radical problem of moral evil in a Christian rather than a Platonic universe. Plato's lover chooses someone worth loving, who is already in some sense beautiful; he would not waste his time on someone unlovely; that would normally be to set himself an impossible task.

According to Plato, we are to retain an unblemished moral core, a thesis that Christians, more realistically, denied, and hence the demand on the Platonic lover is less; he has not to regenerate, merely to spruce up the true self, to reveal beauty, not enable it to grow, or grow back, for which feat no human lover would entirely suffice; if it is possible, it is only possible for God, indeed for God as conceived by Christianity, not on a Platonic or even Plotinian model. In Augustine's view (as in Gregory's and embryonically in Origen's), we need the more-than-mortal lover, the lover who has the powers of a Creator: a radical difference between the Christian position and that of Plotinus.

By emphasizing that God, in Christ, is true beauty, Augustine has set himself problems in some respects precisely opposite to those of Plato. In Plato we find puzzling how we can start from a love of human beings – bodies, then souls – and move beyond the personal to the impersonal world of Forms. How can love, seemingly a relationship between persons, without debasement be transferred to the impersonal object – or to the less-than-personal in the case of Plotinus?

In Augustine we have the opposite problem. Love is primarily of the beautiful, that is, of God in Christ; the object of love is personal. Hence how can one explain the love not only of "lesser" persons, that is, our fellow human beings, but even of "beautiful" physical objects that are wholly impersonal? Would not such love be almost a perversion, and are not such beauties – as the ascetics and puritans have ever feared – whatever their appearance, mere shadows, hardly worthy of the title of beauty at all?

Augustine will make a number of replies to this. First, that all beauties, not least that of the human body[61] (but also physical objects), are beautiful precisely because God, who knows beauty, has made them so; insofar as they are beautiful, they are in God's image. That means that human beauty, especially but not only the beauty of the human soul – the beauty of real virtue (*Sermon* 391.5) and of justice, the beauty of the inner man (*Letter*

---

[61] Cf J. Tscholl, "Augustins Interesse für das körperliche Schöne", *Augustiniana* 14 (1964) 72–104.

120.4.20) – will be at the top of the list of beauties in our physical universe, precisely, again, because we are created in God's image. But that beauty of soul will be lost if we pretend to being not in God's image but our own. Our beauty exists, because we are "in God", but since we are "amphibious" and travellers between two worlds, can be lost if we live away from God – whereas the (lesser) beauty of physical objects cannot be so lost. Then we become ugly and in need of "beautifying".

Thus we have a sequence of beauty in the world: first (potentially) the human soul, then (probably) the human body where the harmony of the parts is such that it is difficult to know whether it was formed on principles of beauty or of utility (*City of God* 22.24.4), then other bodies, then other beauties of nature and of art. This enables the "moral" problem of beauty which had worried Christians and pagans alike to be resolved. Beauty cannot be intelligibly recognized apart from God; insofar as I recognize beauty, I recognize God. But I must acknowledge an "order of love" (*On Christian Doctrine* 1.27.28; *City of God* 15.22) and hence of beauties, loving each beauty in accordance with its sequential beauty. Augustine's frequently expressed low opinion of physical beauty as compared with the beauty of the soul and of God,[62] so far from being mere contempt for the physical world, is – in putting that world into its proper perspective – the only means whereby physical beauty and the love of physical beauty are susceptible of rational (rather than merely emotional) accounting.

The implication of this for aesthetics is that artistic creation is possible without beauty; a clever artist can, in theory at least, create what is ugly for its own sake – I shall return to this question – or to make some point that has nothing to do with the direct expression of beauty.[63] Yet insofar as he is striving to represent *beauty* as the legitimate and inspirational ideal, his goal is only intelligible in the light of the existence of a beautiful God. For Augustine all beauty implies structure, and the perfection of structure points towards the perfection (however limited) of the maker of structure. Insofar as I make a beautiful object, I am beautiful and reflect both God's beauty and the fact that the word "beauty" makes sense and has a specific – ultimate – point of reference. For Augustine, without knowledge of God, beauty – in this like moral good – would be recognizable but inexplicable. Our recognition of it would have to be as a conventional habit or an instinct like the instinct to eat, though less palpably goal-directed; it could only be a brute and primary fact. We could praise something as beautiful because we

---

[62] This is especially emphasized by O'Connell, *Art* 131; cf. *Ep.* 118.4.23; *De Trin.* 8.6.9; 15.5.7; *CD* 1.18, etc.

[63] He might, for example, be trying to expose an ugly truth or to show beauty in contrast with ugliness.

like it, or imagine we do, and our likes and dislikes would remain incomparable and impossible to evaluate or prioritize, thus *inter alia* generating a problem of the relationship between ethics and aesthetics.

We can now see how easy it is for Augustine to speak intelligibly of the beauty of self-sacrifice: God's self-sacrifice in Christ is the act of the supremely beautiful soul, and the martyrs, though apparently ugly and deformed, are beautiful in imitation of that soul.[64] In describing God's self-sacrifice, the familiar texts of Isaiah 53 and Psalm 44 are cited, often linked by Philippians 2:6–8: the Word made itself ugly to save man's soul and make it beautiful (*On Psalms* 103/1.5; cf. *On John's Epistle* 9.9).[65] Also easier to comprehend is the beauty of material objects (*Trinity* 10.1.1). Granted God, their symmetry indicates a designed will to perfection in a natural order. Without God, it remains merely accidentally pleasing symmetry.

3.13 WHAT USE "PAGAN" BEAUTY?

The typical reader of Gregory or Augustine feels no astonishment at the enormous emphasis they put on beauty: on the beauty of God, on beauty as a divine attribute. He finds nothing surprising in their identifying truth, goodness and beauty[66] – as he *should* do if he compares earlier Christian writers. For the first time Gregory and Augustine more or less simultaneously have coupled beauty and inspiration as well as glory and awe as the centre of mainstream Christianity's vision of God. God, always a figure of awe and majesty, is now recognized as also a figure of beauty, and as the source and explanation of beauty. Some Christians – in the spirit of biblical and early Christian literalism – were to object to the possible implications of that, while others took the opportunity to develop Christian theories of art and beauty into a specifically Christian "aesthetic". Perhaps some realized that there could be no alternative "aesthetic" to the platonizing path broadly followed by Gregory and Augustine which would not eventually resolve itself into subjectivism. Iconoclasm is suited only to ghetto Christianity.

In one sense, the original version of the fourth-century solution (so I refer generally to the position of Augustine and Gregory) played for safety. The beauty of nature is a showing or revelation of the beauty of God, and the beauty of God, being personal, enables one to move easily between physical beauty (typified by the transfigured and resurrected Jesus) and beauty

---

[64] E.g., *EnPs.* 32.2.6.
[65] Many texts of this sort are discussed by Harrison, *Beauty and Revelation* 232–238.
[66] E.g., at *DLA* 2.13.35–38.

of character, and thus to moral and spiritual beauty. But, as we have seen, in antiquity the "problem" of beauty, as of "love", was centred on the seductive and hence ambivalent beauty of the human body and, of course, on the painted and sculpted figures of the gods, which might seem to offer the twin temptations of lasciviousness and idolatry and thus promote both immorality and blasphemy.

Perhaps here the fourth-century Christian retrieval of beauty might have ground to a stop, ignoring such "artistic" productions. Indeed, even scenes of non-human nature might need to be redeemed by being placed in a specifically "religious" context – as was much encouraged by the strictly "religious" aspect of the great artistic movement that in medieval Italy drew its inspiration from Francis of Assisi. If Francis did not need to redeem nature from scratch, he at least established a better based and more fruitful redemption than had hitherto been achieved.

But the artistic depiction of the naked human body had been linked not only to sexual laxity but also, via the *de facto* (and originally also *de iure*) worship of Venus as sex-goddess, to the wider problem of paganism. Reactions to anything judged neo-pagan therefore normally entailed hostility to various forms of art, thus in effect helping engender, in a Christianity weakened in the Renaissance and later, varieties of art that the Catholic Church found it unhappily difficult to appropriate. By the time it had more or less done so, secular culture had left Christian neo-prudery behind in progressing at first towards an art and an account of art parallel with those possible within Christianity, then to more and more depersonalized variations, themselves ever harder to Christianize – indeed, in recent versions effectively, and often deliberately, anti-Christian. The problem of "pagan" art – more properly the problem of a failure to distinguish between "true" and "false" inspiration – contributed historically to the contemporary phenomenon of the depersonalized art appropriate to a mechanized, bureaucratic and consumerist age.

I have observed that in classical Greece representations of the naked female form appeared in manifestations of popular culture well before reaching parity with those of males in the public art of the fourth century. But I also argued that, despite Phryne and other representations of feminine perfection, an opportunity was lost: the male form was still thought not only fine but superior. Within Christianity the problem was not entirely dissimilar. Whereas in Greece representation of male nudes had a long and distinguished tradition before the coming of their female counterparts,[67]

---

[67] That is connected, as we saw earlier, with the belief that the male form is the more perfect.

in Christianity, with its fundamental hostility to homosexual practice (as well as to the "heroic" and hence idolatrous image), the problematic beauty of the human form affected the representation of both males and females. Yet the historical parallel can be pursued further: as the marginalia of medieval manuscripts remind us, representation of sexual difference and its biological finality appears in less "public", more popular locations. That is in itself part of a Christian temptation – to which I shall turn in a later chapter – to deny "public space": precisely the space at the centre of classical culture.

As early as the twelfth century legends grew up that various popes – normally Gregory the Great, but sometimes Sylvester in the time of Constantine – were responsible not only for the burning in Rome of major texts of classical antiquity, including the works of Livy, but also for the smashing of statues of pagan gods and goddesses and of eminent figures from the Roman past.[68] Classical divinities were regarded as demons, and in view of the biblical and post-biblical preoccupation of Adam and Eve with their nakedness after the Fall – emphasized by Augustine in book 22 of the *City of God* where only after the resurrection can nakedness be viewed without lust – Venus was (as in some second-century Christian writers) regarded as especially fearsome. According to Ezechiel and other Old Testament writers (16:39; 23:29), nakedness, ritual or other, is uncleanness. Idol or not, however, Venus could not be denied, as we can find in reading twelfth-century texts such as those of a certain Master Gregory who was so impressed by the beauty of the Capitoline Venus that he visited her several times.[69] And this time, she prevailed. Unlike Phryne her physical beauty was not judged inferior to that of males: despite her seductiveness a first step towards a "popular" recognition that she herself, soul as well as body, need not be judged inferior to her male counterpart.

One of the first to retail idol-smashing stories about Gregory the Great was John of Salisbury (d. 1190), who clearly approved of the Pope's supposed actions against demons and idolatry. Soon battle was joined, and growing anger at what began to be considered vandalism is evident among the pupils of Petrarch and in the defence of pagan art by Boccaccio. Often cited is the critique of Ghiberti in his *Commentaries* (1447–1455),[70] echoing – unbeknown to its author – the tirades of ancient pagan Neoplatonists

---

[68] For an introduction to the theme see T. Buddensieg, "Gregory the Great, the Destroyer of Pagan Idols", *JWCI* 28 (1965) 44–65. For wider treatment of medieval attitudes to "idols" see M. Camille, *The Gothic Idol* (Cambridge 1989).

[69] See J. Osborne, *Master Gregory* (Toronto 1987) 26.

[70] Cited by Buddensieg, "Gregory the Great" 44.

against the "enemies of the good and the beautiful". It marks an increasing insistence that in such vandalism the "medieval" Church had shown itself uncivilized, philistine and in need of correction:

The Christian faith achieved victory in the time of the Emperor Constantine and Pope Sylvester. Idolatry was most stringently persecuted so that all the statues and pictures, noble, and of antique and perfect venerability as they were, were destroyed and rent to pieces. With statues and pictures were consumed books, commentaries, drawings and the rules by which one could learn such noble and excellent arts. In order to abolish every ancient custom of idolatry it was decreed that all the temples should be white. At this time the most severe penalty was ordered for anyone who made any statue or picture. Thus ended the art of sculpture and painting and all the knowledge and skill that had been achieved in it. Art came to an end and the temples remained white for about six hundred years.

Such texts reveal several significant facts: that "enlightened" Catholics were beginning to reprove the Church for its non-acceptance of specifically non-Christian art; that in doing so they were implicitly rejecting the "defence" that the destruction of such art is necessary to protect the Christian faith against paganism; that the merit of the works of art themselves is excellent reason for their preservation and thus that "moral", as well as directly religious, pretexts for destruction are unacceptable. I shall return in due course to both the "anti-pagan" and the more generally "moral" arguments, noting first, however, that Ghiberti declined to offer any specifically "iconodule" reasonings for his position. That is, in castigating papal hostility to specific representations of humans or gods – and even to pagan worship of such representations – he did not treat of the biblical prohibition on constructing images of God. Quite the reverse: his position is not "iconodule" but "humanist".[71]

In Ghiberti's time biblical scenes and lives of the saints had long been depicted, so he had no need to resort to an anti-iconoclast defence of art in general. But explicitly Christian art was originally intended to *replace* pagan art,[72] and the question Ghiberti and others raised (implicitly and increasingly explicitly) was whether the two could in some circumstances – but in which and to what degree? – go in tandem, despite the apparent "paganism" of "secular" productions. Ghiberti's view would seem to have been that not only

---

[71] It is important to remember that the attitudes of Ghiberti and others developed at a time when Catholic Christianity and the papacy in particular seemed to many to be in more general need of radical reform. The coincidence of "humanism" with the failure of the theocratic politics of the medieval Church will be discussed in chapter 5.

[72] As Christian culture (of whatever sort) was intended to replace pagan culture in general. I shall return to the matter in discussing John Chrysostom in chapter 5.

are biblical scenes and the lives of the saints fit subjects for art, but all subjects, if well executed and beautiful – we remember Master Gregory's insistence on the *beauty* of Venus – are appropriate to a Christian commonwealth.

Ambrogio Lorenzetti's representation of the just and the unjust city in the Palazzo Pubblico of Siena, often hailed as the West's first secular painting, is nearly a hundred years earlier than Ghiberti's polemic – though Lorenzetti's theme could certainly be defended as allegorically teaching Christian *morality*. By the early 1430s Christendom's first free-standing nude statue in bronze had been sculpted by Donatello, whose David, though biblical, is cast in the heroic mould, with perhaps a deliberate bow to the classical "idol":[73] in effect it is that oldest classical idea of human (and humanist) splendour, the "Greek" male. "Aphrodite", however, had in her ancient form already returned, as we have seen, and she would soon take on new life. The decision whether to appropriate or reject classicizing "pagan" art in general could not be long postponed.

Counter-Reformation times would render the decision agonizing. In the 1580s Pope Sixtus V was responsible, *inter alia*, for removing Trajan and Marcus Aurelius from their Roman columns and replacing them with Peter and Paul, while by 1546 Pietro Aretino was castigating the *"licenzie dell'arte"* of Michelangelo's Last Judgment. In 1565 a certain Antonio Agustin observed in a letter that the Venuses and other lascivious objects owned by Pope Julius III would scandalize the Lutherans and promote apostasy. That comment might be considered prudential rather than moral; at the very least, it shows the pragmatic aspects of a particular debate about the expansion and possible limits of "catholic" culture.

Fundamental to all such disputes are a number of difficulties: about the distinction between liberty and licence in art; about the possible short-term moral disadvantages of "paganism" as against the long-term educational values of an expansion of human and catholic culture. There is also a more basic point about beauty itself. In the twelfth century Hugh of Saint Victor had presented a not untypical Christian thesis whereby all "beautiful" objects are of three kinds:[74] the works of God, visible in his creative act *ex nihilo*; the secondary works of nature; the works of artificers who imitate nature. Hugh's identifying the last group as "adulterous" finds its origin in an "updating" of Plato's restricted critique of art as dealing in images, not reality, as "adulterous", though on a strict interpretation of that trichotomy all works of art, Christian or pagan, would be suspect.

---

[73] So Camille, *Gothic Idol* 345.
[74] Hugh of St. Victor, *Didaskalion* 1.9 (ed. J. Taylor (New York 1961) 59).

Behind all these disputed questions lies the distinction I made in the introduction to the present book, between truth and saving truth. The Christian "humanist" position resolves itself into the thesis that any truth that does not imperil saving truth should become part of Catholic culture. The more "puritan" or sectarian thesis worries both that the risks are too high, and that in every case blasphemy is to be recognized. Historically such ideas have appeared in both Catholic and Protestant guise, in the latter affording a further anxiety among the Catholics, as we have seen. Luther, ever preferring the word to the image, taught that images *contrary* to God's word should be "despised and smashed" by official decree;[75] which among his followers was often taken to include the Catholic (especially Marian) images originally intended – I reiterate the point – to replace their pagan predecessors.

Scriptural commands apart, the "puritanical" position raises a number of questions, for if some are more likely to remain on the straight and narrow path to salvation if they are not exposed to aesthetic seductions, others may fall by the wayside precisely because they see a proposed religious path as too narrow to be worthy of human nature. That is part of the point made by Armstrong as quoted at the beginning of the present chapter. There is no way to resolve such questions at the practical level without directly facing the *justification* of aesthetic as of moral values in a Christian setting. Perhaps also there is no other setting in which they can be adequately justified.[76]

I have left virtually untouched a very practical question which must arise in any discussion of the proper relationship between art and morality, and which lurks below much traditional Christian ambivalence, if not hostility, to art. The essence of the problem can already be recognized in Plato's attitude towards the poetry of Homer and the Greek dramatists, and, although it is rarely broached nowadays, it can be easily approached by reflection on traditional attitudes towards secular vocations judged unsuitable for Christians. One such unsuitable profession was acting, particularly by women.

Since the representation of female beauty began in Greece, especially with Praxiteles, the artist used nude models: in the case of Praxiteles his mistress Phryne to whom I have already alluded. Thus one version of our

---

[75] *Against the Heavenly Prophets in the Matter of Images and the Sacraments* (1525) in J. Pelikan and H. T. Lehmann (eds.), *Luther's Works* XL.2 (St Louis 1958). Camille (*Gothic Idol* 346) gives the impression of attributing Karlstadt's more extreme view to Luther himself. Luther's stance is more moderate; he is happy to see the images fade out, but crucifixes and images of saints may be respected. His principal concern is to discourage disorderly mob action against them.
[76] As I argued in the case of moral values in *Real Ethics*.

problem can be identified in the choice of women to pose for an artist: is that fitting for a Christian or not? And more broadly: is any representation of sexual activity on the stage acceptable? More broadly still, such questions are part of a wider problem which can best be understood in Augustinian terms.

We know (from Augustine's 220th letter) that a career-general, Boniface, on the death of his wife and weary of the ambiguities of a military career, asked Augustine whether he should retire to a monastery. Augustine's answer – expectably – was a firm No, and his reasoning was that distasteful aspects of public life must be humbly accepted by Christians, that soldiers were desperately needed to repel the barbarians, that decisions about how to act in individual cases must be left to the individual, guided, so far as possible, by the traditional teachings of the Church. The theme is further developed in book 19 of the *City of God*, and surely Augustine supposed that "in this darkness of social life" if reasonably good men refused such work, worse would take their place.

The reward of participation in public policy – which may entail killing, even sometimes and unintentionally of the innocent – is the maintenance of a certain vestige of justice. The reward of taking part in the presentation of plays on the stage, or of modelling for an artist, is the production of beautiful works of art. Without such "risqué" activity, humanity is the poorer. Perhaps one must admit that there are areas of social life where a degree of consequentialism – though ever devoid of self-indulgence or self-serving – is necessary even in a society as far as possible Christian.[77]

3.14 AESTHETICS AND ETHICS

I began this chapter by accepting that physical beauty gives pleasure through the senses, and that it may strike us as "sublime", but that its inspirational effects are both important in themselves and provide guidance in determining whether an apparent beauty is "real", and hence whether objectivism in aesthetics is justified. For problems of subjectivism in aesthetics are similar to those in ethics, with the important difference – making subjectivism the more difficult to resist in the aesthetic domain – that in aesthetics there is apparently no "ought".

What ethics and aesthetics have in common is the notion of inspiration (aesthetic or moral), and in the case of great beauties, whether of character,

---

[77] I have discussed some of the more political aspects of this problem in an essay (which will shortly appear) entitled "Practical Reasoning in Utopia".

art or nature, of lasting inspiration. In a godless age, the distinction between inspiration and instinct is easily lost, though the power of inspiration to perdure through many generations would suggest that its appeal is beyond the personally and instinctually preferred or culture-bound. An artist possesses particular skills, and much discussion of art and of beauty has enquired what those skills may be. A "meta-aesthetics", treating of the *conditions* for aesthetics, will ask what happens when the skills remain but the concept of beauty is neglected, set aside or lost.

In earlier sections of this chapter I argued that, following certain leads (*inter alia*) in Plato's *Phaedrus*, Christian writers of the fourth century developed the idea that the personal beauty of Christ represents the revelation of God, and I suggested that this enables them to account for the beauty of nature, the beauty of God as the source of nature, and the moral beauty of man, who, being created in God's image, will reflect the beauty of God in a manner different from that of other beauties of the universe. But in noting that man is morally and spiritually ambiguous, being capable of both virtue and vice, I also observed how, though Christian writers were able to *notice* the physical beauty of man, they frequently found ways of separating this ambiguous beauty from the beauty of man as image.

One favoured way of doing this, adopted especially by Origen in his writings on the Song of Songs and by those who followed him, was by allegory. Thus one Platonic link was snapped: while physical beauty represents spiritual beauty, it is in no sense the way *towards* spiritual beauty. Whereas for Plato and the Platonic tradition it is often physical beauty that, being beautiful – albeit defectively so – is able to recall us to the higher beauties that are genuinely its source, a number of Christians tried to develop a tradition whereby the way to spiritual beauty was to deny physical beauty, especially the beauty of the human body, as seductive and misleading.

That might work if man were to be identified with his soul, but we have seen Augustine (for example) coming to deny that idea, asserting that if anyone says a man is simply his soul, he is a fool. That insight originated in the Christian claim of Jesus' incarnation in human flesh, so that not merely is the soul immortal but the body also is to "rise from the dead". As we saw in relation to the image of God, if we take seriously the claim that man is not to be identified with his soul (as did Aquinas), we must recognize that man's bodily nature, including his sexuality, is no mere appendage, but metaphysically part of a hylomorphic whole. In the spirit of the Viennese psychologist Christian von Ehrenfels, we must recognize that, when we view a human being as the image of God, we recognize his *Gestalt*: that is, the way he presents himself to our mind and senses as a psychosomatic whole.[78] We are not our *Gestalt* but our *Gestalt* is how we present ourselves. The concept of *Gestalt* enables us to recognize in the hylomorphic whole the combination by which man reveals himself not as God but as in God's image: the transcendent and infinite in an immanent and finite "frame". It is not just our soul but our whole being that is in God's image; the belief that it is merely our soul is at least half way to a claim that we are simply divine.

The challenge that faced Christian culture with the revival of artistic interest in the human body and its comparative or idealized beauty was also a theological challenge: are we would-be moral angels or are we potentially beautiful psycho-physical entities? Insofar as the Church tended to deny the latter alternative, it tended toward a denial of what, for want of a better term, we must call Christian humanism, based on the reality of God as creator of humanity. Insofar as the Church abandoned the artistic representation of humanity to the secular sphere, it helped develop a culture in *opposition* to Christianity: a secular culture that appeared to represent the highest artistic aspirations of man – though, as I shall argue, unable to justify the values apparently lying behind such aspirations – so that we find the same sort of foundational difficulties in aesthetics as in ethics.

For though it may seem possible in a secular society to construct a serious theory of obligation and responsibility, as I have argued elsewhere, the metaphysical foundations for such an edifice cannot be established in secular terms: thus ethics will be reduced to post-Kantian formalism or to nihilism in the style of Nietzsche, or to choice-theory, flavoured, if possible, with utilitarian or contractarian maxims designed to keep the lucky ones among us comfortable. Similarly in aesthetics: if "human" beauty is rejected by the Church, the secular world will seem to develop an aesthetics of its own. Its foundations, though, will be flimsy, the ancient association of ethics and aesthetics will be lost and we should be surprised neither at depersonalizations of art – entailing a corresponding decline in its inspirational charge – nor at purely emotivist explanations of beauty.

In a later chapter I shall raise in wider historical context the roots of certain anti-Christian features of the modern world; for the moment it remains to sketch this depersonalization of art, with its emphasis on what would traditionally have been thought of as ugliness, as it has developed *pari*

---

[78] Von Ehrenfels was a pupil of the influential "Aristotelian" Brentano. Perhaps particularly interesting in the context of our present discussion is the fact that he was prepared to speak even of the *Gestalt* of a melody.

passu with the decline of Western Christianity, especially of its full-blown Catholic version. My claim is that in Western society beauty has as little defence against ugliness as morality has against nihilism: indeed, that ugliness and nihilism go hand in hand as Christianity with its Platonic metaphysical features and philosophical justifications is whittled down. As I have already observed, my concern is not with the simple inclusion of ugliness in art – any tragedy will "portray" ugliness – but with its intentionality: with the emotions it arouses, the effects achieved when the ugliness is no longer in the service of a deeper understanding of the beauty of truth.

Classical and medieval theories of art identify the artist as artificer of what can be recognized as "beautiful" or "fine" (in Greek *kalon*). Most earlier "aesthetics" – I limit myself to aesthetics in its modern connotation as reflection on sensed and sensual beauty – is concerned to identify the nature of the inspirationally "beautiful". Albert the Great, Aquinas' teacher, offered a fairly typical definition: beauty subsists in the "gleaming" of substantial form over proportionally arranged parts of matter.[79] Most such definitions, implying a further definition of the artist as the person capable of producing such beauty, are in some degree arbitrary, or rather they are based on an accepted account of value. They suggest that "beautiful" work so defined will produce the *proper* inspiration that is the mark of the "aesthetic", and they assume that the "right kind of person" will experience such inspiration.

Just as in ethics, according to Aristotle, the well-brought-up individual will delight in doing good, while the ill-brought-up will delight in doing harm, so in aesthetics the aesthetically well-trained will be inspired by what is noble, others by what is in fact ugly. For just as Aristotelian ethics assumes it knows how the proper moral individual will behave, so traditional aesthetics (viewed as inseparable from ethics) knows what will inspire the aesthetically well-educated.

That could be a mere conventionalism. The meta-aesthetic question which is my present concern is: How do we know whether good taste in art is any better grounded than good breeding in ethics? Most people are still inclined to believe – albeit not knowing why – that in ethics taste may not be the ultimate arbiter, while allowing it its apparent due in aesthetics: beauty, but at least not all kinds of "good" action, they will say, is in the eye of the beholder.

---

[79] *Opusculum de pulchro et bono* 5.456, cited by R. Tatarkiewicz, *Mediaeval Aesthetics* (Warsaw 1970) 243.

It was primarily in the eighteenth century that the metaphysical basis of both ethics and aesthetics, and of metaphysics itself, seemed to crumble, and with it the sense of the transcendent and any "transcendentalist" justification of beauty. It is worth recalling, therefore, how, in that particular century, the parallel between ethics and aesthetics worked itself out. To do that, we must first return to the historical debate about artistic representation of the human body, then to the theoretical question of whether the production of beauty is the only function of the artist. For it can be argued that if Beauty exists, then in some sense Ugliness exists too (albeit not in a "perfect" form), and that the artist may enable us to expand our appreciation of the beautiful by presenting us with what is not beautiful. But, as I have observed, he might want to present the ugly not to show it up in contrast with the beautiful, but because he is fascinated by ugliness or because he has some reason for presenting it "artistically" or "enticingly". He might, for example, want to corrupt someone's sexual morality. Here again, there may be a parallel with ethics. The good surgeon could be the good torturer; the good artist could be the good pornographer: it depends on the *aim* to which he chooses to dedicate his skill. Perhaps just as there are philosophers and sophists, there are "moral philosophers" and "moral sophists", not to speak of practising "aesthetic" philosophers and "aesthetic" sophists. "X is a good torturer" does not equal "X is a torturer" plus "X is good", unless you approve of torturers.

The development of a complete and universally accepted Catholic account of art was hindered (*inter alia*, and I use it as a paradigm case about cultural growth) by the dispute in the late Middle Ages and during the Renaissance and Reformation about "neo-pagan" presentations of nude and especially of "lascivious" paintings and sculpture. The roots of the problem are both ethical and aesthetic: physical beauty, as we have seen, is ambivalent; it can inspire to good or evil so that it challenges us to be, as it were, either moderate drinkers of it or strict teetotallers. The "teetotaller" has a picture of human flourishing limited to the narrowly moral; the moderate has a more Aristotelian and wider vision of humanity.

Renaissance popes tended to be "liberal" on the matter, as did the majority of their successors in the Baroque period, but the dispute was never theoretically resolved and in the Counter-Reformation, as in much Protestantism, the narrower view prevailed. With the subsequent disintegration of Church authority – and despite the fact that Puritan Reformers certainly had no time for "neo-paganism" – a counter-tradition began to be established outside the jurisdiction of the Church and eventually outside Christianity altogether. As in other aspects of Western society, one effect of the development of Protestantism was the growth of secularism: in art of non-Christian and eventually anti-Christian tendencies.

It would be ridiculous to argue that the dispute about representations of the human body was the cause – rather than a striking outcome – of the collapse of the slowly growing, Augustine-based, Catholic approach to beauty, and of the consequent disintegration of "aesthetics", parts of which process I shall briefly discuss. The attack on transcendent reality was the most fundamental engine of change. What I am arguing is that the dispute about "paganism" is symbolic of the Church's historically conditioned confusion about the development of its own artistic traditions and about how in its understanding of art – in this particular case of how to present the image of God – it could become more fully Catholic. In effect it had to learn to discern what is appropriate for a Christian, uniquely complete, theory of beauty: learn, furthermore, how to decide which among the various accounts of art that developed in the seventeenth and eighteenth centuries might open up new and important avenues of enquiry, even though, in and of themselves, they might be intellectually indefensible.

As with ethics, so with the aesthetics of the early modern period, new proposals offered both intelligible and unintelligible prospects, and the new canons had little theoretical underpinning. Hence in the eighteenth century there developed in many quarters a tendency to fall back on a "value-Aristotelianism", by which is not meant that Aristotle would have approved of neo-classicizing taste, but that those who upheld it asserted, as Aristotle had done in ethics, that right-minded, "educated" people had "the right" taste in art and literature. The (particularly French) canonization of taste was paralleled by theories of proper sentiments in English ethicists of the same period: first Shaftesbury, then, more strikingly, Hutcheson: even Hume. Such canons were open to attack not only from Catholic traditionalists appealing to (even poorly understood) Thomistic theories of beauty, but within the ever-increasing secular orbit by more determined students of "aesthetics".

The canonization of taste was a conventional substitute for a metaphysical theory of art: indeed for precisely that Christian theory of art and beauty, developed out of Platonism, which I have identified in Augustine and Gregory of Nyssa, whereby the beauty of Christ is the justifying metaphysical ground for spiritual and physical beauties, whether natural or artistic, in the created universe. In the absence of such grounding, we are left with the conventionally tasteful view of beauty, and, as was only to be expected, with the roughly contemporary "discovery" of aesthetics as a specific science by Baumgarten. "Art for art's sake" became inevitable, even apparently legitimate, though meaningless in an anti-metaphysical context. The phrase appears to have been first used (slightly later) by Théophile Gautier in *Mademoiselle de Maupin* (1835).

We have reached the age of Kant and it should come as no surprise that his moves in aesthetics parallel those in ethics. He has no time for an aesthetics of taste, nor for such other theories as the notion that beauty can be understood by resort to the authority of Nature, whether individual or communal, whether under-written by a deistic God or in effectively pantheistic or Stoicizing versions. These had been inseparable from that self-creating individual unearthed in embryo by Descartes, developed by Hobbes and Locke: a self whose pretensions grew through the eighteenth century as the claims of God receded.

Kant remained a nominal, if rationalist and anti-dogmatic, "Christian", strongly imbued with the moralism of the Pietists, but his solution to the problems of meta-aesthetics – a shift from conventionalism or naturalism to supreme confidence in the artistic genius as such – carried forward the neo-paganism of the Renaissance ever further even from ancient paganism. For what chiefly distinguishes Renaissance Neoplatonism from the theories of Plotinus and Proclus is the centrality of "divine" man's role in the cosmos: a view clearly supervening on – but subversive of – the Christian doctrine of man created in God's image and redeemed by Christ himself.

The influence of Rousseau on Kant (not least on the latter's account of "genius") is acknowledged, and in later times it contributed much to the drive in art towards "expressivism", which saw the greatness of art in the opportunity it gives man to express his (originally pure and noble) nature. At its extreme this leads to the hyper-Renaissance thesis of Herder that the artist is become a creator-god. That, however, might be read in different ways, depending on whether some vestige of the doctrine of original sin (still accepted by Kant) remains to suggest its weaknesses. Without that, there is no limit to the powers and authority the creator-god might arrogate to himself. In Kant's case this creator-god is still only a "genius"; hence his attitude to his art still is mitigated, acting creatively, but within at least nominally assumed limits. But insofar as Kant, in aesthetics as in ethics, can offer no metaphysical justification for the acts of the artist, beyond the determinations of his own judgments, the way is open for pure assertion of the self: those selves that are more "talented" will provide the standard of artistic excellence.

There are many modern transformations of such views, often influenced directly or indirectly by Nietzsche. An especially informative one (by the American poet Wallace Stevens) is cited by Taylor:[80] "After one has abandoned belief in God, poetry is the essence which takes its place as life's redemption." In this case the ambiguity surrounds the word "redemption". If Stevens means that at least something of a "vision" of a non-consumerist, non-mechanist, non-industrial world is preserved by poetry, there is little difficulty in accepting what he wants to say. But if he thinks that poetic language is self-explanatory, he is mistaken. Poetry as such cannot redeem; it can only point to phenomena such as would be redeeming if there were a Redeemer, and thus offer a "virtual" redemption. Once belief in God has been abandoned, any non-metaphorical redemption has vanished; indeed even "metaphorical" is beginning to become a substitution for "self-deluding". Stevens, in common with many ethical writers, is now relying on a theology and a metaphysic that he has explicitly rejected!

The "post-Kantian" artist is thus not merely creator but is necessarily self-deceiving and hybristic, whether he thinks of himself as a virtual god or merely as seer or prophet. His pre-modern predecessors were members of a community rooted in transcendental values, and spoke, in however personal a vision, out of the values of that community. The reconstructed artist, on the contrary, tries to create his own community, which at its lowest consists of "groupies" (whether or not giving allegiance to the *Times Literary Supplement* or the *New York Review of Books*). In Augustinian terms, he strives out of pride, the primal vice. Modern "aesthetics" (understood strictly as such) has, from its initial identification, been consciously and consistently anti-religious and anti-Platonic.

In the absence of the divine, the self-conscious artist can now only be a seer of himself: of his self; he poses as self-creator, as well as, to whatever degree, creative artist. But though he is indeed a creator, and can be recognized as such, he cannot be a self-creator; if he holds or implies that he is that, he produces art – however fine – as a means to self-glorification (*ad maiorem gloriam Mei*), and thus to self-mutilation. The worship of the artist (at least by élites or would-be élites) has become a replacement for the worship of God. If Augustine is even broadly right in his account of art and beauty, the slogan "art for art's sake" – probably logically indefensible though confusingly suggesting that a work of art, unlike a packet of cornflakes, is irreplaceable – also involves the self-praise and self-worship of the self-creating artist.

The foregoing analysis will enable us to face a more fundamental problem about the possibility of Christian art, the relationship between art and

---

[80] C. Taylor, *Sources of the Self* (Cambridge, Mass. 1989) 493, citing Stevens' *Opus Posthumum*.

beauty and the intelligibility of post-Christian aesthetic theory. Insofar as art is seen as the expression of the self, it will reflect its weaknesses as well as its strengths, and the more unintelligible the ideology of the self, the more unintelligible (and beauty-free) – though not the less immediately seductive – will be its expressions. The fate of such art is to become solipsistic; the groupies will understand less, pretend to understand more, and "at the end of the day" laud unintelligibility and ugliness: such ugliness, as I have noted, that may be presented with great technical skill but will make no pretensions either to show up beauty or to present ugliness as means to the better understanding of beauty's absence.

We have reached that post-modern turn of the road which envisages the disappearance of the self, of the artist or writer, now unmasked as a competent piece of jetsam on the tide of social change. In the course of my account of the development of an all-embracing Catholic theory of art, I argued that the ultimate comprehensibility of art depends on the recognition of the beauty of God which validates, via the Incarnation, both spiritual and physical beauties. In the post-modern world-view, the role of the personal is deliberately undercut; there can be no incarnation, therefore no explanation of beauty in the universe or in human beings. Outside Christian circles the advent of the impersonal can easily be recognized: an advent neither of the beauty of a transcendent God, nor of the immanently beautiful Nature of the seventeenth and eighteenth centuries, nor even of the self-created beauty of the expressivist. One notes the impersonal turn from the Absolute Spirit of Hegel's de-personalized Christianity to the more radical "being there" (*Dasein*) of Heidegger, from which all *necessary* moral as well as aesthetic content has been removed. Heidegger was a Nazi, as it happened, and the banality of Nazi art is well recognized. He could in other circumstances have been a Stalinist, loyal in such a world to an equally banal "Soviet realism".

In these all too rapid remarks on the fate of non-transcendental art, I desire not to be misunderstood. It would be obviously false to say that even great technical advances have not been made in art, literature and poetry since the Renaissance, and it would be even more absurd to suppose that great works have not been produced. My thesis, involving neither of these conclusions, is that, for all the technical advances, no coherent theory of the nature of beauty can be proposed in a world where it is impossible to distinguish beauty from ugliness, but each is an "authentic" expression of artistic achievement. It is also that, where works of great beauty have been produced (usually on an immanent level, but sometimes where the immanent symbolizes transcendence as with the French Impressionists), their greatness cannot be understood in terms of a non-transcendental, non-personal meta-aesthetic theory. Catholic artists can learn from techniques of the post-Christians, just as in ethics Catholic philosophers can learn from the analytic skills of atheists, so long as they can separate the skills from the unintelligible, rationally foundationless ideology, and so long as they resist the arrogant setting of the parameters of legitimate discussion by their opponents.

The art I am expounding is properly concerned (directly or indirectly) with beauty and the inspiration of beauty. But I have argued that there is also a parasitic or sophistic art, of which there are at least two versions: either the "sophist" can deploy great skill in making moral ugliness seem beautiful, a charge which Plato, adducing the falsely heroic behaviour of their gods and heroes, brought against Homer and the Greek tragedians, and which in recent times has been advanced against Leni Riefenstahl's Nazi film *Triumph of the Will*;[81] or – which is my more immediate concern – there are products of "artistic" skill without beauty at all.

Both types of sophistry are identifiable as what used to be called *curiositas*: intellectual and experiential enquiry into what should not be known or experienced and desire for emotions that should not be aroused. Riefenstahl's film seeks to arouse sympathy and enthusiasm for Nazism, by presenting a beautiful but inaccurate representation of its character and of the emotions that it arouses. So we are not inspired but seduced – and, as has always been feared, beauty has always been able to seduce as well as to inspire. Riefenstahl's case shows why, among earthly beauties, beauty and goodness cannot simply be identified – though it is hard to know why they should be, as the example of a beautiful but grasping prostitute would obviously show. As for the second kind of sophistry, no-one is "inspired" to fornicate at a rock-concert, though they may be aroused to fornicate, or to masturbate after viewing a cleverly designed and "artistic" "skin-flick".

So my account, in the end, sees art as an ethical, or, better, as a spiritual phenomenon and necessarily subordinated to spiritual goals and the richness of man's capabilities: that means no *curiositas*. It also refers us back to Plato's *Symposium* and the proper relationship between beauty and goodness. In medieval times philosophers called beauty a "transcendental", but not necessarily a distinct transcendental. Like awesome splendour (with

[81] For interesting comment see M. Devereaux, "Beauty and Evil: The Case of Leni Riefensthal's *Triumph of the Will*", in J. Levinson (ed.), *Aesthetics and Ethics: Essays at the Intersection* (Cambridge 1998) 227–256.

which it has sometimes been confused) it shows a facet of God: not his power as such – which might instil mere fear – but God's creative and beautiful goodness, arousing and inspiring "erotic" longing.

In Greek times *kalon* could signify physical, moral or spiritual beauty. Part of the enduring strength of that piece of linguistic good sense is that it indicates recognition that a proper foundation for ethics will ultimately have to be identical with a proper foundation for aesthetics. For the production of the "fine", as originally construed, involved an appeal to an "end" "seen" by the individual but beyond him or her. Just as in ethics neither emotivism nor formalism, nor the cult of obligation nor utilitarianism, can provide adequate defence against moral nihilism, so in aesthetics neither formalism nor expressivism nor mere engineering will defeat the Gadarene rush towards an ugliness seen as "authentic", "poignant", "deep", and so "beautiful".

But in such an aesthetic the key that is the association between beauty and inspiration has been discarded. Inspiration calls forth an emotion, but not all emotions, however aroused, call forth an erotic desire for the Good.[82] An authentic Catholic aesthetic – deriving, as we have seen, after much trial and error, largely from dialogue with Platonic "paganism" – can still enable us to discern whether emotions are inspirational or not, and so to advance our understanding of beauty; whether it reveals the immanent or conceals (under symbols) the transcendent. But too much must not be claimed for it: no aesthetic theory can tell me whether the *Iliad* is more beautiful than *Hamlet*, let alone whether *Hamlet* is more inspirational than *Lear*.

Finally I return to the beginning. Recognition of God's beauty, to which Origen, Methodius, Gregory of Nyssa and Augustine (in the footsteps of Plato and Plotinus) blazed the Christian way, must go along with the awe and reverence for God's majesty exemplified in the Bible and recognized by such as Irenaeus. *Pace* the iconoclasts and puritans, there is no contradiction and only cultural enrichment in that proposition. The discovery, by Origen, Methodius, Gregory and Augustine, of what – in more contemporary language – can be identified as a Christian meta-aesthetic is one of the best examples of how reflection by serious

---

[82] Kant, by contrast, prefers "disinterested delight"; see *The Critique of Judgment*, section 5, with the comments of Gadamer, *Relevance of the Beautiful* 19. Note in this idea features of an (admittedly incomplete) Stoic aesthetic parallel to much of Kant's near Stoicism of virtue and duty.

Christians on a well-developed but immediately non-Christian thesis can lead to a richer understanding of truth – and may enable others to recognize saving truth. It is laid upon contemporary Catholics not to betray that priceless heritage either by abandoning its transcendentalism or by reverting to a moralist sectarianism.[83]

[83] Readers may wonder why I have hardly spoken of music. The short answer is that this chapter is primarily a study of the appropriation of originally non-Christian ideas within the expanding Catholic tradition. Western music, as distinct from Western art, grew up largely without recourse to non-Christian riches: in its modern forms from Catholic tradition in the work of such as Palestrina and Monteverdi. That alone is enough to refute the fashionable claim – not least by advocates of the European Union – that European culture is to be understood solely as the imposition of Enlightenment values on Greco-Roman achievements. (There is a more full-blown version of this fashion to be identified in the attack on "Eurocentrism" in general: a coded repudiation of Christian, especially Catholic, values by a *déraciné* intelligentsia.)

There are interesting parallels – which cannot be explored here – between the history of music and the history of art, though the former – adapting themes from European literature and culture – moved on a necessarily compressed time-scale: the formally secular theme of Lorenzetti's allegory of just and unjust government finds its parallel in the secular subjects already treated by Monteverdi, as later in Handel's oratorios.

CHAPTER 4

The origin and early development
of episcopacy at Rome

Quis custodiet ipsos custodes?

Juvenal

4.1 THE RELEVANCE OF THE PRESENT THEME

In the contemporary "global village" in which a new and more or less
autonomous Christian church or community is formed almost every
minute, the Roman Catholic Church could not survive intact without a
dogmatic (hence indirectly cultural) centre. That centre is provided by the
Roman see, the principal reason why the "Western" Church, unlike
Orthodoxy, has thus far not fragmented further.[1] By fragmentation I refer
not merely to the existence of autonomous (or autocephalous) churches but
(as with Anglicanism) of autonomous doctrines. To make that case as
strongly as possible would require a book on the history of the see of
Rome – which for both practical and intellectual reasons I could not now
write – to show how its gradual emergence as the ultimate doctrinal centre
of Catholicism has inhibited the disintegration of Christianity, as well as
entailing its own development not only as a doctrinal but also as a juridical
centre. What I can manage, within the limits of the present chapter, is an
argument that the doctrinal role of the Roman see – amid other often more
vigorously intellectual local churches – had already begun to emerge in the
early centuries, though, of course, the development was by no means
complete. Nor, humanly speaking at least, was it yet irreversible. Yet a
pattern had been set which others, from both more and less sympathetic
viewpoints, have shown to have continued to the present day.

The present chapter deals with the emergence and eventual recognition
of a doctrinal centre, but doctrinal questions, in a historical setting, cannot

---

[1] For a full-length study of the history of papal primacy see K. Schatz, *Papal Primacy from Its Origins to
the Present* (Eng. trans. John A. Otto and Linda M. Maloney, Collegeville 1996).

be separated from "political" applications. Hence my next chapter will treat of various (failed or now irrelevant) models of possible relations between a "doctrinal centre" and the "civil" power, while chapter 6 will consider, *inter alia*, some aspects of a possibly fruitful relationship in our own times between our necessary doctrinal centre and the anti-Christian "high" culture by which it is increasingly surrounded in Europe and the West more generally. Here part of my argument will be that, had the "doctrinal centre" not developed, Catholicism (as Christianity itself) would be entirely secularized or marginalized, or more probably both. If secularized then marginalized, for there is little gained spiritually in retaining ecclesiastical dignitaries as court-prelates, whether as political directors like Cardinal Richelieu to Louis XIII of France or as moral consultants of the calibre of the late Cardinal Cushing of Boston to the Kennedys.

If that is so, then a study of the origins of the authority of the Roman see is also a study of the prospects, even the continuing possibility, of the Catholic culture that is the subject of this book. For as Catholic culture has developed, so the doctrinal authority of the Roman see has developed. Hence if the doctrinal authority of that see should decline (whether through over-estimate of its own political skills, cultivated ignorance of the secular society in which it functions, simple old-fashioned susceptibility to flattery or through caving in to *improper* outside pressures), then Catholic culture must correspondingly decline.

The present chapter is historical, the material highly controversial; it is impossible to do it full justice in a short space. Nevertheless, I believe the facts are clear enough to enable me to argue (even if many details must remain unproven) that the institutional growth I describe offers a curious parallel to developments in more theoretical aspects of Christian and specifically Catholic culture. I believe that a form of episcopal authority that can be reasonably described as monarchical – though "monarchy" was still viewed less in terms of power than of authority – was established in Rome only towards the middle of the second century AD, by which time such a form of Church order was common practice. And, of course, by the middle of the third century the monarchical aspects of the see had grown much further and a greater degree of institutional power can be recognized in the bishop's hands. I shall also notice that in the mid second century our present four-Gospel canon was established and various serious threats to the Church in Rome defused.[2] That entails (*inter alia*) that the canon was

---

[2] The final establishment of the canon of the entire New Testament took much longer, but that is not my present concern.

established under the aegis of increasingly monarchical bishops, at Rome and elsewhere.

Those who wish to uphold the divine inspiration of our four Gospels must take note that monarchical bishops presided over the Churches where those Gospels were recognized. Since such bishops did not exist in New Testament times, their successful selection of the inspired texts is a strong argument that they and their office are in direct continuation of the original inspiration of Christianity. However they secured their status – and that is a matter of strictly historical enquiry as far as possible – the effects of their behaviour must form a strong argument, for those who accept the New Testament, for the divine origin and inspiration of their ministry. It would follow that monarchical bishops were not only the product of a natural historical development, but that that development should, by Christians, be regarded as providentially inspired.

Hence arises a further claim: if the development of episcopacy is divinely inspired, the specific development of the see of Rome, in its broad and probably incomplete outlines, must also require a providential as well as a historical and sociological explanation: not least if such development has turned out to promote rather successful ways of handling a series of serious (but ultimately related) doctrinal and (particularly more recently) moral problems in the Church.

I am thinking of development overall. That is not to suggest that every detail, even every important detail, of the process of growth with which I am concerned is providential and unreformable. Here again there are parallels at the conceptual level: just as Church order is both providential and fallibly man-made, so the progression of Catholic thought, though advancing towards truth, cannot be expected to avoid even serious mistakes as it proceeds in overall harmony with such truth.

In many significant respects, the growth of the organization of the Christian community in Rome parallels that in other early Christian centres, though the progress is not simultaneous. My immediate intention, however, being not to discuss the development of episcopacy in general but Roman developments in particular, I shall treat of episcopacy outside Rome only when it is helpful in understanding the Roman experience.[3]

Such historical study is only part of my project in this chapter. The growth of the Roman see carried dangers as well as advantages. It offered prospects that were to turn out to be blind alleys – even enticements to

---

[3] An interesting, though at times necessarily controversial overview – one has to separate news from views – is to be found in F. A. Sullivan, *From Apostles to Bishops* (Mahwah, N. J. 2001).

serious abuse – as well as occasions for service to the Christian cause and to civilization. As I have indicated, the present chapter will set the stage for considering the almost equally controverted issue of the relationship between the growing authority of the see of Rome and the tendency to possible religious domination of civil society by the Church. If what belongs to Caesar is to be rendered to Caesar and the Church is not to dominate inappropriately, what are the Church's proper rights and duties in civil society?: a question still ongoing and increasingly urgent.

4.2 ROME BEFORE THE NERONIAN PERSECUTION

In the year 42 AD the Apostle Peter was arrested in Jerusalem on the orders of King Herod Agrippa I, "miraculously" escaped from prison and disappears not only from the Acts of the Apostles but from the spotlight of historical writing (12:1–19). Accompanied by Mark,[4] to whose mother's house he first resorted after his escape, in all likelihood he went to Rome,[5] from where he probably returned to Jerusalem on the death of Herod Agrippa two years later.[6] There is no reason to suppose that he first brought Christianity to the city of Rome or "founded the Roman Church", though he would have been regarded by Christians and non-Christians alike as the leader of the new movement (and particularly of its mission to Jews (Galatians 2:7–9)) both within the Roman synagogues and in the wider community.

Visitors from Rome are among those astonished at (or mockers of) the linguistic prodigy of the apostles at Pentecost (Acts 2:10). Perhaps some of them were converted before returning and introducing Christianity to the Imperial City. Writing, probably in early 57, to the Christian community in Rome – another man's foundation, as he notes[7] – Paul mentions (among others) Aquila and his wife Prisca,[8] and "the church" which meets at their

---

[4] Mark's Gospel was believed in antiquity to be a record of Peter's original preaching to the as yet tiny Christian community in Rome (see Eus., *H. E.* 3.39 for the evidence of Papias, and Irenaeus, *Adv. Haer.* 3.1 = Eus., *H. E.* 5.8).

[5] Cf. Eusebius, *Ecclesiastical History* 5.6 and the derivative Jerome, *On Famous Men* 3.1. G. Edmundson, *The Church in Rome in the First Century* (London 1913) 52–53, citing Allard and Marrucchi, draws attention to the frequency of representations on sarcophagi from Rome of Peter's release by the angel.

[6] Jerome speaks of a Roman episcopate of 25 years; that perhaps indicates the length of Peter's involvement with the city. The words "episcopacy" in Antioch and "sacerdotal chair" in Rome reasonably indicate Peter's authority. Whatever Jerome thought, they are not to be taken as evidence that the fourth-century sense of "bishop" was current in Peter's time.

[7] One reason for Paul's hesitancy about coming to Rome was that he did not like to interfere in Churches founded by others (Rom. 15:20).

[8] Cf. Rom. 16:3; 1 Cor. 16:19; 2 Tim. 4:19. Acts uses the diminutive "Priscilla" (18:2). Paul apparently first met the couple in Corinth in AD 51 (Acts 19:1).

house (Romans 16:3),[9] as well as Andronicus and Junia[10] "who were prominent among the apostles and became Christians before me" (16:7). That
would put their conversion back to the time of Stephen. It has been suggested
that they originally belonged to the Synagogue of the Freedmen in Rome
(cf. Acts 6:9) and later returned to preach there and "found" a church. As for
Aquila, a Jew from Pontus, he was already a Christian in 49 when, as Acts (18:2)
tells us, he arrived in Corinth, no doubt in company with others expelled
from Italy that year by Claudius – an expulsion almost certainly provoked by
the rioting "about Chrestus" (Suetonius, *Claudius* 25.4).[11]

Whether Peter first met the members of the established Roman Church(es)
in Rome in 42 or later, by the time Paul wrote to them in 57 he was able to say
that their "faith is spoken of all over the world" (Romans 1:8). More to our
present purpose is to enquire how that faith was instantiated. Where did the
Roman Christians meet in those early days and what sort of organization did
they form? It is often claimed that the new communities were structured on
the synagogues, and that, since there were at least a dozen synagogues to cater
for Rome's considerable Jewish community, there must have been a number
of churches each with its group of elders (presbyters) in charge. As with the
synagogues, the argument continues, there would have been no overarching
authority in the Christian churches – except, of course, in the case of the
presence from time to time of an apostle: Peter or Paul. It is clear that the
immediate pre-eminence of the Church in Rome depended in no small
measure on its connection with the combined presence (and martyrs' deaths)
of both these apostles – to the Jews and Gentiles respectively.[12]

---

[9] For the authenticity of chapter 16 and its place in the original letter see R. E. Brown in R. E. Brown
and J. P. Meier, *Antioch and Rome* (London 1983) 106–109.
   Besides the church of Aquila and Prisca Paul himself mentions four other groups. See A. Brent,
*Hippolytus and the Roman Church in the Third Century: Communities in Tension before the Emergence
of a Monarch-bishop* (Leiden 1995) 398–404, often following P. Lampe, *Die stadtrömischen Christen in
den ersten beiden Jahrhunderten* (Tübingen 1989). Brent points to parallels between certain Christian
groups, such as that around Justin, and pagan philosophical schools (especially the Epicureans), but
his assertion (against Lampe) "Given that the church of Rome consisted by the end of the second
century of a number of house-schools . . ." (p. 409) seems an exaggeration. Not all house-churches
would be house-schools in the required sense.

[10] Junia, a woman and not, as earlier believed and widely printed, a man, Junias. So recently,
L. Belleville, "Iounian . . . . episēmoi en tois apostolois: A Re-examination of Romans 16:7 in Light
of Primary Source Materials", *NTS* 51 (2005) 231–249.

[11] For a more accurate account of the details of the edict – not *all* Jews were expelled – see Cassius Dio 60.6.

[12] Cf. (e.g.) Ignatius, *Ad Rom.* 4; Irenaeus, *Adv. Haer.* 3.3; Eusebius, *H. E.* 2.25, citing Dionysius of
Corinth. Martyrs came to be viewed as icons of the suffering and absolving Christ. But at least in
widespread belief Peter and Paul were not the only apostles to suffer martyrdom, so that their deaths,
though giving added prestige and thus helping the recognition of the Roman see, were not unique:
other "apostolic" sees might claim martyr-founders.

Yet there is little hard evidence for claims about Christian structures in Rome in this very early period. I have already noticed Paul's mention in his letter to the Romans of a "church" in the house of Aquila and Prisca. The claim of 1 Peter to be written from Babylon (5:13) and its reference to the "fiery ordeal" (4:12) both suggest a Neronian Roman provenance,[13] and it identifies (5:1) within the body of Roman Christians a number of presbyters who may also, as we shall see – and perhaps from the start – have been called "leaders". In any case it is probable that at least initially Christian missionaries preached in synagogues, and that the rioting in Rome mentioned by Suetonius resulted from this preaching within Jewish communities. What we do not know is the number of "house-churches" such as that of Aquila. According to ancient traditions there was only one other at an early date, that associated with Pudens (mentioned in 2 Timothy 4:21) and his family, though phrases like "and all the brothers/saints who are with them" (Acts 16:14–15) may suggest further informal groupings.

Nor do we know many details of the governance of these house-churches either during the lifetime of Peter and Paul when there was no apostle in the city or when the Roman Church began to pick up the pieces after the Neronian persecution had eliminated the leading apostles and large numbers of others. Probably both house-churches and groups more closely resembling synagogues (the latter certainly presided over by "presbyters") were in operation, but whether the two groups were identical is uncertain and perhaps unlikely, if the house-churches (with their "leaders") were largely Gentile (even if philo-Jewish).[14]

In 62, when Paul first arrived in Rome as a prisoner and met the Jewish leaders, they in general were far from sympathetic. It looks as though an effect of the earlier rioting had been virtually to separate the Christians from their institutional Jewish roots. The Jewish leaders tell Paul that although they will hear his views, all they know of the Christian "sect" (*hairesis*) is that it is everywhere repudiated (Acts 28:22): a grim prediction – at the time of the wave of anti-Christianity in Palestine that led to the death of James, the "brother of the Lord" and local leader of the community – of the hostility to Christians on which Nero was to capitalize a few years later. In the years succeeding the earlier rioting, and now that Jews were safe in Italy under the new Emperor and his "god-fearing" mistress and later wife Poppaea

---

[13] That view has recently been re-affirmed by Rolland, *L'origine* 90–91.
[14] Brown's case for the "moderately" Jewish character of Roman Christianity (more Petrine than Pauline and in direct contact with the supporters of James in Jerusalem) is plausible (see Brown in *Antioch and Rome* 170–171).

Sabina,[15] it is unsurprising that their leaders should be hostile to Christians who might subject the Jewish community in Rome to risks such as the Christians had faced in Jerusalem.

All of which hardly suggests the idea that in the 50s and 60s Roman Christians – even those of Jewish origin, and despite a probably continuing connection with the Church in Jerusalem – would necessarily feel obliged to copy Jewish forms of ecclesiastical order. Gentile converts would have had even less incentive to do so. House-churches must have seemed more attractive than synagogues, and there would be no reason for parallel structures – though such secret and isolated safety could provoke its own dangers. Even if Jews might be suspected of "hatred of the human race", yet the "atheism" (i.e., treasonable refusal of civic religion), orgies and cannibalism with which the "name of Christian" now began to be associated could hardly be supposed features of legally privileged centres of official Jewish worship.

4.3 ROME AFTER PETER: 65–165

According to the lists of the second-century writers Hegesippus and Irenaeus, there was a succession of "bishops" in Rome, after the death of Peter, of whom Linus was the first and Clement the third. Before looking at these compilations, I shall consider earlier sources of evidence about the state of the Roman Church between the Neronian persecution (and the subsequent – more judicial – execution of Paul) and the mid second century. It is often said that there are only three specific pieces of evidence: the first letter of Clement, the letter of Ignatius of Antioch to the Roman Church, and the *Shepherd* of Hermas. There are, however, other sources, while the evidence of these three is rendered somewhat more problematic in that their normally assumed dates are hardly secure and, apart from that of Ignatius, probably mistaken.

A certain amount of information is available in the New Testament, even though there is surprisingly little in 1 Peter, though if that document is Neronian it largely predates our concerns.[16] In any case it merely indicates the presence in Rome (and in northern Asia Minor) of a group of presbyters who are to function as "pastors" (5:1–5).[17] More help may be found in

---

[15] For Poppaea as god-fearing, Josephus, *Ant.* 20.8.11. For her un-Roman burial, Tac., *Annals* 16.6.
[16] See for example F. L. Cross, *I Peter: A Paschal Liturgy* (London 1954) 43f., though Cross's wider claims about liturgy are untenable.
[17] Paul seems to have avoided the term "presbyters" (too Jewish?) in his own Churches, preferring "bishops" ("overseers", Phil. 1:1; cf. Acts 20:28 (Ephesus)) who (cf. 1 Peter 1:1–5) are to be "pastors". In Acts 20:17, however, Luke seems to refer to the same group as "bishops"; probably "bishops" and "presbyters" performed the same "pastoral" (including sacramental) functions.

Hebrews and the book of Revelation, both of which provide specific information about the Roman situation.[18]

According to Tertullian (*On Chastity* 20) – no mean witness – Barnabas was the author of Hebrews,[19] a claim compatible with the view that the destination of the epistle was the city of Rome, though the arguments for Rome are unaffected if Tertullian is mistaken as to authorship. That the letter was written before the fall of Jerusalem and the end of Temple sacrifices seems an obvious deduction from the fact that the author presumes these sacrifices to continue (especially in 11:2)[20] – even though, had they ceased, his case for Christ's eternal high priesthood's being the fulfilment of the levitical system would have been immeasurably strengthened.[21] As for the destination of the letter, those who think that the greeting from

---

[18] A possible further source of information might be the Gospel of Mark, plausibly written in Rome and traditionally held to represent the teaching of Peter. In fact it has little immediately relevant information and I shall therefore leave it (and its problems) aside.

[19] For a challenging discussion of the date and provenance of Hebrews see J. A. T. Robinson, *Redating the New Testament* (London 1976) 200–220; earlier promoters of Tertullian include Harnack, *Chronologie* (= vol. II of *Geschichte der altchristlichen Literatur bis Eusebius* (Leipzig 1897)) 477–479 and Edmundson, *The Church in Rome* 157–160. Other possible authors are widely canvassed: see (for example) Brown, *Antioch and Rome* 139–151, who likens its theology to that of Stephen and the "Hellenists" (which if so might rule out Barnabas). Those consulting Robinson should not be put off by the intemperate and ill-argued reviews of his work by an outraged biblical establishment represented by R. M. Grant, *JBL* 97 (1978) 294–296 and J. A. Fitzmyer, *Interpretation* 32 (1978) 309–313, though Fitzmyer allows that Robinson may have something worthwhile to say about the date of Revelation.

[20] Contrast on a similar theme the *Epistle of Barnabas* (16.4), perhaps to be dated to about 75. Revelation also seems to allude to the continued (though seriously threatened) existence of Jerusalem (11:8), and thus to be datable before 70. (For the extraordinary attempts to evade accepting this obvious reading see Robinson, *Redating the New Testament* 241–242 with my comments in note 19.) Christian tradition consistently, though not universally (see Robinson 224), states (from Irenaeus on) that John, presumed to be the author of Revelation, was exiled to Patmos by Domitian and released by Nerva – Irenaeus says at the end of the reign of Domitian (*Adv. Haer.* 5.30.3) – and that these events took place when Domitian and Nerva were Emperors. The latter assumption is almost certainly a mistake. According to Tertullian, after the deaths of Peter and Paul John was thrown into boiling oil but survived (*Praesc.* 36), and the best explanation of all the evidence is that he was indeed exiled by Domitian (not yet Emperor but acting for his father Vespasian, with consular authority (cf. Tac., *Hist.* 4.3.44ff.), in Rome in AD 70) and was released by order of Nerva, not as Emperor but when consul with Vespasian in 71. The best discussion is still that of Edmundson, *The Church in Rome*.

Note that Clement of Alexandria (also cited in Eus., *H. E.* 3.23) says that after the death of the "tyrant" – perhaps he intended Nero rather than Domitian, though Eusebius assumes a reference to the latter – John was released from Patmos, went to Ephesus (originally a Pauline foundation) and among other vast labours (too vast for a very old man?) appointed "bishops" in Asia.

It is important for our immediate concerns that if Revelation is to be dated to about 70 (celebrating – Rev. 18:20 – the catastrophic events in Rome of the preceding "year of the four Emperors" which might have looked convincingly like Armageddon), the only conclusion to be drawn about the date of Clement of Rome's letter – to which we shall turn shortly – is that it was written no earlier than 71.

[21] For the complete cessation of Temple sacrifice see E. Schürer, *The History of the Jewish People in the Age of Jesus Christ* I (Edinburgh 1973) 522–523.

"those from Italy" (13:24) indicates that it is written to those now in Italy (therefore presumably to a Jewish-Christian group in Rome) are almost certainly right.

As has often been noticed, the author of Hebrews is exceptionally severe on the lapsed, probably not least because lapsing would involve informing on fellow-Christians. Some scholars believe that such informing cost Peter's life, and further indications of it are found in both pagan and Christian references to the Neronian persecution.[22] If a near-Neronian date is correct for Hebrews, we must note, for future reference, the use of the word "leaders"[23] for those who have guided and still guide an incipient Christianity: a terminology that seems to have been applied regularly, and perhaps particularly, to the chief members of the *Roman* Church.

Turning to Revelation, questions of dating are again important, and there is every reason to follow Edmundson in believing that the persecution of which it speaks in Babylon (= Rome) is not that of Domitian, which seems to have been comparatively limited, but again that of Nero, and that the exaltation of the seer who predicts the city's impending fall is to be referred to the events of the year 69.[24]

As already noted, it is Tertullian who proposes Barnabas as the author of Hebrews, and it is again Tertullian who believes that John (supposed the author of Revelation) witnessed the events in Rome which Revelation seems to describe (*Proscription of Heretics* 36.3).[25] Tertullian, it seems, is a good historical witness for events and activities within the Western Christian tradition. Again it is Tertullian who almost alone emphasizes the

[22] Tacitus, *Annals* 15.44; *1 Clement* 6.1; Hermas, *Vis.* 2.2.2; *Sim.* 8.8.1.

[23] *hēgoumenoi*, Heb. 13:7, 17, 24. For Clement and Hermas see below: cf. *1 Clem.* 1.3; *prohēgoumenoi*, *1 Clem.* 21.6; Hermas, *Vis.* 2.2.6; 3.9.7.

[24] In view of the importance of the matter, I cite Edmundson's own words, with the accompanying text of Tacitus, to indicate the happenings in Rome which alone make sense of the seer's claims and hopes.

"The writer" (of Revelation), says Edmundson (p. 169), "had seen it with his own eyes – the storming and burning of the Capitol by the foreign mercenaries of Vitellius, and the subsequent capture and sacking of the city by the infuriated Flavian army under Mucianus and Antonius Primus on December 19 to 21, 69 AD. At no other time, certainly not in the course of Domitian's reign, was it possible to speak of Rome as fallen, or for the Seer to have raised his triumphant cry 'Rejoice over her, thou heaven, and ye holy apostles and prophets; for God hath avenged you on her.'"

An ancient version of some of these events, similar to that of Tacitus and culminating in the lynching of the drunken Vitellius, can be found in Josephus (*BJ* 4.645–654). As for Tacitus, his description runs as follows (*Hist.* 3.83; 4.1): "The city exhibited one entire scene of ferocity and abomination. Here there was fighting and wounds, there baths and taverns. Rivers of blood and heaps of bodies at the same time; and by the side of them harlots, and women no different from harlots. All that unbridled lusts can effect in the wantonness of peace, all the brutalities committed when a city has fallen to a relentless foe – so that you could suppose that the same state was mad with rage and lust at the same time . . . Lamentation was everywhere . . ."

[25] For Tertullian on the authority of Clement see below.

comparatively minor scale of persecution under Domitian when compared with that under Nero (*Apologeticum* 5).

With Revelation dated to the early seventies, I can summarize what the New Testament tells us about Church order around that date, in particular in Rome. Thus I am looking both for some general pattern throughout the Empire and for specific evidence for Rome in the chaotic years on the morrow of the deaths of Peter and Paul, before the Roman Church was able to settle into a period of comparative stability. The general situation is clear. Apostles and apostolic delegates (such as Barnabas) would exert an overriding authority when present in a particular city (as doubtless did Peter and Paul in Rome when they were there), both in those fateful latter years of Nero and in the near interregnum that followed when, despite the Seer, it was Jerusalem that fell and Rome that survived.

Clearly, in all the Churches founded or confirmed (in Rome as well as elsewhere) by apostles, continuity was required when there was no apostle present, or before an apostle arrived, and though at first a number of Christians may have thought that the apostolic founders would need no successors in view of the coming end of the world, that hope must have faded fast in the 60s when the persecutors began to strike more effectively. In Jerusalem James was eliminated in 62 (Josephus, *Antiquities* 20.200–203), an event which doubtless required that a replacement be found to fill the locally monarchical position among the presbyters (Acts 21:18) he had held since Peter's disappearance in 42. An ancient tradition – *ben trovato* if not historical – holds that his successor was a nephew, by name Simeon.[26] But the Church in Jerusalem was soon to dwindle into comparative insignificance, not without leaving a possible pattern – perhaps soon to be developed further in Antioch – for local government in what was once the senior Christian community with, as we have seen, strong links to Rome.

When Peter disappears from the narrative of Acts, among his last instructions are that James and the "brethren" are to be informed of his situation. It is almost a signal that James the Brother of the Lord is to be treated, in the absence of the Twelve, as the leader of the Jerusalem community, the model of other Christian communities at that stage and perhaps until its marginalization when or before Jerusalem was sacked by

---

[26] For evidence see Eusebius, *H. E.* 3.32.1; 4.5.1–4; 4.22.4; Epiphanius, *Haer.* 27.6, etc. According to Eusebius the *Memoirs* of Hegesippus are his source. The election of another member of Jesus' family has sometimes suggested the desire for a continuing "caliphate" or necessary succession of relations, but there is no evidence for this attitude even in the case of James. The question whether the monarchical office developed in Jerusalem under the influence of Judaeo-Christian notions of high-priesthood must remain moot.

Titus in 70. Here we have a model community, and in its leading "presby-ter" a possible model of what was later to be dubbed a monarchical episcopate. James may not have been called *episcopus* (at least in the sense of a monarchical bishop[27]) – and insofar as he had seen the risen Lord and could thus be thought of as an apostle (1 Corinthians 15:7; Galatians 1.19) needed no such title – but insofar as the BISHOP was chief overseer of a local community, James filled a somewhat similar role to those later so desig-nated. James, uniquely both an apostle and successor of the Twelve in their original place of apostolic activity, was struck down in 62.

The ordinary pattern of church life in the absence of the itinerant apostles is clear enough. The communities were normally governed by a group of presbyters,[28] some of whom (perhaps in places heads of families or of specifically Pauline foundations) were also called *episcopi* ("bishops").[29] Normally there would be several presbyter-bishops in each community; thus we would have a *presbyterion*, a college of presbyters either chosen directly by the Holy Spirit working through the Church as a whole and/or on whom "official" hands had been laid (1 Timothy 4:14; 5:22). The terminological link between apostolic pastors and bishops is provided by 1 Peter; here Christ himself is called the shepherd and "bishop" of souls (2:25).

That is as far as the regularly used New Testament evidence takes us, and Hebrews and Revelation add comparatively little to our knowledge apart from the references in Hebrews – in language that we have already observed to be repeated in the Roman authors Clement and Hermas – to the "leaders" (plural) of the Roman Church. Before turning to Clement, Ignatius and Hermas, however, I should consider one further text, the *Didache*: all the more important if it is to be dated before 65, with parts as early as the 40s.[30]

The *Didache*, it is generally agreed, derives from Syria and reflects Eastern conditions.[31] What immediately concerns us is that it also reflects the introduction of a new and localized church order. Its local community is urged to accept the authority of *elected* bishops and deacons chosen from its own number (15.1) instead of, or as a substitute for, itinerant missioners and "apostles" (11.3) – who, as the author is aware, might be fraudsters. Here we

[27] I shall henceforth capitalize these as BISHOPS – though, as we shall see, the authority and power of their "monarchy" will not always be identical.
[28] Acts 21:18 (Jerusalem); Acts 20:17 (Ephesus); cf. Acts 14:23; 1 Tim 5:17–22; Titus 1:5; Jas. 5:14; 1 Pet. 5:1–5; Rev. 4.4.
[29] Acts 20:28; 1 Tim. 3.2; Titus 1:5; 1:7; Phil. 1:1.
[30] Cf. J. P. Audet, *La Didachè: Instructions des apôtres* (Paris 1958). Even if the *Didache*, at least in our present version, is later, most of what follows would stand.
[31] A recent treatment is that of K. Niederwimmer, *The Didache* (Minneapolis 1998).

have hard evidence for a change that must at some point have overtaken every community in the Christian world. Bishops and deacons, we read (15.2), are not to be despised – and they are still in the plural.[32] As yet there are no BISHOPS: an argument either for early dating, or less plausibly for the origin of the *Didache* in an out-of-the-way and therefore undeveloped later community – which is odd if it derives from the ambit of Antioch where there seems to have been at least one BISHOP before the early second-century Ignatius.

So we reach Clement of Rome, and again a problem of chronology – that of the date of his letter to the Corinthians.[33] We can accept that the author is indeed the Clement who later was held to be a "bishop", in some sense of the word, of the Roman Church. In his letter, however, he never claims to be a "bishop" in any sense, merely to speak for the Roman Church. (The singular form "Church" is used in chapter 1.) And we should reject not only the common claim that the letter refers to a persecution under Domitian, but the assumption that it was written in the reign of Domitian at all.[34]

There is even less reason to believe that the apparent references to persecution in Clement's letter merely signify struggles in the souls of individual Roman Christians. That suggestion seems to derive from a widely adopted but egregiously false axiom, largely promoted by Dibelius,[35] that if an ancient Christian author refers to purportedly historical events in a stylized or conventional mode, those events are not historical but *merely* symbolic or metaphorical. Such a principle in the world outside New Testament and post-New Testament studies would lead us to infer, from the contorted language put in the mouth of Pericles (and others) by Thucydides, that Pericles never gave a Funeral Speech in Athens, or – a more recent parallel – that the strained diction of G. M. Hopkins' *Wreck of the Deutschland* indicates only that the poet is airing his psychological and spiritual anxieties or those of some possibly German nuns.

---

[32] The fact that "bishops" are not also designated "presbyters" may indicate that the *Didache* community is largely Gentile, not Jewish-Christian, or at least following Gentile practice rather than that of the synagogue.

[33] Some time after 170 Irenaeus (*Adv. Haer.* 3.3.2) speaks of Clement as the third BISHOP of Rome after Peter and connects him with the letter sent by the Roman Church to the Corinthians; see also the letter of BISHOP Dionysius of Corinth to BISHOP Soter of Rome (166–175) mentioned by Eusebius (*H. E.* 4.23.11).

[34] See the summary and development of some earlier objections to a Domitianic date by L. L. Welborn, "On the Date of First Clement", *BR* 29 (1984) 35–54. The Domitianic date is still affirmed – without discussion or even mention of Edmundson – by (e.g.) P. Henne, *La Christologie chez Clément de Rome et dans le Pasteur d'Hermas* (Fribourg 1992) 10 and by Rolland, *L'origine* 164.

[35] M. Dibelius, *Botschaft und Geschichte* II (Tübingen 1956) 102–199.

In the *Shepherd* of Hermas (to be dated probably to the last quarter of the first century[36]) we read of a Roman Clement who is presumably the same one – providing evidence for the comparatively early date of the *Letter*. There is no clear indication that Clement is a bishop – though he presumably is – let alone a BISHOP, as he presumably is not. According to Hermas he is the individual entrusted with the important task of keeping up communications with other Churches (*Vision* 2.4.3), as he would also appear to be in the *Letter* itself. This confirms the view that he is a presbyter-bishop but not, as yet, a BISHOP. He himself mentions what we can now take to be the standard Church order of bishops (or presbyters) and deacons (appointed, according to Clement, by the apostles) both for Rome (42) and for Corinth (44, 54, 57). Though he has been entrusted with a position of some importance – he is certainly no mere secretary taking dictation – there is no reason to think that he is at this point even a permanently presiding presbyter, let alone that he has been formally consecrated as such.

Presiding presbyters demand more detailed consideration. Most scholars hold that they would have been necessary, at least at times and for particular functions of the Roman Church, but there is little agreement about their status in the first century. It is often accepted that the need, however limited, for such a position, combined with factors that include the model of the original Jerusalem Church – we note the reference to Temple practice in chapter 41 of the letter – points towards the eventual establishment of a BISHOP.

Apart from one perhaps significant point, already noted in connection with the Roman origins of Hebrews, that is all we can derive about the organization of the Church in Rome from *1 Clement* or, for that matter, from the *Shepherd*, for the years between the fall of Jerusalem and the early second century. The further point is that Clement seems to distinguish "leaders" from (probably other) "presbyters", thus seemingly indicating a hierarchy. Let us "respect" (*aidesthōmen*) our "leaders", he insists, and "honour" our presbyters.[37] Hermas too, as we have noted, writes of "leaders" of the Roman Church (*Vision* 2.2.6; 3.9.7).

Before moving to Ignatius of Antioch – who is in no doubt that, in his part of the world, at least, real churches have BISHOPS with some sort of real authority – I revert to the actual *appointment* of presbyter-bishops. What seems to be clear is that after a time of direct appointment or, where

---

[36] That Hermas was the brother of Bishop Pius (mid second century) seems a confusion between the bishop's brother, Pastor, and the name of Hermas' book; see Edmundson, *The Church* 209–211.
[37] 21.6; cf. 1.3, where again "leaders" are mentioned first. Note also *archēgoi* (14).

possible, confirmation by an apostle – at least in Rome, Corinth and the
community of the *Didache* – such appointments were local affairs, even in
the Church in Jerusalem which in its more monarchical structure under
James may eventually have provided a model for other Churches. In the
Didache (15), as we have seen, the community is told to select its presbyters
and deacons. In Corinth, Rome and presumably more generally, at least
according to Clement (44), the original bishops and deacons were
appointed – the reality may often be "confirmed where possible" – by an
apostle, who arranged that after their deaths they should be replaced by
other "approved" men. No appointee either of the apostles or of other
"reputable" men, once "confirmed by the Holy Spirit" through the local
Church, could be removed without good cause.

This passage of Clement has caused much debate. The most serious
difficulty concerns who does the approving and whether the "reputable"
men are presbyters of the local Church (or perhaps one senior such presbyter, i.e., a BISHOP – but it is hard to twist this meaning out of the Greek
plural "men of repute") or whether they are neo-apostolic persons from
outside. In other words, to appoint a presbyter did one need a higher
authority from outside the local community or a chief presbyter (or
BISHOP) from inside? And if a BISHOP were required to appoint a presbyter,
clearly an outside BISHOP or BISHOPS would be required to appoint a local
BISHOP.

It is impossible to be certain what Clement means,[38] but by far the most
natural reading of the Greek in context is that the local presbyters (or some
of them), in the absence of an apostle, are to appoint any new presbyter (or
deacon) with the consent of the local Church as a whole.[39] Clearly, as we
have seen, if a BISHOP either inside or outside the community were needed to
appoint a presbyter, his own successor would have to be appointed by a
BISHOP, but if he is not so needed (not least because he did not exist) this
further problem disappears. Clearly again, when BISHOPS do become a
regular fact of life, there will be a new and special problem of how they
are to be appointed. Eventually consecration by other BISHOPS will be
logically and historically required.

---

[38] E. G. Jay offers a balanced discussion in "From Presbyter-Bishops to Bishops and Presbyters", *The
Second Century* 1 (1981) 129–136.

[39] It should be noted, however, that in one important respect Clement's account of the functions of a
presbyter differs from those desired by the author of Hebrews. Clement emphasizes the role of the
presbyter-bishop as a priest (44.4), that is, as one who offers sacrifice as the successor of the Jewish
priesthood. See the interesting comment of Brown (*Antioch and Rome* 170–171).

The appearance of BISHOPS, or at least the development of their powers, cannot but be related to problems of spiritual as well as organizational authority. It seems as though Roman practice at the time of Clement's letter roughly coincides with that urged in the *Didache*: after the deaths of the apostles presbyter-bishops were appointed by some (perhaps all) of the local "college" with the consent of the local Church as a whole. The Holy Spirit's working was through the local Church – the people of God – seen as the bearer of the apostolic tradition, not least because he had no other historical option!

The passing of the apostles left a peculiarly urgent problem: no succeeding figures could enjoy a similar authority. It is unsurprising that those who wished to solve the problem by promoting an authoritative BISHOP (or claiming to be one) would need serious arguments to demonstrate that he was necessary. When such arguments began to prevail – and well before the resulting emergence of BISHOPS – one or more of the presbyter-bishops, for the convenience of all, would already be functioning as some kind of chairman; from such chairmen the BISHOP would evolve. Cogent reasons, however, not mere power-politics, would be required to justify this development, which would in any case be gradual as spiritual authority (not least in the performance of Christian rites) tended to grow into juridical power. Seeing that the apostles chose to vest their authority and hand on the traditions of their teaching to some (or all) of the presbyter-bishops, these representing the community as a whole, a more "monarchical" change would involve recognizing the BISHOP as legatee of the responsibilities originally vested in the presbyters as a representative group. Such developments might be deferred, but ultimately they would have to be faced.

We have already seen that it is likely that among the presbyter-bishops (or whatever title might normally be used) some would be senior to others. If that were the case, it would be natural that a chairman (and potential BISHOP) should be drawn from this senior group. If such seniors succeeded each other, they would form the basis for what Hegesippus and Irenaeus later identify as a succession of BISHOPS.

There is a curious piece of admittedly late but apparently relevant evidence: according to the *Liber Pontificalis* (1.118 Duchesne) – the source of which may ultimately be Hegesippus in the second century – Peter himself ordained as his successors Linus and Cletus, who at times exercised "episcopal" powers during Peter's lifetime,[40] presumably providing more authority when Peter was away. The *Liber* adds that Clement also was

[40] Linus was assumed in antiquity to be the Linus mentioned in 2 Tim. 4:21.

ordained by Peter.[41] That may be pure fiction, but nothing even in later theories of an "Apostolic Succession" of bishops requires that seniority among the presbyters could not have passed from Peter to Linus to Cletus to Clement in simple sequence; indeed, the historical likelihood is enhanced by this being no necessary claim. If Peter appointed or confirmed the three as presbyter-bishops, they would have special authority in the community and would have formed a senior group from which chairmen of all the presbyter-bishops would be selected when needed. The order of succession within such a group would presumably have been on grounds of age and experience. Clement outlived the others and may have been the youngest.[42]

I shall return to these speculations when considering the lists of supposed BISHOPS produced by Hegesippus and Irenaeus. First, however, we must investigate the arrival in Rome some time between 110 and 135 of Ignatius of Antioch,[43] bishop of the most important see in the East now that Jerusalem had been eclipsed, to consider the picture of church order he presents against the background of authority in the Roman Church insofar as I have been able to identify it. Ignatius was an easterner; apart from his letter to the Church in Rome his correspondence and his experience are with Eastern Churches. But Christianity at this period is predominantly an Eastern religion, at least in terms of its membership, however much Rome is growing in prestige in light of the preaching and death there of the principal Apostle to the Jews and principal Apostle to the Gentiles.[44]

---

[41] The opinion that Clement was ordained by Peter is also voiced by Tertullian in *De Praescr. Haer.* 32. (Tertullian, as we have seen, is an important witness for Latin traditions.) Jerome (*De Viris Illust.* 15) "knows" that most Latins think that Clement immediately succeeded Peter. For an introduction to the complexities of the problem of the first "successors" of Peter in Rome (and their place in the list of Irenaeus as well as that of Hegesippus) see W. Ullmann, "The Significance of the *Epistula Clementis* in the Ps-Clementines", *JTS* 11 (1960) 295–317. Perhaps the problem is slightly simplified if Abramowski is right and Cletus (Anacletus) did not exist; see L. Abramowski, "Irenaeus, *Adv. Haer.*III.3.2: Ecclesia Romana and Omnis Ecclesia, and 3.3: Anacletus of Rome", *JTS* 28 (1977) 101–104.

[42] If Clement was indeed quite young when he was ordained, it is not difficult to see that he could refer to Peter and Paul as of an earlier generation.

[43] A series of weak arguments about Ignatius himself and interpolations in Polycarp have been used to prop up what looks like theological prejudice against BISHOPS among those who propose a date after 135 for Ignatius' allegedly interpolated letters. I would prefer the "traditional" time of around 110, but nothing hangs on this and any time between 110 and 135 is possible. For reliable comment see A. Brent, "The Relations between Ignatius and the Didascalia", *The Second Century* 8 (1991) 129–156, esp. 154–156, and on a wider canvas *Ignatius of Antioch and the Second Sophistic* (Tübingen 2006) esp. 18–30, 312–318. My own view of Ignatius' understanding of the role of a bishop and of its mistreatment by later patristic authors is greatly indebted to Brent's work.

[44] The Synod of Antioch (in 341) indicates how easterners had come to respect Roman as a religious centre: the glory of the Roman Church is that it is the site of the monuments of the apostles and has always been the "capital" of piety, "even though the bearers of the faith came to it from the East" (Sozomen, *Hist. Eccl.* 3.8.5).

Ignatius wrote to the Church at Tralles (3.1) as follows: "In like manner let all men respect the deacons as Jesus Christ, even as they should respect the bishop as being a type of the father and the presbyters as the council of God and the college of the apostles. Nothing is called a church without these."[45] And again to the Church at Smyrna (8): "Let that be held a valid eucharist which is under the bishop or anyone to whom he entrusts it. It is not possible apart from the bishop either to baptize or to hold an *agape*. Whatever he confirms is pleasing to God, so that everything he does is safe and valid." And although Ignatius, in continuation of what we must assume to have been normal practice in Antioch as well as in Jerusalem, always associates the bishop with his presbyters and deacons, there is no doubt that, once and however appointed – he says nothing of laying on of hands or of apostolic succession – the BISHOP has become in significant if unexpected ways their superior: not merely their chairman, but the "type" of God the Father. This superiority is linked to the performance of the sacraments, particularly of baptism and the eucharist, which can only be performed in (or with reference to) a community where there is a bishop. The eucharist in particular is to be celebrated either by the bishop himself or by someone delegated by him.

Nevertheless, the position of Ignatius has often been misinterpreted. He is certainly a BISHOP, but not in the sense that later prevailed; later BISHOPS – naturally but in a different world – assumed that he was strictly "one of us". Yet Ignatius never writes of presbyters and deacons being subject or sub-missive to the BISHOP, as was later the case. He supposes that the relationship between the BISHOP and his priests and deacons will always be harmonious: a mark both of his own early date and of a rather self-flattering view wide-spread among Christian clergy in antiquity – and found even at times as late as Augustine – that their fellow clergy will be free from petty strife, working together in harmony, as Ignatius puts it, like the strings on a lyre.

When writing to the Church in Rome, for which he has tremendous respect, not least because of the presence there of Peter and Paul (4), Ignatius never addresses or even mentions a bishop, let alone a BISHOP. He seems to see his arrival in Rome as part of an eschatological drama, his martyrdom as a re-enactment of the death of Christ, transcending the particulars of day-to-day church life or of church order which are thus of no immediate concern to him.

Ignatius' letter to the Smyrnaeans not only speaks of the BISHOP's superior authority but explains at least in part what justifies it: the need for secure

---

[45] The theme is constant: *Eph.* 3.4; *Philad.* 3.4.7; *Mag.* 3.6, etc.

and valid actions in a unified community. The BISHOP, that is, represents what Ignatius thinks of as orthodoxy (perhaps especially sacramental ortho-doxy), and in view of various threats to orthodoxy of a "pre-Gnostic" and sometimes sexually tinged antinomian type[46] such as are also disturbing to Paul in the Pastorals[47] – not to speak of the author of Revelation who denounces members of the Church at Smyrna (2:15ff.; 3:4, etc.) – we can see the roots of Ignatius' concern. In apostolic times the apostles themselves were the disclosers and guardians of controverted "orthodoxy". In later years when, as we know, the communities (including the presbyters) were still divided, it was hoped that an ultimate single, though consulting, author-itative BISHOP would be able to do what was required to maximize unity (especially of ritual) and orthodoxy in each community.

The stage was thus set for a later act of the drama. What if internal choices lead to the appointment of "heretical" or factional BISHOPS? And what if the duly elected BISHOP of one see disagrees with the duly elected BISHOP of another? And what if a BISHOP, apparently unworthy but with local backing, refuses to stand down? Some non-local input into the appointment – and continuance – of BISHOPS, if they are to be BISHOPS, will seem increasingly necessary. As Juvenal said, *Quis custodiet ipsos custodes?* Who will guard the guards?

All this is still a long way ahead of Ignatius, who seems confident that each local BISHOP will be an adequate guarantor of the "universal" Church (*Smyrneans* 8.1: "Let no-one do anything that has to do with the Church without the BISHOP") – so long as he is surrounded by his deacons and his circle of presbyters who are a "woven spiritual wreath" (*Magnesians* 13), an apostolic council. Here we recognize both a survival and an idiosyncratic development of the idea that it is through the presbyters (i.e., the presbyter-bishops) in concert that the Christian tradition is handed down. Ignatius does indeed teach a triple order of BISHOP, presbyters and deacons, but his vision of their role has no immediate connection with any clear and specific thesis about apostolic succession and its transmission; that was read into him later by Irenaeus and others. What he does want to demonstrate, not least by his own death as a martyr-bishop, is that Christ really died, that any "docetic" Christology, by which Christ did not suffer and die, is false. Ignatius' primary concern, as a bishop, as a "type" of God, is to live out in unity with his community the bloody truth of orthodox theology. His contribution to the later growth of the notion of BISHOP, as we can now see,

---

[46] Jude 3–4, 23; cf. 2 Pet. 2:14ff.   [47] 1 Tim. 1:4; 1:10; 6:3; Titus 1:9.

is not in terms of succession and ordination, but in terms of the orthodoxy – as he understood it – and unity of the faith.

But Ignatius would agree with those who later misread him that the BISHOP is no merely convenient chairman of his community; he is a key leader in maintaining its single-minded orthodoxy. Those who later misunderstood his theology of orders were at least right about his view of the BISHOP as a successor of the apostles insofar as he represented a proper understanding (and indeed in his view a proper re-enactment) of their faith. Ignatius should not be seen as an anachronistically early advocate of a monarchical episcopate of the type that was gradually developing in the second century, but as a BISHOP with his own understanding of the significance of bishops and who thus helped to build up important aspects of what was to become the later consensus.

Ignatius mentions neither a BISHOP nor even bishops in Rome. Certainly presbyter-bishops were to be found there, and presumably a chairman, the successor of Clement in that role, elected by the local community. But the problems of deviant teaching which provided the motivation for the developing powers of bishops in Eastern sees were as yet hardly experienced. We know that apostasy occurred, but the frequently uttered modern claim that all sorts of heretical teaching flowed into Rome – echoing the disgust of Tacitus and Juvenal at the arrival in the city of all kinds of vile Oriental obscenities, religious and other ("The Syrian Orontes has flowed into the Tiber") – though perhaps, in the eyes of mainstream Roman Christians true of *second-century* Christianity in the days of Marcion, Valentinus and Tatian, is in no way borne out by (nor to be back-dated to) first- and early second-century evidence. On the contrary, Ignatius congratulates the holy and enlightened Roman Church on its purity of doctrine (*Romans* 1).

In Ignatius' time, despite the prestige he readily grants the Church in Rome, Christianity, still very limited in numbers, was primarily, as we have noted, a religion of the Eastern Mediterranean where the "faithful", being probably rather more literate and educated than their Western counterparts, were also more open to semi-sophisticated theosophies. Its original home in Jerusalem had now gone. Rome (for all her pride in Peter and Paul) was not yet *consciously* moving into primacy of place, and the memory and practice of the original apostolic centre in Jerusalem were still green.

That original centre, famed for a doctrinal purity going back to the Master himself, had boasted the first residential and "monarchical" bishop in the person of James the Brother of the Lord. A similar "monarchical" structure had perhaps not yet been adopted even at Antioch, where we "know" only the name of a single BISHOP, Euodius, before Ignatius himself

(Eusebius, *Ecclesiastical History* 3.22). Yet a BISHOP, as a bulwark against deviant teachers, is already to be found there by about 90, and there is no particular reason to suppose that he appeared first in Antioch. In the East more than in Rome the proximity to the monarchical situation at Jerusalem – so long as it lasted – could easily indicate that BISHOPS (clearly not "caliphs") were the way forward when unity was threatened.

If this analysis is right, we should expect the appearance of something nearer to BISHOPS in Rome when deviant teaching and the possibility of schism threatened there too:[48] some time, that is, between the death of Clement (whose prestige as chairman among the presbyter-bishops would have been enhanced if he was ordained or confirmed by Peter) and the arrival in the city of Hegesippus, the first to compile a Roman episcopal list, in about 165.

4.4 LISTS OF ROMAN BISHOPS

Clement's fame among the presbyter-bishops may have strengthened the drift towards a fully fledged BISHOP in Rome – together with the recognition of such a BISHOP as bearer of an apostolic authority previously seen as handed on primarily through the presbyter-bishops as a group. By the time of Anicetus, who seems to have ruled the Roman Church from 155 to about 165, BISHOPS have come closer, though they may not always have called themselves BISHOPS, and their power, as distinct from their spiritual authority, was almost certainly less than it was to become in the next hundred years. Irenaeus' reference to BISHOP Polycarp of Smyrna, who died in 156, as "the most blessed and apostolic *presbyter*"[49] may indicate the survival of an older view that the spiritual authority even of a BISHOP resided primarily in his presbyteral office; indeed Polycarp refers to himself as among his fellow-presbyters (*sumpresbuteroi*).[50] Thus it should be borne in mind, when considering the lists of "bishops" in Rome, that even when there is a BISHOP he may still be referred to as a presbyter – which could easily mislead a modern (or even a fourth-century) historian. That would appear to explain why some time after 190 Irenaeus, this time writing to BISHOP Victor of Rome about the date of Easter, refers to the "presbyters who presided over the church which you now rule, that is, Anicetus, Pius,

---

[48] Not only Rome and Corinth but other Western sees were slow to adopt the fully monarchical structure. The salutation in Polycarp's letter to the Philippians (to be dated to about 135) provides no evidence for BISHOPS there.

[49] Eus., *H. E.* 5.20.7; cf. Irenaeus, *Adv. Haer.* 3.2.1.   [50] *2Ep. ad Phil*; cf. 1 Pet. 5:1.

Hyginus and Xystus" (Eusebius, *Ecclesiastical History* 5.24.14). With that in mind let us turn to Hegesippus and the condition of the Roman Church on his arrival in 165.

When Hegesippus reached Rome we can be sure that he found there – as earlier at Corinth – someone whose status approximated to that of a BISHOP, namely Anicetus. Had there not been, it would have been an absurd project to compile the names of those whom Hegesippus at least took to be his predecessors as BISHOP. Hegesippus' language ("I compiled a list") would suggest that he considered himself the first to have done so. We can reasonably continue to assume, however, that the process of identifying the presiding presbyter-bishop as a BISHOP was gradual, and potentially reversible at least until the time when the appointment of the BISHOP had come to be determined by some special rite, perhaps normally and preferably with the aid of clergy from outside the local Church. The earliest possible evidence we have of such proceedings – probably referring back to the end of the second century – is provided by Hippolytus (*Apostolic Tradition* 1.2ff.), who, if his words are no later interpolation, also describes how the laying on of hands (as in 1 Timothy) by a properly consecrated BISHOP is now necessary (though not solely necessary) for the ordination of a presbyter.

In second-century Rome the nature of ecclesiastical authority is shifting, with apparently little serious objection.[51] Previously each presbyter-bishop had derived his commission from his senior colleagues, themselves the "descendants" of the apostles. Eventually the BISHOP came to be viewed as the successor and the presbyters as deriving their authority from him. Such a development of church order is at least partially understood by Irenaeus (who himself, even if apparently consecrated within his local church, is a BISHOP), for he speaks of that "tradition which originates from the apostles, which is preserved by means of the successions of presbyters" (*Against Heresies* 3.3.2) and of the need to "obey the presbyters who are in the church – those who, as I have shown, possess the succession from the apostles, those who, *together with the succession of the episcopate*, have received the certain charism of truth" (4.26.2).[52]

The core of this history was understood as late as Jerome, though he dates the development of full-blown BISHOPS (not least in Rome) too early, makes it too organized and relates it to schism – certainly a problem for Ignatius – rather

---

[51] Lampe (*Die stadtrömischen Christen* 336–337) reasonably stresses that in the second century the increase in poor relief and the power of particular individuals to distribute it would tend to increase the "monarchical" position of certain presbyters.

[52] Cf. Jay, "From Presbyter-Bishops" 153.

than more precisely to heresy. Jerome comments, in characteristically polemical vein, that "the churches were governed by the council of presbyters, acting together. But after each began to think that those whom he had baptized were his, not Christ's, it was unanimously decreed that one of the presbyters should be elected and preside over the others, and that the care of the church should wholly belong to him, that the seeds of schism might thus be removed" (*Commentary on the Epistle to Titus* 1.6–7).[53]

In the process of episcopal appointment described by Hippolytus there must be at least some laying on of hands. Presumably this was originally done by the local presbyters who thereby vested in the developing BISHOP the sum of the powers they themselves had held as a group. I have argued that Jerome is right and that the probable reason for that would be the hope that a concentration of authority in a single individual would ensure a unity of doctrine within the local Church.

It is generally agreed that one of the motives of Hegesippus, and after him of Irenaeus, in composing episcopal lists was to show that in the apostolic Churches – as opposed to the new-fangled conventicles of the Gnostics and Marcionites – the true doctrine had been handed down since apostolic times. It was assumed that the apostolic Churches must, under divine inspiration, have avoided false doctrine and that they must therefore necessarily agree with one another. Hegesippus toured a number of Churches and was able to claim that the same doctrine was taught everywhere: "He associated with very many bishops ... and received the same teaching from them all" (Eusebius, *Ecclesiastical History* 4.22.1).

Exactly the same idea seems to have motivated Irenaeus, and to lie behind a much controverted passage of *Against Heresies* (3.3.2). Irenaeus claims that every Church in which the tradition from the apostles has been preserved will of necessity agree doctrinally with the Church in Rome. And why is the Church in Rome singled out as the point of reference for this necessary agreement among the Churches? Because of its "*potentiorem principalitatem*". In light of the impossibility of enumerating the succession of bishops in all the (apostolic) Churches, this can only mean that the antiquity (*principalitatem*) of the Roman Church has more authority (*potentiorem*), specifically that of the martyrs Peter and Paul (3.3.2). In terms of mere antiquity, the Church at Antioch must have had an equal, indeed greater, claim.[54]

---

[53] Interestingly, Jerome thinks that a bishop differs from a presbyter specifically inasmuch as the latter cannot ordain (*Ep.* 146).

[54] It is unfortunate that L. Abramowski, in her perceptive note on this passage ("Irenaeus, *Adv. Haer.* III.3.2" 101–104), offers no comment on *potentiorem principalitatem*, nor on the implications of the fact

In line with Hegesippus, Irenaeus holds that the uniformity of doctrine taught in the apostolic Churches and guaranteed by the unbroken succession of the BISHOPS of those Churches will expose the theories of Marcion and the Gnostics as alien to traditional belief.[55] That does not commit him to any thesis about the precise juridical powers of the BISHOPS whom he has identified. His concern is with the doctrinal tradition going back to the apostles, and for that purpose he needs only to identify the most prominent presbyters in the Roman Church from time to time. I have already noticed how he regards the title "presbyter", rather than *episcopus*, as the more spiritually based. In brief there is no need to impugn the list of names Irenaeus (or Hegesippus) has produced,[56] but the actual role of the "ruling presbyters" named in those lists remains problematic. The most we can say

that the necessary (that is, for Irenaeus, inevitable) agreement between all the Churches is best seen in the agreement of other Churches with Rome. In this she seems to have followed the misleading advice of J. F. McCue, "The Roman Primacy in the Second Century and the Problem of the Development of Dogma", *TS* 25 (1964) 176, and has herself been followed by Osborn, *Irenaeus of Lyons* 129, who claims that "we have seen Rome rather as emblematic and not prior to other churches". On any interpretation the sort of priority involved is hard to discern from Irenaeus' comments, but the question to be faced is why *Rome* is seen as "emblematic" of the inevitable agreement, and what is to be inferred from its being so. Part of the solution lies with the word *principalitas*; it seems to represent the Greek *archaiotēs*, and to indicate "primitivity", that is, the very early days of the Church. Thus Rome's primitivity is more marked, and therefore more significant. Elsewhere Irenaeus describes Papias, the "companion" of Polycarp, as a man of the early days (*archaios*) (*Adv. Haer.* 5.33.4, cited in Eus., *H. E.* 3.30.1). (There is a more recent and unfortunate German parallel in "Altkämpfer".)

[55] Cf. Irenaeus' attitude to the "apostolic" connections of Polycarp of Smyrna (*Adv. Haer.* 3.3.4). Irenaeus' concern (3.1–2) for the succession of bishops going back to primitive times is paralleled by his concern for a four-Gospel canon (each member of which was probably already known by Justin, who refers to them – perhaps in imitation of Xenophon's memoirs of Socrates – as *apomnēmoneumata*). That four-Gospel canon too is intended at least in part to nullify the claims of seemingly more recent (i.e., non-apostolic) "scriptures". Thus we have simultaneous insistence on the primitivity of the Gospel traditions and of the centres of teaching. For the fourfold Gospel see recently T. C. Skeat, "The Oldest Manuscript of the Four Gospels", *NTS* 43 (1997) 1–34 and "Irenaeus and the Four-Gospel Canon", *NT* 34 (1992) 194–199; G. N. Stanton, "The Fourfold Gospel", *NTS* 43 (1997) 317–346. For more caution about "the oldest manuscript" of the four Gospels see P. M. Head, "Is P[4], P[64] and P[67] the Oldest Manuscript of the Four Gospels? A Response to T. C. Skeat", *NTS* 51 (2005) 450–457. A convenient summary of much of the debate is to be found in G. N. Stanton, *Jesus and Gospel* (Cambridge 2004).
Stanton's discussion is disappointing in one basic particular: although he follows von Campenhausen and others in denying a connection between the establishment of a four-Gospel tradition and the struggle against Marcion in particular (81), he has little to suggest on the crucial question of why the "authentic" Gospels were so determined – except for an appeal to Christian partiality for the codex. But however useful the codex may have been, it can hardly be thought to have, by itself, induced Christians to decide on four and only four Gospels. Far more plausibly it was deemed necessary (by someone) to fix the authentic Gospels and rule out any kind of deviant misinformation, whether from Marcion-style reduction or from attempts to supplement the historical account with more "Gnostic" material.

[56] Remarks like "he [Irenaeus] reinforced his invented line of bishops . . ." (so Hopkins, *A World Full of Gods* 103) must be dismissed as reckless at best, deliberate misrepresentation as more likely.

is that if, as seems certain, there was gradual but persistent growth in the power of the chairman-presbyter, Irenaeus and Hegesippus are largely unaware of it. That should provoke no surprise.

A new and serious problem was caused by the very existence of the episcopal lists. Once they had been taken to be canonical, pressure would obviously arise about future continuity. Hegesippus and Irenaeus both speak of the Church in Rome, but give us no idea as to how the orthodox teachers they listed were selected. Did they all belong to one Roman house-church? In what territorial sense, if any, can we say that Clement, for example, is the "successor" of Cletus? There is no reason to suppose that the presbyter-bishops selected were from the same community within the wider Roman Church, though, since it is quite implausible that Hegesippus simply invented the names, he must have drawn them from church traditions and probably from church documents. The most plausible explanation is that they were identified in documents or tradition as the chairmen of the presbyterate, often from different segments of the community.

Once the lists existed, each time the current chairman died, it would become a matter of great urgency who should be the next overall guardian of orthodoxy. The mere existence of the "official" lists would strongly promote the monarchical tendencies already working themselves out. We might also expect that after the compilation of the lists the successors of Anicetus would be likely to come from his own local church or at least be known to have been favoured by him, and thus to be *his* successors, not only doctrinally but as belonging to his particular group within the wider Christian body. It was probably not by divine choice purely that one of a BISHOP's deacons often became his successor, not least in Rome.

In early third-century Rome, we seem to see such a scenario unfolding in the relationship between Zephyrinus and his eventual successor Callistus – and being resented by other presbyter-bishops. Thus, while the compilation of the lists was doubtless intended to promote unity and orthodoxy – and with some success – their existence may also have encouraged (as in the reaction against Victor, Zephyrinus and Callistus) a tendency (among "conservatives") to schism and to allegations of a self-promotion alien to tradition. That in its turn might encourage imputations of heresy. Furthermore, in the early third century, when the Roman Church began to own property as a corporation, the victor in disputes over the succession, the "orthodox" BISHOP, would have power to seize the ecclesiastical property of his rivals – something not possible while the individual churches merely functioned in public buildings such as bath-complexes (as in about 150 in the case of the group around Justin) or on private property. At all events, by the 240s BISHOP Fabian was sure enough of the new *status quo* to be able to establish in the Catacomb of Callistus a mausoleum specially reserved for the BISHOPS of Rome. In modern times some have even said he had the mausoleum of Augustus in mind; that must be an exaggeration, but the action of Fabian and his successors cannot be overlooked.

4.5 BISHOPS AND DOCTRINE

If Hegesippus and Irenaeus are right to connect an emphasis on an apostolic teaching tradition with the need to combat the growth of deviant doctrine,[57] it is highly likely that increase in the power of the chairman-presbyter was regularly seen as an appropriate response to such doctrinal threats. This would certainly have made it more widely acceptable and, as I have noted, concern about false doctrine would also involve anxiety over the perhaps older problem of schism. This being the case, we can probably identify the period of the rapid development of the Roman chairman's office more precisely – as well as better understand the roughly simultaneous acceptance at Rome of the four-Gospel canon of the New Testament.

In Clement and Hermas there is no indication of substantive doctrinal problems in Rome, merely standard moral difficulties about penance. Ignatius goes out of his way to point to Roman orthodoxy. That suggests that we must identify the time of troubles as beginning in the early to mid second century; we know that the "threat" of heresy is already present in the time of Justin's book against Marcion (Irenaeus, *Against Heresies* 4.6.2). Justin never mentions "bishops", but (some time after 150) speaks of a "president" (*proestos*) at the eucharist (*First Apology* 65–67), who also has responsibility for prisoners and foreigners:[58] clearly a prominent presbyter, but not specifically identified as a BISHOP. The figure to whom Justin refers is perhaps Pius, soon to be identified as a BISHOP in the Muratorian Canon. In a famous text – which I have noted is mistaken about the authorship of the *Shepherd* – we read of Hermas' brother, Pius, recently "sitting in the chair" of the Church of Rome. The Muratorian writer clearly thinks of Pius as a BISHOP, but that his information, or interpretation, is independent of the

---

[57] The same attitude is to be found in Tertullian, *De Praescr.* 32.
[58] Presumably this refers to foreigners resident at least temporarily in Rome. Some responsibility for such was also presumably assumed by "chairmen" – at least from the time of Xystus (*c.* 120) who apparently began the practice of sending a portion of yeast (*fermentum*) to churches in Rome that followed the Eastern custom of celebrating Easter on Nisan 14 (see Eus., *H.E.* 5.24.14). There are some who think that this practice began later, even though the *fermentum* itself was familiar to Justin (*1 Apol.* 65 and 67). For the agreement between Polycarp and Anicetus to live and let live over the date of Easter see Jay, "From Presbyter-Bishops" 149.

lists of Hegesippus and Irenaeus is unlikely.[59] It was Anicetus, the successor of Pius, who was in office when Hegesippus arrived, so we may assume that at least by his time the position of the chairman was sufficiently augmented for Hegesippus to assume that a certain Pius – not necessarily the brother of Hermas – really was a BISHOP.

Let us take it as a reasonable assumption that the authority of a single bishop was considerably augmented during the days of Pius and Anicetus. Is there any other evidence that would point in the same direction? Perhaps there is a straw in the wind, for it seems to have been in the time of Anicetus that the *tropaia* of Peter and Paul were erected on the supposed sites of their deaths, at the Vatican and on the Via Ostiensis: a new assertion of the importance for Christianity as a whole of the Church of Rome – currently recognized in the activity of its BISHOP – as the site of the final *acta* of the Apostle to the Jews and the Apostle to the Gentiles. It is, then, in this crucial period that we must identify the first self-conscious efforts to re-model the chairman-presbyter as what was later to become a BISHOP: that is, in the time not only of Marcion (who also proposed a single Gospel), but also of the Gnostic Valentinus who seems to have been in Rome from about 139 to 165,[60] offering a (Gnostic) *Gospel of Truth* (*Against Heresies* 3.2.9), and in some sense aspiring to the leadership of the whole Roman community – as he could not have done if there was no formal way of identifying such leadership.

The connection between the appearance of "deviant" forms of Christianity at Rome and the formation of the canon deserves further comment. At Rome, at this period, Marcion and various Gnostics seem to have been regarded as a particular threat. The development of episcopal powers as a means of countering such a threat ties in with a concern to establish the canonical Gospels securely. One of the principal results of securing a Gospel-canon would be to emphasize that these and only these Gospels are *historically* authoritative. This would not only dispose of attempts by self-styled authorities to organize the "historical" data in their own interest, but undercut the construction of "Gnostic" Gospels full of fantasies of a "docetic" sort whereby (for example) Jesus was not "really" crucified, nor indeed "really" took on human flesh. The formation of a canon, in these circumstances, might be part of a campaign – of which more authoritative BISHOPS would be organizers – against typical "heresies" of the period.

---

[59] There have been a number of attempts to redate the Muratorian Fragment to the fourth century; they are satisfactorily rebutted by Stanton, *Jesus and Gospel* 68–71.

[60] Iren., *Adv. Haer.* 3.4.3; Eus., *H. E.* 4.11.1.

It is sometimes supposed that, with the new role of monarchical BISHOP finally established by the time of Victor (*c.* 189–199), this explains Victor's high-handed attitude towards the so-called Quartodecimans in Asia Minor, indicating the expanding claims of the Roman BISHOP outside his own see. The dispute was about the date on which to celebrate Easter, and Victor's opponents were defended by Bishop Polycrates of Ephesus who believed he was speaking for a tradition dating back to the Apostle John. It is more likely, however, that Victor's threat of excommunication was aimed at those Asian Christians in the city of Rome itself who followed their native practice, rather than that he was claiming a wider primacy.[61] Presumably it was to them that he declined to send the yeast (*fermentum*), the symbol of unity.[62]

The chief significance of this incident seems to lie in its indication that inside Rome itself there were still widely held to be local rights and practices which the BISHOP had no business to tamper with. Victor's actions should be seen as reflecting the growing development of the bishop's *local* office,[63] but in an area where there was still no agreement as to its limits. Indeed, in this case he seems not to have had his way. In fact, if the role of the BISHOP of Rome developed largely for doctrinal reasons, it is easy to understand why "non-essential" traditions supposedly going back to the apostles themselves would not readily be surrendered to him.

After Victor a similar problem arose over a disciplinary matter, the right of BISHOPS to grant absolution for murder, adultery and apostasy[64] – which led to the appearance of the first "anti-pope" (though the term is anachronistic for the times of the author of the *Refutation of all Heresies*). Though the matter is very uncertain, this "anti-pope" was perhaps not the presbyter Hippolytus but a predecessor in the church Hippolytus later governed, who claimed to be merely an (old-style) "bishop", that is, a presbyter-bishop

---

[61] See McCue, "The Roman Primacy" 161–196.   [62] So Brent, *Hippolytus* 414.

[63] Brent, ibid., would delay this till the early third century, but apart from the evidence already cited, the letter of Dionysius of Alexandria to *the* Roman bishop Soter weighs strongly against him; so M. Simonetti, "Una nuova proposta su Ippolito", *Augustinianum* 36 (1996) 13–46, esp. 17–33.

[64] A similar situation arose at roughly the same time in Carthage, where Tertullian, probably referring to his own bishop, but just possibly to Callistus in Rome, challenged the bishop's juridical power: that is, again, his authority to remit the sins of fornication and adultery (*De Pud.* 1.6–7). Tertullian seems to have come to think of bishops as necessary administrators, but as lacking the "apostolic" charisms of the apostles whose genuine spiritual successors were prophets and inspired teachers: a conservatively utopian thesis which left it impossible to determine which spiritual leaders were genuinely apostolic. Nevertheless, the bishops all derived their authority, in Tertullian's view, from the fact that they sat in the chairs of the apostles (or of "apostolic men") who had founded the individual Churches (*De Praesc.* 36).

(*Refutation* 1 *proem* 6).[65] Interestingly, the "Refuter"'s tactic was to argue, in a doctrinally "sectarian" mode, that his opponents' views were unorthodox as depending on various Greek philosophers. Such charges were regularly made against Gnostic unorthodoxy, and a similar tactic was used by Tertullian in arguing against the misuse of Plato as a general "seasoning" for heresy (*On the Soul* 23).

By the late second century we can assume that in Rome the BISHOP personified a succession from the apostles once seen as more widely distributed among the presbyters. His consecration perhaps involved the laying on of hands by other BISHOPS. Most important of all, his role as heir of the earlier presbyterate – and so as the living representative of the apostolic tradition – was confirmed by his now possessing authority to renew the presbyterate itself. In earlier days his authority would seem restricted in that it derived from his "episcopal" colleagues. We are witnessing a gradual development of the BISHOP's prestige, the primary reason for which was the need to combat doctrine found to deviate from the tradition. The growth of the BISHOP's prestige is contemporaneous with the acceptance (against "deviants") of a four-Gospel canon and the almost inevitable beginning of jurisdiction in "spiritual" matters like penance. For within the Church, to hold "right belief" demanded the authority to enforce the teaching of right belief.

4.6 DEVIANT BISHOPS, DEVIANT CHURCHES

At the period under discussion we can still recognize an assumption that BISHOPS in the apostolic sees, once appointed, will agree "of necessity" with one another, and of course with the Roman BISHOP. Irenaeus, as earlier Ignatius, apparently did not yet envisage the possibility of a "heretical" BISHOP, at least in an apostolic see. That possibility, however, was soon to be actualized, with "deviant" bishops in non-apostolic sees leading the way to "deviance" in the apostolic sees themselves. In 264 it required a council of BISHOPS to depose a BISHOP, Paul of Samosata, at Antioch (Eusebius, *Ecclesiastical History* 7.28ff.). Some sixty years later, at the major doctrinal Council of Nicaea, the legates of the Roman BISHOP, who was not present, voted first, perhaps out of respect for the emperor and his "local" – but also imperial – BISHOP in Rome. As early as 314 Constantine had enhanced the

---

[65] Brent, *Hippolytus passim*. Interestingly the author of the *Refutatio* claimed that Callistus had founded a "school" (*didaskaleion*), that is, a heretical if not near-pagan conventicle (Brent, ibid. 417–424) "against the catholic church". According to the "Refuter" the error of Callistus was to entice into his "school" people excommunicated by other presbyter-bishops for major sins.

authority of the see of Rome, at least in the West, by telling it to regularize a threatened (Donatist) schism in North Africa.[66] Such events, straws in the coming wind, indicated a certain implicit, soon to be explicit, reflection on the position, doctrinal or juridical, of the Roman BISHOP both at councils and in the Church more generally. In the inevitable confusion of doctrinal and juridical power lay much coming history.

Even apart from Paul of Samosata, new scenarios were already under construction in the mid third century. Both Cyprian, BISHOP of Carthage, and Firmilian of Caesarea (*Letter* 75) acknowledged a certain Roman primacy but took exception to attempts by the Roman BISHOP Stephen to extend his jurisdictional powers – in the case of Firmilian over the date of Easter. But with the concern of Constantine and his successors for "One state, one religion" – the imperial early version of *cuius regio eius religio*, though the "details" of that religion might change from emperor to emperor, from "Catholic" to "Arian" – the advance of an increasingly "papal" see of Rome reached a first climax in the authoritative but by no means absolute doctrinal status accorded in 451 to the Roman BISHOP Leo at the Council of Chalcedon.[67] Since in these centuries most active (if not always constructive) theology was the work of generally more educated Eastern bishops – Augustine is the great exception – the recognition of the Latin Leo as a doctrinal authority is especially significant.

But what if a council or a *Roman* BISHOP were to err? And what – ultimately – about the BISHOPS of the other great apostolic sees, Alexandria and Antioch, whose metropolitan supremacy was confirmed by canon 6 of the Council of Nicaea? And what soon of the new "pentarchy" (Rome, Constantinople, Alexandria, Antioch, Jerusalem), with the upstart see of Constantinople given second rank by canon 228 of the Council of Chalcedon and fortified by its succeeding Ephesus as the principal see of the region? (In so doing it took over the prestige of St John as "apostolic" founder – and later confirmed its position with a new legend by which Andrew, brother of Peter, turned out to have been bishop of Byzantium.) And what of the formal condemnation of the heretical teaching of the Roman BISHOP Honorius by the Third Ecumenical Council of Constantinople (680–681)?

We recognize in these questions the seeds of further conflict, further ecclesiastical chaos, further power-struggles, not least promoted by the

---

[66] For the Council of Arles Eus., *VC* 1.44. See T. D. Barnes, *Constantine and Eusebius* (Cambridge, Mass. 1981) 57–58.

[67] See especially Schatz, *Papal Primacy* 41–46. The appeals to Roman authority (whether pragmatic, cynical or doctrinally sincere) of the much-exiled Athanasius, BISHOP of Alexandria, cannot but have fostered respect in the East for the Roman "pope", beyond his earlier Latin "power-base": and even among the "non-Nicenes" who would also have liked his support.

confusion of jurisdictional with spiritual and doctrinal authority, and eventually – surely more by providence than human intention – the clarification of the importance, even the increasingly apparent necessity, of Rome as a doctrinal centre. The present chapter, in effect, has attempted to uncover something of the prelude to that clarification. Some of its later history will form part of the subject-matter of the chapters that follow. That history was to be complicated and confused not least by the Constantinian factor, the existence for centuries of a dominant *Christian* secular authority.

My argument thus far, though I believe it to be both Catholic and catholic, should give little comfort to "traditionists". If a contemporary Church can be regarded as the fully legitimate if unworthy bearer of a tradition that has come down from Jesus via the apostles, it should recognize that to deny the development of Christian institutions – *as to deny the development of our understanding of Christian doctrines and of the Christian culture of which both doctrines and institutions are a part* – is to persist wilfully in ignorance of identifiable historical fact. It is perverse to pretend either that such institutions have always recognized their specific character as they later came to recognize it or that their earlier behaviour and mentality can be identified in detail – as Newman often tried to identify it – from their later comportment, *or* on the other hand that there were complete, "sacrosanct" and thus desirable eternal structures in place in some virtually prelapsarian condition of the "primitive" Church before Christians had to work out defences both doctrinal and institutional against as yet unforeseen attacks on its unity and teaching.

If there is a single axiom to be identified from the history of the early years of the Roman see, it is that the need to defend Christian doctrine, to allow oneself to be guided by what Irenaeus and Tertullian called the rule of truth or the rule of faith, makes it inevitable that such defence will lead to new, organically developed, and hence legitimate forms of church order: indeed that blind adherence to older and inevitably imperfect forms would have been and will always be disastrous. In this we see an example at the institutional level of another axiom recognizable in the history and development of doctrine, namely that the heretic is often the blind conservative while the genuine traditionalist – as distinct from traditionist – is apt, in the words of Jesus in the Gospel, to combine "things old and new".

4.7 WILFUL BLINDNESS AS FAILURE OF DISCERNMENT

One of the lessons to be drawn from historical study is that the understanding of doctrines and the development of Catholic institutions have gone hand in hand. What is to be regretted is that, in the supposed interests of doctrinal truth, historical truth, so far as it is attainable, is often denied. This policy may look convenient in the short term but is certainly inconvenient in the longer (especially when the truth comes out and the "teachers" are exposed, like the Emperor with no clothes). It is also of course in opposition to truth itself. What my reconstruction – if even roughly correct – of features of the early history of the developing "papacy" implies is that, if the present state of that office is not, as many non-Catholics suppose, a historical growth of at best dubious, at worst diabolical, spiritual legitimacy, then it instantiates Christianity's legitimate – though ever improvable – actualization of its developing needs; there is no third possibility.[68] And if it is a legitimate and providential development, it should be avowed as such.

Unwillingness to face historical truth about Christian institutions, so far as it can be recognized, is often motivated by aversion to developmental theory. That aversion is due to another failure, to which I have alluded several times – and which is often motivated by fear – to recognize the radical distinction between theology and the history of theology, between doctrinal truth and its discernment over time. Herein lies the fundamental problem with traditionist Catholic accounts of the origins of the papacy.

Hence arises the urgency to evoke the Christian and Catholic needs that are neglected in any blindness to historical truth about the origins and development of the Roman see. And hence I revert to my argument that the early development of that see was linked to the need to ensure that doctrinal purity kept pace with the inevitable theological adventures which expanding Christianity had to face up to. In our "global village" that need to avoid both "heresy" and "schism" (perhaps ultimately inseparable) is for obvious reasons as great as ever it was.

If it is observed that in the history of the Catholic Church comparably little theological progress has been initiated by the see of Rome – I have noted that the Roman BISHOP, for whatever reason, was not even present at the Council of Nicaea, perhaps the most fruitful council of them all – I would reply that this exactly proves the necessary role of the Roman see: its function, for the most part, has been not to propose theological adventures – for that we look to the "doctors" (Paul, Athanasius, Augustine, Aquinas, Teresa of Avila, Newman, Benedicta of the Cross and the rest) – but to ensure the theological "purity" of proposed new insights and vigorously to promote the regenerated old and new order.

---

[68] My argument, if correct, entails that a far more detailed examination both of the early period and of succeeding ages could only confirm the ineluctable decision between the only two alternatives available.

To this essential, if at times intellectually unexciting role, I shall revert in my final chapter. There have been and will be failures and derelictions of duty in its perfomance – Peter himself, as Augustine often observed, was at times an "incomplete success" both morally and doctrinally – but just as we cannot accept the implications which Cardinal Ottaviani intended in his (apt) observation during Vatican II (that the only "collegial" act of the apostles recorded in the Gospels was at Gethsemane when they all ran away,[69]) so we cannot accept, in a world in which hundreds of new Christian groups come into existence, and often pass away, every year, that we have no need for a BISHOP who represents the historical and doctrinal unity of a Church still more or less in one piece.

Winston Churchill famously remarked that democracy looks awful until we consider the alternatives, and something similar could be said of the papacy: it is the only doctrinal unity available and the purpose of this chapter has been to chronicle an early stage of the gradually dawning recognition of that fact. I have not wished to claim – indeed I would on *a priori* grounds deny – that the motives of those to whom this recognition came, whether in Rome or elsewhere, were guaranteed absolute purity. What I would claim is that the development of the Roman see was essential not only to the maintenance of theological purity but to the possibility of an expanding culture which in all its ramifications was to remain Catholic, that is, universal.

[69] Cited by J. L. Allen, *Pope Benedict XVI* (New York 2000) 46.

CHAPTER 5

Caesaropapism, theocracy or neo-Augustinian politics?

God has given us the papacy; let us enjoy it.

Pope Leo X

John [Chrysostom] elevated the Christian household so as to eclipse the ancient city. He refused to see Antioch as a traditional civic community, bound together by a common civic patriotism, expressed by shared rhythms of collective festivity. He made no secret of the fact that he wished the theater, the hippodrome, even the busy agora, to fall silent for ever. The Antioch of his dearest hopes was to be no more than a conglomeration of believing households, joined by a common meeting-place within the spacious courtyards of the Great Church.

Brown, *The Body and Society* 313

5.1 CHRISTIAN TOTALITARIANISM: A POSSIBLE PROGRAMME

If the reflective study of history is to be more than an account of who did what to whom when (as Aristotle apparently put it), the history of ideas and of their cultural impact must extend beyond what someone said, why they chose to say it and its immediate results, to compass also its longer effects, whether good or bad, and the reasons for them.

It may seem strange to begin a discussion of the Catholic Church's relationship to what we now call secular society by quoting extensively from the views of a proto-Byzantine theologian. But John Chrysostom, though an extremist outside the Western tradition, is all the more informative for that. He represents what was a real possibility for Catholicism, and one which, though now normally rejected, has proved a recurring temptation. Chrysostom essentially looked for a theocratic state – though the place of the Orthodox Emperor remained ambiguous – and the concept of a theocratic state implies not only the subordination of political institutions to those of religion but the inculcation of a theocratic mentality in the citizen-body.

233

Clearly there are many ramifications of such a mentality, and even to begin to sort them out in Chrysostom's case would be beyond my present scope. Nor do I wish to portray Chrysostom as the sole offender; rather as a particularly forceful and articulate one. Chrysostom viewed the social prospects for Christianity in terms of an alluringly "religious" answer to the question: what is the proper relationship, within a Christian political structure, of the civil and ecclesiastical powers, and what are the implications of such a relationship for the life, particularly the intellectual and cultural life, of the Christian community? In an earlier chapter I looked at some of the attitudes – not least a misconceived and outdated fear of what was once "paganism" – that historically inhibited the development of an adequately Catholic and catholic understanding of art, and hence the possibility of a serious critique of contemporary and "nihilist" aesthetics. Now I want to argue more broadly that it is only insofar as the Catholic Church has been able (or been compelled) to escape from Chrysostom-style ambitions for a "Christian" society that progress in Catholic intellectual life – and even in the enrichment of moral and social theory – has become possible. A corollary of my argument is that wherever in Christianity (broadly understood) Chrysostom-style ideals persist, similar problems accompany them.

Defenders of Chrysostom against my reading of the effects of his "totalitarian" mentality and associated anti-intellectualism will point to his undoubted concern for the poor, the oppressed and the exploited (including women),[1] and his desire to give them a much greater degree of what we should now call social security. The same argument can be made about the combination of theocratic theory and philanthropic action displayed by Hamas in the Gaza strip. Concern for the spiritually subjugated poor and marginalized, bought at the price of a contempt for the less immediately "religious" features of human development – especially intellectual freedom – purports to do justice to the ordinances and majesty of God while remaining grossly disrespectful of the reflected dignity of his image in man and woman.

Chrysostom's views on many topics became more realistic when he moved from Antioch to the centre of imperial power in Constantinople. Much of his "fundamentalist" writing, for example about Jews, was compiled in his more youthful days. Yet in other respects the change is less striking: thus his hostility to the abuse of wealth and to an associated contempt for the poor by no means decreased when he moved to the capital; indeed it helped to bring about his downfall there. In any case the activities of the emperors in Constantinople gave little encouragement to his hostility to "public space",

[1] See Brown, *The Body and Society* 315–317.

though more to his anti-intellectualism. What the successors of Constantine wished to achieve was the substitution of Christian public space for the earlier pagan version. That would indicate a public, enforced and universal religion of Christ as successor to the failed imperial worship of the sun which their predecessors Aurelian and Diocletian had tried to enforce. Though unenforceable, "homogenization" (*Gleichschaltung*) was the concept of the day.

Chrysostom's theocratic mentality serves as a useful introduction to more political themes in that it involved *inter alia* the subordination of "academic" concerns to those of "right" belief and wherever possible the elimination rather than the appropriation of rival intellectual traditions. Christianity, as immediately understood and within the context of a Christian Empire, might seem already to be the completion of the past and require no further cultural or political enrichment. Of course, it was easier to reject pagan (or other) culture than to proceed immediately to the construction of a Christian social-political society, since, as we shall see, there was no ready agreement on what institutions such a society should have or how power should be apportioned between them.

Chrysostom's "defensive" mentality has recurred throughout the history of Christianity, and once Constantine had established something approaching a Christian Empire, the question of what freedoms (intellectual and other) were to be allowed to non-Christians or deviant Christians became central. A theocracy demands not only control of the institutions of society but a control as absolute as possible of the mentality of that society. Historically speaking, those who pursue such ideological aims normally want to destroy the intellectual structures of their perceived opponents as well as their institutional bases. We should expect, however, that an attack on intellectual structures thus motivated will be dishonest and itself intellectually shameless: the aim is to destroy, not to convince, and certainly not to learn. Such indeed was the aim of Chrysostom – and that is the reason I discuss him at this point. Misrepresentation of the position of opponents is as much a part of the absolutist mentality (whether in Byzantium, Geneva, Rome, Moscow or Teheran) as is the dismantling of their institutional bulwarks (such as the Athenian Academy, somehow closed by Justinian in 529): error has no rights, intellectual or other.

Such attitudes, with their political accompaniments, are inimical to the development of an enriched and enrichable Catholic culture.[2]

---

[2] Happily Chrysostom's influence in the Byzantine world was to some degree contradicted by that of an earlier bishop of Constantinople (and friend of Basil), Gregory of Nazienzus. Gregory, even more than Basil, knew and appreciated much classical Greek literature, as his modern biographers regularly point out, but he shows no interest in contemporary or near contemporary philosophy, and indeed is more

5.2 JOHN CHRYSOSTOM, OR HOW NOT TO BE A CATHOLIC OPINION-FORMER

Chrysostom believed that philosophers were an intellectual and moral threat to the Christian commonwealth, hence a legitimate target of unscrupulous attack. But whereas in classical antiquity the scurrility of Epicurus' attacks on his philosophical rivals was without benefit of armed force, Chrysostom and those like him were hoping that force could be deployed against their opponents – provided those opponents could be depicted as fundamentally vicious and anti-social enemies of "right" belief.

In launching torpedoes at the philosophers of antiquity, in particular Diogenes the Cynic and Plato,[3] Chrysostom, as a professionally trained rhetorician, was following a well-worn tradition both pagan and Christian, and surely aware that much of his invective followed the patterns of the Cynic diatribe.[4] Philosophers were not his only target, and it might be argued that, like Jews, they were a merely conventional bullseye – though some may wonder whether mere convention was enough to license the claim that down at the local synagogue you could meet whores, thieves and the theatre-crowd, or the flaunting of traditional phrases about "Christ-killers" which in the light of later history have had to be sanitized by his apologists. Such language, it is claimed, is only rhetoric; one has to make allowances for the spirit of the age, prescinding from after-effects unforeseen by the exuberant performer. As a Jewish scholar has put it, "Let Jews and Christians study the nature of rhetoric in antiquity to discern the vigor – and virulence – of speech in that age."[5]

There is undoubtedly something in this. The ancients were more case-hardened to raw abuse in public life than our officially tolerant contemporaries. A distinguished historian of Republican Rome noted that Julius

---

or less hostile to *philosophy* as such. Hence his counter-influence to Chrysostom is evident in his humanistic and literary concerns rather than in philosophy. His theology is redolent of a certain Platonism (deriving from the tradition of Origen) but his evident hostility to the Iamblichan Neoplatonism of Julian and his cronies may have convinced him that the time for *philosophy* (as an intellectual pursuit rather than as a Christian way of life) is over. For a recent sympathetic treatment (which has little to say on philosophy as thought rather than as literature) see J. McGuckin, *Gregory of Nazienzus: An Intellectual Biography* (Crestwood 2001).

[3] P. Coleman-Norton, "St. Chrysostom and Greek Philosophy", *CP* 25 (1930) 305–317 lists the references in Chrysostom to Greek philosophers, but, apart from one or two cases where he indicates a misreading or the use of apocryphal material, his article is simply a helpful list.

[4] See Uleyn, "La doctrine morale de saint Jean Chrysostome". Interestingly a legend grew up according to which Chrysostom was an ardent reader of the "scurrilous" Aristophanes. See Q. Cataudella, "Giovanni Crisostomo imitatore di Aristofane", *Athenaeum* 18 (1940) 236–243.

[5] L. H. Feldman, "Is the New Testament Antisemitic?", in *Studies in Hellenistic Judaism* (Leiden 1996) 288.

Caesar reacted to being attacked by Catullus in a poem of "unparalleled obscenity" by inviting the poet to dinner.[6] And it is arguable that as antiquity drew to its close, the pressure to talk violently and thus indirectly promote violent behaviour increased. In his late fourth-century translation of Origen's *On First Principles* Rufinus could not resist the gratuitous gloss (absent from Origen's original) that unless boys are lashed regularly they will turn into savages.[7]

But it is possible to discount violent rhetoric too easily, then and now: "he may look vicious", runs a relevant adage, "but don't be deceived, he *is* vicious". We need not be too surprised by Chrysostom. Philosophers regularly abused one another; a modern scholar has compiled an article more than twenty pages long listing personal abuse directed at Plato by philosophical rivals or other ill-wishers, many of them Aristotelians: one of the more popular examples was a "homophobic" transformation of his name.

Christians were sometimes more restrained, at least until Chrysostom; though the triumphalist dismissal of "philosophy" (understood as thinking rather than in its new acceptation as a Christian lifestyle) paraded by the youthful Athanasius, "The Churches are full, the philosophical schools are empty," would seem to add lying to contempt, for at that point the schools were still quite full. Chrysostom follows in his master's footsteps, asking, "Where now are the ravings of the philosophers?"[8]

Even in pre-Constantinian days it was regularly remarked by Christian rhetoricians that the foolishness of philosophers is revealed in their mutual disagreements on matters of substance: a jibe often unaccompanied – as we shall see with Chrysostom – by any serious attempt either to understand what the disagreements were about or why one philosopher might be better than another, let alone the possible goodness of thinking as such, where disagreement, it might seem obvious, is the way forward and cosy self-congratulation the enemy of Socratic enquiry! There are honourable exceptions to such early Christian bloody-mindedness – Justin, Tertullian (perhaps surprisingly), Origen – but in the late fourth century anyone

---

[6] R. Syme, *The Roman Revolution* (Oxford 1939) 152.

[7] J. M. Rist, "The Greek and Latin Texts of the Discussion of Free Will in 'De Principiis' Book III", *Origeniana (Quaderni di Vetera Christianorum)* 12 (1975) 97–111.

[8] *Hom. in Acta* (PG 60, 47). It is worth noting that Chrysostom's contempt for intellectual honesty in his arguments with the philosophers is but part of a wider laxity about truth. In his *De Sacerdotio* he suggests unambiguously that deceiving, if with good intent and productive of good results, is wholly admirable. He is not a utilitarian, but he has no sense in such questions of the importance of the distinction between means and ends. For further discussion see P. J. Griffiths, *Lying: An Augustinian Theology of Deception* (Grand Rapids 2004) 133–143.

wishing to draw not only on traditional pagan offensiveness in disputation but on a deep-rooted Christian anti-intellectualism had a good deal of material to work with. "Our boys" – such as those who stripped (of course) and then murdered the philosopher Hypatia – would be aroused by the rhetoric.

Our immediate subject is philosophers as they appear in Chrysostom's homilies: Cynics, Stoics, Plato and Socrates, with a concluding glance at an extraordinary remark about Aristotle. Chrysostom has no wish – nor perhaps in sermons much opportunity – to deal with these people in detail, and no concern to understand them or to present their published views with any real care. In the old philosophical tradition, to which I have alluded, any stick was good enough to beat a dog, particularly if the "dog" is a Cynic.

There are several reasons for Chrysostom's particular hostility to Diogenes, though in a propaganda piece for the monastic life he did once speak kindly of his asceticism,[9] and more in the positive tones of Basil and (sometimes) Gregory Nazienzen: perhaps trying to show that extreme behaviour (such as becoming a professional ascetic) is less of a novelty for sons of the gentry than might be supposed.[10] Yet the most basic of Chrysostom's reasons indicates a wider spectrum of the Christian reformer's ideas.

It has often been observed that Cynics were city people.[11] As we have seen, and Brown has well expressed, Chrysostom evinces dislike for "public space".[12] The vast areas of ancient cities constructed by some powerful or place-seeking benefactor for the shows and entertainments with which the populace must be obscenely, brutally, competitively and regularly entertained – Chrysostom's Promised Land would involve the end of all that and instead the inward-looking family hovels in narrow winding streets centred on the two structures of power, the church (later the mosque) and the palace or castle of the local magnate. This would be a society in which the poor would be looked after, justice would prevail, the arts (good or bad) would wilt, women would be kept in their place and certainly out of the public domain, humour would virtually disappear (given its normal subject-matter), the austerity of the saints would reign: a recurring, if significantly deviant, Christian and also non-Christian ideal which Mullah Omar, as well as Clement of Alexandria and Tertullian, would well have understood.

---

[9] *Against Opponents of the Monastic Life* (*PG* 47, 337).
[10] For Basil and Gregory see M. O. Goulet-Cazé, "Le Cynisme à l'époque impériale", in *ANRW* 2.36.4, esp. 2793–2795. Surprisingly, though also mentioning Theodoret, Goulet-Cazé says nothing of Chrysostom.
[11] So Wayne Meeks, *The Moral World of the First Christians* (Philadelphia 1986) 55.
[12] *The Body and Society* 305–322 – in a chapter appropriately dubbed "Sexuality and the City".

Then what of Diogenes? He too would have understood and approved much of it; for the primary target of the Cynics was always the *tuphos*, the inflated self-importance, the arrogance, the *bella figura* of urban life and its trend-setters. In Chrysostom's day and later, partly reconstructed Cynic preachers still provided competition for their Christian adversaries victorious in Antioch, Alexandria and Constantinople. The apostate Emperor Julian had defended Diogenes against those he condemned as the pseudo-Cynics of his own day. Cynic thought and behaviour was a hot topic in the Antioch of the late fourth century.

So what from Chrysostom's point of view was basically wrong with Diogenes?[13] More importantly, what is the significance of the fact that Cynics – fair game for the moralist – are only an hors d'oeuvre? The answer (for Diogenes and, for more complex and disturbing reasons, all the others) can be seen if we consider whether he would have fitted into Chrysostom's utopia. Clearly he would not; he was, in his own words and deeds, a "free (better "liberated") man": one of the few. For Chrysostom he was out of control, indeed diabolically inspired – and to say that Diogenes was demonized is not metaphorical.[14] Plato was said to have described him as Socrates gone mad.

Diogenes, in Chrysostom's normal view, is a diabolical parody of a Christian hero, and potentially a rival attraction, at least if cleaned up a bit. It is interesting that Chrysostom does not go after Crates (despite his famous Cynic marriage with Hipparchia), who represents a much less foul, less abrasive, even kindly version of the Cynic tradition. In Diogenes' role as diabolical ascetic he is contrasted with the genuine article, the martyred Bishop Babylas, as well as with John the Baptist and Paul. Diogenes exhibits in travesty three Christian virtues: ascetic endurance, freedom of speech, contempt for sexual pleasure. Chrysostom compares his showy dwelling in a barrel to the pointless idiocies of people who eat sharpened nails – apparently an allusion to his supposed death from eating raw octopus. Such acts are wholly unproductive. When Diogenes had his famous encounter with Alexander, instead of asking for a boon for mankind, he told the king that by standing in his light he was preventing him from sunbathing.

---

[13] See generally D. Krueger, "Diogenes the Cynic among the Fourth-Century Fathers", *VC* 47 (1993) 29–49; D. Krueger, "The Bawdy and Society", in A. Bracht-Branham and M. O. Goulet-Cazé (eds.), *The Cynics* (Berkeley/London 1996) 222–243; F. Gerald Downing, *Cynics and Christian Origins* (Edinburgh 1992) 278–297; F. Dorival, "L'image des cyniques chez les Pères grecs", in M. O. Goulet-Cazé and R. Goulet (eds.), *Le Cynisme grec et ses prolongements* (Paris 1991) 419–447.

[14] For comment on Diogenes see *Hom. in Matth.* 10.4; 23.4 (*PG* 57); *Hom. in I Cor.* 35.4 (*PG* 61, 302); *Babylas* (*PG* 50, 545–546).

Misused asceticism is matched by abuse of free speech; the famous Cynic *parrhesia* is properly characteristic of the holy martyrs, who replied boldly to the persecutors, of Adam and Eve (or at least Adam) before the Fall, and of the contemporary ascetics who could again boldly speak with God. In the case of Diogenes, in Chrysostom's view, free speech is paraded only in the service of offensiveness and shocking vulgarity. As for *sophrosunē* (in its restricted sense of sexual restraint and lack of concern for pleasure), Diogenes certainly de-romanticizes and despises sex and marriage (advocating public masturbation and recourse to prostitutes), thereby, in Chrysostom's view, merely – and unnaturally – disregarding common decency. There was a tradition of *ben trovato* tales, or *chreiai*, many of them apparently invented by the Cynics themselves, about this sort of Cynic behaviour; at the drop of a hat Diogenes might at best spit on you, at worst urinate on you.

Well and good, some may say; Diogenes had long been recognized as a pathological exhibitionist and a nihilist, and Chrysostom was right to attack him as such. But what is lacking in Chrysostom – though again he has a tradition behind him – is any attempt to understand what were undoubtedly the surface motives for much of Diogenes' behaviour. This is no place to attempt any psychoanalytic explanation of what Diogenes' "unconscious" motives were, though Chrysostom, in the steps of others both Christian and pagan, thinks he understands them: a love of vulgar fame altogether different from Christian ascetics!

Historically this is almost certainly wrong, giving a populist and merely cynical explanation of the attraction of Diogenes' behaviour and ideas to many more thoughtful and gentle folk. For his own reasons Nietzsche admired the Cynics, but their genuine, if unrealistic, appeal is better understood from their parody of book 19 (173ff.) of the *Odyssey*:

There is a city, Pera [the Cynic's wallet] in the midst of the wine-dark smog (*tuphos*), fair and fertile, thoroughly grubby, to which no fool sails, no parasite or lecher, who delights in a whore's buttocks; but it has thyme and garlic, figs and loaves, which are no cause for its inhabitants to wage war on one another, nor do they take up arms for profit or for fame.

An important philosophical truth about Diogenes is revealed by the stories about the breach of philosophical allegiance between his successor Crates and the latter's one-time pupil Zeno, later the founder of Stoicism. Zeno had learned from the Cynics – in this themselves "pupils" of the earlier sophists – that one should reject convention (*nomos*) in favour of "nature" (*phusis*). But nature seemed to him to be defined negatively: to be natural is not to be constrained by the city's laws and customs. This, Zeno apparently claimed, is philosophically inadequate: if we are to follow nature we should know what nature is.

Diogenes' (and Crates') account of nature fails, as does their account of freedom – which turns out to consist merely in being unconstrained by convention: hence (à la Gide) the searching for ever more risqué acts. But it is the acts themselves, divorced from their cause – namely the desire to "deface the coinage" – that are all that Chrysostom wants to see, and there are problems in condemning what you don't (or won't) understand. Cynics in Chrysostom's day avoided Diogenes' extremism.

Diogenes chose to be unconventional, that is, natural. Why publicly? – and at least by implication the Stoic Epictetus asked that. But how else to make a "statement"? There were no heavy metal groups at the time. In classical antiquity, if not in the late Empire, one practised what one preached or one was ignored. Diogenes and Crates were taken seriously not least because their theories were matched by their actions. If a contemporary Chrysostom had castigated this as *unnatural* or sub-human, Diogenes (or a sympathizer) might have demanded an account of what *is* unnatural, and to be satisfying that account would have had to appeal to argument, not merely to tabloid or populist morality – *even if* such morality could be found to be well based theoretically.

That the problem is not just disgust but that Chrysostom was unconcerned to understand the issues involved becomes clearer if we move from Diogenes to Zeno, another of "Golden Mouth"'s regular targets.[15] Chrysostom probably knew of Zeno, as of Diogenes, only through collections of personal anecdotes or from notoriously salacious selections from his book, the *Republic*, written, so it was said, "on the Dog's Tail", that is in the footsteps of the Cynics Crates and Diogenes. Zeno's *Republic* was apparently composed in part as a reply to the more famous homonymous work of Plato, and unsurprisingly what Chrysostom finds to condemn in it is in part what he dislikes in Plato too: some version of the so-called "community of women and children". This, from the austere Zeno, Chrysostom again finds simply unnatural, without feeling obligation to give reasons since his aim was primarily to arouse indignation. More interesting, then, is the further charge, that Zeno allows incest with mothers and sisters, and says that eating human flesh is something "indifferent", that is, in itself neither good nor bad, but to be judged by the wise man according to the circumstances.

---

[15] For Chrysostom's discussions of Zeno see *Hom. in Matth.* 1 (*PG* 57, 47ff.); *Babylas* (*PG* 50, 545–546).

We do not know whether Chrysostom realized he was over-simplifying and hence misrepresenting Zeno's concerns, which were (and are) genuinely philosophical. Perhaps this time it was a case of ignorance rather than malice. For in considering cannibalism or incest, Zeno (confronting the notorious problem of exceptionless norms) taught that as a rule prohibitions on such actions should be accepted. He is working with what we should call thought-experiments. Suppose (as a limit case) that only two human beings are left alive, a man and his sister. In those circumstances, thought Zeno, to maintain the human race, incest would be permissible.

In judging or misjudging such exceptions to moral rules Chrysostom denies to Zeno the more generous attitude he adopts towards the sexual practices of the patriarchs; as is common among patristic writers when these are unconventional – as the lending out of one's wife or sleeping with a slave-girl – there are godly (often very ingenious) reasons to be found, as that (for example) Abraham only had sex when he wished to procreate, or to procreate an ancestor of Jesus.[16] But for a populist preacher, while "our boys" are always to be given the benefit of the doubt, the pagans are to be read, whether through malice or ignorance, in the worst possible light.

Our knowledge of Diogenes and Zeno is very partial, but when we turn to Chrysostom on Plato's *Republic*, another regular object of obloquy – "Let us now turn to those rotting in the Academy": an allusion to its apparently unhealthy site – we are on firmer ground, as of that we have the full text.[17] Following a tradition not unknown among sceptical pagans and later accepted by Christians, Chrysostom is interested in little more than the sexual regulations in the fifth book. Apart from reincarnation ("Why do we need to hear about the soul of a philosopher becoming a fly?" – which is not in the *Republic* at all but is a travesty of an ironical remark in the *Phaedo* to the effect that those who display a mindlessly conventional or bourgeois morality will be reborn next time as social insects), his charges against the "ridiculous *Republic*" (*PG* 57, 47) are concerned with the arrangements for women; he ignores the fact that Plato refers only to women guardians. Just as Plato is not allowed a joke in the *Phaedo*, so his reform proposals in the *Republic* are not accorded accurate reporting.

The basic charge against Plato's proposals for (some) "women" is that they overturn the God-given subordination of the female to the male; we

---

[16] See the well-argued account of the development of Augustine's thought on the use of "concupiscence" in the case of the eventually "anti-Pelagian" Abraham, in Hunter, "Reclaiming Biblical Morality".

[17] For Chrysostom on Plato see especially *PG* 50, 545ff.; *Hom. in Matth.* 1 (*PG* 57, 47ff.); *In Acta Apost.* 4 (*PG* 60, 47ff.).

recall that Chrysostom denies that women are created in God's image. The mere existence of women has produced, and is producing, the greatest evils among households and cities (as with the Trojan War), because it brings with it the dreaded phenomenon of sexual desire: *eros*, as Chrysostom understands it. Thus Plato's *Republic* proposes the worst of all possible worlds in which women have many of the the same rights and duties as men. They go into the army, wearing armour, and, continues Chrysostom, they do this "fearlessly".

Chrysostom knows Plato's argument for these proposals – and misrepresents it. Plato observes that we give a similar training to male and female hunting dogs; why then do we assume *a priori* that the same rule cannot be applied to human beings? This Chrysostom distorts into a claim that we are just like animals, no different from dogs, ignoring the fact that, even when treating of reincarnation, Plato assumes it is a *failed* human who would be reincarnated in animal form. Plato makes great distinction between godlike men and beasts. Animal liberationists take note.

Obviously the community of women and children is denounced in the case of Plato's *Republic*, as it had been in the case of Zeno's, but even here (where he is on stronger ground, as Aristotle had pointed out) Chrysostom manages to distort the text, attacking Plato for proposing "secret marriages": here he refers to proposals of which in Christian contexts he would only approve, namely that the young do not choose their partners but these are chosen by wiser elders (both male and female). Unless, by chance, he is using the word "marriage" (*gamos*) euphemistically, but that would be inaccurate too.

Chrysostom's populist attention naturally focusses (traditionally enough) on Plato's proposal that the guardian women – Chrysostom specifies them as virgins – strip for gymnastic exercises like men, but what bothers him is that these exercises will be carried on in the sight of men (or, as he explains elsewhere, of the girls' lovers). What worries Plato is quite different: he is aware that if women are to take on the tasks of citizens (including warfare) they need to be fit (and will presumably take what in the military – and probably in Sparta – is sometimes called a "let 'em look" attitude to nakedness). But he thinks that the *older* women may be embarrassed; they will have to put up with the fact that, being wrinkled and suntanned, they are not as beautiful as when they were young.

Again, perhaps Chrysostom has not read the "ridiculous" *Republic*. Perhaps he is deriving his inaccuracies from an old tradition (which certainly existed among pagans as well as Christians). Sometimes, however, his remarks are so bizarre and so philistine that, as in one case about Aristotle, we can only wish that our text were corrupt. Chrysostom claims that Plato and Socrates are worse than Zeno in making pederasty a *part* of philosophy (clearly a sloppy reading of a philosopher who twice, and at length, condemns homosexual intercourse). There is an unhappy modern parallel for this sort of insensitivity in the Rev. Bowdler who called the *Symposium* a "sulphurous breviary of pederasty".

Surprisingly, the most extraordinary claim Chrysostom makes about philosophers is not about Plato, Zeno or Diogenes, but Aristotle, whom elsewhere he rarely mentions and whom in this passage he perhaps confuses with some Stoic or Cynic, or even with a Christian libertine. According to Chrysostom it is grotesque of Aristotle to discuss tasting human semen! One commentator has claimed that this is meant to be an attack on Aristotle's wasting time studying biology. More plausibly it is a misdirected or decontextualized reference, as others suppose, to homosexuality.

Clearly Chrysostom does not wish to debate with the philosophers but to discredit them and misrepresent them. In his view – and he would not be alone – philosophical thinking is inappropriate and out-dated in a Christian commonwealth. In a previous chapter we noticed similar attitudes about art and beauty: if it is dangerous, better suppress it, whatever the stunting effect this may have on the culture. I have examined Chrysostom's attitude to philosophy because it forms part of the background to a struggle that began with Constantine and still continues: what attitude should Christians adopt to a civil (later secular) society? What would the ideal Christian society be like? What place in that society could be found for intellectual life and for art? More briefly, why (historically) was a Chrysostom-style model not adopted, and why (theoretically) was it desirable that it not be?

Before Constantine, Christians tended to prefer the margins of society and, like the Epicureans, not to be noticed if they could avoid it. With Constantine the time had arrived in which basic questions could no longer be evaded: what attitude should Christians, if in power, adopt to the society in which they live? How should they mould it? Should they use force to do so? What indeed should be the relationship between the Church and the Christian or nominally Christian ruler or rulers? In looking at some of the history of these issues, I shall glance at the relationship that has emerged between the Roman Catholic Church and other Christian groups. For the question of the relationship between the Catholic Church and civil society cannot be separated, historically and therefore theoretically, from that of the relationship between Catholicism and other Christian traditions, first of all Orthodoxy. One of the two underlying causes of the split between Rome and Byzantium was the problem of Church and State. The other, less historically significant but perhaps more important theoretically, was the attitude to tradition and doctrinal development.

During the long "post-antique" struggle between the theories of Caesaropapism and the dominance of a theocratic Church, no-one was able to predict that only the coming of an increasingly ex-Christian society, and the consequent impossibility of either of the earlier ideals becoming a reality, would eventually provide the stimulus for a search within the Catholic tradition itself for roots from which might grow a better, more comprehensive set of social and political doctrines, including those on the place of philosophy and culture, as well as on religious freedom and "human" rights. In all of which we may see an example of the well-known Augustinian principle that God knows (and needs to know) how to bring good out of objective and apparent evil.

5.3 ANCIENT (AND MORE MODERN) CAESAROPAPISM

In the previous chapter I sketched something of the history of the see of Rome in the early centuries, largely limiting myself to the development of doctrinal authority but keeping an eye open to the place of the papacy in what was to develop as a Catholic culture. If, however, we want to consider the nature of Christian society – later Christendom – as it began to grow up after the initial rejection of the pagan Roman world by Constantine and its subjection at the end of the fourth century by Theodosius, we need to examine how, circling around doctrinal change, two Christian political possibilities played themselves out in the course of the Byzantine and Western Medieval epochs. Both possibilities proved inadequate, and in their failures left a problematic inheritance with which the Church is only now coming to grips. Yet at the time they must have seemed the only alternatives – even if we allow that hindsight may not easily reveal the attitudes of the participants in the historical drama.

One option was the domination of the Christian Church by the Christian State, the other the subordination of civil authority to ecclesiastical power. In light of the career of Constantine, the former was the more likely, and indeed it outlasted the "universal" Byzantine empire by assuming various national forms. In these versions, however, the straightforwardly political, as distinct from the social and "tribal" aspects of Caesaropapism, faded as Christianity itself declined in the modern age. Among many vestiges of Caesaropapism that persisted primarily in the successor states of the Byzantine Empire, the Church of England provides one of a number of post-Reformation Western parallels.

In all such Caesaropapist societies, with the more recent decline of Christianity, the remnants of the old faith have tended to survive in a tribal form: nationalism, that is, has taken priority over doctrine, which in many cases, though not in all, has become fossilized, a process which had already begun in the Byzantine period. In the Anglican case it is less a matter of the fossilization of doctrine than, as with the mainline Protestant Churches in the West, its ever more rapid disintegration and diminution. In no cases have we seen much development of the sort with which I am concerned in this book. That will suggest that, as in other areas, so with political thought, these Christian groupings will have little new to offer – or at least little that can be called specifically Christian. In the Anglican case there developed a sophisticated society, but a society – despite the revivalist movements of such as Wesley, Pusey and Newman – with steadily decreasing Christian doctrine and hence Christian culture. The culture, indeed, has tended to become aesthetic *rather* than Christian, as typified by the choir of King's College, Cambridge; hence a number of jokes: "No sir, this is not God's house, it's King's College Chapel."

Since Constantine, the self-styled "bishop of the pagans", was a politician rather than a cleric, it is unsurprising that historically the Caesaropapist option preceded the ideal of theocracy. Indeed, it was this option which the Western theocrats who invented the "Donation of Constantine" in the eighth century attempted to undermine. The exact connection between the Donation and the deal between the Frankish king Pépin and Pope Stephen II is uncertain, but there is no doubt that in the supposed spirit of the Donation – in which Constantine recognized the authority of BISHOP Sylvester – Stephen, the new Sylvester, received from the "unauthorized" hands of the king of the Franks large chunks of land in Italy and a more general political authority in the West. The Donation, that is, represented the rejection of Byzantine Caesaropapism, and as such was bitterly resented by the Emperor in Constantinople.[18]

Constantine's conversion to Christianity was a slow process, influenced by the desire to find in the new religion a unifying force for the Empire absent from his family's earlier devotion to the Unconquered Sun. But Constantine quickly discovered that Christianity could divide as well as unite. As I noted in the previous chapter, shortly after his victory in the West he was approached by the soon-to-be schismatic Donatists in North Africa to determine the rightful incumbent of the see of Carthage. To resolve the

---

[18] The "acts" of Sylvester and Constantine are superbly represented in a fresco in the Church of the Santi Quattro Coronati in Rome.

matter he commanded the bishop of Rome to sit in judgment, together with three Gallic bishops, and then report back to himself. Soon after the establishment of his new capital at Constantinople, he found himself faced with the dispute between an Alexandrian priest, Arius, and his bishop Alexander, on the strictly doctrinal, not merely disciplinary, issue of Arius' perhaps conservative subordination of the Son to the Father in the Trinitarian scheme. To restore unity Constantine called a council over which his court-bishop, Ossius of Cordoba, was to preside, though in some cases his place was taken by the bishop of the pagans himself.

The nature of Constantine's ecclesiastical entourage in his later life shows that for him the politics of imperial unity – not theology as the bishops wished – was central. After the "Catholic" success at Nicaea and the departure of Ossius, Constantine was more and more influenced by a group of bishops in varying degrees sympathetic to Arius. They included his official biographer Eusebius of Caesarea, and the latter's astute namesake of Nicomedia (in the next reign translated to Constantinople), who in 337 presided at the Emperor's death-bed baptism.

The emperors succeeding Constantine, down to Theodosius at the end of the century, had to choose: all wished in varying degrees for the religious unity of the Empire, but generally, and particularly in the case of Constantius (sole Emperor from 353 to 361), preferred Arianism as their instrument.[19] But Constantius was basically an "Eastern Emperor", and opposition to his policy, led by Athanasius, was far stronger in the West where the aging Ossius and successive Roman bishops persistently favoured the Creed of Nicaea. When that creed, in a modified version, was imposed by the new dynasty of Theodosius after the Council of Constantinople in 381, a doctrinal split between East and West was postponed, but the signs were there to be read. So long as the emperor was orthodox, he could command the Western bishops, but as we shall see, when again in the 480s he ceased to be, then the East–West split came nearer and Caesaropapism became less likely in the West. And what would happen when in the West there was no longer an emperor?

In 451, at the Council of Chalcedon, the bishop of Rome secured his greatest triumph thus far. The so-called "Tome of Leo", denouncing the Monophysites and proclaiming two natures in Christ, was hailed by the Council Fathers: Peter, they insisted, had spoken through Leo, thus at a stroke both affirming the theological primacy of the bishop of Rome and seeming to accept the basis for that primacy: that the bishops of Rome, as

[19] For a good introduction see T. D. Barnes, *Athanasius and Constantius* (Cambridge, Mass. 1993).

Peter's heirs, had inherited his legal prerogatives.[20] But there was a catch: already at Constantinople (381) it had been decreed that after the bishop of Rome the local bishop had pre-eminence in honour (above the Patriarchates of Alexandria, Antioch and Jerusalem), since Constantinople was the New Rome. At Chalcedon (canon 28), that "secular" principle was restated, to the intense anger of the absent pope. An upstart see, not yet even claiming the patronage of Andrew, Peter's younger brother, as its first bishop, dependent entirely for its authority on the presence of the imperial court, was to become his rival: Caesaropapism was alive and well, and soon to become Monophysite.

The crisis came in 482, shortly after the deposition (in 476) of the last Western Emperor and his replacement in Italy by Gothic kings based in Ravenna. Acacius, patriarch of Constantinople, supported by the Emperor Zeno, tried to find a compromise between the Catholicism of Chalcedon and the Monophysitism of large parts of the Eastern Mediterranean. In pursuance of this Zeno promulgated a document called the Henotikon which laid down the new theological orthodoxy. When this proved unacceptable in Rome, the sees of Rome and Constantinople excommunicated one another and the so-called "Acacian" schism had begun. Rome, in effect, had denied the Emperor's authority in matters of religion. The feud continued for thirty-five years.

This was not the first time an emperor had been excommunicated: Bishop Ambrose of Milan had excommunicated the great Theodosius about a hundred years before for massacring civilians in Thessaloniki. This time, however, the situation was more serious: an imperially backed prelate breaks communion with Rome in alliance with an emperor. And the split lasted, with positions hardening as Rome took the view that – whatever the political cost – doctrinal issues were for Churches to settle by themselves. Pope Gelasius (492–496), who had not even informed the emperor of his election, made the Roman position clear: "There are, most august Emperor, two powers by which this world is chiefly ruled: the sacred authority of bishops and the royal power. Of these the priestly power is much more important, because it has to give account for the kings of men themselves at the judgment seat of God . . ." The dispute was only resolved when a new emperor decided to return to the faith of Chalcedon.

---

[20] For emphasis on the Roman-law aspects of the claims of Leo and later Roman bishops (such as Gelasius I (492–496)) see especially W. Ullmann, *A Short History of the Papacy in the Middle Ages* (London 1972) 14–16, 26–34. An edict of the Western Emperor Valentinian III in 445 already indicates the very different relationship between the Church and the (far weaker) Empire in the West: "Nothing should be done against or without the authority of the Roman Church."

Thus after Constantine's establishment of a Christian Empire, first Arianism, then Monophysitism set the Western Church and the Roman bishop (whose claims as arbiter of dogma – and more – were increasingly explicit) against the imperial authority. In the sixth century, in the absence of a *Western* Empire, the papacy developed more spectacular claims in the civic realm. Nevertheless, the Monophysite problem led to further imperial insistence on the emperor's right to control theological orthodoxy: Pope Vigilius was humiliated by the Emperor Justinian before and after the Fifth Ecumenical Council of Constantinople (553), where he was compelled virtually to repudiate Chalcedon – and as a result was excommunicated by many Western bishops, not least the bishop of Milan. The majority of Western bishops insisted that, while there might be two authorities in human society, the senior, in theological matters at least, was not the "lord of the world" (*kosmocrator*) in Constantinople.

In the seventh century the authority of the "lord of the world" was seriously threatened even in "civil" matters: by the Avars in the Balkans, by the Persians who reached Jerusalem in 614, carrying off the "True Cross", then more permanently by the rising military moon of Islam which extinguished Christian rule in many of the old Roman centres by the end of the century: Antioch in 637, Alexandria in 642, Carthage in 698. Struggles with these adversaries took on the character of holy war, with the assimilation of Church and State in the person of the emperor becoming the mark of the Christian régime. Yet the divisions over Chalcedon needed to be healed if anything like a common Christian front was to be preserved, so the Patriarch Sergius in Constantinople came up with what looked a convenient theological and political solution: though Christ must have two natures, he had only one will. Contrary talk was to be forbidden.

Pope Honorius was taken in by a solution that would enable him to continue his strong support for the Byzantine presence in Italy, achieve Christian unity throughout the Empire and "save" Chalcedon. Encouraged by Roman support, the emperor promulgated an "Ecthesis": one-will Christology was to be the imperial theology. But the new vision proved unacceptable in the West and eventually (after intimidation which caused the deposition and death of Martin I who had organized its condemnation at a Lateran Synod of 649), the emperors gave up the struggle: the Sixth General Council at Constantinople duly condemned "Monothelitism" – as well as Pope Honorius and its other founding fathers. Once again imperial attempts to use theology for political purposes had come to grief – and after much skirmishing, some of which came near to achieving for Pope Sergius I (687–701) the fate of his predecessor Martin, the next and most serious imperial manoeuvres were to prove fatal for the imperial claims in the West, leading directly to the possibility of papal theocracy.

When Constantinople was besieged by the Arabs in 717, national panic led to a phenomenon of theological innovation later to be repeated in Renaissance England. With the support of many of his clergy, Leo III decided that the Empire's troubles were due to national apostasy, in particular to the veneration of images, contrary to Old Testament decree.[21] He decided that all images of the Virgin and Child were to be replaced by the simple cross under which Constantine had originally established the Christian Empire: again indicating how anti-developmental conservatism can turn out "heretical". As with the decrees in favour of the Monothelites, the new policy did not win universal popularity even in the East, and the Western Church, led by successive popes (several of whom were Greek-speakers) rejected it unambiguously: Gregory II told the emperor that with his coarse military mind he had no sense for theology.

In retribution the emperors attempted to weaken the power of the Roman bishop both financially and juridically: partly Greek-speaking dioceses in imperially controlled southern Italy and Greece were removed from his authority and transferred to that of Constantinople, while papal revenues from land in southern Italy and Sicily dried up. Despite this the theological situation in the West remained unchanged, though the popes themselves still maintained a certain loyalty to the Empire. But by the time the Empress Irene convoked the Seventh Ecumenical Council (Nicaea II) in 787 and repudiated Iconoclasm, warmly welcoming papal teaching on the matter, the political situation in the West had changed for ever.

Under pressure from the Lombards the popes had increasingly sought protection from (and eventually, in light of the "Donation of Constantine", claimed authority over) Pépin and successive rulers of the Franks. The year 751 had marked the turning-point: Pope Zacharias had accepted that Pépin's *de facto* monarchy was a monarchy *de iure*, and in the same year the Lombards took Ravenna, former seat of Byzantine rule in Italy. By consecrating Pépin and excommunicating those who refused to accept him, Stephen II, the successor of Zacharias, in effect incorporated the king within the ecclesiastical hierarchy. Hence when Pépin's son Charlemagne, "Patrician of the Romans", finally destroyed the Lombard kingdom in

---

[21] At the so-called "Quini-Sext" Council of 692, Justinian II (besides freeing priests and deacons from the requirement of celibacy) had forbidden the representation of Christ as a Lamb. Pope Sergius I retorted by adopting the Syrian custom of reciting the Agnus Dei at the breaking of bread at Mass. Christ as Lamb was simultaneously restored in mosaic in the apse of the Roman Church of Saints Cosmas and Damian.

773/4, he had in effect replaced the Byzantine rulers in the West, but – at least in the papal view – on the basis of a very different understanding of relations with the religious establishment. Charlemagne confirmed the Donation of Constantine with Pope Hadrian I and was crowned as Emperor by Hadrian's successor Leo III on Christmas Day 800. And here arises an interesting dispute, only the Frankish chronicler claiming that the Pope kissed the ground (Byzantine style) before the king's feet.

On purely theological questions the Pope tried to establish a *modus vivendi* with the king which recalled papal claims against the Byzantine emperors. While tolerating royal control (or at least royal veto) of ecclesiastical appointments, he claimed to exercise a certain veto of his own in matters of doctrine. Within the Frankish Empire, as elsewhere generally in the West, the famous *filioque* had been added to the original text of the Nicene-Constantinopolitan Creed, indicating that the Spirit "proceeded" from both the Father and the Son. This was not accepted in the East, largely on the grounds that nothing should be added or taken away from the creed (another example of the rejection of continuous development), and when the issue was raised in 810 Pope Leo III, while he accepted the *filioque*, took exception to its use without ecumenical approval. Charlemagne, for his part, held that its neglect was just another Greek heresy.

But an ecumenical settlement was increasingly unlikely and, although a formal separation of the Churches of East and West had to wait for the papacy of Gregory VII, the so-called Photian schism was a safe predictor of the future. Again it was the rival claims of religion and political power that provoked the conflict – and this time we can recognize a clear parallel with the origins of the Anglican Church in Henry VIII's version of Caesaropapism in England.

In 858 Ignatius, patriarch of Constantinople, attempted to assert the rights of hierarchy against his emperor. Michael III was accused of incest and refused communion. In response the Emperor deposed the patriarch and appointed in his place Photius, a lay civil servant and scholar. Photius rose through the clerical orders in less than a week. Patriarch Ignatius then appealed to Pope Nicholas I – who had already reasserted the supremacy of the Western Church over the potentially "imperial" pretensions of the Carolingians.[22] Nicholas backed Ignatius, excommunicating Photius and

---

[22] According to H.-X. Arquillière, *L'augustinisme politique: Essai sur la formation des théories politiques du moyen âge* (Paris² 1955) 111, Gregory VII would have been virtually impossible without Charlemagne's (perhaps unconscious) forwarding of the assimilation of ecclesiastical and civil power. Insofar as Charlemagne had partially pushed "rights" in favour of the king, Pope Nicholas I had more than reasserted an ultimate papal predominance in any possible Christian society.

telling the Emperor not to interfere in Church and above all papal concerns. Photius and Michael rejected the Pope's decision and in 867 a synod in Constantinople excommunicated and deposed Nicholas (who died without receiving the news). This time final separation was avoided, but the stage was now set for the mutual excommunications of 1054 which remained in force until 1965.

Looking back at the whole history of the relationship between the Byzantine Empire and the Church, it is clear that the emperors persistently attempted to bend theology for political purposes, and were incensed if ecclesiatics attempted to thwart them in so doing. The imperial view, given tangible expression in their claim to approve ecclesiastical appointments, even the appointment of popes – a claim later echoed by the Ottonian emperors in the West – was that in a Christian commonwealth the Church is an arm of the State and the bishops (especially the patriarchs) are Ministers of Religious Affairs. It is interesting to notice that it was over a question of marriage, where secular and religious themes were interwoven, that the "Photian schism" arose.

There is no need to pursue the historical question of Caesaropapism in its original Constantinian form much further. It is clear that the Catholic Church, centred on the Roman see, rejected the notion of a quasi-divine ruler as head of the Church, and with it the "Constantinian" thesis that the Church is an arm of the Christian State. It is worth noticing, however, that while, as I shall argue, the anti-papalism of the late Middle Ages represented by Marsilius of Padua and William of Ockham showed less a resurgent Caesaropapism than a more radical (and by implication anti-Christian) wish to separate the activities and functions of Church and State altogether, at the English Reformation a more genuinely Caesaropapist scenario was staged. The Henrician revolution in England began because of the dynastic wishes of the king. Like the Iconoclast emperors in his probably genuine feeling of being the victim of divine displeasure (shown in his childless marriage to Katherine of Aragon), and like Michael III in his insistence on being surrounded by ecclesiastics who would do his "Christian" bidding, and in thereby putting political and dynastic considerations above those of theology as traditionally understood, Henry VIII, a once loyal adherent of Catholic orthodoxy, set up his own Church with himself as its "Supreme Head".

There were substantive circumstantial differences in the Henrician case, however. In the earlier disputes about Arianism, Monophysitism, Monothelitism and Iconoclasm (though not the *filioque* clause over which the popes were willing to compromise, at least for a while), the emperors eventually backed down. The sexual arrangements lying behind the Photius affair were not so easily swept under the carpet, though a temporary solution was eventually found. But unfortunately for Christian unity, Henry's dynastic aims were contemporary with the volcanic upheavals of Lutheran and Calvinist theological controversy and, by patronizing the politically more cautious heretics, Henry succeeded not merely in defying the pope but in establishing a new Caesaropapist Church which resembled less the Orthodoxy of the Byzantine Empire than the national and nationalist Orthodoxy that grew up after the fall of Constantinople to the Ottoman Turks in 1453. Luther himself summed up the situation well on Henry's death: "Juncker Heintz insists on being God and does whatever he lusts."

The early leaders of the Church of England, starting with Cranmer, Henry's archbishop of Canterbury, doubtless would have wished for more radical theological reform – which they achieved under the Protestant régime of his successor Edward VI and to a limited if unsatisfying degree under Elizabeth I. But the nature of the Elizabethan "settlement" of religious affairs marked (and still marks) the triumph of a new brand of Caesaropapism in England. The would-be Calvinism of the Elizabethan reformers would always be tempered to the political wishes of the monarch as interpreted by the thugs and carpet-baggers controlled by Lord Burghley – and was soon to be buttressed by revised claims about the divine right of kings. Although the Puritan radicals enjoyed temporary success in the Cromwellian Commonwealth, thus establishing a new form of Caesaropapism in what became a military dictatorship, the restored Anglicanism of Charles II brought the return of the earlier Erastian (and Caesaropapist) system of state-run religion.

The political and religious importance of the Anglican system diminished only when "Caesar" gave way to more parliamentary and democratic forms of government and Christianity began its retreat into private life in response to the ever-growing secularism of the post-Enlightenment age. A certain echo of Caesaropapism, however, can still be discerned in the power of the British prime minister – whether he be Christian, Jew, Muslim, Hindu or atheist – to control (however indirectly) the appointment of senior bishops of the Anglican establishment, theological concerns being left at best on the back-burner. The mark of this national Church, as of its Byzantine forerunner and that forerunner's Orthodox successor states, has been what it must always be: compromise with the prevailing values and concerns of secular (or at least civil) society – so long as the state finds it worthwhile to enforce such compromise. But if Catholicism, with however much difficulty – which I have barely sketched – rejected the Caesaropapist state and

Church conformity to it, what about the other "totalitarian" option for Christianity: a papal or at least an ecclesiastical "commonwealth" that is, in effect, a theocracy?

Before leaving Caesaropapism behind, however, I should notice that in Orthodoxy (as the *filioque* clause well demonstrated) there has been little room for the kind of development in the understanding of doctrine that is a main theme of the present essay. Instead of that development, there has been a tendency among Caesaropapists (religious or tribal) to a rigid "traditionism", or, as in the Anglican case, to an actual erosion (rather than development) of foundational Christian beliefs. Caesaropapism will naturally find fertile ground in such anti-developmental societies, not least because in the absence of the development of doctrine there is no real place for theology, and the typical "theologian" offers nothing more than an echo of supposedly fixed formulae – unless he or she becomes an apologist not for theological development but for state- or society-sanctioned retraction of fundamental Christian claims. Insofar as Christianity will continue in such an environment, where religious thinkers have abnegated their responsibilities, the state (Caesaropapist or other) will move to fill the vacuum.

5.4 PAPAL (AND OTHER) THEOCRACY

Caesaropapists have no necessary objection to Chrysostom's disrespect for thought. They want a "Christian" state, but with a secular ruler, endowed with quasi-divine authority, ultimately controlling it and the Church, in some sense, a branch of the divine Empire. If, however, the alternative is a more or less modified theocracy or some sort of hierocratic model, intellectual and artistic life will still have to be rigidly controlled – and we looked at "aesthetic" controls in an earlier chapter. We should expect that in some circumstances would-be "Caesaropapists" would assist rebels against that theocracy, less in light of concern for intellectual or artistic freedom than hoping to enlist intellectuals in the battle against Church control of their political and social aims. And so it was to prove in the later Middle Ages.

I have noted the increasing awareness of the popes of the early Middle Ages that they must retain a certain independence of the Byzantine Empire, as later of the developing Carolingian power in the West: certainly in matters spiritual and increasingly in matters temporal. The more or less permanent break between East and West during the pontificate of Gregory VII helped to ensure an increasing papal ascendency in the West. This I do not need to chronicle in detail, merely to note the rise and fall of papal "monarchy", and the currents underlying political events which seemed to offer the chance of a developing political theory for Christian society in the period of high scholasticism.

From the time of Gregory VII papal claims to sovereignty both civil and spiritual grew steadily, perhaps culminating in the reign of Innocent III and dipping dramatically with the humiliation of Boniface VIII at the hands of the king of France in 1303 and the subsequent beginning of the "Avignon Captivity" in 1309. Bernard of Clairvaux may be taken as the principal theoretician of the movement. Dedicating his *De Consideratione* – a treatise on how the papacy should be run – to Eugenius III (1145–1153), he castigated the increasing worldly bustle of the curia while upholding the "vicar of Peter" and "vicar of Christ" – the latter title became more or less official with Innocent III – as the "supreme priest and king" whose job is to watch over the macro-problems of Christian society. The pope, he maintained, possesses the "two swords" (book 4), but has delegated civil power to secular rulers whose primary function is to operate in accordance with papal wishes.

The catastrophic failure of the Second Crusade, which Bernard preached, revealed the underlying weakness of such "top-down" notions of Christendom, while the fury of Innocent at the transformation of the Fourth Crusade in 1204 into the sacking of Constantinople was a further instance of the inability of the papacy to control Christian rulers. The fate of Boniface VIII and its consequences marked the beginning of the end for papal pretensions of the Gregorian sort: there followed the "Captivity", in which the increasingly "nationalist" French monarchy demonstrated that even in spiritual matters the idea of a Church independent of the state, let alone master of the state, was looking increasingly implausible. Yet the migration of the popes to Avignon was not the result of direct pressure by King Philip IV of France; a vicar of Christ might seem less bound to Rome than a mere vicar of Peter, and Clement V (1305–1314) hoped that by remaining in the comparative safety of Avignon he might also encourage the French and English kings to prefer a new crusade to the prospect of constantly warring among themselves.

Once ensconced in Provence, however, the popes became increasingly controlled by the French monarchy. All the "Avignon popes" were French, as were all but twenty-two of the 134 cardinals they appointed. Clement managed to resist pressure to condemn his predecessor, Boniface, of heresy and sodomy, as Philip wished, but was obliged to give way over the Order of Templars which was duly suppressed, to the great advantage of the French exchequer. Heresy and sodomy were again among the charges, established by confessions extracted under torture by drunken thugs. Far from being arbiter of Christendom, the papacy had been reduced – not for the last time – to condoning a royal master's sins.

The conflict between Boniface and Philip was fought at the intellectual as well as the crudely political level. As we shall see in more detail – and contrary to much still conventional wisdom – the coming of "Aristotelian" political theory in the thirteenth century had little immediate effect in disturbing the traditional "Augustinian", or "politically Augustinian", approach to politics: Aristotle could easily be absorbed, but it was political events then, as often, that provoked changes in theory, and the war between Philip and Boniface was echoed by a contemporary and growing view – typified by John of Paris in his *On Royal and Papal Power* – that the role of the state was not merely to provide peace and security but (as the genuine Aristotle wished) in and of itself actively to promote the life of virtue.[23]

There were more radical developments to come: the Augustinian – or would-be-Augustinian – bases of Christian society were to be further challenged by William of Ockham and Marsilius of Padua, who recast the Aristotelian theories of society of high scholasticism in a "utilitarian" mould, declaring that the state (concerned only with security and material prosperity) is naturally separate from the Church, and that the power that devolves upon princes is derived ultimately from the people, the Church itself being little more than a Ministry for Religion in a national (and potentially democratic) state. In accordance with such ideas, in 1328 Louis of Bavaria was crowned Emperor in Rome not by the pope but by a Roman layman. Before turning, therefore, to more theoretical questions of political philosophy, medieval and other, it only remains to sketch the latter stages of the decline of the Gregorian ideal down to the pontificate of Nicholas V (1447–1455), the first "humanist" pope – and as such a clear witness to the failure of the theocratic ideal.

In 1377 Gregory XI had fulfilled one of the two demands of Catherine of Siena: that he bring back the papacy to Rome. The other demand, that he call for a new crusade against the Turks, remained an aspiration. But his successor, "probably clinically paranoid" according to a recent historian,[24] proved intolerable even to the cardinals who had chosen him; they elected the bishop of Geneva in his place who, as "Clement VII", immediately returned to Avignon. For the next forty years there were two popes and two curial bureaucracies – until a group of cardinals, meeting at Pisa, elected a third to replace both the Roman and Avignonese incumbents. But both refused to go, so that until a second council at Constance elected Martin V (1417–1431), the Church boasted three "popes", and to many the authority

---

[23] Cf. M. S. Kempshall, *The Common Good in Late Medieval Political Thought* (Oxford 1999) 287–288.
[24] E. Duffy, *Saints and Sinners: A History of the Popes* (New Haven 1997) 127.

of the council that eventually resolved the matter seemed higher than that of any of them.

Martin had to fight to retain his position against the conciliarists, and the Council of Basle (1431–1439) – many of whose members were not even bishops – attempted to depose his successor, Eugenius IV. By the time Nicholas V took over in 1447, not even Eugenius' temporary success in reuniting the Churches of East and West on Roman terms could save Constantinople from the Turks – it fell in 1453 – or restore more than the shadow of papal prestige. In 1438 the king of France had legalized the so-called "Pragmatic Sanction": councils are superior to popes, papal control of ecclesiastical appointments is to be drastically reduced.[25] And in 1440 Lorenzo Valla had demonstrated that the Donation of Constantine, one of the pillars of theocratic claims by the papacy, was an eighth-century forgery.[26] The story of the new Catholic humanism under Nicholas and his successors, together with the reduction of the popes in politics to little more than posturing figure-heads even in the eyes of the Catholic monarchs of Europe – a role brutally dramatized in 1773 by the pathetic agreement of Clement XIV to suppress the Jesuits – must be left for brief comment in the next chapter. The stage has been well enough set for me to review the theoretical bases of Western (that is, Catholic) political thinking as they developed after Gregory VII.

5.5 AUGUSTINE AND POLITICAL AUGUSTINIANISM

The fountainhead of medieval political thought in the West is Augustine, so we must identify the bishop of Hippo's political views as a preliminary to separating them from what has come to be called "political Augustinianism", which, it may be conceded, has a certain claim to roots in Augustine.[27] Of course, there is a sense in which there is no political theory in Augustine: no

---

[25] The Sanction was annulled in 1516, but only when the Concordat of Bologna handed over to the French Crown the right to appoint bishops and abbots – while permitting the restoration of annates and papal claims to supremacy over general councils. Similar concordats, usually conceding the appointment of bishops to secular authorities (as in that with Spain in 1753), were later to become common practice as the papacy (still seen largely as a would-be secular state in decline, yet still inclined to hark back to the dreams of Gregory VII and Innocent III) continued to lose prestige among Catholic as well as Protestant powers. Gregory VII himself was canonized by Paul V in 1606 and in the same year Paul placed the Republic of Venice under an interdict which was totally ignored.

[26] Valla also argued – though for conclusive proof we had to wait till 1895 – that the writings of Dionysius "the Areopagite" (now pseudo-Dionysius) could not go back to apostolic times: another foundational text of the medieval world order brought into apparent disrepute, at least with many of the learned.

[27] So Arquillière, *L'augustinisme*.

theory of the state, little specific discussion even of the burning question to which I have already devoted several pages, the relationship between the imperial government and the Church. Perhaps between 405 and 415 Augustine indulged some Eusebian triumphalism about "Christian times"; if so, his more realistic side soon reasserted itself.[28] There can be good Christian emperors, but there is no guarantee that a Christian government will behave in a Christian fashion, and after a brief period of hesitation Augustine resolutely refused the Constantinian option – leading towards Caesaropapism – of any "sacralization" of the state. Yet he spelled out no clear political alternative and the key problem of "political Augustinianism" was not yet on the table: that is, whether the "fullness of (secular) power" should reside with the Church (in practice the pope), with the Empire or its successors, however desacralized they might become, or with neither.

Augustine's problem is not how Church or government shall act together politically in the name of Christ, but what attitude a Christian should adopt towards political life. Underlying this dilemma is the premiss that all political activity is the activity of human beings after the Fall, that is, of human beings in a state of *concupiscentia* (at best a weakness for the morally undesirable, at worst a lust for it) and ignorance. Politics is conducted in a fallen world in which, without divine aid, men will behave badly, and even given such aid will fall far short of perfection in this life. The politician lives in a world where he must regularly make choices he should regret. The Platonic ideal, of a possibly perfect government in a state itself highly conducive to virtue, has disappeared.

Instead, in Augustine there is much concern with the character of the Christian who becomes a politician, administrator or general,[29] and rather little with the Christian state: the gap which "political Augustinianism" attempted to fill. Insofar as political Augustinianism has a theoretical basis – and in this resides much of its claim to be Augustinian – it is that politics is a branch of morality, that in politics as in private life all decisions are going to affect the state of one's immortal soul. And who better than the Church and its representatives – primarily, in the West, the bishop of Rome – to determine the good of one's soul?

In this perspective the leading politician, whether king or emperor, is no different from the ordinary man; he can and should be told when he sins.

---

[28] For further introductory (and limited) comment see Rist, *Augustine* 208–209.

[29] This is emphasized by R. Dodaro, *Christ and the Just Society in the Thought of Augustine* (Cambridge 2004), to which much of the following discussion is indebted. Those seeking a fuller account of Augustine's view of political life should refer to this study.

But the implications of such correction grew as time passed. In the fourth century Ambrose imposed public penance on the Emperor Theodosius (whose pious humility is duly praised by Augustine (*City of God* 5.26.1)) as the price for his return to communion with the Church, but there was no possibility of Ambrose's threatening to depose him. The history of political Augustinianism is of the growth of the idea that deposition too is within the power of the Church and the pope.

I have already considered how the Byzantine emperors took a very different view – and at least insinuated an alternative political theory. So far from being dependent on the Church for legitimacy, the emperor should retain the power to control all ecclesiastical appointments, originally including that of the bishop of Rome as well as the patriarch of Constantinople. Such power, indeed, went back to Constantine. But in dealing with the barbarian kings in the West the popes had no such counter-tradition to overcome. Political Augustinianism is the name for the course they took against the (originally) weaker challenge of the Church's less established secular rivals.

The failure of papalist theories was tied to the development of alternative accounts of the relation of Church and State, whereby political life is ultimately free of moral – and more immediately ecclesiastical – control. But such theories are not unrelated to the lacunae in Augustine's political views themselves and to his concentration on the moral behaviour and attitudes of the individual Christian politician. In considering this, I shall also want to look back to the "anti-intellectualist" tendencies and narrowly authoritarian vision of Christian society desired by such as John Chrysostom as a much less attractive alternative which still lay on the theoretical table.

We can see something of why that alternative returned to favour in some quarters – and not only among Catholic Christians – if we recognize how late medieval and partly post-Augustinian revisions of political theory were associated with an abandonment of the Augustinian (and more generally ancient) blending of "arts", "philosophy" and "theology" in an all-embracing Christian wisdom and culture. If we recognize the significance of that abandonment – however necessary and beneficial it may have been in the short run – we shall be able to understand the importance of more recent and gradually more realistic and honest efforts to undo its ill effects on Christian (and other) intellectual, cultural and political life.

5.6 POLITICAL THEORY: AUGUSTINE AND ARISTOTLE

For Augustine the Christian politician must always remember his direct relationship with God; for the political Augustinians that relationship is

seen as with the temporal and spiritual power of the Church. But what is the
nature of the society in which the Christian politician is to work and what
must he hope to achieve? For Augustine political society is an effect of the
Fall, and in the consequent hierarchical world around us we can recognize
the objects of two loves: City of God and earthly city. As motifs, these cities
represent the effects of love of God and love of self, which latter will take the
political form of lust for power: over the souls as well as the bodies of others.
The primary purpose of political activity (as of "fallen" domestic governance, of which politics is a large-scale examplar with a similar blending of
love and fear) is the maintenance of "earthly" peace and security (*City of God*
19.14–15), but the use of force which this requires is liable to be peculiarly
corrosive for the individual, insofar as he is given substantially increased
opportunities for the "sweet taste" of sinning (*Against Gaudentius* 1.19.20;
City of God 5.26): in particular, that is, opportunity to control the souls of
his fellows (*On Music* 6.13.41). In Augustine's view the lust for power (*libido
dominandi*) is one of three basic and recurring weaknesses of humanity.[30]

Augustine proposes two kinds of remedy: first a rigid (too rigid) distinction between public and private life; second, the constant need for the
Christian to meditate on his proposed courses of action in the light of that
peculiarly Christ-like virtue of humility – whereby we recall that we are
wholly dependent for our virtue and ultimately for our salvation on the
grace of God, who alone can act among men without arrogance (*Confessions*
10.36.59). The first "remedy" tells us that there are actions involving the use
of force, which public officials are licensed to perform but are forbidden to
the private citizen. Augustine observes in *Letter* 47 that he disapproves of
killing even in self-defence but that this is permissible for a soldier or a
public official because such people, acting for others or for the state as a
whole, have lawfully received the authority so to act.

The infliction of penalty by the state, its soldiers and officials is permitted, but those responsible (as we hear especially in book 19 of the *City of
God*) must always bear in mind when they so act that they too are sinners,
liable to pride and its political manifestation, the lust for power. Their
public acts are sanctioned as necessary evils in this "darkness of social life"
(*City of God* 19.6) because without them peace in the fallen world cannot be
preserved, civil strife cannot be averted, hierarchy cannot be maintained –
and the alternative is the brutish savagery of the vendetta (*privata licentia*,

---

[30] The others are the unbridled lust for sex and the desire to know what it is wrong to know (*curiositas*).
In chapter 1 I introduced the gods of Sex and Power – Venus and Jupiter – as the primary divinities of
the world into which Christianity was born.

Letter 47). Perhaps civil law too can to some degree mitigate the lust for domination which is the ultimate *raison d'être* of the earthly city. Though the "peace" it can secure is never stable (*On Psalms* 85(84).10), it can restrain vice, secure the safety of the relatively innocent and perhaps induce wrong-doers to call on God (*Letter* 153.6.16, to Macedonius). In *On Free Will* Augustine argues that human law codes (as distinct from the moral law) deal with the distribution, protection and preserving of "private goods"; we are inhibited from indulging any desire for the temporal goods of others (1.15.32).

Augustine seems to assume that the autocratic political world he knows is more or less permanent. Though he is aware that elsewhere in time and place there have been other sorts of régime, he thinks that no radical systemic improvement is possible; the individual Christian will always, almost hopelessly were it not for grace, be facing the same problems. Such an outlook affects the important question as to why he has virtually nothing to say about a Christian society as such. A society in which all the members love the same genuine good is considered by Augustine an unrealistic hope in a world where the classical thesis that perfection can be attained, at least by individuals, has been abandoned.

Augustine supposes that political activity began only after the Fall; in our "natural" social condition there would be no need for it. That is not to say that before the Fall there would have been no authority, no rule of the superior over the less gifted (such as that of men over women).[31] But such authority would not have needed the element of coercion that necessarily marks political societies, the aims of which are primarily to repress the more obnoxious vices. The authority of the ruler would once have resembled that of an ideal father, without need for coercion where the less well endowed respect the role of their superiors. Society would have been paternal, governed by a proper authority with no threat of force, like a well-run household. But now the key to political action is that "the primary and everyday power of a man over a man is that of a master over a slave".

If Christian society cannot generate goodness, merely help to eradicate the more obvious vices and obstacles to earthly peace and security, pagan society cannot hope even for that. We recall Augustine's strongly held belief that pagan "virtues" are not really virtues at all.[32] Though they bear some external resemblance to real virtues, they are delusory because no virtue is

---

[31] For comment and texts see R. A. Markus, *Saeculum: History and Society in the Thought of St Augustine* (Cambridge 1970) 202–205.

[32] Rist, *Augustine* 168–170; Dodaro, *Christ and the Just Society* 184.

possible without correct motivation, and correct motivation is nothing less than the love and worship of the true God: an impossibility for pagans. The implication of that is that any generalized "political theory" will be relatively useless. Without the Christian theological virtues of faith, hope and love, no society can promote true goodness.

That enables us to understand the claims of "political Augustinianism", for if the Church is the only authority on earth fitted to prescribe what is necessary for virtue, it has every claim to a "plenitude of power". Augustine's own view of the Church as a "mixed body", a blend of the divine and the all-too-human, would rule out this solution.

Since there would have been no politics had Adam remained natural and innocent, and since the primary function of political life and of the state is the repression of vice rather than the promotion of virtue, the lack of any significant treatment of better or worse constitutions in Augustine is hardly surprising: all political order is ultimately unnatural. Any such treatment could only be based on the premiss that the choice of one régime rather than another would greatly enhance the possibility of virtue, but Augustine himself is inclined to assume that for the suppression of vice a strong autocratic rule is likely to be the most effective.

I want to argue, however, first that this view is in conflict with Augustine's own theological claim that, with God's help, man, not being wholly corrupted, is capable of advancement in goodness, and, second, that the Church has eventually abandoned Augustine's apparent preference for autocracy. It is worth noticing that some of the social *implications* of Augustine's position – though less spelled out – are similar to those of Chrysostom with which I began this chapter: that "fallen" society should consist of collections of private family dwellings "controlled" by the ecclesiastical and political authorities – each in their respective spheres – and that otherwise there should be no (necessarily pagan) "public space".

While "classical" Greek and Roman political theories emphasized the role of the city (or its equivalent) as educator of humanity and of the statesman as the active promoter of this goal, Augustine's view of both is more limited. The *polis*-ideal has virtually disappeared, while the hope of the statesman can only be to deliver a more conscientious and humble administration within the dreadful parameters such administration requires. Yet in contrast to those Christians of his day who followed Eusebius in promoting the sacralization of a Christian power, Augustine was more "classical". Power, including in Christian hands, is highly suspect, and the sort of "sacralization" implicit in the policies of a Constantine (and even of a Theodosius), let alone the Caesaropapism which was their logical and historical conclusion, is for him out of the question.

So long as Augustine held sway as the ultimate source for political morality, and so long as his distrust and suspicion of institutions operating in the world and in the secular domain, including the Church itself, pertained, political Augustinianism or Caesaropapism might understandably be thought of as the only foreseeable solutions to pressing political problems, while theocracy might seem the only way to preserve the Church's independence of the state. But Augustine's distinction between "genuine" (Christian) and "false" pagan virtue became more controversial with the return of Aristotelian political theory – unknown of course to Augustine himself – in the twelfth century.

It has often been claimed that the coming of Aristotle revolutionized medieval political thought and advanced the process of secularization that culminated in the humanism of the Renaissance (and further on of the Enlightenment),[33] since according to Aristotle politics did not arise, as Augustine held, from the Fall of man, but is a natural human condition; hence it is primarily the function of government to advance the "virtue" of all the citizens. But it is important to consider more precisely the sort of changes Aristotelianism brought about. Argument over the effect of Aristotle's political writings at the end of the thirteenth century centred less on the question of whether politics is a natural activity – in the sense that it would be needed even had there been no Fall – than on its corollary concerning the end and purpose of political activity: whether, as Augustine held, its sphere is the repression of vice and the maintenance of peace, or whether it can, in and of itself and indeed necessarily, promote the virtue of the citizens and the common good.[34]

The Aristotelians held that grace perfects nature and that, since man is naturally social, there would have been a place for political life in our original natural condition; that means that politics can be discussed without necessary reference to our fallen condition, in which the state must be associated with domination and compulsion, albeit at its best for our own good.[35] And since our original nature has not been wholly deformed by sin, there still remains room for constructive political activity with regard to the (admittedly damaged) character we presently display.

---

[33] See especially the writings of W. Ullmann, such as *Principles of Government and Politics in the Middle Ages* (London 1961).

[34] Note the remarks of Kempshall, *The Common Good* 292, 351–362.

[35] Note the interesting comments of Markus on Albert the Great in *Saeculum* (218) and on Aquinas (219–220). Aquinas follows the Aristotelian approach in distinguishing "domination" as a mark of evil régimes from "government" indicating good ones.

Although Augustine's opinion that pagan virtues are not true virtues remained as an axiom, its significance was changed. Aquinas, for example, will allow that only the infused virtues of faith, hope and love are truly perfect and rightly to be called virtues (because they point us to our final end of the knowledge of God (*ST* Ia IIae q 15, a 2), but will allow the traditional cardinal virtues to point us to our lesser end, namely human flourishing as understood in the Aristotelian mode. Such virtues are possible within non-Christian societies and to promote them is the proper business of political life. Other thinkers take the same view: James of Viterbo (for example) accepts Augustine's position as strictly correct, but adds that virtues can also be understood in terms of "more and less". Even though "pagan" virtues (and thus the virtues of political society in general) are strictly vices, it is natural and right – we recognize here a Stoic language that Augustine himself would not have repudiated – that we pursue those which are the more "virtuous". Kempshall has aptly summed this up: "Temporal peace is not illegitimate if it fails to be directed towards eternal beatitude, it is simply imperfect; moral virtue is not illegitimate in the absence of grace and *caritas*, it is simply incomplete."[36] One might add that the supposed absence of grace from any "better" act depends on the ancient and medieval assumption that explicit admission to the Christian community through baptism is necessary for the entry of grace into human life. We no longer need to accept that assumption.

But if Augustine's views could be modified in such ways, and an important measure of Aristotelianism accepted within a prevalently Augustinian political outlook, the possibility of a "natural" politics allows for questions that for good reasons lay largely outside Augustine's own concerns. These include the problem of the best form of political society in a world where political activity is still to a degree a natural good and conducive of human excellence. More fundamentally, however, given the appropriateness of political life to all societies (perfect no doubt before the Fall but still capable of improvement in our present state), a question arises which, undercutting any possible "Augustinian" outlook, seems to posit a *subversive* Aristotelianism in allowing even the end or purpose of political life to be debated freely. Could the goal of political life (and therefore of the state and its government) be not the promotion of virtue but merely what is *useful in present material circumstances*? "Usefulness" might be much wider than – and even alien to – the bases of civilized life with which Augustine himself was concerned. Hence in a questioning of the source of political authority – is

[36] Kempshall, *The Common Good* 350.

it God, or reason, or the mere will and decision of various groups of individuals as to their own interest? – we pass from the medieval to the modern world.

Even in strictly Augustinian terms – seeing as we are not, in Augustine's view, completely fallen – it would be reasonable, not least if political life would have existed had Adam not fallen, to enquire into its nature and goals. The results of such an enquiry, however, would only be of "Catholic" interest if the goals identified involved both the spiritual good of the individual man and the good of the society to which he belongs, and could be associated with the development of human excellence. In that sense the response of Aquinas is Augustinian, since for him the imperfect happiness which political life is concerned to promote is certainly based on the pursuit of virtue.

As for Aquinas' determination of the related problem of the best form of political society, he is able to remain comfortably in the Aristotelian world, in which, again, the goal is human excellence. Ideally perhaps monarchy is to be preferred, but it may be better in practice to avoid the risk of autocracy by introducing a more democratic element. Aquinas certainly thinks that all human beings are in some sense equal,[37] and perhaps one might deduce from that that some theory of popular sovereignty would suit his book (*ST* I 109.2), but he is also fully aware of our dramatically different talents and holds that it is expedient that those best fitted to govern should do so (*SCG* 3.81; *ST* I 96 a), other things being equal: an expectably Aristotelian conclusion.[38]

Aquinas' position on this key issue remains thus unclear[39] – not least because he upholds the Aristotelian thesis (which he attempts to blend with Augustine's view of the limited role of government in the promotion of excellence) that it is a function of the ruler to promote the virtue of the citizen. Yet we can see in his "Aristotelian" hesitation the effect on "Augustinianism" of the arrival of Aristotelian ideas. So long as the aim of government remained the promotion of human goodness, however, a basically Augustinian framework could be maintained. The real challenge

---

[37] I have discussed some interpretations of such comments in chapter 1.
[38] Note the remarks of B. Tierney, "Public Expediency and Natural Law; A Fourteenth Century Discussion on the Origins of Government and Property", in B. Tierney and P. Linehan (eds.), *Authority and Power: Studies Presented to W. Ullmann* (Cambridge 1980) 167–182, esp. 174. Note Tierney's comment (note 25): "Modern authors, by emphasizing one set of texts or the other, have been able to present Aquinas as an extreme theocrat or an extreme democrat."
[39] In characteristically a-historical mode Finnis attempts to smooth away Aquinas' well-grounded hesitations (*Aquinas* 258–266).

came when not virtue but utility (as with Marsilius of Padua[40]) was proclaimed the aim of government. For Marsilius (as indeed for Ockham) political structures have no moral purpose. The view of Aquinas certainly allows for a degree of autonomy for the government vis-à-vis the Church, thus ultimately pointing towards the emergence of an independent secular authority, but the Marsilian move towards utility both forwarded and revised that development substantially.

The dispute between Boniface VIII and Philip the Fair brought many matters to a head. Thus in Philip's defence John of Paris argued for the state as a promoter of virtue, invoking Aristotle as a defender of the autonomy of secular power. But Marsilius went much further,[41] preaching the total subordination of the Church to the civil authorities. Yet Marsilius is far more than an extreme advocate of the power of kings or emperors over the Church. His version of "Aristotelianism" is transmuted into a system whereby men's natural inclination towards political life (*Defender of Peace* 1.5.2) is merely towards effective functioning and has nothing to do with any natural progress in virtue. Despite our natural inclination towards political associations, Marsilius never calls man a "political animal". The Marsilian state is not "natural", but the product of self-serving human artifice (*Defender of Peace* 1.5.2), and wholly severed from the family, which in its turn is not to be thought of as "political".

Apart from complete control of the Church by the state and the removal of the state from morality, from the point of view of Catholic political theory, the principal significance of the *Defender of Peace* is Marsilius' overriding concern for the state's preservation. In this combination we see a forerunner of the contemporary theory of the state as guarantor of a "level playing field" – "natural" behaviour being in and of itself largely outside the moral orbit, related only to economic and other individual needs.

Marsilius also denies any divine source of political authority. Ultimately the source of authority is the people, who invest it in whichever ruler best preserves "peace" and their personal interests. Yet he also rejects out of hand the old Aristotelian notion that ideally the rulers should be the few more politically astute. No-one, he insists, can be trusted not to be corrupted by power (*Defender of Peace* 1.13.5).

From the point of view of our present enquiry, the overall significance of Marsilius is that he marks the beginning of the end of a long period in which

---

[40] Cf. Kempshall, *The Common Good* 354–360.
[41] For a full-scale introduction (to be used with caution) see A. Gewirth, *Marsilius of Padua* (New York 1951): note especially 88, 99, 131, 205, 207, 235.

the concern of Christian thinkers was whether ultimate authority should reside with the Church or with a lay ruler or group of rulers – and with the appropriate limits to be imposed on those two sources of power. Marsilius' solution, whether or not intentionally so, could appear as an apology for political absolutism combined with unreasonable and incoherent assumptions about the non-corruptibility of monarchs or other rulers when handling "spiritual" – and other – matters. As such it is certainly to be discarded, for no Christian should tolerate the Church being reduced to merely the religious office of a civil government. Yet the historical working out of Marsilius' ideas in the Erastian Churches of Protestantism and in the failed "absolutist" reaction of the Catholic Church – to which I shall briefly return later – affords us the opportunity to see what, from the historical experiments and jetsam of the first fourteen hundred or so years of Christian history, can be (and is being) developed into a contemporary Catholic approach to politics: one which avoids past mistakes and necessities while learning better to define the Church's proper role.

5.7 HUMILITY PLUS HUMAN RIGHTS

It is legitimate to ask which parts of a traditional Catholic political and social outlook can and should be maintained in an era where the "basic" question to which I have devoted much of this chapter has become irrelevant. That question was, what is the proper relationship between a "Catholic" state and the Catholic Church? First, and perhaps primarily to be retained, is Augustine's emphasis on the desideratum of humility in Christian politicians or other public figures, and his insistence that in this "darkness of social life" – not least in the necessary suppression of crime – we should all be aware of our own sinfulness, and should derive no complaisant satisfaction in performing actions which, though necessary, are deeply regrettable. For while neither Caesaropapism nor papal theocracy ("political Augustinianism") is a proper development of Augustine's own ideas, his emphasis on humility as a Christian virtue – not least for men of state – was and should have been defended against "Aristotelian" attacks in the Middle Ages.[42]

Medieval society, being both Christian and hierarchically organized, was in many respects ill suited for such an Augustinian disposition. It was not difficult – as the Franciscans in particular emphasized – to advocate

---

[42] For full historical discussion see R. A. Gauthier, *Magnanimité: L'idéal de la grandeur dans la philosophie paienne et la théologie chrétienne* (Paris 1951), esp. 451–465.

humility before God or to argue that ecclesiastical authority should be purely spiritual, but the problem remained of the attitude of the Christian Church and the Christian statesman to ordinary men and women, and a probably misrepresented Aristotle offered an un-Augustinian solution which could easily pass as Augustinian, namely that one can be humble towards God and magnanimous towards men[43] while insisting on one's rights and privileges as conventionally handed down within society: this was to become too attractive to the powerful and too liable to attack by those whose motivation was only partly, and often only minimally, humane.

To understand the theoretical aspects of the problem we must first look at Aristotle himself. In the fourth book of his *Nicomachean Ethics*, emphasizing that the good and magnanimous man must demand neither more nor less than his deserts, Aristotle assumes that the good man's self-estimate will be accurate. It would be an offence against truth, that is, if one evaluated oneself lower than is correct, as much as it would be if one overestimated one's own excellence. Yet in an Augustinian world of weaknesses after the Fall, it is precisely this ability to be honest about oneself that is in question, and a medieval Augustinian was prone to over-correct. Hence, in rejecting Aquinas' "Aristotelianizing" attitude to such difficulties, Bonaventure thinks in terms of a traditional "*contemptus et miseria mundi*" [44] (to use the language of Pope Innocent III), thus "playing safe" and tending to disregard the sparks of virtue that for Augustine remain in fallen man. For Bonaventure, the Thomist attempt to mediate between a proper attitude to God and Aristotle's vision of human magnanimity can only lead to false claims to human autonomy – to something like the position, it might have seemed, of Augustine's old opponent Julian of Eclanum who was willing to speak of man's freedom as entailing a proper "autonomy" in respect to God.

But the difficulty goes deeper. Augustine's position depends on the standard patristic doctrine that man has been created in God's image and likeness, and although that doctrine was never abandoned in the Middle Ages, I have already identified two considerations that militated against its further development: the *contemptus mundi* (marking an extreme Augustinianism) on the one hand and the "Aristotelian" notion of magnanimity on the other. This second factor became of increasing importance during the Renaissance, contributing first to treatises on the dignity of man – one of the earliest examples was by Pico della Mirandola in 1436 – and then to man's elevation to the rank of demi-god (not least, as we have seen, in his role as creator-artist) in the Florentine Academy of which Pico

43 See Gauthier, *Magnanimité* 451–465.   44 Cf. ibid. 480–486.

was a prominent member. The master of that Academy, Marsilio Ficino, addressed humanity: "Know yourself, divine race in mortal dress"!

It is easy with hindsight to portray this development as originally anti-Christian – as eventually in the Enlightenment it became – but in its origins and its purported revival of Neoplatonism (the first manuscript of Plotinus was brought to Italy by Ambrogio Traversari early in the fifteenth century, and 1494 marked the successful completion of Ficino's Latin translation) quite the opposite was the case. Renaisssance Neoplatonism was supposed to free the Church from its enslavement to a decadent scholasticism distinguished only by endless logic-chopping, though its exaltation of man, so far from being an authentic revival of more "humane" attitudes from antiquity (Christian or other), would have been regarded by Plotinus as arrogant over-valuation of man's place in the cosmos: the sort of pride and self-exaltation which ancient Neoplatonists considered "Gnostic" and (later) Christian.[45]

If, however, the new emphasis on man's dignity and quasi-divine status as a creator (not yet as self-creator) posed a threat to traditional but still necessary accounts of the virtue of humility, it contributed substantially to the development of a Catholic response to a peculiarly modern part of social and political ethics: the problem of inalienable human rights. That problem had in the sixteenth century taken on a new urgency in the Catholic world over the rights (indeed the humanity) of the indigenous peoples of America – but it reached centre stage in the newly Protestant states of northern Europe, especially England and Holland. In England the collapse of the Catholic hierarchy and then of the monarchy itself – together with its dependent bishops of the new Anglican communion – was accompanied by the rise of levelling movements of dissent with millenarian beliefs about a return to the happy days "when Adam delved and Eve span" and there were no "gentlemen". When combined with the pride of Renaissance humanism and its more scientific development in England and France, that could generate a demand (which in their very different ways Hobbes and Locke tried to satisfy) for greater emphasis on a well-articulated *theory* to explain why, if *all* humans should enjoy an equal dignity, that dignity (whether or not attributable to God) entails that all possess inalienable human rights.

Concern about human rights as such, however, was no invention or discovery of the early modern period. Its origins stretch back into medieval

---

[45] For a general introduction to the problem of the relationship between ancient Neoplatonism and its Renaissance successor see J. M. Rist, "Plotino, Ficino e noi stessi: Alcuni reflessi etici", *Rivista di filosofia neoscolastica* 86 (1994) 448–467.

times, though less to the world of medieval philosophy than to canon law where, in a twelfth century widely recognized as seeing the growth of various forms of "individualism", canonists needed to argue in detail the rights of popes and emperors to varying but specific degrees of authority.[46] I have already outlined the political working out of some of these "macro-historical" disputes, while for reasons of space neglecting other and less traditionally central instances: the growing concern of lords for their rights against kings, bishops against lords, city guilds against feudal powers. Then, as now, rights-claims are divisive, often even pointing away from the common good in asserting the rights of the individual.

Nevertheless, in our own day official Catholic moral and political teaching sounds less and less "medieval" about rights: one has only to look at chapter three ("The Human Person and Human Rights") of the recent *Compendium of the Social Doctrine of the Catholic Church* (Vatican City 2004). The immediate catalyst of this change has been the developing post-Christian society: there for more than three centuries there has been an endless emphasis on human rights, even of inalienable human rights – and in ever-increasing numbers[47] – though good arguments to establish them have proved elusive and the shadow of Bentham's comment that they are "nonsense on stilts" haunts the desperate and often dishonest debate. In Catholicism, on the other hand, the recently perceived need to *justify* inalienable rights is one major factor behind the renewed interest in the old (and patristically favoured) language of man's creation in the image of God.

Many secular claims encouraged Catholic recognition of this perceived need, but two themes deserve special if brief attention: religious toleration and the historically associated idea of the separation of Church and State.[48] Early modern ideas of religious toleration particularly aimed to allow variant versions of Christianity (though in Protestant states usually not

---

[46] See B. Tierney, *The Idea of Natural Rights: Studies on Natural Rights, Natural Law and Church Law 1150–1625* (Atlanta 1997), who traces much rights-talk (along, of course, with talk of responsibilities which were the preferred subject of philosophers) to the twelfth century. It is a mistake (involving what we can now recognize as a characteristic "Catholic" confusion of the potential with the actual) of many Catholic writers – I earlier cited Finnis' *Aquinas* in this connection – to overestimate the "origins" of rights in Aquinas and other *philosophers* of the medieval period. The very fact that rights-debates were more prominent in canon law than in philosophical texts provides some explanation of why rights *seem* to our contemporaries so undeveloped before the "modern" period. Most of us, even the professional historians of ideas, look in the wrong place.

[47] I have alluded to Hobbes, Locke and the early modern debate, and will do so again, but space is lacking to deal in detail with the question, which in any case has been widely canvassed elsewhere.

[48] For what follows see especially the discussion of S. Schloesser, "Against Forgetting: Memory, History, Vatican II", *TS* 67 (2006) 275–319.

Catholicism) to flourish unhindered. But toleration within Christianity pointed towards toleration of religions beyond Christianity, in the first instance that of the Jews.

Throughout the nineteenth century Catholicism resisted this development, the arguments being that such toleration encourages "indifferentism", that error has no rights and that (as Leo XIII put it) "Justice forbids the State to be godless". The tone had been set by Gregory XVI in *Mirari vos* (1832), which came out strongly against religious liberty; one should be "free" only to believe the truth. Such thinking certainly impeded any recognition in the same period of the merits of democracy – Pius XII in 1945 was the first pope to approve it – since democracy would seem to entail a separation of Church and State and the prospect that "Catholic" states would no longer exist. Especially, however, in opposition to Bismarck, the Church began to recognize that its insistence on the right to be Catholic might entail – at least for pragmatic reasons – a limited toleration of others. Yet the fear of indifferentism stoked a powerfully *intégriste* hostility to Jews and Judaism – especially in France – until the Holocaust, the consequent discrediting of the anti-semites and the end of the Second World War.

Vatican II's documents *Nostra aetate* and *Dignitatis humanae*, with their assertions of respect for Judaism in particular and other religions more broadly, marked the end of an era – and a genuine revolution in Catholic thought on the rights of the person first to live the religion he wished, then to possess a dignity which must imply the right to error. But if religious freedom is to be one of a series of inalienable rights for all, how is the Church to justify it? For the echo of Bentham, we recall, was still telling the secular world that its much-vaunted rights-claims were nonsense on stilts. And if the Church was to admit that it had been mistaken about religious freedom, what were the implications of this further example for theories about the development of an understanding of Catholic doctrine?

Such is the background to the first section of chapter three of the *Compendium of the Social Doctrine of the Catholic Church* – entitled "Creatures in the image of God" – where the *Catechism of the Catholic Church* is cited: "Being in the image of God the human individual possesses the dignity of a person, who is not just something but someone. He is capable of self-knowledge, of self-possession and of freely giving himself and entering into communion with other persons . . ." The term "person" has been treated in an earlier chapter of this book, and will require further examination – not least because it should recall the persisting need for an Augustinian humility as well as for rights-claims – but more immediately we must recognize in the *Catechism* moves to establish that *justification* of rights which secular society has long been seeking.

There is little doubt that within official Catholic teaching it was two encyclicals of Pope John XXIII, *Mater et Magistra* and especially *Pacem in Terris*, which in modern times first unambiguously connected rights (including women's rights, *PT* 41) with man's created dignity, though the connection has more recently been frequently re-emphasized. The ground for it had been prepared by detailed study of the theological emphasis on image and likeness in patristic times by a long series of scholars, the majority of them French. In light, however, of my earlier discussion of the importance of the papacy in the development of Catholic society, the initiative of John XXIII on this particular "cultural" question deserves further attention.

Until recently most basic Catholic doctrine has been formulated in the pronouncements of councils, while the underlying arguments can be discovered in the personal writings of influential churchmen: Irenaeus, Athanasius, Basil, Augustine, Aquinas, Newman, etc. Among these churchmen are occasionally to be found bishops of Rome, above all Leo the Great. The pronouncements of councils, however, and even more those of popes, tend to be prophetic propositions. Yet, as I argued earlier, the views of the see of Rome on doctrinal orthodoxy grew steadily in importance as unity of doctrine became both more urgently important and recognizably harder to achieve – even though the arguments for that orthodoxy were usually developed elsewhere than in Rome.

To some extent that process has intensified as doctrinal development has shifted in recent times from Trinity, Christology and grace to social and generally moral teaching. A good recent example is Paul VI's notorious *Humanae Vitae*, a text whose "prophetic" significance has become clearer as the years pass, and which can be defended by rational arguments, some of the more interesting of which have been proposed *ex post facto*.

If one looks at the *Compendium of the Social Doctrine of the Church*, it is striking that almost all the authorities cited, apart from Scripture, are documents of the last hundred years; indeed a great number are speeches and writings of John Paul II. There are twenty-six (mostly rather obvious) citations of Aquinas, one of Thérèse of Lisieux and a mere fifteen from the whole body of patristic literature. None of these fifteen relates to image and likeness, nor to their possible connection with theories of rights.

On the one hand this reminds us of the role of John XXIII in treating of the connection between man as image and human rights, on the other of the fact that although the Church, especially in its law codes (not to speak of its preaching), has been aware of the problem of rights – not least its own rights – it has found no need to offer much theoretical justification of them. Indeed the manner in which the connection between rights and the image was made by Pope John was, as traditional, that of the prophetic teacher rather than the thinker proposing arguments in support of his position – in this case in favour of the view that only a *theological* defence of rights can save them from Bentham's contemptuous dismissal.

Be that as it may, and discounting the fact that modern papal documents tend only to cite the text of Vatican II, or of personal papal initiatives and material for which the papacy is directly responsible (like the new *Catechism*), one cannot deny that the formalization (as distinct from the origins) of Catholic *social* teaching in general is a comparatively modern phenomenon that has been specifically promoted world-wide from the Roman centre. As the *Compendium* puts it (section 72), "The Church's social doctrine was not initially thought of as an organic system." Indeed the very phrase "social doctrine", though foreshadowed in Leo XIII's *Rerum Novarum* (1891), was popularized only in 1931 by Pius XI in *Quadragesimo Anno* (section 179).

Nor is it an accident – indeed with hindsight it should have been expected – that the process of formalizing "social doctrine" began when two conditions had been met: there was sufficient external challenge to demand a response from the magisterium, and the papacy itself (even if kicking and screaming – not least about the Papal States) had no option but to distance itself from the two social and political scenarios I have been treating in the earlier sections of this chapter: that of being subordinated to a Christian state (and Catholic states were already ceasing to exist), and that of running a Christian society (or a Christian sub-society within a non-Christian state) in a theocratic mode: engrossing, that is, both "spiritual" and "temporal" power.

From the time of the Risorgimento, if not from that of Napoleon or earlier, popes have needed a new "secular" role both for themselves and, insofar as they could achieve or accept this, for the Church which they were in considerable measure still able to control. The opportunity to discover that role – a discovery which is ongoing – was offered by the growth of "post-Christian" ideologies, first in Europe, then in North America, as a result of the Industrial Revolution and its continuations and of their social and economic ramifications.

Since the modern body of Catholic social doctrine thus developed out of external challenges, it is not surprising that it responded first to those it judged to be critical, only later reflecting on the underlying principles of its own development. In this respect the growth of social doctrine from

Leo XIII to the social encyclicals of John XXIII, Paul VI and John Paul II parallels the development of Trinitarian doctrine from the simpler and less excogitated theses of the Council of Nicaea (325) to the more developed Creed of Constantinople (381), backed as it was by a large body of philosophical and theological argument. Thus Leo may be considered the Athanasius of social doctrine, John XXIII and John Paul II its Basil and Gregory Nazienzen.[49] Needless to say, the work is still far from complete, particularly at the theoretical level of harmonizing social and political philosophy with traditionally Catholic metaphysics and philosophy of man. The solution of old problems has ever the knack of generating new.

Leo XIII was far from original in identifying the evil effects of the Industrial Revolution: the greed of the capitalist "bosses" and their neglect of the social effects of their new industries, the new social structures that developed in the industrial towns, the degraded condition of the newly proletarianized work-force, the abuse of women and children, the "labour question" and the demands for unionization. Not only Marx and his followers but several generations of Protestant (later ex-Protestant) reformers who, especially in Britain, worked to abolish the slave-trade, improve conditions in the factories and mines, promote the incipient trades-union movements, preceded him. Yet it was in part fear of Marxist exploitation of the just grievances of the dispossessed that impelled Leo to speak out.

Nevertheless, *Rerum Novarum* – apart from being a prime example of how the Church could be impelled by the good example of others, in this case non-Catholic humanitarians, as well as by the call of the dispossessed and exploited themselves, to draw on its own somewhat neglected resources – was a remarkable document from an organization that had for centuries been viewed as a bulwark of the ancien régime. Its appearance – apart from short-term practical effects – as a document of a highly centralized Church which looked for comparative uniformity of practice and belief could not but promote what Leo probably did not foresee: an understanding of the contemporary social and institutional chaos – and by implication similar brutalizing conditions in the past – as the product not only of acts of evil or misguided individuals but of the evil and self-perpetuating social and political structures that such individuals leave behind them.

---

[49] Much of the best explanatory work on the Trinity, however, was done by the till recently neglected Gregory of Nyssa (brother of Basil). If we seek those who helped supply *justification* for the social teaching of Leo XIII and John XXIII, contemporary parallels to Gregory of Nyssa are available. Much of the work, however, remains "pastoral", lacking in essential intellectual rigour.

It might be supposed that the Church would always have been aware of such things; after all – to mention just one example – not merely Henry VIII but the institutional Church structures which he established (and which sucked many good men into their orbit and from the Catholic point of view corrupted them to a greater or lesser degree) had always been viewed as dangerous and as matter for condemnation. Yet to view the institutions of social life in the same way as those of religious life in that they too can become the source of "systemic injustice" – of what Paul VI called "structures of sin"[50] – required a leap of the imagination.

Catholics now condemn slavery as such; in the past they normally only called on slave-owners to behave decently to their slaves. Yet the fact that with hindsight we recognize "structures of sin" should not blind us to the significance of Pope Paul's formal identification of it: it is said that after the invention of the wheelbarrow people could not believe that they had not been in use for centuries. We are now taught that only by identifying "structures of sin" – systemic injustices – as well as the sins of the individuals who form and continue to promote them (*Compendium* 117) can a "civilization of love" – again the language of Paul VI[51] – be advanced (*Catechism* 2212). John Paul II even spoke of a "communion of sin".[52]

As we have seen, modern Catholic social doctrine, though based on traditional claims in moral theology, only began to take organic form with Leo XIII. Leo's concern with the sufferings of the new urban proletariat, however, was not yet expressed in the language of rights: not least perhaps because, despite its early background in medieval times, especially among the canonists, by the end of the nineteenth century such language was widely considered to be of secular origin and might suggest too much of a compromise with the liberalism and socialism that Leo rejected. And in Pius XI's *Quadragesimo Anno* – followed in 1937 by encyclicals against both the Nazi and the Communist solutions to contemporary economic and social ills – the rejection of both unrestricted competition and "liberalism" in economic and political theory might still indicate that talk of rights rather than only of responsibilities should be avoided. The theological and philosophical ground for such talk was not clearly prepared, or at least was not in the forefront of most Catholic minds. Although, as I have observed, there was much medieval discussion of rights – which became a matter of urgency

---

[50] Cf. John Paul II, *Sollicitudo Rei Socialis* (1988) 36, 37. Credit should be given to earlier contributors in the matter, not least the little-known French Jesuit, Augustinian thinker and victim of Nazism, Yves de Montcheuil. For an introduction to his work see D. Grumett, "Yves de Montcheuil: Action, Justice and the Kingdom in Spiritual Resistance to Nazism", *TS* 68 (2007) 618–641.
[51] Cf. John Paul II, *Centesimus Annus* (1991) 10.   [52] John Paul II, *Reconciliatio et Paenitentia* 16 (1985).

in the sixteenth century – it is necessary to identify how they became central not only in much Western ethics but eventually in a specifically Catholic context.

Pre-modern Catholic discussion of rights always saw them as secondary to duties, while duties were themselves dependent on obedience to the divine law. Hence when modern writers attribute an implicit theory of rights, say to Aquinas, what they should mean is that, because of Aquinas' account of objective duties and justice, one could infer a corresponding subjective right of all human beings as such. Thus we would identify a possible theory of rights, an implicit theory of rights, but no specific emphasis on rights, and certainly nothing approaching the dicta of modern secular theorists like Dworkin that in ethics "rights are trumps" – or parallel bids to regard rights rather than virtue or divine law as the first principle of political ethics. Quite the contrary (and in Kant's view self-servingly), most pre-modern ethical theory properly was concerned with virtue and being virtuous – and, insofar as virtue was directed towards others, it involved doing good to them, treating them rightly rather than respecting their rights. If A has a right, he has a claim on B, and older thinkers (most clearly represented in this case by Aristotle) would suppose that merely restoring what is claimed as due is a very minimalist account of the virtue of justice.

The canonists and their later medieval and modern successors (Marsilius, Ockham, Grotius, Suarez, Vitoria and the rest) are well aware of the distinction between legal rights and natural rights (as well as between passive rights – the right to enjoy protection, for example – and active rights such as the right to use one's talents). Throughout this period legal rights are supposed to depend on natural rights, given under divine law. That situation still pertained in the case of the English Levellers and later of Locke. The novelty of their claims was the *extension* of rights to all and the equalization of rights as against a hierarchical society. For all their social and political radicalism Locke and the Levellers were in many respects carrying further a theoretical process begun by the canonists of the twelfth century.

The more radical theoretical change in modern discussion seems to be twofold, and especially connected with Hobbes and a growing atheism and consequent non-providentialism in the England of the seventeenth and eighteenth centuries. In this period the essentially modern features of the debate about rights emerged clearly: first that rights may be or must be basic in ethics and political theory: that is, that they are at least as important, if not more important, than duties, the pursuit of virtue and responsibilities. And, second, if God, originally in various ways the foundation of rights, is to be removed from the ethical scene, how can one defend any notion of natural, as distinct from positive or legal, rights? It is from that dilemma – how to defend rights without reference to God and transcendent justice – that the modern and apparently endless contemporary debates about rights derive. We want (most of) Locke's conclusions about inalienable rights without Locke's theological or metaphysical premises.

Some have supposed that we can get what we want from Kant's view that man's potentiality for autonomy enables us to infer that human beings should always be treated as ends, never merely as means. But that solution, as I have argued elsewhere,[53] still depends on Christian assumptions that persons as such have value, since, as Hume had already noted, human value cannot merely be inferred from natural or this-worldly characteristics. In other words, Kant has no answer to the challenge of atheists such as Hobbes that we make deals for our "rights" since in principle we are all equally without value. What contemporary *Catholic* thought is beginning to realize is that, with God removed, and the doctrine of man in his image thus ruled out, natural rights theory is indeed indefensible.[54]

By the end of the Second World War, inalienable rights were a constant theme of secular ethics and jurisprudence, though there was no convincing argument on the table to elude Benthamite denunciation. As time passed, all sorts of desperate attempts were offered to get round such difficulties. Though dialectically dubious, inalienable rights seemed obvious, attractive and politically necessary; even utilitarians proposed defences which they just hoped would work.[55]

One of the more interesting, characteristic and widely persuasive strategies – deriving in many respects from medieval times, but without the key medieval assumptions about God and objective justice – was recently reformulated by Alan Gewirth roughly as follows:[56]

1 I do X for end or purpose E.
2 E is good.

---

[53] See Rist, *Real Ethics*.
[54] Much good sense about the secular nature and poor argumentation of most modern rights-theory is to be found in the article of J. A. Henley, "Theology and the Basis of Human Rights", *Scottish Journal of Theology* 39 (1986) 361–378. But though Henley notes (373) that Moltmann points to the Christian heritage of the doctrine of God's image, he seems to think that this suggests that human rights are "swallowed up in the sovereignty of the Creator and so were not in the full sense *human*". That in its turn would seem to suggest that to be in the full sense human entails to be not merely autonomous but to be able to *flourish* independently of the Creator: the position (again) of Julian of Eclanum. Henley, however, is right to point to the eschatological hope which a theory of inalienable rights must entail.
[55] So W. Sumner, *The Moral Foundation of Rights* (Oxford 1987).
[56] A. Gewirth, *The Community of Rights* (London/Chicago 1996) 16–20.

3 My freedom and well-being are necessary goods for action.
   (Since freedom and well-being are the proximate conditions of any
   (moral) agent's acting as such he must accept (3).) Hence
4 I must have freedom and well-being. Hence
5 I have rights to freedom and well-being.

(1) and (2) are fine. (3) is fine so far as it goes. If a (moral) agent is to act as
such, he needs a degree of "well-being" and a certain freedom of action.
(4) however is problematic: it must be reformulated as "If a would-be agent
is to be able to act as such, he must have freedom and well-being." The
problem is that, although such an agent necessarily wants to act, indeed it is
"natural" for him to want to act, there is no logical necessity that he should
be able to do so. And finally the move from unreconstructed (4) to (5) is
therefore improper. The facts that I need freedom and well-being to be able
to act and that I want to act do not entail *per se* that I have the right to
freedom and well-being, even if I live and cannot avoid living in what
I choose to call "moral space". Simply because I want something (even
something that enables me to act in pursuit of what I judge "good") gives
me no "right" to have it. At best it entails that it would be "good" for me (in
some unclear and probably self-serving sense of "good") to have it. It
certainly does not entail that I have any moral right to it.[57]

Here we are back on familiar ground. Intended targets of genocide or
other human rights abuses do not suppose that it is merely convenient (for
themselves or anyone else) that they should not be killed or abused, nor that
their survival intact merely promotes the greatest good of the greatest
number. They believe that it is wrong that they be killed or abused. The
question that secular rights theorists have ever failed to resolve is *why* it is
"wrong". All they can do is argue that it is distressing or inconvenient or
perhaps that we have developed a "merciful" sensibility at the present stage
of some unplanned evolutionary process, or they can just assert it is "morally
wrong" without being able to explain what such a claim could mean.
Following others (not least Elizabeth Anscombe) I argued in *Real Ethics*
that they are merely spending capital derived from a discarded Christian
metaphysics and theology, to which, as atheists or agnostics, or just persons
unwilling to appeal to the role of God in a moral universe, they have no
rational entitlement.

---

[57] A similar critique could be levelled at Martha Nussbaum's defence of (women's) rights. She infers
rights from capabilities in *Women and Human Development: The Capabilities Approach* (Cambridge
2000) 83. For critical comment see J. Porter, *Nature as Reason* (Grand Rapids/Cambridge 2005) 149.

There is a certain excuse for such secular attitudes, and a certain blame to be attached to their Christian critics. Far from pointing to the weakness of secular arguments for rights-claims to which they themselves wished to subscribe, Christians often neglected the concepts within their own mental world that enable an argument for rights to get off the ground. Perhaps they have behaved thus irrationally in the hope that they can show their rivals that on rights at least a common ground can be found not only in practice but also in theory. If so, the manifest failure of secular arguments – of which that of Gewirth is as good an adaptation of early theologically based theories as any – should show that the time has come to recognize that the common theoretical ground is missing, and inalienable rights can be *justified*, as distinct from being *proclaimed*, only by the theist: indeed not even by every kind of theist, as we shall see. Truths about rights may be inscribed on the human heart (Romans 2:15–16); justifications of those truths are not so readily identified. For such justifications, *qua* Christian and *qua* intelligible, will demand an account of a "person" possessed of rights which also entails that persons stand in need of an "Augustinian" humility towards the divine Persons of whom they are an image.

Especially during and after the Second World War, Catholic thinkers began to insist that human rights must be included in their social programme, but they failed to realize that to include them effectively would entail a radical updating of their traditional sources. They needed to show not only that rights-theory is generally compatible, say, with the work of Aquinas (many began to claim that it is already explicit there), but how specifically it could be set within a framework not of modern secular individualism (and eventual choice-theory) but of more traditional accounts of the common good. On the latter of these questions they generally failed to take into account that a wholesale importation of secular ideas about rights could leave them with the same difficulties as the secularists – not the least of which is the difficulty of determining any sort of hierarchy of rights and indeed of distinguishing between legitimate and illegitimate claims. Writers such as Jacques Maritain, in his *Man and the State* (Chicago 1951), led the way, pointing to the need to talk about rights but largely unaware of the problems such ideas might introduce for the coherence of their political and social theory as a whole. Eventually such problems began to be realized, but even now it is widely unrecognized how far rights-talk needs to be "catholicized" before it can be made coherent.

Among modern ecclesiastical documents the two encyclicals of John XXIII, *Mater et Magister* (1961) and especially *Pacem in Terris* (1963), mark the first extended treatment of Catholic social theory in terms of rights as well as duties. As the *Compendium* (95) puts it (somewhat disingenuously in historical terms), "*Pacem in Terris* contains one of the first in-depth reflections on rights on the part of the Church." And Pope John was in no doubt about the missing premiss in secular arguments about rights such as those of Gewirth. Human rights, he emphasized at the outset of *Pacem in Terris* (3), depend on the nature of man as created by God in his image and likeness (Genesis 1:26); in the words of Psalm 8:5–6, God has created him "little less than a god". That theme – though not in Ficino's aberrant version – was soon to be taken up in Vatican II where *Gaudium et Spes* (27) observes that the roots of human rights are to be found in the dignity that belongs to each human being.

5.8 RIGHTS AND PERSONS

Human dignity is sometimes identified as our dignity as "persons", where "person" is a theological term of art. A "person" is frequently understood, even outside theological circles, in terms of the famous attempt at definition offered by the sixth-century thinker Boethius (*Against Eutyches* 3). According to Boethius, "a person is an individual substance of a rational nature".[58] As a definition, however, that does not do justice to the theological (and metaphysical) sense of "person" which I have already discussed in chapter 1. It suggests that human beings (I leave other possible persons aside) are simply to be understood as rational agents. That is satisfactory as a partial *description* – human beings are recognizable as to some degree rational – but not as a *definition*. Metaphysically and theologically, "persons" are not merely rational.

Whatever Boethius himself may have thought, his description is also (at least to modern ears) "value-free". Hence to base human rights-claims on such a description would be to fall into a mistake similar to that of Gewirth and many others since the time of Kant. A "person" may indeed be understood as a rational individual possessed of free will or autonomy (however defectively after the Fall), thought of as the most excellent of human attributes.[59] But pre-modern accounts of a "person" maintain – at least implicitly – that he is further to be viewed as (or as in) the image of a divine "Person",[60] as a "spiritual individual", and hence as sharing in the nature of God himself. More recent discussion has helped to make that thesis explicit.

---

[58] For a similar notion of the *persona* as an individual rational substance in Augustine see P. Burnell, *The Augustinian Person* (Washington 2005) 193.

[59] Cf. *Catechism* 1705.

[60] Cf. *Compendium* 132, 134 (citing *Catechism* 1706), 270, 391 (citing *Catechism* 2212 and *Pacem in Terris*).

The theological concept of a "person" took its earliest form in the second century in certain proposals of Tertullian (*Against Praxeas* 27). Arguing against Praxeas' "monarchian" account of God, in which the terms Father, Son and Spirit merely indicate ways of viewing a "unitarian" Godhead, Tertullian offered the formula that God is "one substance and three persons", using the word *persona* (Greek: *prosopon* – which originally means a theatrical mask) to denote not merely a role which God "plays" but a being with internal substantial relations which "plays" it. Thus it is correct to say not that God the Father (for example) became incarnate, but that God the Son became incarnate.

In the fourth and fifth centuries the notion of *persona* was further developed,[61] both in regard to God and – more immediately our concern, though the two concerns cannot be separated – in regard to man. Christian thinkers began to treat of Persons in relation to the Trinity – there are three "Persons" – but also in relation to the character of the Second Person: Christ, though one Person, has two "natures". It is an extension of such ideas, powerfully developed by Augustine in a letter (137) to a pagan official by name Volusianus, which helps identify a "person" more precisely – though in my discussion in chapter 1 I considered the metaphysical and theological rather than the ethical implications of the theme.

Augustine uses the term *persona* to refer to the inexplicable "blend" of body and soul that constitutes each human being.[62] *Persona* indicates a "mixture" of substantial elements in which neither is swamped by the other. Thus it would be inaccurate to say either that I am just my soul or that I am just my body; I am a soul–body unity. Analogously it would be incorrect to say that Christ is just divine or just human, or that "Father" is merely a way of looking at the "Son" or the "Spirit". In more technical Christological language, Christ is an "unconfused blend" of the divine and the human.

"Persons", therefore, whether human or divine, are relational unities, and insofar as man is in the image of God he is relational both insofar as he cannot be described merely as a soul or as a body and also insofar as he is created as a relating being in "parallel" with the unity of the relating beings

---

[61] The following account is obviously only a summary, and I have not commented on the very substantial contributions made by the Cappadocians to the eventual Chalcedonian formulae.

[62] Cf *Ep.* 169.8, where Augustine speaks of soul–body and (in Christ) Word–man as one *persona*. Although – as noted in chapter 1 – Augustine's view of *persona* fails to answer various philosophical problems about the soul–body relationship, it introduces features of the spiritual nature of man on which hylomorphism by itself has nothing to say. For further comment see Rist, *Augustine* 100–101, where reference to more detailed discussion is to be found: especially to Drobner, *Person-Exegese und Christologie*. For part of the pagan background to *asunchutos henōsis* see Rist, "Pseudo-Ammonius and the Soul–Body Problem".

of the same "substance" who are God. And the Persons of God (imaged by human persons) are constituted not least by their loving (and, with respect to humanity, compassionate) relationships to one another.[63] Underlying this notion of "person" is that of a complex unity, instantiated primarily in God and secondarily in man. It is clear that such a notion is much richer than the Boethian "definition" would suggest and cannot be reduced to it. It is also clear that this greater richness may help resolve difficulties – not least about rights – on which the Boethian "definition" itself has little to contribute.[64]

For if man is just such a "theological" person, it is easy to see how a doctrine of rights can be derived.[65] Man has rights as a "person" precisely because he is godlike; he could have them inalienably in no other way. We may further see from this how important it is that women also are created as persons and of such a godlike nature: that is, parallel to men in their "blend" of female body and soul: a thesis which, as we saw, it has taken long for the Church fully to accept.

It is easy to point out that the Church has always taught that man is created in the image and likeness of God, and to suppose that the medieval scholastics, and especially Aquinas, were fully aware of this – and that, when Las Casas and Vitoria defended the right of the native peoples of America to be treated as human beings and not as "natural slaves", it was to precisely such theology that they were able to appeal. That history, however, does not quite explain John XXIII's linking of rights, persons and the image of God. What does explain it – granted his familiarity with the tradition – is his recognition that the modern concern with rights was a "sign of the times"

---

[63] For compassion see Burnell, *The Augustinian Person* 122, 187 (on *De Trin.* 7.5.10–7.6.11).

[64] It should be noticed that, in the work against Eutyches itself, Boethius is aware of the richer aspects of the notion of *persona*. He knows, for example, of the comparison of the soul–body problem with the problem of the two natures in Christ. And he knows about relations, though his thought was brought to a much greater degree of clarity in the twelfth century by Richard of St. Victor. For a useful introduction to this see E. Peroli, *Essere persona: Alle origini di un'idea tra grecità e cristianesimo* (Brescia 2006), esp. 55–61.

[65] In contemporary debate, other accounts of being a "person" are available to explain why certain human beings (though conceived by human parents and sometimes capable of language) do not qualify as "persons", and thus are not necessarily possessed of rights. Various characteristics of "personhood" may be invoked; perhaps the most popular is that persons must be self-aware, or that they must be capable of making "free" choices. Such variations are primarily developed to justify disallowing rights-claims for the unborn, very young children, the senile or those in a "vegetative state". They are arbitrarily selected for specific social purposes, and can as easily be rejected, depending as they do on arbitrary claims about what makes life "worthwhile" for someone else. Such thinking about personhood often underlies arguments about whether in the past particular individuals or societies have had the concept of a "person": thus C. Gill, "Is There a Concept of Person in Greek Philosophy?", in S. Everson (ed.), *Companions to Ancient Thought 2: Psychology* (Cambridge 1991) 166–194.

and that the doctrine of image and likeness is needed to justify the legitimacy of contemporary claims about human autonomy; further, that *only* if man is by nature "godlike" – oriented towards the good by divine fiat – is it unnatural to deny inalienable rights and correct to hold that such claims about what is unnatural are more than wishful thinking or human aspiration with only human authority behind them, but statements about the will and nature of God the Creator.

Thus what the twentieth century saw was renewed discussion of ancient Christian theories of man as created in God's image and likeness, and thus of his "dignity": a revival of traditional thought of which John XXIII could not have been unaware.[66] But the boldness of his solution, and that of Vatican II which followed, is particularly significant in that it overrode concern about the two notable and opposite threats to which the "image" theory had been exposed since the Middle Ages. During the Renaissance – as I have noted and as I will consider further in the next chapter – man as image was discussed in such terms as to make him appear not merely like a god (the language of the Psalmist) but as a god himself. An inflated Renaissance Neoplatonism recognized the splendour of man's achievements, especially in the realm of artistic production, but, in tending *de facto* (and in some quarters and later *de iure*) to deny the existence of sin and the Fall, it helped revive the alternative danger: a de-humanizing reaction among Protestants and later among Jansenists and suchlike rigorist Catholic groups.

In denying man's divine status, such thinkers rejected not only much of the Renaissance, but in anticipation much of the Enlightenment as well – and did so in exaggerated fashion. The full-blown conclusion of their thinking was Calvin's claim that in the Fall the image and likeness of God have been wholly lost, for which appeal was falsely made to the authority of Augustine, thus striking at the very roots of Catholic theology and culture as it had developed. Hence when John XXIII insisted that even now, after the Fall, man's dignity depends on his creation in God's image – if the image is wholly lost man would indeed be only worthy of Calvinist reprobation, and in saving him God would in effect have to create him anew, thus

---

[66] But neither should anachronistic pictures be drawn: Finnis (*Aquinas* 126) attributes to Aquinas the view that rights indicate what is due to persons formed in God's image and likeness. John XXIII may have subscribed to similarly unhistorical beliefs. Among non-theological writers analogous claims are sometimes to be found for a virtually explicit rights-theory in Aristotle, as in F. R. Miller, *Nature, Justice and Rights in Aristotle's Politics* (Oxford 1995). For objections see R. Kraut, "Are There Natural Rights in Aristotle?", *RM* 49 (1996) 755–774 and M. Schofield, "Sharing in the Constitution", ibid. 831–858.

philosophically separating the "new" and the old human individual – he trod a narrow path between two extreme reactions (and two historically recognizable dangers) in Christian thinking. But in so doing he achieved what otherwise was impossible: to offer justification, via man as in the divine image, for his possession of inalienable rights. Yet since he is only possessed of such rights as an image, he must always remember that he is a fallen image, needing an Augustinian humility. The defence of inalienable rights and the insistence on man's humility in face of God are inseparable one from another.

I conclude by emphasizing two particular features of this Catholic position: first that it demands the theology of the image; second, that it offers no account of itself to be generated by reason alone. If John XXIII and others seem at times to suggest that their thesis is rationally demonstrable to all men of good will, that is not correct: such men may recognize its truth but will be unable to do more than accept that (given God's existence and self-revelation) the Christian claim is logically sound. Without the actuality of those "givens", we are back in a position like that of Gewirth: of a truth in search of a justification.

5.9 POLITICAL STRUCTURES

Finally we return to political structures, and the emergence in modern times of a certain Catholic endorsement, with significant qualifications, of representative democracy. Such a shift seems light-years away from the Caesaropapism and quasi-theocracy which we have seen dominating Catholic political debate in earlier epochs. Twentieth-century thinkers like Jacques Maritain, albeit understandably naively, pointed the way, but the change will appear less total if we think again of Augustine. *Gaudium et Spes* (3) emphasizes that the Church "is inspired by no earthly ambition" – which, though perhaps verbally acceptable to St Bernard or Innocent III, gives a very different emphasis from theirs. The same document insists that the Church favours no particular political system (76), and proclaims that earthly progress towards a "civilization of love" (39) is to be distinguished from the coming of the kingdom of God by its lack of an explicit eschatological dimension: a distinction repeated in more recent papal utterances.

The modest Aristotelianism of Aquinas (but not of Marsilius) has also persisted in the recent emphasis on the sovereignty of the people, though this is to be balanced against an equally repeated (Aristotelian) insistence that the mere will of the majority is no more adequate than that of a monarch or of a minority in determining what is just and right. The

Compendium (407) is emphatic that ethical relativism is a perversion of democracy (though it may dominate the ideology of much contemporary democratic theorizing), and that it tends, via a dictatorship of the majority, to totalitarianism: the language here used is almost that of Talmon in his *Origins of Totalitarian Democracy.*[67]

Again (as in *Compendium* 416) there is an increasing awareness that a democracy can be merely in name – that is, that we may live in a society in which everyone has the right to vote while knowledge of the facts of political life is so closely controlled by the media and by special-interest lobby groups that informed judgments by the public are impossible, democratic choice thus becoming a sham. What this all amounts to is that democracy is the preferred political system as being the most worthy of the aspirations of man – but that it cannot legitimately claim to overturn the truths of the moral order since it is a *means* to human flourishing rather than the *end* of social life. Without recognition of truth, human freedom (as understood in the Christian tradition), justice and "solidarity" (a term promulgated by the Gdansk shipyard revolt and in wide use to mean the social friendship of all properly oriented human beings[68]), merely apparent democratic processes will lead to anti-human ends.[69] In any case, democracy (as the Byzantine imperial system) should not be divinized. Even if it avoids the barbarism of mass taste, it can easily reduce to a cocktail of egalitarianism, ignorance and hedonism: giving opportunity for unrestrained individualism and universal pleasure-seeking rather than a vision of happiness as active engagement and the pursuit of goodness.

As an institution, the Church has now largely withdrawn from attempting to act as a direct political – as distinct from social – agent, but it ever claims spiritual authority with the right and duty to speak out, without fear or favour, on political and social issues: in an Augustinian sense, an authority that calls upon all – not only Christians – to live in the service of "spiritual" goods and their earthly instantiation, so far as possible, in social and political structures. The Augustinian presumption that advocacy of the primacy of the spiritual and of its application to social and political life is to be offered in a spirit of service and with a recognition that all humans, including ourselves, are fallen from their once-created excellence is now regularly re-asserted, though disappointingly the peculiar emphasis on the

---

[67] Harmondsworth 1952.
[68] For a brief history of the concept, with many recent examples, see *Compendium* 194.
[69] The word "democratic" should properly be used to describe a political system in which both the means and the ends are democratic. See chapter 6 for further comment.

humility of the Christian in politics – prominent, as we have seen, in Augustine himself – appears to have slipped out of many contemporary documents and needs to be retrieved and preached as a compulsory part of the story.

One of the causes of change in recent Catholic political thought has been a more sincere acceptance of the distinction between Church and State. It is true that even in the theocratic vision there were allowed to be two separate "swords", but the spiritual "sword" was so viewed as to present a constant threat that the secular would be reduced to a merely executive role. What the Church now claims, in the words of the *Compendium* (426), is "the freedom to express her moral judgment on this [human] reality, whenever it may be required to defend the fundamental rights of the person or the salvation of souls". In that sort of gloss, the political community and the Church are viewed as mutually independent and self-governing.

I conclude that, after all the temptations to earthly power that the Church was offered by Constantine and his successors, it has returned to a position more like that of its Founder. Jesus distinguished what belongs to Caesar from what belongs to God, fully aware that that left him unable to enjoy the congenial lifestyle of the successful power-broker. It is appropriate for an image of God to follow his or her spiritual Master rather than a political master – though this leaves one facing the Augustinian question: what should my attitude be to political structures and to society? I have tried to discern the Church's emerging answer to that question: it is neither quietism nor political manipulation; above all it is a concern with fearlessly telling the truth both about Caesar and about God.

If we have reached a new stage in the relationship between the Catholic Church and national and international bodies, in that relationship the Church claims the moral right to judge the actions of the state when it errs, and to call for rectification. It is legitimate to ask how far the reverse could also be the case and the Church learn from civil society about improving its own internal governance. There is no need for a preference for political democracy to entail a demand for ecclesial democracy – which would be wholly in conflict with Christian traditions going back to the Church's beginnings. That in its turn, however, does not mean that, just as the Church was able to develop its own superior accounts of human rights from observing the development, use and abuse of that concept in historical societies, so certain features of contemporary societies cannot help the Church humbly and integrally to develop its social, political and spiritual role.

As an example it might be argued that in the investigation of heresy a number of obviously just features of civil jurisprudence could be developed further. There is no need for clergy or laity to be investigated without their knowledge, or for them to be unaware for long periods of what precise charges are being brought against them. In this regard there are changes on the horizon that will be considered more generally in my final chapter. Suffice it to say that the ever-increasing role of an educated laity in thinking about the nature of the Church and of Catholic culture – and the corresponding dilution of the role of the clergy – means that new ideas will circulate in Catholic society which cannot so easily be "policed" by ecclesiastical authorities.

To some extent and increasingly, this is already true in philosophy, and one can assume it will be increasingly true in theology as well – if this anti-Augustinian distinction is to be maintained in however mitigated a form, and if theology is eventually to emerge from its current crisis of identity. That could indeed have its advantages: we could be rid of a situation where a licensed clerical teacher is uncertain on which of two stools he wants to sit – is he to teach theology as it has been transmitted or to teach what he thinks should to whatever degree replace it?

An advantage of such a reform would spring from recognition of one of the greatest lacks in contemporary Catholic culture: the lack of a serious knowledge of history among those who teach the tradition. If we do not know what the tradition is, we can neither hand it on nor correct it. And to know that tradition, not least in its social and political aspects, is to know not only where the Church in the past has lived up to its programme, but also where it has not.

If we could come nearer to this happy stage of understanding our own past, we would have no time for the anti-intellectualism – indeed the lack of concern for truth – which in the early part of this chapter we observed in the "golden mouth" of Chrysostom. That would look like a cul-de-sac from which we have escaped – though in this "darkness of social life" there will always be those longing to return to it, and who will argue that all thought is culturally driven sophistry – forgetting what Plato in particular should have taught us: that "much" does not mean "all".

Anti-intellectualism is a peculiar danger for the contemporary Church. It has flourished under periods of Caesaropapism as well as those of would-be theocracy, and the advocates of those systems often have preferred it to flourish. Now that Catholic social teaching has begun to define its transcendence over transient forms of social order, it is further able to draw attention to the dangers of an anti-intellectual democracy: that is, a democracy where the half-educated (or half-uneducated) control access to most information. In extending such criticism the Church can exercise a more soundly based influence over human beings aware of their human dignity and its origins than could have been dreamed of in more authoritarian times. It is the job of the Church not to depose political criminals, but rather to maintain its right to denounce their actions as criminal and where appropriate to excommunicate. But we should not deceive ourselves on that matter either; its judgments, not least if governed by either a residual clericalism or a new-fangled admiration for secular success, may often be fallacious. Such spectres will haunt the remaining pages of this book.

CHAPTER 6

The Catholic Church in "modern" and "post-modern" culture

There is a bit of everything in everything.

Anaxagoras

6.1 WHERE THE HELL ARE WE NOW?

By the end of the Middle Ages Western Christian thought and culture had been growing for more than two thousand years. Much of its metaphysical underpinning derives from Greek philosophy as it developed since before the time of Socrates. The structure that still existed, in all its essentials, in the year 1450 – though constantly shaken, especially in its political manifestations – seemed to most Europeans the permanent face of humanity as understood in Christian terms. Yet within the next two hundred years the foundations of an alternative culture were being laid, often unbeknown to its architects: a culture which, in Europe and still much influenced by Christian origins which as yet it was uninclined to deny, was to become first the rival, later the successor of Christianity as the apparently dominant mode of human perception. In earlier chapters I noticed some of the political, social, ethical and aesthetic effects of this new culture. In the present chapter I want to look at some of its principal anti-Catholic features before considering what attitude Catholicism has taken and should take towards it. Over the last five hundred years during which anti-Christianity was still comparatively weak even where anti-Catholicism was strong, the Catholic Church has been on the defensive. In our own times, in view of the call by John XXIII and the Second Vatican Council for an *aggiornamento*, an updating of the Church to confront the contemporary and secular anti-Catholic culture, what are we to expect?

Two possible avenues are open, of which is neither is satisfactory. Some advocate what amounts to a radical abandonment of tradition in order to make the Church "acceptable" or "relevant". Such a call would only be tenable if the *raison d'être* of the Catholic Church should bear no relationship to objective truth, but to a subjectivism dependent on the wishes and aspirations, whether traditionally moral or immoral, of each age. The other road, followed in various versions since the Reformation, is to retain a purely defensive and "traditionist" posture, ultimately amounting to a denial of the intellect and a conviction that we have no further truth into which to be led. In view of what the Church has learned – some of it documented in the present study – from outside itself (as well as from those who temporally came before it) this seems as implausible as unattractive.

If neither of these solutions is desirable, what we need is a better understanding of the forces confronting us for, unless we understand the main features of modern and post-modern anti-Christianity, we shall be unable to evaluate them, unable to know when we should learn, when we should go on the defensive, and when we can be sure – as I have argued is already the case with human rights – that we already have a much superior programme demanding no denial of significant parts of human experience.

At the centre of the debate is the "God-question", and first a caveat: God – of some sort or sorts – is very much alive outside the "progressive circles" of Europe and North America, and the future of Catholicism is far from merely a matter of the ideological or religious fate of Europe and the United States. Nevertheless, there is little reason to believe that the alternative secular Western culture, not least because of the power and attractiveness of its science and technology which seem to promote not merely more satisfactory health and comfort but a more hedonistic – especially in sexual choices – *dolce vita*, will not continue to provide the most substantive, perhaps the only viable, challenge to Catholic Christianity. And if that Catholic Christianity is to be overwhelmed in many parts of the world besides Europe by another and far more militant religion, Islam, that will be thanks in no small measure to the use that religion can make of Western anti-Christian ideology in combination with the weapons of war or terrorism which are the product of Western scientific development, as well as to the self-indulgent defeatism and self-abasement previously displayed in European confrontations with Hitler and Stalin, and also – among those few who took him seriously – with that even more successful mass murderer, Mao Tse Tung.

6.2 FROM THE RENAISSANCE AND REFORMATION TO SCIENCE AND SCIENTISM

If we go back to the year 1450, the Christian God, understood in terms of Catholic metaphysics and theology, seemed secure, and man was understood in relation to him. That largely homogeneous Christian society, within the parameters of which, we remember, the philosophical synthesis of Thomas Aquinas was developed, was soon to fragment, losing in the process many of its key elements. Some of that fragmentation has been treated in the present essay; I shall now attempt something of a précis of the effects produced, first on accounts of God, then of his universe and particularly of man, by the Renaissance and the Reformation. That will enable us to recognize some of the foundation blocks of modern and post-modern culture.

Many of the revolutionary developments of the new spirit derived from over-correction of the Catholic past. I have alluded to an important example: the growth of the idea of the splendour and dignity of man, as recognized in his powers as a creative artist fully aware of the significance of physical beauty – not least of the human body – led philosophy to an unconscious re-writing of some of the Neoplatonic roots of Augustinian Christianity. Now the near-worship of man's creativity was seen as part of a Neoplatonic replacement for a dreary scholasticism. By ancient Neoplatonists, pagan even more than Christian, that near-worship would have been dismissed as "Gnostic" arrogance, an attempt to identify man too closely with God. If man is seen as a god, what place for God? Put extremely, we have a move from the excessive debasement of fallen man to his exaltation to a degree which could soon make God redundant. That was far from the intentions of Marsilio Ficino and his friends in the Florentine Academy who did not foresee what, in the absence of God, has been styled the "Promethean humanism" which gained ascendency with the ideologies of the nineteenth century.

When we turn to the Reformation, there is a curiously parallel development. Luther disliked what he thought of as the neo-paganism of the Roman Church, and also rejected its supposed (and sometimes actual) Pelagianism. (As any preacher should be aware, "Pelagianism", the attributing of man's moral success to his own efforts rather than to God, is an ever-present challenge.) In that sense (and besides his more professed aim of going back to the Bible and the Fathers) Luther was rejecting the vision of the Christian humanists of the Renaissance in favour of the harsher, more Augustinian view of man preached by St Bernard and Pope Innocent III. The strongly iconoclastic tendencies of the Reform movement may be seen as part of the same trend.

Perhaps more immediately relevant are two other Reformation emphases: the revised versions of the doctrine of predestination by which God has ordained at his good pleasure the fate of individuals, consigning them to hell or heaven, before the formation of the world; and the characterization of Christianity as a religion "of the Book" by the doctrine of "Scripture alone". These two doctrines in combination, though intended by their preachers to reinforce and therefore perpetuate true Christianity, had the opposite effect, when in time the denial of predestination and the dissolution of Scripture by historical scholarship would be major factors in the construction of an anti-Christian counter-culture that became the "culture" of modern and post-modern society. As with the Neoplatonizing Christianity of the Renaissance at the other end of the theological spectrum, so this outcome was far from what Luther and Calvin would have wished. They did not foresee how their movement, blending with the new science, mainly developing in Protestant states, was to become "scientific" or "empirical" humanism.

Thus the Reformation was no mere revolution in theology and the success of Evangelical and Reformed theology was far from solely due to its own merits or intellectual and religious attractiveness, nor to revulsion against Romish worldliness, paganism or the abuse of "indulgences". Just as the effects of the new theology were to fragment Western Christianity at the theoretical level, so its advocacy – often self-serving – by kings and princes became a source of political division. The old battles between "theocracy" and "Caesaropapism" took on new form with the Erastian state in England and the dictatorship of the presbyters at Geneva, while the combination of political and religious fragmentation meant in effect that religion would be subordinated to the state (*"cuius regio eius religio"*): a principle that continued to flourish even when the state had become non-Christian and "secular". In such régimes, as we have seen, pressure has mounted to render Christianity itself first private, then marginal.

"Scripture alone", a more basic Protestant doctrine than predestination, seems likely to outlast most of the "mainline" Protestant churches and in the long run has done more harm to Christianity. There was now effectively no place for natural theology. Scriptural exegesis and explication were to replace metaphysics, often imagined to have been a substitute for biblical reflection; a reconstructed Jerome was to replace Augustine. Preaching was to replace the sacraments as the heart of Christianity and church furniture was re-arranged accordingly.

The sting in the tail, however, was provided by exegesis itself, leading both to multiple interpretations of biblical texts (each one self-evident to its interpreter) and eventually, with the nineteenth-century application of historical-critical methods to Scripture, to the discrediting of the Bible as a historical authority, and with it an undercutting of the ultimate basis for Protestant ecclesiology – though biblicist fundamentalism remained as a popular option, necessarily based on historical ignorance.

The danger could have been perceived in the days of Luther himself, who prided himself as an exegete but supposed that if the Bible were translated into vernacular languages – as he himself translated it into German – the ordinary, even unlettered Christian could readily understand it, with no priestly mediator. Yet when others, not least his immediate rival, Zwingli – to say nothing of the "fanatical spirits" in the Anabaptist wing of the Reform – interpreted the sacred texts in a way that differed from his own, he could only explain it in terms of wilful stupidity, "popish" prejudice or diabolical inspiration. It became clear that though a Church-authorized approach to the Scriptures might be at times in error, it at least ensured an approximately uniform version of the faith. When interpretation was carried forward with little or no respect for the authoritative version and the mainline Protestant groups set themselves up so far as they could as new authorities, it was inevitable Christianity would fragment indefinitely, with a corresponding loss of authority in the increasingly secular society.

One might have supposed with many of its first adherents that the coming of new authority in the form of the historical-critical method would have pointed to a new and more learned uniformity: that in religion too "science" would replace "myth"; yet the sceptical aspects of the movement, when combined with a tendency to wishful thinking inducing special-interest groups to read into the texts whatever they wanted to find, rendered such hopes illusory in a society that had lost almost all contact with the ancient world where Christianity began and either knew nothing of the historical Jesus or remade him in its own image when the historical data were unavailable or easy to invent or misread.

As for predestination, the second major aspect of Protestantism to which I have drawn attention, the ultimate damage was less severe and of a different nature, but for all that substantial. Already in the early seventeenth century a "heretical" group of Calvinists was outlawed by the Synod of Dordrecht for disowning "double" predestination – which, it must be allowed, has often given huge confidence to those facing hard times while recognizing themselves as among the elect. But the increasing "moralizing" of Christianity – due partly to the disillusioning effects of the Wars of Religion, partly to the decline of metaphysics, partly to a desire to find a more tolerant God and a more tolerant society – led to the indictment of the God of predestination on moral grounds: does it make sense to suppose that God damns people before the creation of the world, through no foreseen fault of their own?

Some, in irrational terror, sought refuge from such fears in suicide and others were driven mad; yet others merely lost confidence in a God whose moral characteristics did not add up. A further growing suspicion that the doctrine of hell was not easily to be squared with a compassionate God made predestination all the more problematic. If hell, and above all predestination (understood in the Calvinist sense) were what Christianity is about, then there were, it seemed, moral objections to religion itself. At a time when "Promethean man" was beginning to emerge (originally in beneficent form, like Prometheus himself, not yet beyond good and evil), moral objections to God – in comparison with exalted man – were calculated to promote atheism and agnosticism. It is not surprising that the revulsion against Christianity in many formerly Calvinist countries (for example Scotland) has been angry and bitter.[1]

As the old Christian metaphysics, and eventually the old Christian Bible, disappeared from the modern world, the new man of Renaissance fantasies would soon be equipped with scientific and technological dreams to take their place. And since metaphysics is no immediate empirical help to scientists, the growing prestige and success of the new science has contributed to pushing us towards a world where metaphysics has no longer to be repudiated but can be safely ignored, with few to feel the loss.

It is not only in Protestant countries that the virtual disappearance of metaphysics, entraining further erosion of any sense of the transcendent, has occurred. Some of the greatest advances in early modern science took place in Catholic countries – one thinks particularly of the Polish Copernicus and the Florentine Galileo – but because of the Church's failure rapidly to come to grips with the new discoveries scientific and technological development proceeded faster in Protestant states. Gradually, however, the new science spread throughout the Western world, bringing with it its apparently anti-metaphysical, anti-transcendental implications. If God for some had become morally disreputable, in the eyes of others he became an obstruction to scientific progress – and not yet because he might seem to place *ethical* restraints on certain forms of enquiry. The radical separation in the seventeenth and eighteenth centuries of what was left of metaphysics from that "scientific" enquiry manifested itself in the abandonment of such questions as "What is this for?", "Why are things here?" which point to God's nature as final cause. Instead the more "immanentist" question "How does this function?" became a major impetus to the tremendous advances in what was coming to be known simply as "science".

There is a certain parallel between the sad results of the hesitations of the Church to embrace the celebration of beauty and those of its catastrophic blunder – not least in lasting "PR" effects – over the heliocentric theory of Copernicus and the consequent condemnation of Galileo. In both cases

---

[1] The same might be said of the reaction to "Catholic Calvinism" (i.e., Jansenism or some less educated equivalent) in France (and even more in Québec) and in Ireland.

no small part of the problem was caused by biblical literalism: in that of Galileo because of a failure to determine the scope of the biblical text.[2] Galileo himself claimed, both in a letter to Grand Duchess Cristina and in his defence of *Two Chief World Systems* before the Roman Inquisition, that the subject-matter of the Bible and of scientific enquiry is distinct – though he himself muddied the waters by concluding, as a good Catholic, that if the results of scientific enquiry contradicted the Scriptures, faith must prevail.

What he needed, in effect, was that the approach to apparently "scientific" material in the Bible should be analogous to that which, since patristic times, had been followed in treating apparently "immoral" or "unworthy" texts, especially from the Old Testament: passages such as those describing Abraham lending out his wife and Lot offering his daughters to the Sodomites to protect his guests – or showing the unchangeable God getting angry. But Galileo did not express himself like that, contenting himself with arguing that the Bible does not teach science but the road to salvation. Yet, without an explanation as to how inadequate "scientific" passages got into the text and a proposal as to how they should be handled, his case looked far from convincing.

For the difficulty is lack of clarity about what precisely the Scriptures are intended to teach. Psalm 103:5, for example, proclaims that God fixed the earth for ever, and Duchess Cristina knew that Joshua had ordered the sun to stand still – implying that it was previously in motion – and on the basis of such texts it looks easy to "show" that the heliocentric theory conflicts with the Bible, as Galileo's adversaries were quick to point out. It is worth noticing that even in 1893, when in his encyclical *Providentissimus Deus* Pope Leo XIII made proposals similar to those of Galileo about the separate subject-matter of science and biblical revelation, the fuzziness was still there; it is helpful to point to the different areas of competence of the scientist and the biblical author only if we know what specific competence the biblical author has and what should be done with texts that seem to exceed that competence. If the biblical author has a literal inerrancy, the scientist (or the historian) stands condemned; if not, we need a principled account of wherein his competence – *scilicet* for the salvation of souls – actually lies.

Not Leo XIII in 1893; only with Pius XII in *Divino afflante spiritu* (1943) does the magisterium of the Catholic Church seem to have grasped this. Pius understood the nature of the authority of the Bible in terms of the

---

[2] Protestants too had their own potentially anti-scientific literalists; in 1650–1654 the fanatically anti-Catholic Archbishop Ussher argued for the creation of the world in 4004 BC on the basis of adding up the ages of the Old Testament patriarchs. He had, however, less opportunity than the Roman Inquisition and the Congregation of the Index to enforce his views.

circumstances of composition – thus in effect separating the Old from the New Testament – and more generally concerned himself with the *context* in which scriptural texts were composed. But by 1943 failure to recognize in particular the historical *growth*, in the Old Testament, of man's understanding of God's word had already led to the problems that had arisen about Galileo rearing their heads once more in the case of Darwin.

What a theologian is qualified to say about science is not that scientific knowledge – so far as we can achieve it – in apparent contradiction to Scripture is false, but that an understanding of Scripture (and by the same token of Church tradition) may tell us that certain methods of acquiring scientific knowledge (as well as the pursuit of certain scientific goals) are immoral: in other words, a judgment of value, not of fact. Here again we note a parallel with the story of the Church and art. The Church has learned to accept artistic representation of, say, the life of a prostitute on stage or screen, but would be justified in objecting to the role being played by a fourteen-year-old girl.

Contrary to much seventeenth- and eighteenth-century belief, there is no necessary conflict between science and metaphysics – many great scientists (Aristotle, Galen, Descartes, Leibniz, Whitehead, etc.) have also been metaphysicians – but there is necessary conflict between Catholicism and a *philosophy* of science that claims that the *only* mechanism for clear thinking is the scientific method and that methodologies that cannot be reduced to logic, mathematics and empiricism are of no value. Of this claim it should first be noticed that it is itself not a "scientific" claim of this order; thus rationally speaking it is self-refuting. But to disprove it at the intellectual level is far from defeating it at the level of social acceptability. And we should notice that it appeared in different but also recognizably similar versions both in France (and hence in "continental" philosophy) in the positivists and Auguste Comte, and (later) in extreme versions of Anglo-Saxon "verificationism".

Comte, who coined the term "sociology" and expected the study of the community to be carried out "scientifically", thus greatly encouraged the use of the impersonal methods of the hard sciences as a substitute for metaphysics, with all the Procrustean reductionism that such an approach must imply. In the Anglo-Saxon world, the importation of logical positivism from Vienna in the 1930s by such as A. J. Ayer combined with cruder versions of Humean empiricism to influence the intellectual mentality of the age.

It is true in philosophy as a whole that, while virtually no philosophical claims have been definitively defeated, they have regularly disappeared from societies (usually to re-emerge later) that did not want to know about them, or preferred to write them off as irrelevant or obscurantist. Hence, while philosophers of science have failed to show why the empirical and experimental methods of modern science are valid for every intellectual enquiry, that has little effect on a populace that gapes in awe at some scientific discovery and inclines to the near-worship of a practitioner whose work promises to make their personal lives more comfortable through advances in computer technology, medicine or birth control. All that will check such adulation – and women will throw themselves at scientists with almost the same readiness as at soccer-players or other "celebrities" – is when some wonder-drug turns out to have unhappy side effects: as, pregnancy sickness is lessened but thalidomide babies are born.

Two further effects of the concepts of the scientific revolution on the mentality of the modern world must be noted: their dependence (even in ultra-mathematical form) on being formulated as clear and distinct ideas, with clear and distinct relationship to "truth"; and their "analytical" nature – this point is closely linked with the supposed demise of metaphysics – which permits us to speak of the structure and composition of substances but not of their nature as a whole. Of course, some would dissolve any possible problem here by claiming that, beyond the analysis of an object's structure, there is nothing further to be said: we, and everything else, are the exact sum of our parts – except insofar as we can be considered part of some larger structure. Of what is beyond the scientific universe, as Wittgenstein seemed to put it (however ambiguously), there is nothing to be said, and so we must be silent.

The demand for purely analytic reflection on reality marks a striking alteration in the traditional understanding of cognition. In ancient and medieval times philosophers always made a distinction between discursive reasoning and an intuitive grasp not only of individual objects seen "as a whole", but of the universe as a whole. Although such notions were common-place in earlier ages, the third-century philosopher Plotinus is recognized as one of their clearest exponents: he distinguishes between *logismos* (discursive reasoning) and *nous* (immediate apprehension) and urges those in pursuit of a "higher" spiritual life to "see it whole" (*Ennead* 5.5.10.10; 6.7.34.35).[3] Only by such immediate grasp can the nature of an object and its status in the universe be possibly recognized – as more, that is, than as a "cog in a machine". It is strange that this form of cognition has lost its prestige in contemporary

---

[3] Typical of the "modern" mood is the debate about whether "non-discursive" thought among the ancients is "paradoxical": see A. C. Lloyd, "Non-Discursive Thought – an Enigma of Greek Philosophy", *PAS* 70 (1969) 261–274, also "Non-Propositional Thought in Plotinus", *Phronesis* 31 (1986) 258–265; R. Sorabji, "Myths about Non-Propositional Thought", in M. Nussbaum and M. Schofield (eds.), *Language and Logos: Studies in Greek Philosophy Presented to G. E. L. Owen* (Cambridge 1984) 295–314. The root of the disagreement lies in the question whether all "thought" is propositional: which if true would probably imply that poetry is not thought at all.

philosophical fashion, since it denotes an activity in which we engage every day, not least in our personal relations.

If I say I know a friend F, I do not imply that F is merely the sum of his qualities. Perhaps I cannot grasp what it is that makes F attractive to me, but I would reject out of hand any suggestion that a, b, c, etc. are all there is to F. And the implications of rejecting "holistic" approaches in philosophy are serious: they lead us to suppose not just that F cannot be "grasped", but that there is simply no point in asking what F is for, but all objects and states in the world are simply "brute facts". And yet that is a mere assertion. The only reason one might suppose it to be true is if one held that all genuine thought is analytic: hence one can legitimately ask what Frank's arm is for, but not what Frank is for. To claim that is not merely to claim that we do not or cannot know what Frank is for; it is to claim that the question "What is Frank for?" is a non-question. Were that to be the case, the religious answer, "To proclaim the glory of God," would be simple nonsense, and any religious claim about the providential ordering of the cosmos meaningless and absurd.

Thus the identifying of analytic thinking with thinking in general, which in its extreme form is a mark of "modern" culture, is in clear contradiction with the possibility of a religious explanation of the universe and any traditionally "spiritual" variety of human "cognition". But such analytic accounts of the world are challenged by key moves both within analytic philosophy itself and in "post-modernism": the latter a phrase I have as yet left undefined.

The "analytic" objection is associated particularly with Saul Kripke:[4] it introduces the term "rigid designators" to indicate that words may be intelligibly used with particular kinds of reference in fixed contexts. Thus, I may use the word "iron" with or without particular understandings of iron. I may or may not know its molecular composition, for example, but either way I may, in the relevant circumstances, be able to make it clear what I am talking about when I use the word "iron". If we apply such ideas to what scientists are doing when they identify, say, the chemical components of a human being, we need in no way be tempted to suppose that when I, as a layman, say "F is a human being," I mean that I know either his chemical make-up or any other scientific fact about him. I may merely want to indicate that I like him or that he might be identified as being my father. In other words analytic data (of whatever kind) about a subject can offer no answer, whether positive or negative, to the apparently reasonable questions, "What is F, all in all?", or "Is that all there is to be said about F?"

---

[4] Cf. S. K. Kripke, *Naming and Necessity* (Oxford 1980).

When turning to "post-modernist" observations on this theme, I want to prescind from the question of whether all propositions (even scientific ones) are "really" some form of power-play. What is of more interest is the claim that one can understand a question only if one understands why it is asked; which would at least imply that there could be other comments on the facts (or objects) in question that have not been introduced into the frame of discussion being undertaken. What is important about this is not the claim that a question can only be answered if one knows why it has been asked, but that we again meet the notion of the incompleteness of any specific form of intellectual (including scientific) investigation. Needless to say there is no reason to follow those "post-modernists" who want to infer from such incompleteness that there is no such thing as truth, for truth might (and often appears to) pertain independently of our ability to discern it.

If we now turn to the second of the characteristics of the scientific mentality to which I drew attention, the need for "true" propositions to be expressed in clear and distinct ideas, much less need be said. Except that if those clear and distinct ideas are, as they must be in science, applied to the experimental verification of hypotheses, then such a mentality will tend to be more comfortable with godlessness. I do not mean that scientists are necessarily godless; indeed the reverse is often the case. But scientists may often be satisfied with a rather ill-thought-out notion of God; they direct their intellectual energies elsewhere. What I mean is that, if verificationism is applied, for example, to the possible workings of providence, then providence must seem uncertain.

I am not merely thinking of the extreme forms of what is now called "verificationism", whereby all propositions that cannot be empirically tested are held to be uninteresting. Rather, I note that throughout his *Confessions*, for example, Augustine sees himself as drawn, at times much against his will, in a "noble" direction which he is able to recognize only by hindsight. He himself would attribute this to providence; others would object either that this is to introduce a further cause in defiance of Occam's Razor (explanatory factors are not to be multiplied beyond sufficiency) or that it is hard to demonstrate that providence (rather than chance or happenstance) is at work.

6.3 ANTI-PERSONALISM

One of the features of empirical and experimental science that contributes to godlessness in modern society is its impersonalism; science – and for Comte and his successors social science – necessarily works by measurement and in general terms. The scientific aim is to show that everything we properly call water is H_2O. It aims to understand the sort of things things are: human beings like all else. It considers the ("normal") human belly, not the belly of JMR *qua* unique. In medicine it applies these generalized norms to particular cases; thus if the surgeon wishes to operate on (and normalize) the belly of JMR, he does so with reference to the knowledge he has acquired of bellies in general. The patient is related to a list of similar patients.

Such a necessary mentality can have nothing to say (unless perhaps that certain features are "normal" or "abnormal") about the belly of JMR *qua* belly of JMR. Any claim to personal uniqueness is irrelevant to the kind of knowledge medical science is able to deploy or to discover. But a development of the idea of a person, namely as a unique member of the species man – earlier identified as an individual substance of a rational nature – has been a mark of recent Catholic social thought, being based on fundamental propositions about each man being created in the image of God. Indeed, this understanding of a human person is derived from the notion that we are each an image of God in the special relational form of the divine Persons of the Trinity.[5]

The weakness of the "purely" scientific approach I am trying to pin down can be seen in the well-known "philosophical" question of whether the average patient would prefer to be looked after by a duty-driven or by a love-driven nurse – given that their scientific skills are equal. The question was originally posed in criticism of Kantian morality and it serves to bring together three anti-Christian features of "modern" thought. First there is the hostility to metaphysics and transcendence: much "professional" rejection of traditional metaphysics depends on Kant's view that it relies on an indefensible objectivism, not least about the existence of God. Then there is the attempt to develop a rational morality without reference to such transcendence, but based exclusively on the notion of man as a rational animal. Finally there are the consequent "impersonal" features of such a reductionist view of human nature which – QED – tailor it to the "scientific" and "empiricist" presuppositions I have identified, enabling it to be manipulated like any other object.

Kant's moral theory fails not least because he is unable properly to justify the claim that human beings should be treated as ends and not as mere means. His defence of it smuggles in the Christian view that persons *qua* persons are

---

[5] I have already noted the fourth- and fifth-century origins of these ideas, and the role in their development played by such as Gregory of Nyssa and Augustine – the latter at least looking back to the erratic genius of Tertullian. The growth of modern Catholic developments of "personalism" was greatly influenced by non-Christian thinkers such as Martin Buber and Max Scheler.

of value, but his attempt to justify it falls foul of Hume's objection that statements of value cannot be derived from statements of fact: in this case the "fact" that humans are rational.

The assumption that rationality is intrinsically "valuable" falls foul of a similar objection. "Scientifically", to be rational or not is a brute fact with no implications as to value that in a world of brute facts has no place. In any case, since humans are not equally rational, humanity cannot therefore be described simply as rational, or, if perfect rationality is made the standard valuable.[6] Finally it is interesting to note that, where in "continental" philosophy there have been attempts to revive a form of metaphysics with a largely Kantian framework setting the parameters within which such questions may be discussed, there has been a marked tendency to reduce the importance of the "personal": as I have noted, while Hegel – who subverted Aristotle's view that human beings are naturally social by the similar-seeming claim that without society human beings would not be human – was yet still willing to talk (albeit more or less immanently and perhaps inconsistently) of Spirit, Heidegger preferred a more unambiguously impersonal mode well suited to his moral "neutrality" (to use no harsher term).[7]

Thus the "continental" reaction to Kant has (perhaps necessarily) moved in the same impersonalizing direction as the more empirical world of Anglo-American thought, where already in the seventeenth century the writing was on the wall in the reformulation of traditional natural law – increasingly since Grotius seen as merely a version in human beings of patterns to be observed in non-human nature – which certainly made it easy for Hume. It has been insufficiently observed, not only that Grotius' "*Etsi Deus non daretur*..."[8] is an attempt to argue that the obligations of natural law can be found even in a scientific context from which at least a transcendent God has been removed (though perhaps a shadow of "Stoic" vitalism survived in the newly mechanistic science), but also that God's removal set in train the elimination of special significance from the human person.

I observed in chapter 3 how in a wider cultural setting all such impersonalizing moves not only eviscerate morality but render the search for aesthetic beauty redundant. Modern political ideologies also are impersonal, so we should not be surprised to find "Socialist realism" displaying the

---

[6] These matters are discussed in more detail (*inter alia*) in Rist, *Real Ethics* 173.
[7] For helpful comment on the related "amorality" of Heidegger see A. MacIntyre, *Sartre: A Collection of Critical Essays* (New York 1971) 26.
[8] *On the Law of War and Peace*, prolegomena, paragraph 11.

same banality as its Nazi counterpart. Many have seen the same effect in Western consumerist art.[9]

I conclude that contemporary anti-personalism represents both a failure and a consummation of the Enlightenment project. I have already suggested that Enlightenment ideas of freedom and autonomy – including autonomy from God – are themselves extensions of the individualism, the cult of the "divine man", that flourished in the Renaissance, to be continued in the Enlightenment, culminating perhaps in Kant's worship of genius. Politically it failed, and the replacement of the noble individual by the General Will of the mass – foreshadowed by Rousseau – took on a lethal aspect with the tyranny of the Jacobins, followed by the dictatorship of Napoleon – and similar movements developed elsewhere in the Europe of the nineteenth and twentieth centuries.

While the ideal of the Renaissance and many of its Enlightenment successors was personal freedom, one of the more lasting social effects of such views can be seen in the worship no longer of the individual man, but of Man or of "Society". Thus a spurious love of Humanity came widely to replace love of men as individuals – a love of Humanity so liable to abuse by power-hungry politicians and money-grubbing advertisers as to make words like freedom regularly obscene. *Arbeit macht frei* read the grandiose slogan that welcomed the victims to Auschwitz; "freedom of choice" is the slogan of about every contemporary Western political party. The former pretends to promote a renewed humanity; the latter represents the economic if not the political manipulation of the mass by what *ceteris paribus* can still be regarded as vanguard-groups. Hobbes' struggle of all against all has emerged in a revived form as the struggle between such groups all the way to declarations of enforced bankruptcy – all such struggles being rhetorically justified as dedicated to the good of (impersonal) Man the Consumer.

6.4 HUMANISM OR NIHILISM

In recent sections of this book I have perhaps seemed to shift without due concern from the "modern" to the "post-modern" world. I do not wish to diminish the significance of the "post-modern" turn, by which I primarily refer to the rejection (often under the influence of Nietzsche) of "Cartesian" objectivism: rejection, that is, of the search for objectively clear and distinct ideas whereby to govern the way we live and think, in favour of the imperative constantly to "unmask" the "real" motives of human acts, at

---

[9] The satirically inclined reader may consult *Private Eye*'s "Young British Artists" strip-cartoons.

the same time recognizing that the process is endless and that "truth" cannot be found – least of all in the scientific wisdom and learned compilations to which the nineteenth century was addicted.[10]

Nevertheless, for present purposes there is good reason to treat modern and post-modern ideas together, since although, as I have observed, they are distinct, they circulate together as part of the mental furniture of individuals in Western society and as part of a wider mélange of ideas from disparate sources, which, if we think about them, we can recognize are incompatible. Indeed it is worth recalling that it is not only the unsophisticated who act "irrationally" in such matters. If a thinker dislikes the views of an opponent, he may offer a battery of opposing arguments incompatible one with another; an oft-quoted early example was the Epicurean Lucretius who proposed some forty *ad hominem* objections to the immortality of the soul, of which, if some might be valid, others must fail.

The inconsistency of a typical product of contemporary Western culture can be palpable. Hostile to or uninterested in Christianity, he will sometimes aver that it is scientifically implausible, thus using "verificationist" arguments (at least in germ) against it, while simultaneously holding that scientific truths are to be pursued not for their own sake but for the "post-modern" reason that their discoverers win power and prestige – or, more immediately, sexual conquests among adoring graduate students. In another case he may be a devotee of a popular novelist – say Jeffrey Archer – while in his more "learned" moments pontificating on the "death of the author" who is no more than a pen in the hands of destiny. Or, if an author himself, he may sue an authorized translator of his writings for plagiarism. Or, alarmed by the murderous activities of a paedophile, he may assert that it is time to bring back the death-penalty – and in the next earnest conversation insist that we cannot help being born the way we are, the society into which we arrive, the portion of "genetic soup" we have inherited.

Such examples – all of which I have met – could be endlessly multiplied, but what is most important about them is not that they are common – significant though that is in daily life – but that they depend on an unwillingness to reflect on inconsistency. Rather than give up an opinion we like and think of almost as an old friend in favour of another, people – including professors! – prefer illogically to maintain both. At a more fundamental (and revealing) level I have argued that it is a mark of the modern enlightened mentality to maintain "inalienable human rights" and to deny the

---

[10] For comment see A. MacIntyre, *Three Rival Versions of Moral Enquiry* (London 1990), esp. chapter 8, and the subsequent "literature".

metaphysical presuppositions that alone make them intelligible. For most, being comfortable is more important than being logical or truthful.

Two particular features of the modern world make such attitudes all the easier to adopt: advertising (and the media generally) and globalization. The former means that we are constantly surrounded by a mixture of half-truths, inventions and untenable assumptions which leave us with the belief that we can make up our own minds when we are frequently unable to know even what we are supposed to make them up about. (As I write, I hear the BBC World Service inviting its listeners all over the globe to send in e-mails about the effectiveness or otherwise of relief efforts in New Orleans: their defence would presumably be that to invite such "input" is democratic – fair enough *if* "democracy" entails the deliberate encouragement of ignorance.)

As for globalization, one of its many mixed blessings is that we are confronted with numbers of spiritualities from different cultures, often mediated through Westerners who misinterpret them for ideological reasons or Easterners in search of quick financial rewards from the gullible. These "spiritualities", being levered free from most of their cultural moorings, have great appeal to those in revolt against an institutionalized religion often presented ignorantly even by its own adherents and readily described as authoritarian, paternalist, patriarchal – or merely as an old-fashioned restraint on "natural" instincts. In the rootless condition to which globalization contributes, we are often in a position to evaluate neither alien traditions nor our own. Our reaction is often to suppose either that a "new" (and non-Western) spirituality can release us from our hypocritical and banalized ways, or at best that each and any tradition is as good as any other – a notion often promoted by nominal Christians who have lost sight of their own *raison d'être*. We are then invited – here we are back to the media and the advertisers – to choose for ourselves.

What kind of options are we invited to choose between? They may be summarized as "modern" or "post-modern" varieties of humanism which, the more logically they are pursued, the more nihilist they look: intelligibly enough, since their own logic will carry them further and further away from a Christian (or more broadly theistic) alternative. Such "humanisms" will vary with their notions of the nature of man, to range from "Promethean" man as an image of God (and virtually a god himself) to the post-modern self which has disappeared. We have seen how the "ultra-divine-image" first appeared – when the earlier Christian view was nearer the general consciousness and what seemed to be required was merely the correction of an excessive pessimism about man's miserably "fallen" state and a recognition that select ideas of a non-Christian origin (such as the erotic love of beauty) are not incompatible with Christianity, indeed are confirmatory enrichments and expansions of a specifically Christian culture.

"Promethean" humanism began as an exaggeration of a genuinely Christian humanism, but the role of God diminished until – by the time of Voltaire – he is seen as a mere enemy of human progress. So the divine man began to take total control as creator of those values which originally were defensible at least within the older theological account. Unbounded (if mindless) optimism replaced traditional image-theory, while human dignity resolved itself into human autonomy. But with God sidelined, the credentials of "Promethean" or its variant "romantic" humanism began to be seriously called in question by latter-day versions of Christian thinking. For the partisans of so-called Covenant theology, man, so damaged by the Fall, is entirely at the mercy of the unimaginable divine power which has, however, made with him a solemn covenant, seen as parallel to the contractual relationships between men which replaced the part-Aristotelian, part-Christian emphasis on man as *naturally* social.

With God sidelined, it is easy to see how such contracts would soon be understood solely in terms of power-relationships. Hobbes again led the way, but in Hobbes contracts – hence theories of power – arise because man grows aware that he cannot safeguard his life without them; they are seen as an effective way by which the isolated and non-social individual that is man may survive. In post-modern versions of power-theory, the arrangement of power-structures is the only primal activity for man; so rights, for example, are simply what we can enforce for ourselves. While Hobbes thinks that the best – the most rational – strategy for mankind is to make the best kinds of deals each person can rationally accept as in the interest of his own survival, the post-modernist replies that all "moral" thinking is a veiled or naked pursuit of power.

That is one example of how scepticism began to corrode the earlier humanist visions of man. We can summarize the development as: in the theistic age of Europe, man, the social animal, sought God's laws and the moral law planted in his heart. By the time of Hobbes, whatever moral laws are to be followed are already, for some, man-made. By post-modern times all moral laws, whether supposedly from God or from human convention, are masks for power-plays and man knows that he lives in a moral-free universe. If he thinks at all, he becomes a nihilist. Nihilism thus is the last stage of humanism.

I argued in *Real Ethics* that this last stage of the abandonment of objective morality had already been foreseen by Plato in fourth-century Greece, and he immortalized its apologists in the person of Thrasymachus, who would have regarded Socrates' other opponent, Callicles of the *Gorgias*, as merely confused – in that he promoted some version, albeit "immoral" and certainly impersonal, of a law of nature: namely that the stronger can and should, by a presumed law of rational obligation, do as he likes. In one respect, however, Thrasymachus and Callicles speak the same "modern" language: they both regard other people as units to be manipulated, abused, and – especially true for Thrasymachus – deceived by those who have the ability to do so. Human beings are not "persons" but malleable objects. It is worth recognizing one special contemporary instance: a modern Thrasymachus (unlike the typical medieval philosopher) would say that he has the absolute right to do what he likes with what is "his own" (including his own body – and indeed soul if he had one) – and with whatever he can make his own. No Thomist – nor even "Green" – nonsense about man being a steward of the earth here!

In the worlds of Thrasymachus and Callicles (and of their modern avatars) only power remains: there is no room for beauty, justice or truth. I argued in *Real Ethics* that Thrasymachus marks the end of the logical road. But there is a sense in which Callicles cannot merely be written off because logically incomplete, more especially in a book not about logic but about rival cultures. Callicles' *in*complete cynicism about human nature and objective truth is in a sense more human than the logical extremism of Thrasymachus (though even Thrasymachus makes mistakes in his argument that depend on his inability *qua* nihilist to keep his logical end clearly in view).[11] Insofar as Callicles is confused, he might be the more likely to find imitators – at least if I am right in thinking that not least in our own times there are myriad incentives to avoid the honest attempt to think things through.

If we assume for a moment that the Catholic world-view is largely correct, there is further reason to think that a Calliclean mentality will attract some who shun the sheer emptiness of a Thrasymachean universe and prefer to fill it with more "bourgeois" goods. That helps to explain why in the *Gorgias* Callicles wants "natural law" to equal the pursuit of pleasure. In the dialogue itself his application of power to the securing of intensity of pleasure leads him – because he is unable or unwilling to offer criteria to distinguish one thrill from another – to embarrassment. Socrates is able to challenge him with the pleasure of being buggered, which he wants to disown while not having the intellectual means to do so.

---

[11] It might be argued that Plato "invented" nihilism in the way in which some think that Augustine invented "Pelagianism" (and as Cardinal Ratzinger invented liberation theology). In each case what is attacked is the logically coherent "last stage" of a set of claims and a mentality. Thus Pelagius need not have held all the propositions of "Pelagianism" (though logically he should have), nor Boff all the entailments of liberation theology.

Yet Callicles' attempt to identify pleasure as a real good is evidence from a hard-core realist that we all want to recognize some good. Callicles' confusion might even be taken as evidence that, in spite of the logic of nihilism, there remain traces of the desire for a human good not made by man implanted in the human. For all the apparent absurdity of such a claim, there seem to be few of us without a single redeeming feature – even if not a few seem to try hard to falsify that proposition.

6.5 CHURCH AND SOCIETY: CORRUPT SURVIVAL IN A SECULAR WORLD

In earlier chapters I showed how, especially in medieval times, the Church has seen itself, necessarily, against the problems of its contemporary background. Thus the "political" issues it faced were generally of the relationship between the Church and the Christian political régimes of the day. As a result of such necessary involvement it was inclined to adopt the attitudes of society and apply them within its own structures and self-awareness. Thus the growth of papal "monarchy" accompanied the development and strengthening of "secular" monarchies, and Ignatius of Loyola organized his Jesuits on quasi-military lines: soldiers of Christ in emulation of soldiers of the king of Spain. Such reflections of civil society need not be harmful to Catholicism; in some cases they represent the Church's willingness to learn from outside structures and ideas. But such assimilation of "outside" material is not always beneficial, and in at least two ways can be seriously damaging. The Church may take on board ideas that have temporary usefulness but should later be jettisoned, yet institutional inertia inhibits their rejection. Or newly accepted ideas may be harmful but seem immediately attractive. In either case the process of taking them on board can occur deliberately or by mere osmosis.

All this is only to be expected and is theologically intelligible; Augustine had already learned from the unorthodox Donatist Tyconius that the Church is a *corpus mixtum* (a "mixed body"), and Vatican II and subsequent documents[12] have stated that the Church of Christ "subsists in" the Catholic Church, not that it is identical with it. In the past deviant "Catholic" behaviour can be documented and there is no reason to suppose that similar weaknesses – with similar effects – are not to be found within the Church of today. Here I want to consider a number of ways in which the contemporary Church (that is, its members as distinct from its "deposit of faith") tends

---

[12] E.g., *Dominus Iesus* 17.

to copy features of the surrounding society (especially its intellectually and politically dominant features), with, it may be, the idea of being able to "talk" to that society or seem to be "relevant" to it – or just to be more comfortable in being unthinkingly seduced by what is regarded as normal, modern and progressive "outside".

In recent years there has been considerable anxiety in the Church about "liberation theology"; on the grounds that, apart from its emphasis on the necessity of class conflict, it distorts Church doctrine in trying to promote the kingdom of God on earth, losing sight of the transcendental message of Christianity. There has also been anxiety about "religious pluralism", on the grounds that it compromises the historical reality of salvation-history and the unique person of Christ. Of these concerns the first is about secularism, the second about religious relativism. But the second is also about secularism at a deeper level, the suspicion being that intellectual tolerance of many religions must ultimately entail little valuing of any one rather than another, thus comfortably devaluing the missionary activity in which the Church has to engage, hence eventually Christianity itself.

Underlying these concerns, and more basic than either of them, is the situation that in the present world the dominant power, the United States, as well as many of the European second-raters, are democratic, and not least as a result of the American experience – felt beyond its national boundaries – Church reform has been taken to mean more democratization. Up to a point this is reasonable and indeed follows traditional patterns whereby in the age of monarchies, for example, the Church took on board certain monarchical features helpful (at least in the short term) to its continuing development. But, as we have seen, the characterization of the Church as yet another monarchy would have been an abandonment of its mission, and there is no reason to believe that democratization does not pose a comparable threat.

There has long been a tendency within the United States to suppose that there should be a "truly American" Church, and this has resulted in the appearance of such specifically American institutions as the Latter Day Saints, Jehovah's Witnesses, Christian Science, even Scientology. In the nineteenth century "Americanism" in the Catholic Church itself attained the status of an official heresy. But movements of a specifically national sort need not immediately arise outside a mainstream ecclesiastical structure; they can also develop within such a structure in the form of theological progress deriving its initial impulse (and its theological and financial potency) from features of secular society. That is not, of course, to deny that they may be enriching: the admirable – if naive – document on religious freedom (*Dignitatis humanae*) produced by Vatican II was largely the work of an American theologian. But theological ideas deriving from the most powerful, most influential, most self-confident society in the world need to be scrutinized with particular care if *aggiornamento* is not to degenerate towards the wholesale replacement of tried and tested ideas by popular fads.[13] In particular, such new ideas need to be defended on strictly theological and philosophical, not merely "social", grounds.

Part of the problem is less that "democratic" ideas need theological evaluation if they are to be applied in an ecclesiastical setting, but – as I have noted – that the merits and demerits of democracy itself are left unexamined while it is even left unclear what sort of régime is properly to be labelled democratic. It is loosely supposed, for example, that a democratic society is one in which every adult has the right to vote without fear of intimidation. Certainly that is a minimal condition for such a society. But democracy is not an end in itself, and it is misguided to describe a state as democratic if it uses democratic means to undemocratic ends. It makes little sense to suppose it democratic to vote for a totalitarian régime – which was essentially what happened in the election of the Nazis in Germany in 1933. Similarly it would not be democratic for a Muslim state "democratically" to vote in a theocratic constitution by which, for example, women were to be deprived of the right to vote – let alone that no future elections should be held since the desired "theocracy" had already been attained.

So the first point about the influence of "democracy" on the Church is "What kind of democracy?" And the second is that as a method of governance democracy – even understood as the use of democratic means for democratic ends – still leaves much to be desired. But even granted that we are thinking only of a democratic society by which the well-being of the citizens, material and spiritual, is to be promoted directly or indirectly, it does not follow that democratic procedures are appropriate to ecclesiastical structures, though sometimes they may be. And if a democracy is to be understood – as with much contemporary liberalism – as a society that wishes to maximize choice, even at the expense of truth, it is least of all suitable to the religion dedicated to "catholic" truth.

As a test case let us return once again to the question of rights. I have argued in the previous chapter that secularists are right to hold that there

---

[13] Such critical observations should not be taken as any participation in the wash of unthinking anti-Americanism currently spreading in Europe. In the coming years much good can and should be derived from American energy in the Church, with its importation into ecclesial life of a willingness to "put your ass in gear".

are – or should be – inalienable rights, but have no adequate justification for identifying them. Christians – and Jews – on the other hand, have retained, and developed, the fundamental tenet that man is created in God's image, legitimate ground for acceptance of inalienable rights. But which rights? It would seem absurd to assert that every household has the right to own a refrigerator; it is generally admitted that rights-claims have got out of hand, and the very word "claims" explains why this has happened. For the ground for such a "claim", in a secular society, is simply that I advance it, or that I persuade other people, somehow or other, with or without a valid argument, that I have such a right. If I say that rights are simply the construct of a law that recognizes "legitimate" needs (but who knows what is legitimate?), I have not even begun to explain why such rights should be inalienable. In fact, quite the reverse: if mere "law" gives a right, then law can take that right away.

Consider in the ecclesiastical sphere a woman's "right" to be a "priest": this must be either an inalienable right or a legal right. It has not been a right in Catholic canon law – hence that law might be considered incomplete on this point – so if women (or some women) have an *inalienable* right to ordination, that could only be connected with their existence in God's image. But even for men the priesthood is not a right. Any unwed Catholic male can apply, but only has a right if he has a vocation tested by the Church. One might claim that a woman has a similar right to be tested and theoretically that might be upheld; still, as of now there would be no legitimate ground for complaint merely because on every occasion a woman was turned down – as certainly she would be, as would her male counterpart, if her claim to be ordained was based on a supposed *right* independent of a tested divine call. In other words, merely in virtue of being in God's image she (as he) has no right to ordination: which does not entail that at some time she might not be ordained – canon law might be defective in failing to recognize the full implications of her being created in God's image – only that she cannot be considered a fit candidate for testing as feminine humanity is currently understood, certainly in part defectively, by the Church.

I mention rights in order to argue that, though it might seem that what would be a "right" in a secular society should also be a right in the Church, the conclusion does not follow. A random appeal even to legitimate civil rights cannot be assumed to be compelling for any desiderate revision of canon law. Always the case needs to be made whether "civil" rights of an inalienable sort should or should not pertain in ecclesiastical structures. The Church must ask whether or not they are defensible within traditional theological structures, or compatible with legitimate and logical developments of those structures.

The wider question of the influence of democracy, in some form, is not limited to institutional structures; it is now frequently introduced into debates on doctrinal matters, sometimes matters of Christology and Trinity, more commonly matters of morality: in our times, for reasons which we must briefly consider, especially sexual morality.

Those of us who have passed through the "Sexual Revolution" of the Sixties – as well as younger generations – cannot be unaware of its impact on traditional civil and Christian society in the West (and increasingly elsewhere): the licence of women to behave sexually more as men have traditionally behaved, as a (supposed) further stage in their social emancipation; the increased opportunities offered by the pill to exploit women sexually now that resulting pregnancies can be taken care of by the women themselves; the massive increase in the number of abortions and the great strengthening of an (ill-founded) claim that abortion is "a woman's right" (since rights depend on choice); the related drastic reduction of the control of parents over the behaviour of their children – itself tied to the "democratic" pressure to reduce the age of consent such that the concept of a "minor" for whom someone else is responsible has tended to disappear;[14] the pressure by many schools on their pupils for ever earlier sexual experience; the severe demographic crisis that is hitting Europe, with anticipated (if as yet not fully realized) economic and social effects; the claimed legality of homosexual acts, as well as sado-masochistic versions of sexual behaviour between consenting parties.

All this depends not only on technological innovation and the legitimate demand of women to be viewed under the law and in social life as possessed of an autonomy similar to that of men – and thus on the rejection of a misused concept of "modesty" to justify their reduction to second-class citizens or even chattels – but ultimately on those pillars of modern democratic secularism: tolerance of anything that cannot be "demonstrated" to be harmful and the construction of morality by the consent of parties or groups. And since this implies a common denominator, we have the *de facto* acceptance of pleasure ("Which most people want") as the goal of life. "Morality is about sex, ethics is about money," and the aim of both is pleasure, which we all can "agree" is good and which therefore (we falsely infer) is to be directly sought.

---

[14] As well as being attractive to those who want less (or no) responsibility for others, such trends are often a legitimate but exaggerated reaction to abuses in the treatment of children, especially in institutions. But in an age that prefers historical ignorance, deliberate distortions of history (whether motivated mischievously, ideologically, by the financial rewards of sensational reporting by the media or by corrupt specialists) mean that the non-specialist is even less able than in the past to distinguish comparative fact from obvious fiction in his historical judgments: witness *The Da Vinci Code* and indeed the average Hollywood "historical" film.

The Sexual Revolution, more than anything else, has produced a crisis of authority and confidence in the Church. Many thought (and taught) that the Church could hardly survive unless it took on board most of its effects, good, bad or indifferent. In 1968, however, Pope Paul VI published his encyclical *Humanae Vitae* in which he reasserted the Church's ban on artificial contraception, both by means that are actually abortifacient and more controversially those that are not. In doing so, he may have anticipated the howls of anger provoked in a secular world that saw it as an attack on personal freedom, especially that of women, by an aging and celibate cleric careless of the problems involved (especially for married couples), and also as socially irresponsible in view of the massive increases of population in many parts of the world.

Having overruled his own commission's recommendations favouring some relaxation of the ban on artificial contraception, at least for married couples, Pope Paul appears to have been wholly taken aback by the storm he provoked within the Catholic community itself. His misjudgment was probably partly induced by non-recognition of the increasing demand after Vatican II from the laity (especially when their ranks were swelled by substantial numbers of ex-priests and ex-nuns) for a much larger voice in Church decision-making. But the challenge was not only, and perhaps not even primarily, from the laity. Hundreds of theologians protested, and were supported more or less openly by many bishops and senior members of religious orders. It is often supposed that the intensity of this reaction was the direct cause of the fact that Paul never published another encyclical.

For although the bishops more or less fell into line (at least in public), the ban was widely ignored – indeed rejected in principle – by the laity, especially in more "advanced" parts of the world – Europe and North America – where sophisticated theology was increasingly taken to be that which followed "obviously" progressive secular trends.

Conclusions were quickly drawn: the Church was hopelessly out of touch with the realities of the contemporary world and its pronouncements on sexual ethics (and by implication much more widely) must be ignored. Hence demands for the full sexual (and implicitly if not explicitly anti-family) programme of Western secular society: acceptance of masturbation, pre-marital (even occasionally extra-marital) sex, homosexuality. Even the cause of women priests was indirectly advanced by what was taken to be the Vatican's anti-feminist stance. And the problem was exacerbated by two factors: first a tendency in official circles to link contraception too hastily with abortion, though a reasoned condemnation of either has to keep them separate in the first instance; then the "prophetic" character of the encyclical itself: Paul doubtless had arguments to hand, but did not deploy them successfully in his document. He and those who advised him probably thought that, in an encyclical on a matter of such importance, to pronounce was enough.

Those who later, in the papacy of John Paul II (including the Pope himself), defended *Humanae Vitae* would supply (or discover) some of the necessary argumentation. In one respect this was highly satisfactory since it drew attention to the need for much rethinking and revising of traditional attitudes to women and to the sexual aspect of marriage (and of life in general). It also enabled Catholics, with benefit of hindsight, to recognize effects of the "contraceptive mentality" that Paul – whether or not he understood them – had little opportunity to see working themselves out in the Western world. Contraception led to a view of marriage in which children were a dispensable luxury and where the physical experience of "successful" sexual love – "good sex" – tended to replace the goodwill of the partners – Augustine's *amicitia matrimonialis* – as the fundamental feature of the marriage bond.

But if Paul did not foresee immediate trouble, still less did he see some of the wider consequences, which may be unique in Church history. Predictably, some left the Church over *Humanae Vitae* – as the Old Catholics had done over Papal Infallibility – only this time they often moved, at least temporarily, to some other ecclesial community; but many remained in the Church while rejecting the encyclical, and with it much of Church and especially papal authority. One of the effects of *Humanae Vitae* was to leave within the Church a potential anti-Church which would easily move from rejection of Church teaching on sexuality to rejection of much else, especially in the social domain. And since the offenders were laymen and laywomen, it was impossible to punish them directly without denying communion to millions: clearly a non-starter in the contemporary world. Although the Church, with a little justification, tried to shift the blame to punishable dissident clergy, it was in fact faced with a "democratically" based lay rebellion. The option of surrendering to the age having been dropped, the Church did not know how to deal with the new situation.

The problem of authority generated by *Humanae Vitae* has been particularly sharp in the United States, where tendencies to a split between conservatives and liberals were greatly exacerbated. At least three reasons for this can be identified: first that the "revolt" seemed to be democratically based – as the will of a large number, if not a majority, of the Catholic population. Second, there is normally, in American society, a tendency to think that laws are made by agreement between consenting parties. Third, American society prides itself above all on being modern and progressive: although the country dates back some four hundred years, widespread is not merely an ignorance but an unawareness of history – especially of other parts of the world – as well as a sense of its irrelevance even among the Catholic population. The very notion of the handing on of unbroken tradition from time immemorial can seem out of keeping.

All this cannot be kept separate from the widely accepted (and anti-religiously applied) "secular" tenet of the radical separation of Church and State. This theme, developed in the seventeenth century from a weariness of religious wars and the almost universal abuse of power by religious groups, and fostered by the especially Lutheran tendency to treat religion as a purely private matter, had always made loyal American Catholics uneasy; as elsewhere,[15] not least in their country of origin, they feared to be held unpatriotic subjects of the Pope rather than of the Republic. This helped generate what might be called "Kennedy Catholics": Catholics, that is – or at least tribal Catholics, being often of Irish descent – whose ambition for personal advancement led them to compromise their Catholic doctrine, especially in matters of morality, when standing for public office.

The typical example might be photographed embracing groups of nuns while promoting abortion in his public policy.[16] Under the flag of tribalism, religious and nationalist, such figures were to be seen in company with "court-prelates", from the rank of Cardinal down, who apparently made no attempt to encourage them in even remotely Catholic morality. Their "ethical" policies, where they coincided with Catholic teaching (such as in the movement for Civil Rights) drew their origin not from Catholicism but from the secular order and a desire to win the favour of the *ben pensanti* and of their media. And their numbers were such as to appear to be a "grass-roots"

---

[15] One recalls the dilemma of English Catholics after the pope's excommunication of "good" Queen Bess in 1570, and their disintegration after the – probably to a considerable degree government-inspired – "Gunpowder Plot" of 1605.

[16] Of course, the phenomenon was not limited to the United States. In Canada liberal abortion laws – and abortion is often the best test of practical Catholicism – were introduced by a government with a Catholic Prime Minister, a Catholic Minister of Justice and a Catholic majority in the Cabinet. Such behaviour can sometimes be attributed to a branch–plant mentality, or a fear of being "left behind" in the latest "progressive" social reform (though more recently Canada may be seen as a laboratory for testing "liberal" social programmes); or it is cynically excused as a pre-emptive strike to prevent something worse. Governments make analogous moves in other areas; thus a university may be induced to make drastic cuts in its programmes for fear (they leak) of something more drastic being imposed from above. The government gains twice over from such supineness: the pre-emptive move by the university secures the cuts the government wants, while the obliquy is passed on to the lower institution. "I do not want to cut your throat, here is a knife for you to cut only half of it."

Catholicism such as would replace the fogies of Old Europe (especially in Rome) and their obscurantist allies at home.

Together with such politicians and opinion-formers went the institutions from which they emerged. Before the Sexual Revolution and other movements of the Sixties, Catholic universities in the United States had – often deservedly – a low reputation in the academic world: their programmes damned as "pastoral", their staff as narrow-minded and tame. Frequently the "Kennedy Catholics" and their would-be followers avoided them, preferring the superior power-base of the Ivy League. This set the Catholic institutions a problem in a world of *aggiornamento*; they recognized that they had to change; the question was how. Ashamed to go on as they were, they tended to over-react and attempt to turn themselves into copies of the dominant secular schools. Few chose the option of radically improving a genuinely Catholic education in all its potential breadth and historical strength.

In the ensuing Gadarene rush, theology departments, now often devoid of adequate work – since apparently Scripture studies had been destroyed by Protestant form-criticism and the magisterium and its traditions were held merely obscurantist – embarked on a period of intellectual stagnation which there is no need to chronicle here; it was admirably summed up in my presence by a distinguished priest-professor of philosophy. Asked how priests should be educated, he replied, "Well, if you want to stop them thinking, teach them theology." Nor did he have Thomistic theology, even at its manualist worst, in mind.

The problem was not only with theologians. One of the expectations arising at and from Vatican II was that Vatican I would be completed: that is, that after the definition of the authority of the pope, the job would be finished by various affirmations about collegiality among the bishops and the bishops' personal authority. This was supposed to represent a "decentralizing" of power to match the apparent centralization promoted by the "infallibility" – in whatever sense – of the papacy. And indeed the conservatives at Vatican II, who saw Cardinal Ottaviani as their natural leader, fought hard to prevent this from coming about. They appeared to fail, and it was widely held that, as was apparently the wish of Paul VI, a far more decentralized "magisterium" would follow. But this did not happen.

Factors contributing to that non-event are legion, not least the effects of the media and of "globalization". It had become easy for conservatives to appeal over the heads of their local bishops to Rome – and there seems to have been a certain encouragement for them to do so. But the principal single cause of the failure of "decentralization" was the failure of the said bishops to do their job, especially over moral issues and especially over the crucial test of abortion, infuriating more energetic laypeople who felt that, despite expending much time, effort and money, they had been left high and dry.

Why did this occur? There may be a single underlying cause to which I have alluded already and to which I shall return, but in the short run there were many other obvious factors, of which I can briefly present a few: first, the rapidly declining prestige of Christianity in general in the West and the sense of isolation in which bishops (let alone their far less sheltered diocesan clergy) found themselves obliged to live. In Ireland – to take an extreme example – from being given inordinate respect they began to receive inordinate hostility and contempt among the new intelligentsia, opinion-formers, and gradually the public at large. Educated people who remained Catholic generally preferred to keep their heads down in the new situation. Old "scandals", old abuses of authority could now be excavated and at times deliciously exaggerated; new scandals, especially of a sexual nature – now hard to cover up – kept the pot boiling.

Second – and perhaps in fear of their newly isolated state – many bishops began to surround themselves by *faux amis*, by just the people they should have avoided: chiefly ex-priests and ex-nuns whose new and "advanced" theological skills – combined with exciting experiments in non-clerical living – may have seemed to offer a certain protection against the tidal wave of secularist "truth", while in fact laying them open to charges of dithering impotence and temporizing which served to encourage those happy to delate them to Rome.

Among Catholics the new lack of confidence rarely reached the levels it did among Anglicans, whose disbelief in central doctrines of traditional Christianity – even sometimes disbelief in God, or at least belief only in a God of human projections – was widely "known" to an increasingly cynical public. In the seventies and eighties there was immense interest among learned Anglicans – and then there were still many such – in the fourth-century heresy of Arius, the Alexandrian priest who denied the divinity of Christ, though still treating him as by far the first of all created things. But their interest in Arianism related not so much to the fourth-century "heresy" as to the Christianity of the twentieth century. Was not some form of Arianism the logical next stage of advanced biblical criticism and the abandonment of Church tradition, of the longed-for "demythologization" of Christianity to which the "wise men" of their day looked forward? Or perhaps not the last, for beyond lay agnosticism, atheism, and the appearance of avowed anti-Christians among the teaching staff of seminaries. Among Catholics things rarely went that far, but the warnings were clear enough.

We come last to the major "institutional" problem to which I alluded. It concerns a mentality which has certainly caused great difficulties in the past, but which in the present century has become so serious that it must be faced directly. I have no wish to discuss exactly how "clerical" early Christianity was, but there is no doubt that "clericalism" increased greatly as Christianity expanded and as the civil authorities found it necessary and convenient to allow bishops and other clerical leaders ever-increasing political power. And the prestige of the clerical state was further augmented by the growing numbers of "religious", who represented a foretaste of paradise on earth, a life beyond that of mere laymen, even of mere mortals. But in practice in the West, where Christian thought is still largely developed, and not least in the United States where probably more people study what is taken to be theology than anywhere else on the planet, the contrast, or at least the nature of the contrast, between the clerical and the lay state has been changing. Yet while the social and political implications of this are increasingly recognized on paper – statements are issued that priests should not enter party politics and that political and social aspects of the Christian life should largely be left to laymen and women – older habits of clericalism frequently prevail.

A feature of political life inadequately recognized both inside and outside the Church is the normal course of revolutionary action. Those possessed of civil as well as ecclesiastical power normally delude themselves that they can contain the situation: just leave it to us; we can at least look after our own interests.

The kind of revolutionary actions I have in mind have always existed, but at least since the French Revolution have taken on a new totalitarian dynamic. In France Mirabeau was succeeded by Robespierre, in Russia Kerensky by Lenin. In the Germany of the thirties the situation was somewhat different. Hitler, by what he styled "originality plus brutality", eclipsed his nationalist rivals and made fools of those conservatives who thought he could be used and discarded – probably among them Cardinal Pacelli (later Pius XII) whose legitimate fear of communism led him to underestimate the nearer threat. By their Concordat with Hitler the Vatican authorities of the age undercut (indeed destroyed) the lay Catholic opposition to Hitler; they seem to have thought they knew how to handle things better than those on the spot. The principle "My enemy (communism) is your enemy" proved too simple to be an effective defence, and the Church was tricked by Hitler into supposing that its local interests would be protected if he was given more of a free hand in dealing with non-Catholic activists and institutions. Time was to show how this naive and ignorant policy (shared, of course by wishful thinkers throughout Europe) was to fail disastrously.

"Peace-makers" – and obviously the Vatican will try to be a peace-maker – are always liable to make such mistakes: typically, alleged moderates will be found – or invented – with whom we can talk; Stalinists were right to call such temporizers "useful idiots". In the contemporary world clerics, sometimes over-concerned about the historical effects of Church policies, are particularly liable to earn this designation, remembering "Peace be with you" and forgetting "I come not to bring peace but a sword". Balancing these two is not easy, and hard-bitten individuals in the secular world are more likely to understand their even more hard-bitten opponents than are those whose proper job is to preach the truth rather than dirty their hands with its practical applications. In its coming dealings with Islam the Church will need to avoid such well-intentioned errors.

Neither by misplaced generosity, verging on wishful thinking, nor by sitting on the fence ("until the iron enters into their souls", as Lloyd George put it), but by honest observation and firm action will the Church stand any chance of recovering the respect of the secular world which it has largely lost – and in so doing it may achieve some at least of its social objectives. And there is a final hazard, the "ecumenical" and inter-religious aspects of which should not be taken lightly. Support for the view that one should "turn the other cheek" to political oppressors is often drummed up by the Gandhi-myth. Gandhi, it is said, overcame British India by non-violence. This is wrong on two counts: first because a genuinely brutal Empire would have killed him, non-violent as he was; second, had the British done so, a *latent* threat of violence on which he relied would have burst out into massive terrorism and slaughter – as it did when the Indian subcontinent was partitioned.

There is a story told of St Basil who, approached by an imperial official and asked to do something compromising, refused. The official was astonished: no bishop before has refused when I asked him, he complained. Basil told him, "You have not yet met a real bishop." So was Bishop Fisher of Rochester the only bishop to resist Henry VIII. If such models were now to be followed, there would be far less problem with the centralization and bureaucratization of the Church – in themselves marks of its unnecessary assimilation to the secular and largely godless world beyond its doors.

CHAPTER 7

Looking at hopes and fears in the rear mirror

We need a Caliph who would chop hands, cut throats, stone people in the same way that the messenger of God used to chop hands, cut throats and stone people.

Ayatollah Khomeini

7.1 CURRENT THREATS AND FUNDAMENTALIST RESPONSES

I have argued in the preceding chapters that, just as we can identify development in Christian doctrine, so we can see a development in our understanding of the role of the Church and – a particularly illuminating example – of the see of Rome, as well as the ever-widening possibilities of the socio-political, moral and aesthetic aspects of Christian culture. Instead of shrinking within some fundamentalist core of "saving truth" we need to further the growth of all the implications of that saving truth: that is, of all that is compatible with it. Newman's identification of the development of Christian *doctrine* concerned itself with distinguishing between legitimate growth and the growth of abuses within the strictly religious – that is, salvational – sphere; and within those limits it has been of immense value, despite some weaknesses, notably the privileging of the state of doctrine in the fourth and fifth centuries to the extent of reading such ideas back into the first three centuries of the Christian era. Newman's theory was worked out largely in the context of a defence of the Church of Rome against Protestantism, viewed as pervaded by the spirit of individualism, of a "pick-and-mix" Christianity.

The world has changed since Newman's time and the main problems of the Catholic Church are far less the old Reformation debates, but indeed far more serious, as can be symbolized by one in particular: the potential capitulation of Catholicism's European base before the combined forces of a resurgent Islam and a head-in-sand hedonism which could even allow the decimation of the Christian and ex-Christian populations of Europe and their significant replacement, without any overt use of force, by the followers of Mohammed. The old Christian centres of the southern side of the Mediterranean, Antioch, Alexandria and Carthage, were Islamized by the conquering might of Mohammed himself and later his generals, and a contempt for Christianity and its European heritage can lead to the less immediately warlike overwhelming of Christian society on the northern side of "our sea". European demography is not in favour of Christianity nor of Catholic culture, and it is hardly science-fiction to imagine the transformation of St Peter's into a mosque as was the fate of Santa Sophia in "Constantinople" – with the consequent destruction not only of its religious influence but of its cultural and artistic treasures and those dependent on it – to say nothing of the wider art-treasures of Italy and in the long term of Western Europe more generally. In those circumstances a new and more extended "Avignonese" captivity – perhaps to Washington – could ensue.

If Catholicism – and ultimately all Christianity – is to be successful against more or less severe versions of such challenges, it cannot afford to be merely a rigorist sect. In any case, for it to revert even to the cultural mentality of the earliest Christians would be a betrayal of a culture that has engendered the poetry of Dante and Shakespeare, the art of Michelangelo and Leonardo, the music of Bach, Mozart, Haydn and Beethoven. Development not only of doctrine but also of culture – the cultivation of all that is true and beautiful and "of good report" – within a Catholic purview is the only way to persuade non-believers that religion itself is no dusty, morbid relic of the past, serving only guilt-ridden neurotics. Catholicism, as I have argued, not only can but must continue to be culturally expansive, and in my various chapters I have looked at different forms its expansion has taken – with greater or less degrees of success – as well as indicating areas where further advance is obviously needed.

But since various barbarians are at the gates and threats to such humane culture loom, and since ultimately "saving truth" may seem to satisfy a minimalist view of religion, the temptation remains not to an expansive but a contracted Catholicism. The choice, then, culturally as well as dogmatically, lies between development without dogmatic subtraction and fundamentalism. So we need to take a little time considering the weakness of the fundamentalist case, from even a pragmatic point of view – and also sketching an improved version of fundamentalism to counter the current interpretation of the term as it has developed historically. For many forms of fundamentalism are not only a threat to Catholic dogma in that they rightly bring Christianity itself into contempt; they also belittle the development of

Catholic culture and civilization and do their best to inhibit if not proscribe its future growth.

"Fundamentalism" is regularly on our lips, as we perform in the socio-political circus, and when we use the word we milk it for emotional effects of various sorts – depending on whether we want to be identified as fundamentalists or not, or as particular types of fundamentalists. The question "What is fundamentalism?" is a legitimate candidate for Socratic and philosophical enquiry, especially if we assume that the word has historical origins but has extended beyond them and is now widely used in the mindless and uninformative way of terms like "fascist", "imperialist", or "democrat".

The word "fundamentalism" seems to have been coined around the time of the First World War to describe the attitudes and practices of a group of Northern Baptists in the United States who, according to the *Oxford English Dictionary*, proposed a "bigoted rejection of all Biblical criticism, a mechanical view of inspiration and an excessively literalist interpretation of Scripture". By the 1950s its application had spread: to religious revivalists both Hindu and Muslim in the newly independent states of India and Pakistan, thence in particular to the Ayatollah Khomeini and his fellow clerics in Iran. By the 1980s "fundamentalist" Jews could be so described (by other Jews) insofar as they were hostile to descriptions of religious history in which scenes from the New Testament were depicted alongside those from the Old.

From our dictionary definition, widely interpreted, several features of what is usually understood as fundamentalism can be identified:

1 "Fundamentalism" is basically a religious phenomenon, though the word can be extended readily enough to cover various para-religious or totalitarian beliefs: one can infer a Nazi fundamentalist. Normally, fundamentalists rely on some "sacred" text or at least some set of "divinely given" – hence unchangeable – precepts or traditions.

2 Where such texts exist, fundamentalists (as distinct from other members of the same religious group) will interpret them literally: thus the universe, as Archbishop Ussher insisted in the seventeenth century, began at 10 o'clock in the morning, some time in the year 4004 BC – a date guaranteed by the addition of the divinely authenticated ages of the Old Testament patriarchs. Perhaps a more disturbing example is that Christians must somehow square the evidence of Matthew about the date of the birth of Jesus (before Herod's death in 4 BC) with that of standard editions of Luke, who states it was "when Quirinius was governor of Syria", i.e. AD 6 – which is impossible, except that all things are, for the fundamentalist, "possible with God".

3 Historically, fundamentalism is a conservative *reaction* arising when traditional positions seem threatened, often by some form of "rational" enquiry.
The first identified fundamentalists were Protestants, and a key theme of
original Protestantism was "Scripture alone". This may have been excus-
able, even in historical terms, in the sixteenth century, but nineteenth-
century biblical scholarship, beginning in Germany, seemed to undercut
the biblical text, first of the Old Testament, when Mosaic authorship of
the Pentateuch in its entirety became more and more implausible. The
New Testament was the next to suffer: are the Gospels really reconcilable?
Did Paul write Ephesians and if not would he agree with it? Is Galatians
compatible with Acts? But beyond the details was the problem of the
history of the text itself. As it became historically understood that our
four-Gospel canon is a second-century production, and hence that there
was a period in the history of Christianity in which there were "orthodox"
Christian Churches but no Christian Bible, what was the Protestant to do?
One answer: turn fundamentalist. And what was the fundamentalist to do?
Answer: deny the value of historical investigation (whether of the Bible or
of dinosaurs) altogether.

It seems that a common, if not ubiquitous, element of fundamentalism
(as I have argued can also be the case with accounts of the early history of
the Roman see) is a degree of wilful ignorance sometimes called faith.

4 Finally, it is important to notice that fundamentalism is not only a theory;
it is also a way of life, a praxis, often of a morally severe and rigid sort.
Contemporary Islamic examples may be invoked: under Shari'a law mutilation is the prescribed penalty for theft, stoning for adultery in women.
How then should we react to such punishments? A reasonable start would
be to agree that theft and adultery are sins and/or crimes, but that cannot
be enough for the Islamic fundamentalist who must prescribe mutilation
and stoning because they are "in the Book", and the Book is quite literally
the word of God. I should add that Christians *in the past* had similar more
or less official views of judicial mutilation,[1] as of the use of torture, and
similarly supported by fundamentalist readings of Scripture. Nowadays we
can avail ourselves of the more developed social and political doctrines
whose origins and necessity I have tried to indicate.

In such circumstances what other religious possibilities exist? One would
be to accept the Book's basic claim as a universal truth – adultery and theft
are crimes – but to argue that the means of dealing socially with such crimes
are conditioned by specific cultures. In thinking about death by stoning for

---

[1] See Aquinas, *ST* II-II, 64 2c and ad 3 in favour of mutilation as a proper penalty.

adultery, Christians cannot but recall the biblical "woman taken in adultery" and Jesus' reported reaction to her situation. The liberal response is to say that she is forgiven (and therefore presumably should not be stoned); Jesus' response was to say that she is forgiven and that she should not sin further. The fundamentalist says that, even if she repents and is forgiven, she must be stoned (or mutilated or whatever the local practice happens to be) – even if no-one (except God?) is righteous enough to do the job – *pour encourager les autres*.

One can see objections to my position. Even if we cannot be biblical fundamentalists, we must be fundamentalists of some sort. There must be some positions on which we cannot compromise; we cannot, for example, follow those "Christians" who compromise on the divinity of Christ or the Resurrection. A partial defence of this kind of "traditionalism" is that if we do so compromise we are playing with words: Christianity as traditionally understood is actually denied if its uniqueness is denied, and we may add that one thing simple logic – not to speak of the growth of scientific knowledge – teaches us is that truth is not identical with our knowledge or understanding of truth. There is no logical reason why there cannot be truths (such as the Resurrection) that our minds are largely incapable of comprehending – which is no excuse for not trying to comprehend as much as we can, or as much as we are empowered to, or for wilfully failing to recognize a possible truth's explanatory power.

Which leaves us with two problems: how do we identify the bases on which we cannot compromise? – or, rather, how did Christianity identify the bases on which it could not compromise? – and how, in identifying such bases, do we free ourselves from the charge of fundamentalism, pejoratively understood? – by which I mean fundamentalism that feels constrained to deny observable and discoverable truths by a mere act of will. Again one must insist that the only religious answer to fundamentalism is some theory of the development of our understanding of doctrine; the only logical answer is to show that, unlike the fundamentalists, we hold positions that are more, not less, rationally coherent, when taken as a whole and without partiality, than those of either secular rationalists or religious fideists.

There is a sense in which we might be biblical fundamentalists after all, for if the Church has authenticated our New Testament canon, then from that point on, some might say, the Bible has been declared to represent literal truth. But in adopting the canon the Church told us which books to accept, not how to interpret them, and the history of Christianity shows very clearly that it required challenges over time to show how such interpretation should proceed. If, for example, the second-century Christians who accepted the four-Gospel canon had read the decrees of Chalcedon or even of Nicaea, they would have required a lot of thought, study, prayer and reflection before understanding them, for the core elements of Christian understanding are in process of constant development, always of a specific and retrospectively recognizable kind.

In the document *Dominus Iesus*, the Congregation for the Doctrine of the Faith denied the title of sister churches not to those whose view of Christian truth was, in the view of the authors of the document, not brought up to date, but to those who had *subtracted* from the faith of the Church. For if reformers who subtract from tradition, let alone from the Bible itself, remain in some full sense Christian, the implication is that one can take away parts of the developed faith. The Reformers Luther and Calvin would have been insistent that someone who denies the Resurrection or the divinity of Christ is no Christian, nor would they even have conceded them to be persons "of good will", that being a concept they would have found difficult. In short, the history of Catholic Christianity shows that our comprehension of the truth of faith is agglutinative. Moreover, a full understanding of Christianity presumably has existed, at least thus far, only in the mind of God.

Which enables me to state the logic of my argument. An oddity of current religious debate in the West is that most Christian thinkers are so demoralized by the insistence of the neo-pagans – backed by media and political élites – and so used to retiring within their own walls to talk among themselves, as to have come to think that, because they cannot produce knock-down arguments for, say, the existence of God (or the immorality of abortion), they had better withdraw from face-to-face debate and at best denounce from a safe distance. In this situation the sophistic methodology used against them has meant that, just as they are often afraid to oppose abortion openly for fear of being labelled "misogynist" or "fascist", so they fear to insist on the intelligibility of the concept of God for fear of being labelled "fundamentalist". We are confronted here with a crisis *not* of the intellect, but of self-confidence and of the virtue of courage. At the level of intellect, all we need to do is produce arguments to show, not the divinity of Christ as we show that two plus two is four, but that the Christian view of the universe, without any resort to a mindless fundamentalism, biblical or other, is more coherent, more wide-ranging, altogether more intelligible than any rival view.

If I have implied that crude versions of fundamentalism are defence-mechanisms damaging to the intellect, misuses of the will and in some hands leading to a coarsened, brutal and brutalizing handling of human frailty, it is to show the proper correction to them is not to doctor doctrine to suit the whims of any particular age, but on the contrary is an adequate theory of the *development* of doctrine and its reception, coupled with a slowness to see God's "moral" beauty – and such a term is permissible – in terms of the limited psychological understanding of particular epochs.

These are deadly matters, and yet there is a sense in which – as I observed in my Introduction – those who concern themselves with *la comédie humaine* should not take themselves too seriously. In the last scene of Plato's *Symposium*, a major work of this greatest of philosophers, Socrates is drinking and debating with a tragic and a comic poet, and he is trying to persuade them through an alcoholic haze of a thesis that had not yet seen its application on the Greek stage: namely that the same poet should be able to write both tragedy and comedy – arguably because both arts depend on our lack of self-knowledge which can be exploited to both tragic and comic effect. The greatest of the playwrights, the crypto-Catholic William Shakespeare, understood the point,[2] and rightly found the fundamentalists of his day – the Poloniuses, the Malvolios, the Angelos – both tragic and comic. In these cases we can see the pity and terror of Aristotle also turned into a smile, even a guffaw.

7.2 THE NEXT NECESSARY PHASE OF CULTURAL DEVELOPMENT

Banning things is a mark of practical fundamentalism; that seems to offend against our desire to be "adult", to be able to make up our own minds, to be able to choose between good and evil. However, the fundamentalists' wish to ban is not entirely senseless, even if autonomy must be substantially respected. Few would commend *Mein Kampf* or *The Protocols of the Elders of Zion* as reading for schools. The difficulty is to know the limits of desirable control of such books and who is to be trusted to ban them. No clear answer can be found for such difficulties, and it is the apparent obligation of any culture, not least that of Catholicism, to arrive at the best it can. At times it will fall short, and history will condemn its failures, while apologetic and

---

[2] Perhaps the most convincing evidence in the build-up for Shakespeare as a "church Papist" – that is, as a person who, at times at least, conformed externally to the Church of England while sympathizing with (and acting for) the Catholic opposition – is the identification of the two subjects of the strange poem "The Phoenix and the Turtle" as the Catholic martyr Anne Line and her exiled and beggared husband Roger (see J. M. Finnis, "The Phoenix and the Turtle", *TLS* (18 May 2003) 12–14). For the subject more generally, aside from the pioneering work of the Comtesse Clara de Chambrun and P. Milward, see recently T. C. K. Rist, *Shakespeare's Romances and the Politics of Counter-Reformation* (Lewiston/Lampeter 1999) and Clare Asquith's almost recklessly brilliant tour-de-force, *Shadowplay: The Hidden Beliefs and Coded Politics of William Shakespeare* (New York 2005).

hagiography will find ways of condoning them. The alternatives might seem to be a cynical hostility or a mindless permissiveness.

I have no proposals to make here about non-Catholic cultures, insofar as they can be regarded as cultures – and I would so regard them by reference to my concept of what a Catholic culture should be. But in Catholicism, as our various studies have shown, there will always be a tension between retaining the past – and with it the unity that such a past represented – and looking towards the future, whether doctrinal or cultural, in the hope either of improving on what we have achieved or of embarking on new courses that we can show to be compatible with the ideals and beliefs we have tried to live up to.

Just as in theology some of Aquinas' insights were originally condemned, while Augustine's account of God's salvific will was substantially modified, so boldness in the artistic, literary and musical sides of Catholic culture will risk incomprehension and ill-thought-out condemnation (dependent in part on the "spirit of the age" in which they are developed). There will always be tension between the desire to advance and the need to retain "communion" with what has already been achieved. That need to preserve in unity has been the primary characteristic of the papacy itself, and I have tried to show how such a role lies beneath its historical (and often culture-driven) claims to a more than spiritual authority. For in the desire to retain will always linger the residual danger of a collapse into fundamentalism, while in the desire to advance will always lurk the threat of a simple abandonment of the past. That threat will be the greater in our current age where ignorance of a past held to be irrelevant is even hailed as a virtue.[3]

I now turn – without, as we shall see, leaving fundamentalism entirely aside – to certain ambivalent features of a very recent and more originally secular development, as well as the problems it raises for the present and future of the Church. The theme of the position of women and the so-called Sexual Revolution has already assumed considerable proportions in the present book and is a phenomenon of the past half-century which will increasingly determine the fortunes of the Church and wider society. It amounts to an almost unparalleled shift in human mentality in excess even of the effect of the new Aristotelianism on the intellectual presuppositions of the thirteenth century or of the later "Copernican turn". With this major shift all religions will have to come to terms.

---

[3] Typical was the utterance of a recent British Minister of Education against the study of Medieval History.

When Islamic terrorists select whom to murder in Algeria, they tend to fix on two classes of civilians: primary-school teachers and librarians. For if education is promoted, their "ideal" society is undercut, and more especially if that education is extended to women. That is an extreme case,[4] but it highlights a problem facing all "Abrahamic" religions – and I have no present need to look further afield. Such religions have grown up in a necessarily male-dominated world, where the need to protect the weaker and more vulnerable female – before the invention of the handgun *et al.* – has extended into a far-reaching control of her role in society and in the practices of religion itself. The first chapter of this book indicated the difficulty Christianity had in accepting the idea that woman is created in the image of God, not least because those who first began to think through their religion were largely men and they supposed that man was not only the stronger but the superior type of human being. They often concluded that to be saved a woman had to be "masculated".

There is reason to believe that, after the political emancipation of women in democratic societies and the Sexual Revolution with the "pill" to enable them to live more or less as promiscuously as men,[5] the fortunes of women will indicate both the nature of tomorrow's society in general and the future of religion, not least of Catholicism. As regards the modern notion of gender – understood as the effect of "nurture" and culture on basic reproductive differences now understood, one would hope, both physiologically and psychologically, in a corrected Aristotelian mode – the future remains uncertain, and it is fundamental for the well-being of Catholicism's self-awareness as a religion for the whole of humanity that it face up to the options in light of its developing traditions.

As in many areas, there are two basic options, though in practice there may be intermediate – and probably necessarily illogical and inexplicable – half-way houses. The two "extreme" positions are easily recognizable, both in terms of one of the themes of the present book and as observable in historical and literary texts. They are on the one hand that barring reproductive roles (which may in any society be at least theoretically optional and which will increasingly be manipulated by technology) there is no significant difference between men and women. That may have been something like Plato's view. The other alternative is that women are radically different

---

[4] Members of al Qa'eda prevent teenage girls attending school in Iraq, and the Taliban operated similarly, also forbidding music.
[5] The idea was well represented by a Sixties slogan: "A nymphomaniac is a woman with the sexual desires of the average man."

intellectually and morally and therefore necessarily must have a different status in society. If women's differences indicate a wide-ranging inferiority, their social status should be correspondingly inferior. Needless to say, it is hard to square that kind of conclusion with recent Catholic teaching that men and women are equally created in the image of God and are equally valuable in God's eyes and therefore, if we are Christians, in ours.

One of the major effects of the "Sexual Revolution" is that it has made possible an almost complete separation of the "unitive" and "reproductive" uses of sexuality. Since the unitive effects of sexuality may only be temporary, and in an age widely encouraged to be frightened of long-term commitment, a predictable effect of the separation of these two functions of sexuality is to lower the birth-rate, even, as in modern Europe and Japan, to unsustainable levels. It is pointless to deny the cultural implications of such a change, or the connection between a lack of commitment to founding a family and the desire to exploit the "unitive" aspect of sexuality as a mere opportunity for hedonism.

The challenge of hedonism is not as trivial as is often supposed. Human beings have always been tempted by it, but the unusual feature of its modern version is that it appears to many to be the only reasonable goal. What Callicles in Plato's *Gorgias* took to be the proper aspiration of the "strong" – the person who can pursue power as a means to pleasure – has come to seem the analgesic panacea for an increasingly large section of the population of Western Europe and its satellite cultures. For although Plato and his various "transcendentalist" successors may argue that it will not "ultimately" – or even immediately – bring happiness, they are not readily believed, and in any case short-term advantage normally is preferred to long-term prudence. Indeed, as Plato well knew, the Greeks' favourite proverb was that only by suffering does learning come (more especially in moral and spiritual matters).

Such considerations affect "gender"-development, not least for newly emancipated women. Imagine a world in which one does not know whether one is the same person as one was five years ago, in which one must switch from one job to another as readily as from one partner to another – and probably, especially for the élites and opinion-formers, from one country to another; in which we live with the threat of AIDS or its successor, of massive global warming producing the widespread flooding of long-inhabited cities, of atomic or biological weapons in the hands of terrorists, of a sense of globalized powerlessness in face of ever more intrusive bureaucracies, of countless local wars fuelled by the unstoppable proliferation of powerful weaponry by no means *only* of "mass" destruction. And imagine that scenario coupled with a growing belief in the existence of no God other than one we can conjure up for ourselves as a spiritual hobby or to suit some passing whim or local resentment. *Carpe diem*: hedonism, now thanks to the "pill" easier for women to pursue, even if recognized to be only short-term, could never look better as the only rational course – at least for those who have, for a time, more than enough to eat.

The present hedonist option fuels the rigorist alternative, and in rigorist alternatives the suppression of women – the denial *in effect* of their status as fully human – is one of the expectable results. The end of both Christian Caesaropapism and of papal theocracy should rule out such an extreme alternative, but not for members of other religions. One of the touted features of the "Great Satan" is the freedom of women to make immoral choices similar to those made by men, for in the "satanic" society a primary spur to hedonism *is* the emancipation – or rather its abuse – of women. For a future Catholic culture one *démarche* is clear enough: to dissuade from hedonism while retaining emancipation.

Clearly no advance on this question is possible until the more basic question of the relationship between biological sex and socialized gender is well resolved, and normatively as well as descriptively, so that we will be brought back to some revised version of a natural-law theory. More specifically, how far should we foster a culture that allows for gender-development at the expense of reproductive differentiation? The rigorist (and normal Muslim) answer is that gender-development must always be wholly determined by the conjugal and reproductive role of women. Women exist for reproductive *purposes* – and regardless of whether individual specimens are even capable of reproducing (or still reproducing).

Interestingly, the Christian institution of the religious life for women – in which the explicitly sexual is renounced – puts such a radical subordination of gender to sex out of court. A woman, that is, is properly Christian and properly human as created in the image and likeness of God whether or not she chooses (or is forced) to be sexually active.

If the possibility of a proper life apart from marriage in no way diminishes female value or lessens female sexuality, then those who marry are in no way diminished either, since human value – and the image of God – is not dependent on the performance or non-performance of genital acts. For a woman to marry, in Catholic terms, is normally for her to devote her sexuality in the context of the vows and sacrament of marriage. Viewed thus, that way of life depends on her female sexuality, but that sexuality does not make her the property of her husband, to be guarded from the eyes of other men, but a free agent able to rejoice in being female. Which brings us back to Plato and to certain aspects of his proposals for women in an ideal society.

If a married woman is exclusively the property of her husband, and an unmarried one of her father, then her value is entirely dependent on her at least potentially reproductive role. In all other respects she is not to be publicly female at all: hence bans on female athletics, not to speak of swimming, at least in full view of men. In Plato's *Republic*, as I noticed earlier, where female athletics are practised naked so that women can perform what is deemed a non-reproductive but useful role in society, women wear what is deemed appropriate for the activity in which they happen to be engaged. Their value depends not on being someone's property but on their being useful and full members of the society as a whole.

Plato has an inadequate account of the holistic nature of the human person, but what he understands is that there is nothing wrong with women looking like women, that their sexuality is not the trophy of a husband but a signal feature of their being. On the other hand, as we have seen, he makes the opposite mistake: for him women are *only physically* different from men, in an ideal culture. In a properly Catholic culture, however, with its properly Catholic account of all human beings as created in God's image and likeness, women will be of equal value with men but live not as men but as women, and readily accepting their female gifts, just as men must choose to accept theirs as men. They will be different from men (in greater or lesser ways) but no more than men will be different from women. They will make decisions as effectively as men, but it may be differently – in some areas at least – just as men will make decisions as effectively as women, even though in some areas they will make them in different modes. Thus will their final decision-making be the surer.

The greatest theoretical challenge the Church faces as it moves into the present century is to advance its understanding of this question, rejecting the rigorist model – whether in its Islamic form or otherwise – while at the same time insisting that in general terms it matters that men are not meant to be women[6] and that women neither are nor should pretend to be men. However it solves the problem of rigorism, the Church will have to avoid both the hedonism to which "emancipation" can point, and any temptation to insist that there is no significant difference between men and women, to which "emancipation" can also point. Curiously enough, both of the options to be rejected entail the same undesirable if not disastrous consequence, namely

---

[6] Apparently "sex-changes" are more often desired by males than by females.

that separation of the unitive and reproductive aspects of sexuality which leads any society to breed itself out of existence.

As for the broader picture – how are sex and gender roles to be blended in women in the future – we must remember that the advancement and emancipation of women is a very recent phenomenon.[7] We have as yet rather little empirical evidence as to how this emancipation can best be extended for the benefit of both individuals and society. What we do know, however, is already enough to show that Plato's insights in the *Republic* were substantially correct, and that only now are we in a position to take advantage of them and apply them in a specifically Christian context where woman is known to have been created in the image of God.

And if the current failure to reproduce continues in Europe, the result will go beyond the collapse of pension funds or even the destruction of European culture as it has developed (despite its failures) over the centuries, to entail the simultaneous weakening of the Catholic Church "at home" and of the influence of that Church beyond Europe's boundaries. For although increasingly Catholics derive from the "third world", the cultural and intellectual heart of Catholicism will for some time necessarily remain with Europe and its cultural satellites. In terms of "saving truth" all these things may seem less than important, but in terms of the Church's ability successfully to preach that saving truth after such cultural impoverishment they will surely be disastrous. An enlightened understanding as to how both men and women are created in the image of God – and what this implies about the analogously imaged God – is integral to this further development of Catholic culture.

Perhaps Plato's nudity for exercise is more fitted to an ancient Greek cultural climate, but despite the "sex-market economy" that disfigures the West[8] Islamists (and others) can rightly conclude that every time a "Western slut" in a bikini (or less) lies sunbathing on a beach in a Muslim or semi-Muslim country, a blow has been struck against any religion that denies equal value to women. If women are to be neither some man's chattel nor mere imitators of men, they cannot afford to be afraid of looking like women. It would still be absurd to see women in bikinis in a philosophy class or (more like Phryne) in a court of law, or at Mass where such dress would be inappropriate because distracting and irrelevant. Appropriateness – not

---

[7] For some helpful if summary documentation see L. Scaraffia, "Socio-Cultural Changes in Women's Lives", in *Men and Women: Diversity and Mutual Complementarity* (Pontificio Concilio Per i Laici, Vatican City 2006) 15–22.

[8] The phrase is from E. Bornemann (cited by M. Lutz, "Changes and Crisis in the Relations between Men and Women", in ibid. 47–61, at p. 56).

unconnected to the Aristotelian mean – is a neglected virtue, but it is the fitting response to rigorism and the master–slave culture it promotes.

7.3 BOLDNESS AND CAUTION IN CATHOLIC CULTURE

Aristotle argued that a virtue is a mean between two exaggerations. He was not referring to a safe middle road; indeed he made it clear that the mean itself is an extreme: a position that is supremely correct. In discussing the emancipation of women as a secular concept and their recognition by the Church as fully in the image of God and hence, through the dignity that confers, fully the bearers of rights, I identify what I regard as perhaps the most significant area for the further development of Catholic culture: an area in which the ideal mean falls between the extremes of rigorism and hedonistic exploitation.

In the second chapter of this book I investigated disputes, still to some degree unresolved, about the relationship between God's mercy and God's justice. I indicated that the Church eventually sought to avoid certain extreme developments of Augustine's position that lead, via the doctrine of double predestination and related themes, to serious doubts – partly exposed already by Julian of Eclanum – about the intelligibility of God as a loving Father. I also maintained, on the other hand, that Augustine was right to insist that the doctrine of original sin, whatever its difficulties (many of which he himself recognized), is an essential aspect of Catholic Christianity that cannot be "developed" away.

Augustine himself, pointing *inter alia* to the frequent miseries of "innocent" children, drew an attention – which itself would be perverted – to the inadequate moral inheritance of human nature. For unless God is simply blind and unconcerned with evil – an obvious impossibility for a Christian – Augustine has probed human behaviour and the thin veneer of "civilization" that scarcely disguises, and often fails to disguise, the inhumanity of man to man. Though leavened by many acts of goodness and lovingkindness, that inhumanity shows itself (to take contemporary examples) in the hundreds of wars laced with atrocities against the living and the dead which disfigure the African continent in particular – where it can indeed seem that old savages have new guns; in the millions of abortions, in mutilations and tortures inflicted on thousands daily in the majority of countries on the planet; in the apparently unstoppable outbursts of violent crime, often driven by the largesse to be obtained by killing children and adolescents with addictive drugs. In this patent mix of brutality and kindness which is the human character, Augustine's picture of a race seriously maimed but still able to walk with God's help emerges from the conflict which his original formulations of God's justice and mercy provoked.

My next chapter presented an analogous story about beauty, and is linked itself to the theme of woman as in God's image. Beauty may be an inspiration to the love of God – a phenomenon of the world which Christians came to recognize helped them represent and worship God's splendour and awe-inspiring goodness – or a temptation to worship the creature in exploitative eroticism, or (earlier) in fertility cults, rather than the Creator without whom beauty can be experienced but not accounted for.

The ensuing political and social chapters point up a similar message. In coming to recognize its inspirational and evangelical role in society, the Church has learned that it must avoid the two extremes: domination over legitimate secular authority and servile subordination to it. It must preach, not command, the commandments of God, precisely as God's commands. In these matters, as in the others I have examined, the Church has had to advance, and in advancing to take risks, while never losing sight of the advances it has already established and refusing to give them up in the face of the prevalent *Zeitgeist*. It can be – historically – that it has been the peculiar function of the Roman see to represent this cautious application of theological boldness to Catholicism's traditional deposit. Averted from this international focus, hierarchies and groups of bishops have ever fallen away – to become, in some cases, actual enemies of Christian unity if not (as Talleyrand) *de facto* friends of secular cynicism.

Culturally, then, the Church has exhibited what in the political domain is known as "progressive conservatism", and one would expect that, not least in the realm of dogma, the "non-progressive" conservative, that is the man frozen in the past, the mere reactionary, would be left behind, in the useful if unpopular former term, as a designated heretic. It is worth recalling a few examples of this phenomenon.

In the early fourth century, Arius was condemned for subordinationism. Had he lived a hundred years earlier he might have passed unnoticed, for it is hard to find a single pre-Nicene writer who shows no trace of subordinationism. In the fifth century many Eastern bishops separated from the Church of the Council of Chalcedon because, in their zeal to recognize the saving divinity of Christ, they lost sight of his humanity. Yet before that council, and even in many orthodox figures after it, tendencies to "Monophysitism" were widespread, though often formally condemned in various specific versions, while in the Western Church a continuing tendency in that direction was checked not least by the Franciscan re-emphasis – against more conservative trends – on the very humanity which the Monophysites had formally denied.

In modern times, however, the humanity has, partly in reaction, been again over-emphasized so that Christ's divinity and transcendence – indeed even the transcendence of God the Father – has virtually disappeared in many apparently Christian quarters and Jesus has conveniently come to be regarded merely as, at best, an outstanding teacher among others. In the seventies and eighties of the last century such "neo-Arianism" seems identifiable among a number of prominent Anglican theologians.

But in the twentieth century the most conspicuous example of the "conservative-heretical" phenomenon has been the movement, presenting itself as "real Catholicism", of the late Archbishop Lefèbvre, whose followers demand that the Church, which has always accepted the authority of councils, deny the authority of Vatican II. Thus Arius and Lefèbvre, in their own inimitable ways, provide excellent examples of the heretic or schismatic who gets left behind, because he does not recognize the *developmental* view. He or she is the stranded "traditionist" who will learn neither from the richness of established tradition nor – God forbid – from what is compatible with that tradition but is seen as lying outside its narrower boundaries.

Yet such "heretics" have a point. To develop is a risky process, whether in theology or in culture as a whole, and it will involve clashes, sadnesses and, at the personal level, the partings of friends. Jesus himself said that he came not to bring peace but a sword and to set members of households against each other. It seems then that what is called for – while the end is not (at least quite) yet – is a confidence in providence and, what is perhaps the most difficult of all the virtues in Augustine's "darkness of social life", the virtue of hope that we may avoid "Aristotelian" extremes and walk the narrow path between them.

7.4 THEN IS IT MERELY NOSTALGIC TO PREACH ABOUT THE COMMON GOOD?

An underlying theme of the present book has been that, in any study of the development of Catholic culture and of its relationship with other cultures past or contemporary, no purpose is served by lack of frankness. We need to tell the truth about ourselves as well as about others. That might seem obvious but unfortunately it is not, and I am thinking less of deliberate lying or falsification of historical realities than of an unwillingness to tell the whole truth about them. It is comfortable to our consciences to omit unpleasant truths about our own culture, past or present, and also an easy massage to our sense of our own goodwill and of the comparative ease of the tasks before us to ignore the even very serious deficiencies of others: an attitude often defended as respecting their cultural autonomy. One of the more interesting areas in which these matters have come under scrutiny is in discussions of the traditional theme of the common good in Catholic public policy and social thought. It is worth while looking at what, after coy lies and euphemistic presentations have been removed, remains of that concept.

The history of the common good goes back to the Greek *polis*. It was discussed by Plato and in detail and more influentially by Aristotle. The theory was that in a comparatively small society there is a common good to be recognized which has higher claims on the loyalty of the citizens than their private interests, but which affords them a specific opportunity to develop virtue. The common good was seen in shared responsibilities which ensured both individual moral and material advantages and a unique possibility of engaging in common public activity. It was not to be seen as a mere aggregate of individual benefits but presupposed a general recognition of the requirements of a common welfare.

But it had more than one problematic side. First, it demanded a small society; it was agreed that large conglomerates such as the Persian Empire could not develop the concept, and even within the city-state participants in the common good were free adult males only: no slaves or resident foreigners, though Plato at least wished to enlarge the full subjects of the common good to include female citizens.

Such a concept must not be confused with the benevolent autocracy that came to replace it in the mind of Stoic-seeming Roman emperors such as Marcus Aurelius, in whose "dear city of Zeus" the active citizen-participation in the legislature and the judiciary, as originally demanded, had lapsed. Later, when that Aristotelian concept was revived in the Middle Ages (not without some influence from Augustine's refusal both of theocracy and of "private religion" in the *City of God*), we again find participation restricted to a comparatively small and hopefully homogeneous community, to be designated Christendom – though even there, as in antiquity, large slave and serf classes – not to mention women – would be outside the social though not the eschatological pale.

A second problematic aspect of emphasis on the common good is that it demands sacrifice: that is, self-sacrifice, in extreme cases of one's own life.

The beginning of the dismantling of the concept of the common good was probably the substitution by Marsilius and Ockham of utility for virtue as the goal of the state – which marked the origins of the current notion that the state should hold as among its primary duties the preserving of a "level playing-field" for the advocacy of every sort of social experimentation. And it is widely acknowledged that the concept of the common good suffered

substantial further damage from the destruction of Western religious homo-
geneity in the Reformation, with the ensuing "privatization" of religion,
especially – but eventually not only – in the emerging Lutheran countries.
A common purpose, especially in matters of religion, was no longer obtainable
by common assumption or even consent and, after attempts to reimpose it
(or to impose a revised version) by force had failed, the era of toleration (from
which some groups, notably Catholics in England, Scotland and Ireland, were
originally excluded) eventually became something of an ideal for all.

With toleration came a widespread acceptance of the view that not
merely was religion – given the chance – likely to prove divisive, but so
was a common good to be associated with the excessive power of religious
or ideological groups who would wish to impose their view of it on the rest
of societies eager to eschew demanding public religions and ideologies.
Hence developed what has been well dubbed a "liberalism of wariness".

More recently, the cult of toleration has been seen to have its limitations. It is all very well to tolerate other people's practices so long as they
are "harmless", though the "Lockean caveat" – so long as what I do leaves
equal opportunities to others, indeed does them no injury – is much harder to
interpret than is widely supposed, and is open to abuse, not least by courts
of law, where a clear abuse may be deemed to be "non-demonstrable". Hence
toleration becomes far more problematic when your own clear view –
whether or not founded on religious belief – tells you that particular practices
harm, though not "demonstrably", not only those who perform or promote
them, but the wider society.

It is generally assumed that when within the secure limits of their own sub-
culture certain groups in the United Kingdom perform human sacrifice, this
is to be held as beyond the limits of toleration. A few might dispute this – the
pure nihilist or choice-theorist indeed ought to do so – but, even without a
concept of the common good, such are likely to remain a minority, even
if they argue that freedom to act in such ways is not the prerogative of an
individual, but only of a culture. For what then is to happen to the views of
an individual within the human-sacrificing group who rejects such culture-
driven freedom? Presumably his or her views are not to be tolerated; that is, an
individual is not to be allowed to try to reform his community, but must
formally leave it – which might also carry risks. Thus absolute toleration is
shown to be an impossibility, like absolute scepticism.

In our "global village", which now in the West may well be directly
affecting our local and individual villages, an older problem has come back
to haunt us in new guises. Whether or not pursuit of the common good is to
return, what is to be done with those who reject toleration (unless perchance

for themselves) and aim to impose their beliefs on others? It is in dealing with such groups that in much of the prevailing culture of the West – and I do not exclude many well-meaning Christians from such an indictment; indeed they are often among the worst offenders – respect for the views of others, however obnoxious, takes precedence over a willingness to face exactly what it is these others do and want to do.

Such unwillingness exists at the level both of individual morality and of the presentation of more formal "cultures". There is as little willingness to face the nature and implication of homosexual acts (such as their early association with the spread of AIDS), or of partial-birth abortions, as there is to recognize the real aims of anti-tolerant groups religious or political. Had Western leaders and the Western public been willing to face the patent goals of Nazism in 1933, we might have been spared the Holocaust and even the Second World War. If we are unwilling to face the fact that Islam always has been spread by force; that Mohammed and his followers – as the Ayatollah Khomeini has rightly and regularly said – were military men for whom mercy was merely a tool to be resorted to when brutality in "God's" cause seemed inappropriate; that it is fundamental for Islam that any territory once historically conquered but subsequently lost should be returned to the Ummah, then we may yet incur further catastrophes.

Against a background of economy with the inconvenient truth, toleration of certain cultures (as of private violence), far from being the right answer, makes massive slaughters and destruction the more likely. How can one pursue a common good in company with those who have a wholly divergent view of it – and one that is, if necessary, to be imposed by force? When an observant Muslim talks of human rights, he is frequently referring to the right of a woman to half of the value of a man in civil society. Which is not to deny that a "Westernized" – dare I say "semi-Christianized"? – Muslim may dream of reforming his religion.

Nor does it avail for Catholics to write about these questions as though the common good of Christian (or ex-Christian) Westerners can be squared with the cut-throat politics of other cultures. Toleration in politics cannot be a one-way street, unless we are to give our opponents the right to decide which one-way we are to drive or be driven. Nor is it adequate for people like the Jesuit political scientist David Hollenbach to point out[9] – rightly – that toleration by itself will not solve problems of poverty in the inner cities of the United States. There are too many other problems that he conveniently – lest the liberal élites of the West be offended – neglects, ranging from the culture

[9] *The Common Good and Christian Ethics* (Cambridge 2002).

of death in private life, symbolized by the abortion holocaust, to the demands for the imposition of Shari'a law (viewed as Khomeini correctly views it) on or within our own culture. To reject such monstrosities, we do indeed need a notion of the common good – the developed Catholic view – and to proclaim it without fear of offending those ready to resort to intimidation or outright violence.

I have argued that Catholicism has learned, by hard experience, to abandon the discredited ideas of Caesaropapism and papal theocracy – with their accompanying religious violence – that have disfigured it in the past. Fortunately, with a theory of the development of our understanding of social as well as other forms of doctrine, we do not have to live in the twelfth century. Consequently I have pointed to the growth of a purified prophetic role for the Church in the public sphere: a role in which her accumulated experience can be forcefully deployed without the backing of physical force, and in which she must continue to insist on her principles while leaving the laity to apply them sedulously in the bitter decisions required in public life.

That does not imply an abandonment of the idea of the common good. On the contrary, the ideals of community, the richness of achievement to which it can lead individuals and civilizations, are needed as never – and also as ever – before. Man has not ceased to be an Aristotelian political animal, and he has no possibility of living richly without the opportunities that community life provides. The ideals of the common good must now be preached not merely to the adult males of classical Athens or the inhabitants of a medieval Christendom, but to the human race, all of whom, as St Paul observed, have the inborn ability to recognize them, if they have not been inhumanely deformed by their families and cultures.

But just as those who, like Hollenbach, are willing to speak of a new Augustianian politics must point to the humility Augustine demands of his public figures, so they must also recognize two unpleasant truths which, neglected, make preaching the common good a waste of breath. The first I have already mentioned: the necessity to tell the truth without fear or favour, particularly without fear of religious or political violence, while the time remains in which it can be usefully told – while it is 1933 and not yet 1939. The second is to recognize that the Aristotelian concept of the common good was developed in a philosophical culture with a less clear recognition of human weakness and sins than its Christian successor.

That hard-won Christian learning should not be lightly cast aside. Aristotle and his successors held that the common good is achieved by active citizenship: that is, by citizens willing to lay aside their personal needs, when duty and responsibility require, for the public good, for the *res publica*, the

commonwealth. Their common good, insofar as it benefited them indivi-
dually, was understood more as shared opportunities to serve and develop
within the parameters of a common society than merely as imparted rights.
But service, as already noticed, requires self-sacrifice, and that entails, *inter
alia*, that we be prepared to undertake commitments, for example to mono-
gamous marriage. In the past, at least the desirability of such commitment
was taken for granted; at the present time in Western individualist culture
it is not. The word "sacrifice" itself – like its equivalents in other Western
languages – now regularly suggests not hard or loving duty but a whining
complaint at giving up luxuries for someone else's more basic benefit.
Those who talk of the common good without due awareness of what it
implies, what it demands and the wide unacceptablity of its demands are
whistling in the wind.

The acquisition of better attitudes in such matters is more difficult than
Aristotle supposed, not least in a globalized society. Political and social
failures and crimes do not arise solely through mistakes, through "human
error"; they frequently arise through wickedness, through our propensity to
sin – a word that hardly appears in the texts of Catholic progressives such as
Hollenbach. Tolerance of itself will at most preserve a few of the privileged –
for a while. Whatever its merits in the seventeenth century, it cannot be
treated as a panacea for our woes in a pluralistic society where what divides
us is our common inhumanity and what unifies us our vestiges of common
humanity. Tolerance today leads to the search for the goods of private life:
the leave-me-alone-and-I-will-leave-you-alone which again denies commitment. From the Catholic point of view it also entails ignoring not the foibles
of others but often, in effect, their sins – as long as they do not impinge on
me or, as often regrettably in the past, on "my" Church.

As such, tolerance is the opposite of a pursuit of a common good, as of
truth, and in a humane society – let alone a society worthy of images of God
both male and female – no substitute for it. As has been said of individuals,
so for institutions, especially one that claims an ever fuller catholicism,
if you won't stand up for others no-one will stand up for you – to paraphrase
Bonhoeffer. But if those others are oppressors, not least oppressors of half
the human race, they are not be tolerated but *converted* by those who are
insistent to tell the truth. If their belief-systems are rigid and, by definition,
non-reformable, that too cannot be left in silence. If they say they can
reform, they must be challenged to do so, and if they succeed they will move
closer to a developing Catholicism.

As for Catholics, not least Catholic bishops, when talking traditionally
about the Common Good they need to recognize that most of their hearers

have lost all concept of it, and that if they had not, they would certainly be feeling the pressure to give up many of their current shibboleths, not least that all religions are equally beneficial or equally harmful. This might be painful but would introduce them to a (Roman) world of God and humane culture which, despite all many of its advocates can do, has lost neither its natural appeal nor its potential to develop.

7.5 TRUTH AND SAVING TRUTH REVISITED

If we look at the state of Christianity in the contemporary world, we recognize that the Roman Catholic Church is generally flourishing (even if not in Europe) and that there is a second growth area represented by various evangelical, charismatic and fundamentalist forms of Christianity that are making strides both in the "first world" and – fuelled by American money – even more notably in the "third". I want to conclude the present study by briefly setting this phenomenon and its implications against the background of the distinction between truth and saving truth that I outlined in the Introduction.

I have argued throughout this book that Catholic culture has grown in parallel to Catholic dogma, and that the pair, in combination, offer both the salvation of Christ and a rich vision of humanity – plus the intellectual resources to resist secularism and nihilism without recourse to fideism. I have insisted, however – both here and elsewhere – that such resistance is possible only if Catholics decline to argue from preconditions set by their opponents which guarantee that those opponents will win the ensuing debate. I have also argued that for Catholics (and Christians more generally) there remain only two alternatives: a theory of the development of dogma *and* culture on the one hand, and a biblicist fundamentalism and literalism on the other. And the latter option – to be applauded for staunch maintenance of aspects of Christian morality – can in the end fight secularism only with ignorance and a denial of history and rationality.

I also claim that, by its very ability to assimilate the best of human achievement wherever it originally appears, Catholicism is able to demonstrate the richness of God's spiritual and cultural gifts to humanity – and thus also to indicate something of the richness of the divine nature. In other words, Catholicism is able to offer an account of God and of salvation that includes not only redemption from sin but a rich concept of the possible nature and greatness of that humanity which Christ has redeemed.

The vision offered by that other growth area – evangelical or fundamentalist Protestantism – is far more restrictive. It limits itself to "saving" truth and, if pursued to its logical limits, can only be and has only been moralizing, iconoclast, anti-intellectual and fideist. It thus presents two of the faces of a possible "Christianity" that Catholicism in my vision of it has outgrown, and in effect rejects the strenuous efforts of Catholic theoreticians – not to speak of Catholic (and non-Catholic) writers and artists from Origen through Augustine and Aquinas to the present day – to build a redeemed human culture which, in its fullest capabilities, shall be a worthy interpretation of the age-old thesis that men and women are created in the image of the unimaginable creator God: a God of truth, as we must still tell Pilate, whether he waits for an answer or not.

Bibliography

(Limited to secondary works cited in the text)

Abramowski, L., "Irenaeus, *Adv. Haer.* III.3.2: Ecclesia Romana and Omnis Ecclesia, and 3.3: Anacletus of Rome", *JTS* 28 (1977) 101–104

Allen, J. L., *Pope Benedict XVI* (New York 2000)

Armstrong, A. H., "Plotinus on the Origin and Place of Beauty in Thought about the World", in R. Baine Harris (ed.), *Neoplatonism and Contemporary Thought* (part 2) (Albany 2002) 217–230

Arquillière, H.-X., *L'augustinisme politique: Essai sur la formation des théories politiques du moyen âge* (Paris² 1955)

Ashley, B., "Gender and the Priesthood of Christ: A Theological Reflection", *The Thomist* 57 (1993) 343–379

Aspegren, K., *The Male Woman: A Feminine Ideal of the Early Church* (Uppsala 1990)

Asquith, C., *Shadowplay: The Hidden Beliefs and Coded Politics of William Shakespeare* (New York 2005)

Audet, J. P., *La Didachè: Instructions des apôtres* (Paris 1958)

Baer, R. A., *Philo's Use of the Categories Male and Female* (Leiden 1970)

Balthasar, H. U. von, *Theo-Drama* I–VI (1973–1983; Eng. trans. Graham Harrison, San Francisco 1990)

The Glory of the Lord (Edinburgh 1982–1991)

Bammel, C., "Adam in Origen", in R. Williams (ed.), *The Making of Orthodoxy: Essays in Honour of Henry Chadwick* (Oxford 1989) 62–93

Barnes, T. D., *Constantine and Eusebius* (Cambridge, Mass. 1981)

Athanasius and Constantius (Cambridge, Mass. 1993)

Barth, K., *Church Dogmatics* (Eng. trans., Edinburgh 1961)

Baumgarten, A., *Reflections on Poetry* (Halle 1735)

Beatrice, P. F., "L'union de l'Ame et le Corps: Némésius d'Emèse, lecteur de Porphyre", in V. Boudon-Millot and B. Pouderon (eds.), *Les Pères de l'église face à la science médicale de leurs temps* (Paris 2005) 253–285

Beattie, T., "Sex, Death and Melodrama: A Feminist Critique of Hans Urs von Balthasar", *The Way* 44 (October 2005) 160–176

Behr, J., *Asceticism and Anthropology in Irenaeus and Clement* (Oxford 2000)

Belleville, L., "Iounian . . . episēmoi en tois apostolois: A Re-examination of Romans 16:7 in Light of Primary Source Materials", *NTS* 51 (2005) 231–249

Bird, P. A., "Sexual Differentiation and the Divine Image in the Genesis Creation Texts", in Børresen (ed.), *Image of God and Gender Models* (Oslo 1991)

Blanchard, Y.-M., *Aux sources du canon: Le témoignage d'Irenée* (Paris 1993)

Blumenthal, H. J., *Plotinus' Psychology* (The Hague 1971)

Bonner, G., "Rufinus of Syria and African Pelagianism", *AS* 1 (1971) 31–47

"Augustine's Doctrine of Man: Image of God and Sinner", *Augustinianum* 24 (1984) 495–514

Borden, S., *Stein* (London/NewYork 2003)

Børresen, K. E., *Subordination and Equivalence: The Nature and Role of Women in Augustine and Thomas Aquinas* (Washington 1981)

"Imago Dei, privilège masculin? Interpretation augustinienne et pseudo-augustinienne de Gen. 1,37 et 1 Cor. 11,7, *Augustinianum* 25 (1985) 213–234

"In Defence of Augustine: How femina is homo?", in B. Bruning, M. Lamberigts and J. van Houten (eds.), *Collectanea Augustiniana: Mélanges T. J. van Bavel* (Louvain 1990) 263–280

"God's Image, Man's Image? Patristic Interpretations of Gen. 1,27 and 1 Cor. 11,7", in *Image of God and Gender Models* (Oslo 1991) 188–207

"Patristic Feminism: The Case of Augustine", *AS* 25 (1994) 139–152

Børresen, K. E. (ed.), *Image of God and Gender Models* (Oslo 1991)

Boulnois, M.-O., "L'union de l'Ame et du Corps comme modèle christologique de Némésius d'Emèse à la controverse nestorienne", in V. Boudon-Millot and B. Pouderon (eds.), *Les Pères de l'église face à la science médicale de leurs temps* (Paris 2005) 451– 475

Boylan, M., "The Galenic and Hippocratic Challenges to Aristotle's Conception Theory", *JHBiol* 17 (1984) 83–112

Bremmer, J. N., "Pandora or the Creation of a Greek Eve", in G. P. Luttikhuizen (ed.), *The Creation of Man and Woman* (Leiden 2000) 19–33

Brent, A., "The Relations between Ignatius and the Didascalia", *The Second Century* 8 (1991) 129–156

Hippolytus and the Roman Church in the Third Century: Communities in Tension before the Emergence of a Monarch-bishop (Leiden 1995)

Ignatius of Antioch and the Second Sophistic (Tübingen 2006)

Brisson, L., "Bisexualité et médiation en Grèce ancienne", *Nouvelle Revue de Psychanalyse* 7 (1973) 27–48

Brown, P., "Sexuality and Society in the Fifth Century A.D.: Augustine and Julian of Eclanum", in E. Gabba (ed.), *Tria corda: Scritti in onore di Arnaldo Momigliano* (Como 1983) 49–70

The Body and Society (New York 1988)

Augustine of Hippo (London² 2000)

Brown, R. E. and J. P. Meier, *Antioch and Rome* (London 1983)

Buddensieg, T., "Gregory the Great, the Destroyer of Pagan Idols", *JWCI* 28 (1965) 44–65

Bürke, G., "Die Origenes Lehre vom Urstand des Menschen", *ZKTh* 72 (1950) 1–39

Burnaby, J., *Amor Dei* (London 1938)

Burnell, P., *The Augustinian Person* (Washington 2005)

Camelot, T., "La théologie de l'image de Dieu", *RSPT* 40 (1956) 443–471

Camille, M., *The Gothic Idol* (Cambridge 1989)

Capboscq, A., *Schönheit Gottes und des Menschen: Theologische Untersuchung des Werkes "In Canticum Canticorum" von Gregor von Nyssa aus der Perspektive des Schönen und des Guten* (Frankfurt 2000)

Cataudella, Q., "Giovanni Crisostomo imitatore di Aristofane", *Athenaeum* 18 (1940) 236–243

Cavadini, J. C., "Feeling Right: Augustine on the Passions and Sexual Desire", *AS* 36 (2005) 195–217

Cipriani, N., "Echi antiapollinaristici e aristotelismo nella polemica di Giuliano d'Eclano", *Augustinianum* 21 (1981) 373–389

"La dottrina del peccato originale negli scritti di S.Agostino fin all' Ad Simplicianum", in L. Alici, R. Piccolomini and A. Pieretti (eds.), *Il mistero del male e la libertà possibile IV* (Rome 1997) 23–48

"*L'altro Agostino* di G. Lettieri", *REA* 48 (2002) 249–265

Clark, E. A., *Jerome, Chrysostom and Friends* (New York/Toronto 1979)

Cohen, S. J. D., "'Those who say they are Jews and are not': How do you know a Jew in antiquity when you see one?", in S. J. D. Cohen and E. S. Frerichs (eds.), *Diasporas in Antiquity* (Atlanta 1993) 1–45

Coleman-Norton, P. R., "St. Chrysostom and Greek Philosophy", *CP* 25 (1930) 305–317

Colish, M., *Ambrose's Patriarchs: An Ethics for the Common Man* (Notre Dame 2005)

Cross, F. L., *I Peter: A Paschal Liturgy* (London 1954)

Crouzel, H., *Théologie de l'image de Dieu chez Origène* (Paris 1956)

"La doctrine origènienne des corps ressuscités", *Bulletin de littérature ecclésiastique* 81 (1980) 175–200, 241–266

Daley, B., "Apocatastasis and the 'Honourable' Silence in the Eschatology of Maximus the Confessor", in T. Heinzer and C. Schönborn (eds.), *Maximus the Confessor* (Fribourg 1982) 309–333

Daniélou, J., *Platonisme et théologie mystique* (Paris 1944)

"La chronologie des oeuvres de Grégoire de Nysse", *Studia Patristica* 7, TU 92 (1966) 159–169

L'être et le temps chez Grégoire de Nysse (Leiden 1970)

D'Arcy, M. C., *The Mind and Heart of Love* (London 1962)

Dean-Jones, L., *Women's Bodies in Classical Greek Science* (Oxford 1994)

de Keyser, E., *La signification de l'art dans les Ennéades de Plotin* (Louvain 1955)

de Moor, J. C., "The Duality in God and Man: Genesis 1:26–27", in J. C. De Moor (ed.) *Intertextuality in Ugarit and Israel* (London 1998) 112–125

De Salvo, C., *L'oltre nel presente* (Milan 1996)

De Solenni., P. F., *A Hermeneutic of Aquinas's Mens Through a Sexually Differentiated Epistemology: Towards an Understanding of Woman as Imago Dei* (Rome 2003)

Devereaux, M., "Beauty and Evil: The case of Leni Riefensthal's *Triumph of the Will*", in J. Levinson (ed.), *Aesthetics and Ethics: Essays at the Intersection* (Cambridge 1998) 227–256

Dibelius, M., *Botschaft und Geschichte* (Tübingen 1956)

Dideberg, D., *Saint Augustin et la première epître de saint Jean: Une théologie de l'amour* (Paris 1975)

Dillon, J. M., *The Middle Platonists* (London/Ithaca, N.Y, 1977)

"Aisthēsis Noētē: A Doctrine of Spiritual Senses in Origen and Plotinus", in *The Golden Chain* (Aldershot 1990) essay XIX

Dodaro, R., "The Secret Justice of God and the Gift of Humility", *AS* 34 (2003) 83–96

Christ and the Just Society in the Thought of Augustine (Cambridge 2004)

Dorival, F., "L'image des cyniques chez les Pères grecs", in M. O. Goulet-Cazé and R. Goulet (eds.), *Le Cynisme grec et ses prolongements* (Paris 1991) 419–447

Downing, F. G., *Cynics and Christian Origins* (Edinburgh 1992)

Drobner, H., *Person-Exegese und Christologie bei Augustinus* (Leiden 1986)

Duffy, E., *Saints and Sinners: A History of the Popes* (New Haven 1997)

Dunphy, W., "Pelagius in Carthage, 411–412", *Augustinianum* 45 (2005) 389–466

Dünzl, F., *Braut und Bräutigam: Die Auslegung des Canticum durch Gregor von Nyssa* (Tübingen 1993)

Duval, Y.-M., "La date du 'De Natura' de Pélage", *REA* 36 (1990) 257–283

Edmundson, G., *The Church in Rome in the First Century* (London 1913)

Eilberg-Schwartz, H., *God's Phallus* (Boston, Mass. 1994)

Elm, S., *'Virgins of God': The Making of Asceticism in Late Antiquity* (Oxford 1994)

Elsner, J., "Late Antique Art: The Problem of the Concept and the Cumulative Aesthetic", in S. Swain and M. Edwards (eds.), *Approaching Late Antiquity* (Oxford 2004)

Exum, J. C., *Plotted, Shot and Painted: Cultural Representations of Biblical Women* (Sheffield 1996)

Feldman, L. H., "Is the New Testament Antisemitic?", in *Studies in Hellenistic Judaism* (Leiden 1996) 277–288

Finnis, J. M., *Aquinas: Moral, Political and Legal Theory* (Oxford 1998)

"The Phoenix and the Turtle", *TLS* (18 May 2003) 12–14

Fitzmyer, J. A., Review of Robinson, *Redating, Interpretation* 32 (1978) 309–313

Flasch, K., *Die Logik des Schreckens: Augustinus von Hippo, Die Gnadenlehre von 397* (Mainz 1990)

Ford, D. C., *Women and Marriage in the Early Church: The Full View of John Chrysostom* (South Canaan 1996)

Fredriksen, P., "Beyond the Body/Soul Dichotomy: Augustine on Paul against the Manichees and the Pelagians", *REA* 23 (1988) 87–114

Fuchs, E., "L'homme à l'image de Dieu: L'anthropologie théologique, du point de vue de l'éthique", in P. Bühler (ed.), *Humain à l'image de Dieu* (Geneva 1989) 309–320

Gaça, K., *The Making of Fornication* (Berkeley/Los Angeles/London 2003)

Gadamer, H.-G., *The Relevance of the Beautiful and Other Essays* (Cambridge 1986)

Gauthier, R. A., *Magnanimité: L'idéal de la grandeur dans la philosophie paienne et la théologie chrétienne* (Paris 1951)

Gerson, L. P., *Plotinus* (London/New York 1994)

Gewirth, A., *Marsilius of Padua* (New York 1951)

The Community of Rights (London/Chicago 1996)

Giakalis, A., *Images of the Divine: The Theology of Icons at the Seventh Ecumenical Council* (revised edition, Leiden 2005)

Gill, C., "Is There a Concept of Person in Greek Philosophy?", in S. Everson (ed.), *Companions to Ancient Thought 2: Psychology* (Cambridge 1991) 166–194

Gillette, G., "Augustine and the Significance of Perpetua's Words: And I was a man", *AS* 32 (2001) 115–125

Gleason, M. W., "The Semiotics of Gender", in D. M. Halperin, J. Winkler and F. I. Zeitlin (eds.), *Before Sexuality* (Princeton 1990) 389–415

Goulet-Cazé, M. O., "Le Cynisme à l'époque impériale", in *ANRW* 2.36.4, 2720–2833

Gourevitch, D., *Le mal d'être femme: La femme et la médecine dans la Rome antique* (Paris 1984)

Grant, R. M., Review of Robinson, *Redating*, in *JBL* 97 (1978) 294–296

Griffiths, P. J., *Lying: An Augustinian Theology of Deception* (Grand Rapids 2004)

Grumett, D., " Yves de Montcheuil: Action, Justice and the Kingdom in Spiritual Resistance to Nazism", *TS* 68 (2007) 618–641

Guillaumont, A. and C. Guillaumont, *Evagre le Pontique: Traité pratique*, *SC* 170, (Paris 1971)

Gunton, C., "Trinity, Ontology and Anthropology: Towards a Renewal of the Theology of the Imago Dei", in C. Schwöbel and C. Gunton (eds.), *Persons, Divine and Human* (Edinburgh 1991) 47–61

Guyer, P., *Values of Beauty: Historical Essays in Aesthetics* (Cambridge 2005)

Hadot, P., "L'image de la Trinité dans l'âme chez Victorinus et chez s. Augustin", *Studia Patristica 6, TU* 81 (Berlin 1962) 409–442

Halperin, D. M., "Why is Diotima a Woman? Platonic Eros and the Figuration of Gender" in D. M. Halperin, J. Winkler and F. I. Zeitlin (eds.), *Before Sexuality* (Princeton 1990) 257–308

Hamman, A. G., *L'homme, image de Dieu* (Paris 1987)

Harl, M., "Recherches sur l'origénisme d'Origène: La satiété (kóros) de la contemplation comme motif de la chute des âmes", *Studia Patristica 8, TU* 92 (Berlin 1966) 373–405

Harnack, A. von., *Geschichte der altchristlichen Literatur* (Leipzig 1897)

Harrison, C., *Beauty and Revelation in the Thought of Saint Augustine* (Oxford 1992)

Harrison, N. V., "Women, Human Identity and the Image of God", *JECS* 9 (2001) 205–249

"Woman and the Image of God according to St. John Chrysostom", in P. Blowers *et al.* (eds.), *In Domenico Eloquio: In Lordly Eloquence: Essays in Patristic Exegesis in Honor of Robert Louis Wilken* (Grand Rapids 2002) 259–279

Head, P. M., "Is P^4, P^{64} and P^{67} the Oldest Manuscript of the Four Gospels? A Response to T. C. Skeat", *NTS* 51 (2005) 450–457

Henley, J. A., "Theology and the Basis of Human Rights", *Scottish Journal of Theology* 39 (1986) 361–378

Henne, P., *La Christologie chez Clément de Rome et dans le Pasteur d'Hermas* (Fribourg 1992)

Hölscher, L., *The Reality of the Mind: Augustine's Philosophical Arguments for the Human Soul as a Spiritual Substance* (London/New York 1986)

Hollenbach, D., *The Common Good and Christian Ethics* (Cambridge 2002)

Hopkins, K., *A World Full of Gods* (London 1999)

Horowitz, M. C., "The Image of God in Man – Is Woman Included?" *HTR* 72 (1979) 175–206

Hunter, D. G., "The Language of Desire: Clement of Alexandria's Transformation of Ascetic Discourse", *Semeia* 57 (1992) 95–111

"The Paradise of Patriarchy: Ambrosiaster on Woman as (not) God's Image", *JTS* 43 (1992) 447–469

"Augustinian Pessimism? A New Look at Augustine's Teaching on Sex, Marriage and Celibacy", *AS* 25 (1994) 153–177

"Reclaiming Biblical Morality: Sex and Salvation History in Augustine's Treatment of the Hebrew Saints, in P. Blowers *et al* (eds.), *In Domenico Eloquio: In Lordly Eloquence: Essays in Patristic Exegesis in Honor of Robert Louis Wilken* (Grand Rapids 2002) 317–335

Inwood, B., "Why Do Fools Fall in Love?", in R. Sorabji (ed.), *Aristotle and After* (London 1997) 55–69

Irigaray, L., *Speculum of the Other Woman* (Eng. trans., Ithaca, N.Y. 1985)

Jay, E. G., "From Presbyter-Bishops to Bishops and Presbyters", *The Second Century* 1 (1981) 129–136

Jeauneau, E., "La division des sexes chez Grégoire de Nysse et chez Jean Scot Erigène", *Eriugena, Studien zu seinen Quellen* (Heidelberg 1980) 33–54

Jenkins C. (ed.), "Origen on 1 Corinthians", *JTS* 9 (1908) 231–247, 353–374

Jensen, R. M., *Face to Face* (Minneapolis 2005)

Jervell, J., *Imago Dei* (Göttingen 1960)

Kahn, C. H., "Aeschines on Socratic Eros", in P. A. Vander Waerdt (ed.), *The Socratic Movement* (Ithaca, N.Y./London 1994) 87–106

Plato and the Socratic Dialogue (Cambridge 1996)

Kannengiesser, C., "L'infinité divine chez Grégoire de Nysse", *RSR* 55 (1967) 55–65

Kanyaroro, J. C., "Les richesses intérieures de l'âme selon Plotin", *LTP* 59 (2003) 235–256

Karras, V., "Male Domination of Women in the Writings of John Chrysostom", *Greek Orthodox Theological Review* 36 (1991) 131–139

Kegley, C. W. (ed.), *The Philosophy and Theology of Anders Nygren* (Carbondale, Ill. 1970)

Kempshall, M. S., *The Common Good in Late Medieval Political Thought* (Oxford 1999)

Kilmer, J., "Genital Phobia and Depilation", *JHS* 102 (1982) 104–112

Kinder, D., "Clement of Alexandria: Conflicting Views on Women", *Second Century* 7 (1990) 213–220

Knust, J. W., *Abandoned to Lust* (New York 2006)

Kobusch, T., "Kann Gott leiden? Zu den philosophischen Grundlagen der Lehre von der Passibilität Gottes bei Origenes", *VC* 46 (1992) 328–333

Kraut, R., "Are There Natural Rights in Aristotle?", *RM* 49 (1996) 755–774

Kripke, S., *Naming and Necessity* (Oxford 1980)

Krueger, D., "Diogenes the Cynic among the Fourth-Century Fathers", *VC* 47 (1993) 29–49

"The Bawdy and Society", in A. Bracht-Branham and M. O. Goulet-Cazé (eds.), *The Cynics* (Berkeley London 1996) 222–243

Lamberigts, M., "Julian and Augustine on the Origin of the Soul", *Augustiniana* 46 (1996) 243–260

"Augustine on Predestination: Some Quaestiones Disputatae Revisited", in *Mélanges offerts à T. J. van Bavel* (*Augustiniana* 2004) 270–305

Lampe, P., *Die stadtrömischen Christen in den ersten beiden Jahrhunderten* (Tübingen 1989)

Laqueur, T., *Making Sex: Body and Gender from the Greeks to Freud* (Cambridge, Mass. 1990)

Lévy, A., "Aux confines du créé et de l'incréé: Les dimensions de l'épectase chez Grégoire de Nysse", *RSPT* 84 (2000) 247–274

Lietaert Peerbolte, L. J., "Man, Woman and the Angels in 1 Cor. 11: 12–16", in G. P. Luttikhuizen (ed.), *The Creation of Man and Woman* (Leiden 2000) 76– 92

Lilla, S. R. C., *Clement of Alexandria* (Oxford 1971)

Lloyd, A. C., "Non-Discursive Thought – an Enigma of Greek Philosophy", *PAS* 70 (1969) 261–274

"Non-Propositional Thought in Plotinus", *Phronesis* 31 (1986) 258–265

Loader, W., *The Septuagint, Sexuality and the New Testament* (Grand Rapids/ Cambridge 2004)

Loraux, N., "La race des femmes et quelques unes de ses tribus", *Arethusa* 11 (1978) 43–89

Lössl, J., "Augustine on Predestination", *Augustiniana* 52 (2002) 241–272

Lutz, M., "Changes and Crisis in the Relations between Men and Women", in *Men and Women: Diversity and Mutual Complementarity* (Pontificio Concilio per i Laici, Vatican City 2006) 47–61

MacIntyre, A., *Sartre: A Collection of Critical Essays* (New York 1971)

Three Rival Versions of Moral Enquiry (London 1990)

Marafioti, D., "Alle origini del teorema della predestinazione (*Simpl.* 1.2.13–22)", *CIA* (1987) 257–277

Markschies, C., "Die platonische Metapher von 'innerem Menschen': Eine Brücke zwischen antiker Philosophie und altchristlicher Theologie", *ZKG* 105 (1994) 1–17

Markus, R. A., "'Imago' and 'Similitudo' in Augustine", *REA* 10 (1964) 125–143

Saeculum: History and Society in the Thought of St Augustine (Cambridge 1970)

Masai, F., "Les conversions de s. Augustin et les débuts du spiritualisme en Occident", *Le Moyen Age* 67 (1961) 1–40

Mathias, P., *Plotin. Du Beau, Ennéades 1.6 et 5.8* (Paris 1991)

May, G., "Die Chronologie des Lebens und der Werke des Gregor von Nyssa", in *Ecriture et culture philosophique dans la pensée de Grégoire de Nysse* (Leiden 1971) 51–67

May, G., *Creatio ex Nihilo* (1978; Eng. trans. A. S. Worrall, Edinburgh 1994)

Mayer, A., *Das Gottesbild im Menschen nach Clemens von Alexandrien* (Rome 1942)

McCool, G. A., "The Ambrosian Origin of St Augustine's Theology of the Image of God in Man", *TS* 20 (1959) 62–79

McCue, J. F., "The Roman Primacy in the Second Century and the Problem of the Development of Dogma", *TS* 25 (1964) 161–196

McGowan, R. J., "Augustine's Spiritual Equality: The Allegory of Man and Woman with Regard to *Imago Dei*", *REA* 33 (1987) 255–264

McGuckin, J., "The Changing Forms of Jesus", in L. Lies (ed.), *Origeniana Quarta* (Vienna 1987) 215–222

Gregory of Nazienzus: An Intellectual Biography (Crestwood 2001)

McLeod, F. G., *The Image of God in Man in the Antiochean Tradition* (Washington 1999)

The Role of Christ's Humanity in Salvation: Insights from Theodore of Mopsuestia (Washington 2005)

McQueen, D. J., "Augustine on Freewill and Predestination: A Critique of J. M. Rist", *Museum: West African Review of Theology* (1974) 17–28

Meeks, W., "The Image of the Androgyne: Some Uses of a Symbol in Earliest Christianity", *History of Religions* 13 (1974) 165–208

The Moral World of the First Christians (Philadelphia 1986)

Merki, H., ὉΜΟΙΩΣΙΣ ΘΕΩΙ: *Von der platonischen Angleichung an Gott zur Gottähnlichkeit bei Gregor von Nyssa* (Freiburg in der Schweiz 1952)

Meyer, M. W., "Making Mary Male: The Categories 'Male' and 'Female' in the Gospel of Thomas", *NTS* 31 (1985) 554–570

Miller, F. R., *Nature, Justice and Rights in Aristotle's Politics* (Oxford 1995)

Mitterer, A., "Mann und Weib nach dem biologishen Weltbild des hl. Thomas und dem der Gegenwart", *ZKTh* 57 (1933) 491–556

Moltmann, J., "Christian Faith and Human Rights", in *On Human Dignity* (London 1984) 19–36

Mortley, R., *Womanhood: The Feminine in Ancient Hellenism, Gnosticism, Christianity and Islam* (Sydney 1981)

Mosshammer, A. A., "The Created and the Uncreated in Gregory of Nyssa "Contra Eunomium 1", in L. F. Mateo-Seco and J. Bastero (eds.), *El "Contra Eunomium 1" en la producción literaria de Gregorio de Nisa* (Pamplona 1988) 353–379

Mothersill, M., *Beauty Restored* (Oxford 1984)

Motta, B., *La mediazione estrema: L'antropologia di Nemesio di Emesa fra Platonismo e Aristotelismo* (Padua 2004)

Mühlenberg, E., *Die Unendlichkeit Gottes bei Gregor von Nyssa* (Göttingen 1966)

Murphy, F. A., *Christ the Form of Beauty* (Edinburgh 1995)

Murray, M. C., "Art and the Early Church", *JTS* 28 (1977) 303–345

Narbonne, J.-M., "Action, Contemplation and Interiority in the Thinking of Beauty in Plotinus", in A. Alexandrakis (ed.), *Neoplatonism and Western Aesthetics* (Albany 2002) 3–18

Niederwimmer, K., *The Didache* (Minneapolis 1998)

Nolan, M., "The Defective Male: What Aquinas Really Said", *New Blackfriars* 75 (1994) 156–166

Noort, E., "The Creation of Man and Woman in Biblical and Ancient Near Eastern Traditions", in G. P. Luttikhuizen (ed.), *The Creation of Man and Woman* (Leiden 2000) 1–18

Norelli, P., *Esposizione degli oracoli del Signore* (Milan 2005)

Nussbaum, M., *The Therapy of Desire: Theory and Practice in Hellenistic Ethics* (Princeton 1994)

"Eros and the Wise", in J. Sihvola and T. Engberg-Pedersen (eds.), *The Emotions in Hellenistic Philosophy* (Dordrecht 1998)

Women and Human Development: The Capabilities Approach (Cambridge 2000)

Nygren, A., *Agape and Eros* (trans. P. S. Watson, Philadelphia 1953)

O'Connell, R. J., *Saint Augustine's Early Theory of Man, AD 386– 391* (Cambridge, Mass. 1968)

Art and the Christian Intelligence in Saint Augustine (Cambridge, Mass. 1978)

Osborn, E., *Ethical Patterns in Early Christian Thought* (Cambridge 1976)

Tertullian: First Theologian of the West (Cambridge 1997)

Irenaeus of Lyons (Cambridge 2001)

Osborne, C., "The Repudiation of Representation in Plato's *Republic* and Its Repercussions", *PCPS* 33 (1987) 53–73

Eros Unveiled: Plato and the God of Love (Oxford 1994)

Osborne, J., *Master Gregory* (Toronto 1987)

Pelikan, J. and Lehmann, H. T., (eds.), *Luther's Works* (St Louis 1958)

Peroli, E., *Essere persona: Alle origini di un'idea fra grecità e cristianesimo* (Brescia 2006)

Perrone, L., "La passione della carità: Il mistero della misericordia divina secondo Origene", *Parola, Spirito e Vita* 29 (1994) 223–235

Pinckaers, S., "Le thème de l'image de Dieu en l'homme et l'anthropologie", in P. Bühler (ed.), *Humain à l'image de Dieu* (Geneva 1989) 47–163

Pinto de Oliveira, C. J., "Image de Dieu et dignité humaine", *Freiburger Zeitschrift für Philosophie und Theologie* 27 (1980) 401–436

"Homme et femme dans l'anthropologie de Thomas d'Aquin", in P. Bühler (ed.), *Humain à l'image de Dieu* (Geneva 1989) 165–190

Pisi, P., "Peccato di Adamo e caduta dei NOES nell'esegesi origeniana", in L. Lies (ed.), *Origeniana Quarta* (Innsbruck 1987) 322–335

Porter, J., *Nature as Reason* (Grand Rapids/Cambridge 2005)

Prigent, P., *L'art des premiers chrétiens* (Paris 1995)

Prinzivalli, E., *L'esegesi di Metodio d'Olimpo* (Rome 1984)

Magister Ecclesiae: Il dibattito su Origene fra III e IV secolo (Rome 2002)

"L'uomo e il suo destino nel Commento a Giovanni" in E. Prinzivalli (ed.), *Il Commento a Giovanni di Origene: Il testo e i suoi contesti* (Villa Verruchio, RN 2005) 361–379

Rad, G. von, *Genesis* (London 1972)

Rahner, K., "Le début d'une doctrine des cinq sens spirituels chez Origène", *Revue d'Ascétique et de Mystique* 12 (1932) 113–145

Refoulé, F., "Julien d'Éclane, théologien et philosophe", *RSR* 52 (1964) 42–84, 233–247

Ricken, F., "Nikaia als Krisis des altchristlichen Platonismus", *Theologie und Philosophie* 44 (1969) 321–341

Rigby, P., "The Role of God's 'Inscrutable Judgments' in Augustine's Doctrine of Predestination", *AS* 33 (2002) 213–222

Rist, J. M., *Eros and Psyche* (Toronto 1964)

"Mysticism and Transcendence in Later Neoplatonism", *Hermes* 92 (1964) 213–225

Plotinus: The Road to Reality (Cambridge 1967)

"Augustine on Free Will and Predestination", *JTS* 20 (1969) 420–447, reprinted in R. A. Markus (ed.), *Augustine*, Modern Studies in Philosophy (New York 1972) and E. Ferguson (ed.), *Studies in Early Christianity: Vol. 10, Early Christian Doctrines of Human Nature, Sin and Salvation* (Hampden, Conn. 1993)

"The Greek and Latin Texts of the Discussion of Free Will in 'De Principiis' Book III", *Origeniana (Quaderni di Vetera Christianorum)* 12 (1975) 97–111

"Pseudo-Ammonius and the Soul–Body Problem in Late Antiquity", *AJP* 109 (1988) 402–415

The Mind of Aristotle (Toronto 1989)

"Ps-Dionysius, Neoplatonism and the Problem of Spiritual Weakness", in H. Westra (ed.), *From Athens to Chartres: Festschrift E. Jeauneau* (Leiden 1992) 135–161

Augustine: Ancient Thought Baptized (Cambridge 1994)

"Plotino, Ficino e noi stessi: Alcuni reflessi etici", *Rivista di filosofia neoscolastica* 86 (1994) 448–467

"Plato and Professor Nussbaum on Acts 'Contrary to Nature'", in M. Joyal (ed.), *Studies in Plato and the Platonic Tradition: Essays presented to John Whittaker* (Aldershot 1997) 65–79

"Augustine: Freedom, Love and Intention", in L. Alici, R. Piccolomini and A. Pieretti (eds.), *Il mistero del male e la libertà possibile (IV): Ripensare Agostino* (Rome 1997) 7–21

"Why Greek Philosophers Might Have Been Concerned about the Environment", in L. Westra and T. M. Robinson (eds.), *The Greeks and the Environment* (Lanham 1997) 19–32

On Inoculating Moral Philosophy Against God (Marquette 2000)

"Love and Will: Around *De Trinitate* XV 20,38", in J. Brachtendorf (ed.), *Gott und Sein Bild* (Paderborn 2000) 205–216

"Plutarch's *Amatorius*: A Commentary on Plato's Theories of Love?", *CQ* 51 (2001) 557–575

"Desiderio e azione", in L. Alici (ed.), *Azione e persona: Le radici della prassi* (Milan 2002) 29–44

Real Ethics (Cambridge 2002)

"Luke 2.2: Making Sense of the Date of Jesus' Birth", *JTS* 56 (2005) 489–491

"Practical Reasoning in Utopia" (forthcoming)

Rist, T. C. K., *Shakespeare's Romances and the Politics of Counter-Reformation* (Lewiston/Lampeter 1999)

Robertson, M., *A History of Greek Art* (Cambridge 1975)

Robinson, J., *The Mass and Modernity* (San Francisco 2005)

Robinson, J. A. T., *Redating the New Testament* (London 1976)

Rolland, P., *L'origine et la date des évangiles* (Paris 1994)

Rudhart, J., "Pandora: Hésiode et les femmes", *Mus Helv* 43 (1986) 231–246

Runia, D. T., *Philo in Early Christian Literature* (Assen/Minneapolis 1993)
Scaraffia, L., "Socio-Cultural Changes in Women's Lives", in *Men and Women: Diversity and Mutual Complementarity* (Pontificio Concilio per i Laici, Vatican City 2006) 15–22
Schatz, K., *Papal Primacy from Its Origins to the Present* (1990; Eng. trans. John A. Otto and Linda M. Maloney, Collegeville 1996)
Schindler, D. C., "Reason in Mystery. Gestalt: Knowledge and Aesthetic Experience in Balthasar and Augustine", *Second Spring* 6 (2004) 23–33
Schloesser, S., "Against Forgetting: Memory, History, Vatican II", *TS* 67 (2006) 275–319
Schofield, M., "Sharing in the Constitution", *RM* 49 (1996) 831– 858
		The Stoic Idea of the City (Chicago 1999)
Schürer, E., *The History of the Jewish People in the Age of Jesus Christ* (Edinburgh 1973)
Scola, A., "L'*imago Dei* e la sessualità umana", *Anthropotes* 1 (1992) 61–73
Scola, A., *The Nuptial Mystery* (1998; Eng. trans. M. K. Borras, Grand Rapids/ Cambridge 2005)
Sedley, D., "The Ideal of Godlikeness", in G. Fine (ed.), *Plato 2: Ethics, Politics, Religion and the Soul* (Oxford 1999) 309–328
Sesboué, B., *Hors de l'église pas de salut: Histoire d'une formule et problèmes d'interprétation* (Paris 2004)
Sfameni Gasparro, G., "Image of God and Sexual Differentiation in the Tradition of Enkrateia", in K. Børresen (ed.), *Image of God and Gender Models* (Oslo 1991) 138–171
Shaw, T. M., *The Burden of the Flesh: Fasting and Sexuality in Early Christianity* (Minneapolis 1998)
Siegel, J., *The Idea of the Self: Thought and Experience in Western Europe since the Seventeenth Century* (Cambridge 2005)
Simonetti, M., "Una nuova proposta su Ippolito", *Augustinianum* 36 (1996) 13–46
Sissa, G., "The Sexual Philosophies of Plato and Aristotle", in P. S. Pantel (ed.), *A History of Women* I (Cambridge, Mass. 1992) 46–81
Skeat, T. C., "Irenaeus and the Four-Gospel Canon", *NT* 34 (1992) 194–199
		"The Oldest Manuscript of the Four Gospels", *NTS* 43 (1997) 1–34
Solignac, A., "Le salut des paiens d'après la prédication de saint Augustin", in G. Madec (ed.), *Augustin prédicateur (395–411)* (Paris 1998) 419–428
Sorabji, R., "Myths about Non-Propositional Thought", in M. Nusssbaum and M. Schofield (eds.), *Language and Logos: Studies in Greek Philosophy Presented to G. E. L. Owen* (Cambridge 1984) 295–314
Sorabji, R., *Emotion and Peace of Mind* (Oxford 2000)
Sorabji, R., (ed.), *Aristotle Transformed* (Ithaca 1990)
Spanneut, M., *Le stoicisme des Pères de l'église* (Paris 1957)
		"L'apatheia chrétienne aux quatres premiers siècles", *POC* 52 (2002) 165–302
Stanton, G. N., "The Fourfold Gospel", *NTS* 43 (1997) 317–346
		Jesus and Gospel (Cambridge 2004)
Stein, E., *Self-Portrait in Letters (1916–1942)* (trans. J. Koeppel, Washington 1993)

Strola, G., *Il desiderio di Dio: Studio dei salmi 42–43* (Assisi 2003)

Stroumsa, G. G., "Caro salutis cardo: Shaping the Person in Early Christian Thought", *History of Religions* 30 (1990) 25–50

Studer, B., *The Grace of Christ and the Grace of God in Augustine of Hippo: Christocentrism or Theocentrism?* (Collegeville 1997)

Sullivan, F. A., *From Apostles to Bishops* (Mahwah, N. J. 2001)

Sumner, W., *The Moral Foundation of Rights* (Oxford 1987)

Svoboda, K., *L'esthétique de saint Augustin et ses sources* (Brno 1933)

Syme, R., *The Roman Revolution* (Oxford 1939)

Talmon, S., *The Origins of Totalitarian Democracy* (Harmondsworth 1952)

Taranto, S., "Esiste una 'doppia creazione' dalle origini in Gregorio Nisseno?", *Adamantius* 8 (2002) 33–56

Tatarkiewicz, R., *Mediaeval Aesthetics* (Warsaw 1970)

Taubes, J., "La giustificazione del brutto nella tradizione cristiana delle origini", in *Messianismo e cultura: Saggi di politica, teologia e storia* (Cernusco 2001) 255–281

Taylor, C., *Sources of the Self* (Cambridge, Mass. 1989)

Tch'ang Tche Wang, J., *Saint Augustin et les vertus des paiens* (Paris 1938)

Temkin, O., *Galenism: Rise and Decline of a Medical Philosophy* (Ithaca, N.Y. 1973)

Teske, R., "Vocans Temporales, Faciens Aeternos: St. Augustine on Liberation from Time", *Traditio* 41 (1985) 24–47

"St Augustine on the Humanity of Christ and Temptation", in *Mélanges offerts à T. J. van Bavel* (*Augustiniana* 2004) 261–277

Teugel, G. M. G., "The Creation of the Human in Rabbinic Interpretation", in G. P. Luttikhuizen (ed.), *The Creation of Man and Woman* (Leiden 2000) 107–127

Thonnard, F.-J., "L'aristotélisme de Julien d'Eclane et saint Augustin", *REA* 12 (1965) 296–304

"Justice de Dieu et justice humaine selon saint Augustin", *Augustinus* 12 (1967) 387–402

Tierney, B., "Public Expediency and Natural Law: A Fourteenth Century Discussion on the Origins of Government and Property", in B. Tierney and P. Lineham (eds.), *Authority and Power: Studies Presented to W. Ullmann* (Cambridge 1980) 167–182

The Idea of Natural Rights: Studies on Natural Rights, Natural Law and Church Law 1150–1625 (Atlanta 1997)

Torchia, N. J., *Creatio ex Nihilo and the Theology of St. Augustine* (New York 1999)

Tscholl, J., "Augustins Interesse für das körperliche Schöne", *Augustiniana* 14 (1964) 72–104

Uleyn, A., "La doctrine morale de saint Jean Chrysostome dans le 'Commentaire sur saint Matthieu' et ses affinités avec la diatribe", *Revue de l'Université d'Ottawa* 27 (1957) 5*–25*, 99*–140*

Ullmann, W., "The Significance of the *Epistula Clementis* in the Ps-Clementines", *JTS* 11 (1960) 295–317

Principles of Government and Politics in the Middle Ages (London 1961)

A Short History of the Papacy in the Middle Ages (London 1972)

Unterseher, L. A., "The Mark of Cain and the Jews: Augustine's Theology of Jews", *AS* 33 (2002) 99–121

van Bavel, T. J., "The Double Face of Love in Saint Augustine. The Daring Inversion: Love is God", *CIA* III (Rome 1987) 69–80

"Woman in the Image of God in St Augustine's 'De Trinitate XII'", *Signum Pietatis* (Würzburg 1989) 267–288

van den Hoek, A., "Endowed with Reason or Glued to the Senses: Philo's Thoughts on Adam and Eve", in G. P. Luttikhuizen (ed.), *The Creation of Man and Woman* (Leiden 2000) 63–75

van Eijk, T. H. C., "Marriage and Virginity, Death and Immortality", in J. Fontaine and C. Kannengiesser (eds.), *Epektasis: Mélanges patristiques offerts au Cardinal Jean Daniélou* (Paris 1972) 209–235

Vogt, K., "'Becoming Male': A Gnostic and Early Christian Metaphor", in K. E. Børresen (ed.), *Image of God and Gender Models* (Oslo 1991)

"'Becoming Male': A Gnostic, Early Christian and Islamic Metaphor", in K. E. Børresen and K. Vogt (eds.), *Women's Studies of the Christian and Islamic Traditions* (Dordrecht/Boston, Mass./London 1993) 217–224

Völker, W., *Das Vollkommenheitsideal des Origenes* (Tübingen 1931)

Der wahre Gnostiker nach Clemens Alexandrinus (Berlin 1952)

Walgrave, J. H., *Theological Resources: Unfolding Revelation* (London 1972)

Wellborn, L. L., "On the Date of First Clement", *BR* 29 (1984) 35–54

White, T. J., "Von Balthasar and Journet on Grace and Freedom", *Nova et Vetera* 4 (2006) 633–665

Wojtyła, K., *Love and Responsibility* (New York 1981)

Zagdoun, M.-A., *La philosophie stoïcienne de l'art* (Paris 2000)

Zeitlin, F. I., "The Economics of Hesiod's Pandora", in E. Reeder (ed.), *Pandora* (Baltimore 1995) 49–56

Zorzi, M. B., "La reinterpretazione dell'eros platonico nel *Simposio* di Metodio d'Olimpo", *Adamantius* 9 (2003) 102–127

Desiderio della bellezza (Rome 2007)

Index

355